C0-CDP-736

Estimating and Analysis for Commercial Renovation

Edward B. Wetherill

Illustrations by Carl W. Linde

©Copyright 1985

To obtain additional information concerning
Means products referenced in this manual please contact:

R.S. Means Company, Inc.
Construction Consultants & Publishers
100 Construction Plaza
Kingston, MA 02364
617-747-1270
234567890

Library of Congress Catalog Card Number Pending
ISBN: 0-911950-81-8

No part of this publication may be reproduced, stored in a retrieval system, or transmitted
in any form or by any means without the prior written permission of R. S. Means Co., Inc.

Foreword

In new construction, the developer, architect, and estimator have the advantage of being able to plan and analyze a project completely on paper before estimating and construction. There are relatively few unknown variables. Commercial renovation, however, poses an entirely different set of problems, and the estimator must approach it more carefully. Without proper analysis and estimating, a commercial renovation can easily become a project with cost overruns and time delays.

The object of this book is to establish proper methods to analyze and estimate a commercial renovation project. The first section of the book, The Estimating Process, focuses on the analysis of commercial renovation and provides a step by step explanation of the estimate. The book will deal primarily with applications and problems uniquely associated with commercial renovation.

Two estimating examples are presented. The first, Unit Price Estimating, is arranged according to the sixteen major divisions of the Uniform Construction Index (UCI) as adopted by the American Institute of Architects, the Associated General Contractors of America, Inc., and the Construction Specifications Institute, Inc. The second estimating example of the book, Systems Estimating, uses a "Systems" format that groups all the functional elements of a building into twelve "uniformat" construction divisions.

This book is intended for contractors, architects, engineers, designers, developers, and building owners. A better understanding of the commercial renovation process by all persons involved will establish a basis for a more efficient and cost effective project.

All prices and construction costs used in this book are found in R.S. Means Co., Inc., *Repair and Remodeling Cost Data*, 1985. Many pages of this annual publication have been reproduced to show the origin and development of cost data. Please note that these pages are referred to in the text by Table Number, not by UCI Division numbers. The *Repair and Remodeling Cost Data* book is an up-to-date and thorough source of construction costs for commercial renovation.

No guaranty or warranty is made by R.S. Means Co., Inc., the author, or the editors as to the correctness or sufficiency of the information in this book. R.S. Means Co., Inc., the author, and the editors assume no responsibility nor liability in connection with the use of this book.

Table of Contents

List of Figure Numbers

Introduction
Before Starting the Estimate

In new construction, the estimator is provided with a set of plans and specifications from which he can prepare a complete estimate. Even in the planning stages, when all details have yet to be determined, the parameters are flexible and the options are many. Commercial renovation, however, requires more knowledge and experience of the estimator. Even the best set of plans and specifications for a renovation project cannot anticipate or include all conditions or possible pitfalls that contractors and design professionals encounter when renovating an existing structure. Commercial renovation poses the greatest challenge to the estimator in the exercise of his skills and professional judgement.

In this book, the term "estimator" is used as an all-inclusive title that should be read to include the contractor, architect, owner, or any person involved in the renovation process, as well as the individual preparing the estimate. Before starting the actual estimate, the estimator must be able to analyze the structure, to determine the existing conditions, and to know how they will affect the work to be performed, and therefore, how they will affect the estimate. The estimator must also decide what type of estimate is appropriate for the proposed renovation project. This decision should be based upon:

1. The amount of information supplied to the estimator.
2. The amount of time allowed to perform the estimate.
3. The purpose of the estimate.

How many times has the client given the estimator a small sketch on scrap paper or a vocal description and said, "I need to know how much this will cost, right away!"? Although this may be an extreme, it does happen. On the other hand, the client may give the estimator forty sheets of plans, a specification book two inches thick and a month to complete the estimate. Most commercial renovation projects fall somewhere between these two extremes. Depending upon the above factors, the estimator must choose the type of estimate best suited for the project.

Introduction
Types of Estimates

All estimates break down a construction project into various stages of detail. By determining the quantities involved and the cost of each item, the estimator is able to complete an estimate. The units used to determine the quantities can be large in scale, like the number of apartments in a housing renovation, or very detailed, like the number of square feet of drywall. The type of estimate to be used is determined by the amount and detail of information supplied to the estimator, the amount of time available to complete the estimate, and the purpose of the estimate, such as for a project estimate or a construction bid. Depending upon these criteria, there are four basic estimate types that can be used:

1. Unit Price Estimates. This type requires working drawings and specifications. It is the most detailed and takes the greatest amount of time to complete. The accuracy of a unit price estimate for commercial renovation is plus or minus (+ or -) 10%.

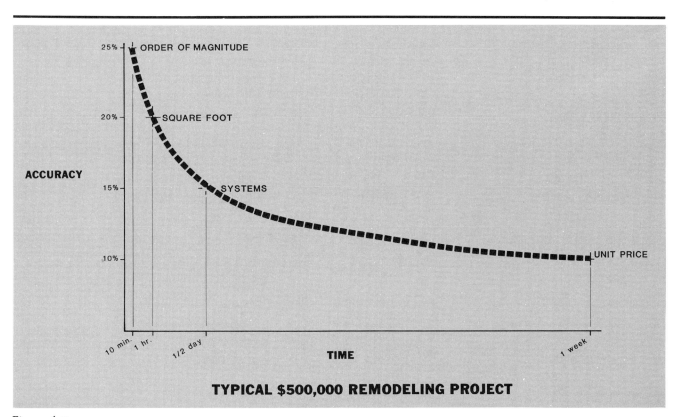

Figure A.1

2. Systems Estimates. A Systems Estimate is used when certain parameters of a renovation project are known such as building size, general type of construction, type of heating system, etc. Accuracy is + or - 15%.
3. Square Foot and Cubic Foot Estimates. This type is used when only the size and proposed use for a renovation is known. It is much faster than unit price or systems estimates and provides accuracy of + or - 20%.
4. Order of Magnitude Estimates. These are used for planning of future renovation projects. Accuracy is + or - 25%.

Variables in the estimating process and in commercial renovation projects are responsible for the spread in estimate accuracy. Figure A.1 shows a graphic relationship between the time spent preparing an estimate and the relative accuracy for each type of estimate. The accuracy described is based upon an "average of reasonable bids," assuming that there are a number of competitive bids for a given project.

Unit Price Estimates

Unit Price Estimates are the most accurate and the most detailed of the four estimate types and therefore take the most time to complete. Detailed working drawings and specifications should be available to the estimator. In these estimates, all decisions regarding materials and methods for the renovation project have already been made. This effectively reduces the number of variables and "estimated guesses" that can decrease the accuracy of an estimate. The working drawings and specifications are needed to determine the quantities of material, equipment, and labor. Current and accurate costs for these items, or unit prices, are also necessary to complete the estimate. These costs can come from different sources. Wherever possible the estimator should use prices based on experience or cost figures from similar projects. No two renovation projects are alike, however, so prices may be determined instead from an up-to-date industry source book such as R.S. Means' *Repair and Remodeling Cost Data.*

Because of the detail involved and the need for accuracy, Unit Price Estimates take a great deal of time and expense. For this reason, Unit Price Estimating is best suited for construction bids. It can also be effective for determining certain detailed costs in conceptual budgets or during design development.

Most construction specification manuals and cost reference books such as R.S. Means' *Repair and Remodeling Cost Data,* 1985, divide all unit price information into the sixteen Uniform Construction Index (UCI) divisions as adopted by the Construction Specifications Institute, Inc.:

Uniform Construction Index Divisions:
Division 1 - General Requirements
Division 2 - Site Work
Division 3 - Concrete
Division 4 - Masonry
Division 5 - Metals
Division 6 - Wood & Plastics
Division 7 - Moisture-Thermal Control
Division 8 - Doors, Windows & Glass
Division 9 - Finishes
Division 10 - Specialties
Division 11 - Equipment
Division 12 - Furnishings
Division 13 - Special Construction
Division 14 - Conveying Systems
Division 15 - Mechanical
Division 16 - Electrical

This method of dividing the various components of construction provides a standard of uniformity that is widely used by the construction industry. Since a great number of architects use this system for specifications, it makes sense to base estimates and cost data on the same format. An example of a page from the Unit Pricing Section of R.S. Means' *Repair and Remodeling Cost Data*, 1985, is shown in Table A.1. This page lists various types of painting. (Please note that the heading "9.8 Painting and Wall Covering" denotes the UCI classification for these items in Division 9 - Finishes.) As can be seen, each page contains a wealth of information that can be used in Unit Price Estimating. The type of work to be performed is described in detail: what kind of crew is needed, how long it takes to perform the unit of work, and separate costs for material, labor, and equipment. Total costs are extended to include the installer's overhead and profit.

Figure A.2 is an R.S. Means' Condensed Estimate Summary form. This form can be used after each division has been separately estimated. It provides a check list to assure that estimators have included all divisions, and a concise means for determining the total costs of the Unit Price Estimate. Please note at the top of form the items: Total Area, Total Volume, Cost per Square Foot, Cost per Cubic Foot. These items can prove valuable when the estimator needs Order of Magnitude or Square Foot and Cubic Foot Estimates for budgeting and as a cross-check for similar projects in the future.

Systems Estimates

Rising construction costs in recent years have made budgeting and cost efficiency increasingly important in the planning stages of renovation projects. Also, design costs have been rapidly increasing. Never has it been so important to involve the estimating process in the initial planning stages. Unit Price Estimating, because of the time and detailed information involved, is not suited as a budgetary or planning tool. A faster and more cost effective method is needed at the planning stage of a renovation project. This is the Systems Estimate.

The "Systems" method offers a different approach to the estimating process. Instead of the sixteen UCI divisions used for Unit Price Estimating, the Systems Estimate reorganizes separate trade items to reflect a logical sequential approach to how a renovation project is constructed. The result is twelve divisions that break the renovation project into components, or systems. They are listed below:

Systems Estimating Divisions:
Division 1 - Foundations
Division 2 - Substructure
Division 3 - Superstructure
Division 4 - Exterior Closure
Division 5 - Roofing
Division 6 - Interior Construction
Division 7 - Conveying
Division 8 - Mechanical
Division 9 - Electrical
Division 10 - General Conditions
Division 11 - Special
Division 12 - Site Work and Demolition

Each of these "Systems" divisions may incorporate items from different Unit Pricing divisions. For example, when estimating an interior partition using the "Systems" approach, the estimator uses Division 6 - Interior Construction as

9.8 Painting & Wall Covering

		CREW	MAN-HOURS	UNIT	BARE COSTS MAT.	BARE COSTS LABOR	BARE COSTS EQUIP.	BARE COSTS TOTAL	TOTAL INCL O&P	NOTES
19										
420	Wood shingles, oil base primer coat, brushwork	2 Pord	.006	S.F.	.07	.12		.19	.26	
440	Spray		.004		.07	.07		.14	.19	
500	Paint 2 coats, brushwork		.014		.10	.26		.36	.51	
520	Spray		.008		.10	.14		.24	.33	
650	Stain 2 coats, brushwork		.014		.13	.26		.39	.54	
700	Spray	↓	.008	→	.13	.14		.27	.36	
800	For latex paint, deduct				10%					
21-001	WALL AND CEILINGS									
002	Labor cost includes protection of adjacent items not painted									
010	Concrete, dry wall or plaster, oil base, primer or sealer coat									
020	Smooth finish, brushwork	1 Pord	.004	S.F.	.04	.08		.12	.16	
024	Roller		.004		.04	.07		.11	.15	
028	Spray		.002		.04	.03		.07	.09	
030	Sand finish, brushwork		.005		.05	.09		.14	.19	
034	Roller		.004		.05	.07		.12	.16	
038	Spray		.002		.05	.04		.09	.12	
080	Paint 2 coats, smooth finish, brushwork		.008		.09	.15		.24	.33	
084	Roller		.007		.09	.13		.22	.30	
088	Spray		.004		.09	.07		.16	.20	
090	Sand finish, brushwork		.010		.11	.18		.29	.40	
094	Roller		.008		.11	.14		.25	.34	
098	Spray	↓	.004	→	.11	.07		.18	.22	
150										
160	Glaze coating, 5 coats, spray, clear	1 Pord	.009	S.F.	.50	.17		.67	.80	
164	Multicolor	"	.009		.60	.17		.77	.91	
170	For latex paint, deduct				10%					
180	For ceiling installations, add			→		25%				
190										
200	Masonry or concrete block, oil base, primer or sealer coat									
210	Smooth finish, brushwork	1 Pord	.005	S.F.	.06	.09		.15	.20	
218	Spray		.002		.06	.04		.10	.13	
220	Sand finish, brushwork		.006		.07	.11		.18	.24	
228	Spray		.002		.07	.04		.11	.14	
280	Paint 2 coats, smooth finish, brushwork		.010		.10	.18		.28	.39	
288	Spray		.004		.10	.07		.17	.21	
290	Sand finish, brushwork		.011		.11	.20		.31	.43	
298	Spray		.004		.11	.07		.18	.22	
360	Glaze coating, 5 coats, spray, clear		.009		.50	.17		.67	.80	
362	Multicolor		.009		.60	.17		.77	.91	
400	Block filler, 1 coat, brushwork		.006		.08	.11		.19	.26	
410	Silicone, water repellent, 2 coats, spray	↓	.009	→	.04	.17		.21	.30	
412	For latex paint, deduct				10%					

For expanded coverage of these items see Means' *Interior Cost Data 1985*

Table A.1

CONDENSED ESTIMATE SUMMARY

PROJECT	TOTAL AREA	SHEET NO.
LOCATION	TOTAL VOLUME	ESTIMATE NO.
ARCHITECT	COST PER S.F.	DATE
OWNER	COST PER C.F.	NO. OF STORIES
QUANTITIES BY PRICES BY		CHECKED BY

NO.	DESCRIPTION	MATERIAL	LABOR	EQUIPMENT	SUBCONTRACTOR	TOTAL
	SITE WORK					
	Excavation					
	CONCRETE					
	MASONRY					
	METALS					
	CARPENTRY					
	MOISTURE PROTECTION					
	DOORS, WINDOWS, GLASS					
	FINISHES					
	SPECIALTIES					
	EQUIPMENT					
	FURNISHINGS					
	SPECIAL CONSTRUCTION					
	CONVEYING SYSTEMS					
	MECHANICAL					
	Plumbing					
	Heating, Ventilating, Air Conditioning					
	ELECTRICAL					
	TOTAL DIRECT COSTS					
	CONTRACTORS OVERHEAD					
	Performance Bond					
	Profit & Contingencies					
	TOTAL BID					

Figure A.2

shown in Table A.2, a page from R.S. Means' *Repair and Remodeling Cost Data, 1985*. When estimating the same interior partition using the "Unit Price" approach, the estimator might consult Division 6 (for wood studs and baseboard), Division 7 (for insulation) and Division 9 (for lath, plaster, and paint). Conversely, a particular Unit Price item like Cast in Place Concrete (Division 3) may be included in different Systems divisions: Division 1 - Foundations, Division 2- Substructures, Division 3 - Superstructure. The "Systems" method better reflects the way the contractor views the construction of a renovation project. Although it does not allow for the detail involved in the Unit Price approach, it is a faster way to develop the estimate.

A great advantage of the Systems Estimate is that the estimator/designer is able to vary components of a renovation project and quickly determine the cost differential. The owner can then anticipate accurate budgetary requirements before final details and dimensions are established.

In the Unit Price Estimate, final details regarding the renovation project are provided for the estimator. When they use the Systems Estimate, particularly for renovation projects, estimators must draw on their skills and knowledge of Building Code requirements, design options, and the ways in which existing conditions limit and restrict the proposed building renovations.

The Systems Estimate should not be used as a substitute for the Unit Price Estimate. While the "Systems" approach can be an invaluable tool in the planning and budget stages of a renovation, the Unit Price Estimate should be used when greater accuracy is required.

Square Foot and Cubic Foot Estimates

Square Foot and Cubic Foot Estimates are appropriate when a building owner wants to know the cost of a renovation before the plans or even sketches are available. Often these costs are needed to determine whether it is even economically feasible to proceed with a project or to determine the best use (apartments, offices, etc.) for an existing structure.

Historical data for square foot costs of new construction are plentiful (See R.S. Means' *Square Foot Costs*). In commercial renovation, however, every existing building is different, so Square Foot and Cubic Foot Estimating may not be effective. One building might have a two-year-old heating system while another has none. One building might need a new roof, and another might need new floors added in a high ceiling area. These variations in each commercial renovation challenge the estimator. A site visit to determine and evaluate existing conditions is critical to Square Foot and Cubic Foot Estimates. Please refer back to Figure A.2, noting the items at the top of form: Cost per Square Foot, Cost per Cubic Foot. The best data available to the estimator are figures from past projects. Calling on experience, the estimator is able to compare projects. Only with an understanding of the variables involved and the differences between projects is the estimator able to use Square Foot and Cubic Foot Estimates effectively for commercial renovation.

Order of Magnitude Estimates

Order of Magnitude Estimates require the least amount of time to complete. The information required is the use of the building and the number of units (apartments, hospital beds, etc.). Table A.3 is a page from R.S. Means' *Square Foot Estimating*. Please note under "Garages, Parking" and "Hospitals" that the final line items give cost per unit. This type of estimate is used primarily for planning purposes for new construction only. The complexities of commercial renovation make the Order of Magnitude Estimate ineffective unless costs from similar renovation projects in similar existing buildings are available.

SYSTEM	LINE NO.	DESCRIPTION	QUANTITY	COST PER S.F.		
				MAT.	INST.	TOTAL
	01	Gypsum plaster, 2 coats, over 3/8" lath, 2 faces, 2" x 4" wood				
	02	Stud partition, 24" O.C. incl. double top plate, single bottom plate, 3-1/2"				
	03	Insulation, baseboard and painting.				
	04					
	05					
	06	Gypsum plaster, 2 coats	.22 S.Y.	.63	2.41	3.04
	07	Lath, gypsum, 3/8" thick	.22 S.Y.	.48	.62	1.10
	08	Wood studs, 2" x 4", 24" O.C.	1 S.F.	.24	.41	.65
	09	Insulation, 3-1/2" fiberglass batts	1 S.F.	.22	.15	.37
	10	Baseboard, 9/16" x 3-1/2", painted	.2 L.F.	.13	.35	.48
	11	Paint, 2 coats	.2 S.F.	.20	.50	.70
	12	TOTAL	S.F.	1.90	4.44	6.34
	13					
	14	For alternate plaster systems:				
	15	Gypsum plaster, 3 coats	S.F.	2.13	4.93	7.06
	16	Perlite plaster, 2 coats		1.90	4.79	6.69
	17	3 coats		2.24	5.45	7.69
	18					
	19					
	20	For alternate lath systems:				
	21	Gypsum lath, 1/2" thick	S.F.	1.94	4.82	6.76
	22	Moisture resistant, 4' x 8' sheets, 1/2" thick		2.15	4.85	7
	23	5/8" thick		2.25	4.90	7.15
	24	Metal lath, 2.5 Lb. diamond		1.79	4.79	6.58
	25	3.4 Lb. diamond		1.90	4.87	6.77
	26					
	27					
	28					
	29	Cut & patch to match existing construction, add, minimum		2%	3%	
	30	Maximum		5%	9%	
	31	Dust protection, add, minimum		1%	2%	
	32	Maximum		4%	11%	
	33	Material handling & storage limitation, add, minimum		1%	1%	
	34	Maximum		6%	7%	
	35	Protection of existing work, add, minimum		2%	2%	
	36	Maximum		5%	7%	
	37	Shift work requirements, add, minimum			5%	
	38	Maximum			30%	
	39	Temporary shoring and bracing, add, minimum		2%	5%	
	40	Maximum		5%	12%	
	41					
	42					

This page illustrates and describes a plaster and lath system including gypsum plaster, gypsum lath, wood studs with plates, insulation, baseboard and painting. Lines 06.1-692-06 thru 12 give the unit price and price per square foot for this system. Prices for alternate plaster and lath systems are on Line Items 06.1-692-15 thru 25. Both material quantities and labor costs have been adjusted for the system listed.

Example: Perlite plaster, three coats as an alternate system; choose Line Item 06.1-692-17, $2.24 MAT., $5.45 INST., $7.69 TOTAL. This price includes all materials compatible with the original system. For alternatives not listed, use the selective price sheet for this section (page 353, 354, 356). Substitute the new prices from the price sheet into the typical system and adjust the total to reflect each change.

Factors: To adjust for job conditions other than normal working situations use Lines 06.1-692-29 thru 40.

Example: You are to install the above system during evening hours only. Go to Line 06.1-692-38 and apply this percentage to the appropriate INST. costs.

Table A.2

S.F. C.F. and % of TOTALS 14.1-200		UNIT	UNIT COSTS			% OF TOTAL		
			1/4	MEDIAN	3/4	1/4	MEDIAN	3/4
272	Plumbing	S.F.	3.34	5.10	6.90	5.10%	8.50%	11.30%
277	Heating, ventilating, air conditioning		4.32	7.08	9.32	9.40%	10.30%	13.80%
290	Electrical		3.24	4.33	6.90	7.20%	9.50%	10.40%
310	Total: Mechanical & Electrical	↓	10.40	18.80	23.30	24.20%	30.40%	33.30%
38	FUNERAL HOMES	S.F.	41.60	52.30	74.90			
002	Total project costs	C.F.	2.90	4.20	4.70			
272	Plumbing	S.F.	1.48	2.29	2.50	3.50%	4.30%	5.50%
277	Heating, ventilating, air conditioning		3.05	3.70	4.46	5.80%	9.90%	10.40%
290	Electrical		2.03	3.22	5.34	4.40%	7.70%	10.60%
310	Total: Mechanical & Electrical	↓	4.91	9.90	11.51	10.60%	22.90%	27.20%
39	GARAGES, COMMERCIAL	S.F.	21.20	35.80	51.80			
002	Total project costs	C.F.	1.54	2.20	3.23			
180	Equipment	S.F.	1.55	2.51	6.95	2.70%	6.30%	16%
272	Plumbing		1.42	2.35	5.03	4.90%	6.90%	11%
273	Heating & ventilating		1.53	2.24	4.10	4.20%	7.10%	8.50%
290	Electrical		2.10	3.66	5.15	7.10%	9%	12.60%
310	Total: Mechanical & Electrical	↓	5.46	8.87	15.50	19%	24.20%	31.40%
40	GARAGES, MUNICIPAL	S.F.	26.80	38.90	58.60			
002	Total project costs	C.F.	1.92	2.60	3.81			
050	Masonry	S.F.	3.60	4.15	8.38	12%	13%	20%
114	Roofing		1.81	3.54	4.86	6.50%	8.90%	10.10%
272	Plumbing		1.94	3.28	5.16	5.20%	7%	8.90%
273	Heating & ventilating		2.89	3.76	5.85	6.60%	8.20%	11.90%
290	Electrical		2.64	3.66	5.02	6.60%	8%	10%
310	Total: Mechanical & Electrical	↓	6.34	12.60	14.50	19.10%	24.40%	31.50%
41	GARAGES, PARKING	S.F.	14.70	18	30.50			
002	Total project costs	C.F.	1.01	1.64	2.36			
272	Plumbing	S.F.	.26	.51	.69	2.10%	2.70%	3.50%
290	Electrical		.58	.81	1.43	3.70%	5.10%	6.50%
310	Total: Mechanical & Electrical	↓	.89	1.42	1.80	7.40%	8.30%	10.10%
320								
900	Per car, total cost	Car	4,620	6,290	8,350			
950	Total: Mechanical & Electrical	"	320	497	610			
43	GYMNASIUMS	S.F.	41.70	51.80	65.80			
002	Total project costs	C.F.	1.92	2.44	3.41			
180	Equipment	S.F.	1.04	2.30	4.55	2.20%	3.40%	8.20%
272	Plumbing		2.77	3.40	4.65	5.30%	7.70%	10.20%
277	Heating, ventilating, air conditioning		3.88	5.61	7.22	7.60%	11.10%	13.50%
290	Electrical		3.39	4.26	5.79	6.50%	8.90%	10.70%
310	Total: Mechanical & Electrical	↓	10.10	13.10	15.80	21.50%	25.70%	29.40%
46	HOSPITALS	S.F.	81.80	102.80	135.40			
002	Total project costs	C.F.	6.16	7.30	9.24			
112	Roofing	S.F.	.65	1.40	1.95	.60%	1.20%	2%
132	Finish hardware		.79	.86	1.06	.60%	1%	1.10%
154	Floor covering		.57	1	1.05	.50%	1.10%	1.20%
157	Tile & marble		.30	.43	.64	.20%	.40%	.60%
158	Painting		.78	1.14	1.92	1%	1.30%	1.60%
180	Equipment		1.93	4.55	6.43	2%	4.10%	6.10%
272	Plumbing		8.43	10.80	13.80	7.50%	9.10%	11.70%
277	Heating, ventilating, air conditioning		12.80	16.30	25	12.50%	16.60%	19%
290	Electrical		9.91	12.50	17.60	11.30%	13.90%	15.20%
310	Total: Mechanical & Electrical	↓	31	39	51.20	36.60%	40.10%	44%
900	Per bed or person, total cost	Bed	27,300	44,000	64,500			
950	Total: Mechanical & Electrical	"	23,600	39,400	57,100			

Table A.3

Part I:
The Estimating Process

Part 1
Introduction

In commercial renovation, it is of the utmost importance for the estimator to conduct a site visit and evaluation before performing the estimate. The estimator must become familiar with each project by inspecting the existing conditions. The extent and detail of the plans and specifications supplied to the estimator are an important factor in the site visit and in the proper completion of the estimate. As stated previously, this information can be minimal or extensive. Before conducting the site visit, the estimator should examine all information provided. As important as it is to perform the site evaluation before making the estimate, it is just as important to know what the project entails before visiting the site. For example, the specifications may state:

> "All existing mortar joints shall be scraped to a depth of at least 1/2," using hand tools only, before tuck pointing individual joints. Care shall be taken not to allow new mortar to stain existing porous bricks."
> or:
> "Clean and patch existing masonry joints."

Obviously, the two statements have entirely different implications. If involved in the planning and supervision of the project, an architect will answer most questions about methods and materials. If an architect is not involved in the supervision of the project, then the estimator is responsible for the interpretation of the plans and specifications. In commercial renovation, the estimator should not make assumptions or hasty interpretations without the experience or knowledge to make the correct choices for each different project.

In the discussion of the Site Visit and Evaluation below, the reader should note that the architect will normally supply some of the information to the estimator. This information should be treated accordingly. It is important, however, for the estimator to be aware of the processes involved in planning commercial renovation. Thus, this information is included.

When an architect is not involved at all, it is often the responsibility of the estimator to make sure that all items are included in the estimate and that the roles of the subcontractors do not overlap. This is especially important in renovation, where such omissions or overlaps can often occur. For example, wood backing for plumbing fixtures could be included in both carpentry and plumbing subcontracts. Conversely, providing holes through existing walls for sprinkler piping could be omitted, assumed by each trade to be the responsibility of another. This type of problem is less likely to occur in new construction where all parties are familiar with established precedents. It cannot be stressed enough, however, that each commercial renovation project is different and requires special attention and diligence.

If possible, subcontractors and engineers should accompany the estimator on the site visit. Undoubtedly questions will arise specific to certain trades. The estimator should know how existing conditions will affect the work to be performed.

Commercial renovation projects are often in urban settings. Access for delivery of materials and placement of equipment can be difficult. Often scaffolding must be erected over busy sidewalks. These and many other factors described below add to the intricacy of commercial renovation. Knowing the applicable Building, Fire, and Energy Codes helps the estimator to anticipate any requirements that may not be included in the plans and specifications. It should be noted that Building, Fire, and Energy Codes for existing structures are often different from those for new buildings.

The estimator should be familiar with former types of construction, like mill-type wood construction built before extensive use of steel and concrete, or the terra cotta-encased structural steel method introduced with the advent of fire resistant construction (See Figure I1.1). Different types of construction will require different methods of work.

After the site visit and evaluation, the next step of the estimating process is the quantity take-off. Working from the plans and specifications, the estimator must determine the quantity of materials for all the types of work to be performed, such as cubic yards of concrete, square feet of partitions, or number of doors. This phase of the estimate must be executed carefully and with the knowledge gained from the site visit. After determining the quantities involved, the estimator extends the costs of the individual items, using current construction costs determined either from experience on past projects or from an industry source such as R.S. Means' *Repair and Remodeling Cost Data*, 1985.

It is important throughout the whole estimating process to be diligent and organized. Minor errors in initial calculations can grow to larger errors in the final stages of the estimate.

The next section describes the site visit and evaluation. One text cannot possibly describe all the variables in commercial renovation. This book, however, will attempt to establish a way to approach the evaluation of an existing building so that the estimator will know what to look for and what to anticipate.

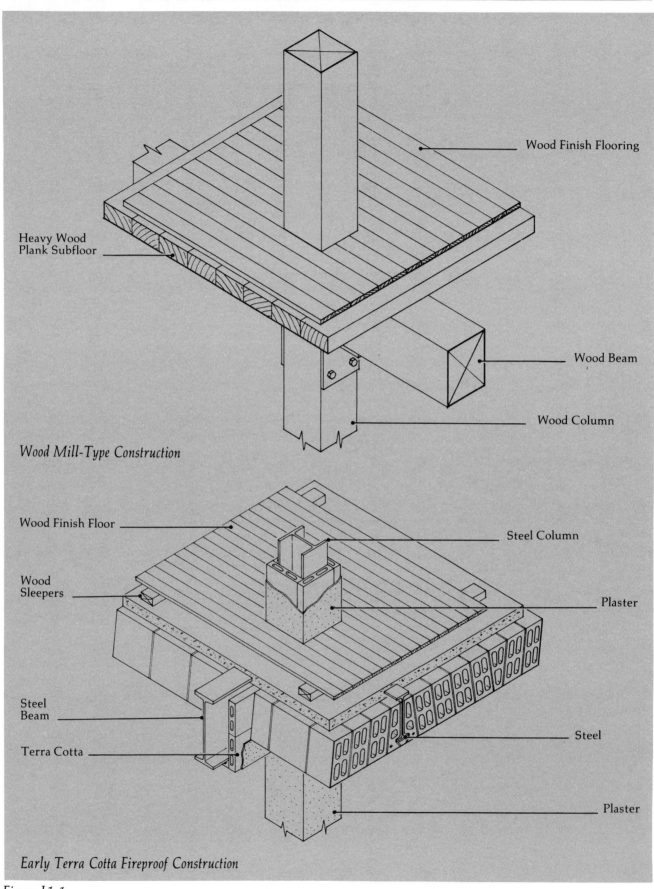

Wood Finish Flooring

Heavy Wood Plank Subfloor

Wood Beam

Wood Column

Wood Mill-Type Construction

Wood Finish Floor

Steel Column

Wood Sleepers

Plaster

Steel Beam

Terra Cotta

Steel

Plaster

Early Terra Cotta Fireproof Construction

Figure 11.1

Chapter 1.
The Site Visit and Evaluation

The best way to approach an existing structure is from the bottom all the way up to the top. The basement of a building often contains the "guts" of the structure. By starting the inspection of the existing conditions at the bottom, the estimator can observe the structure as it was built. Structural elements can be identified and followed up through the building. The core of mechanical and electrical systems can also be traced from below to better understand the distribution above. Throughout the site visit and evaluation, the estimator should always remember how the building is going to be renovated and what the ultimate use is going to be. It is important for the estimator to note any conditions or potential problems that may not have been incorporated into the plans and specifications. The estimator should always consult the architect or owner on any questionable conditions.

The following evaluation is based upon the twelve divisions of the "Systems" approach, listed in the logical way that a building is constructed, from the bottom up. This does not mean, however, that the evaluation is appropriate only for the Systems Estimate. It is merely a way to examine an existing structure and can be used for all estimate types.

Throughout the discussion of the site visit and evaluation, the person performing the inspection is referred to as the estimator. This reference is used primarily for consistency. The inspector could be the building owner or any professional involved with a renovation project, such as the architect, engineer, or contractor. It is helpful to the project if all involved parties do perform a site visit to gain a better understanding of the renovation process.

1.1 Foundations

The foundation of an existing building can be of many types: stone rubble, concrete, wood piles, or another material. Before modern developments in structural engineering techniques and materials, foundations were often massive structures. The material of the foundation and, if possible, its thickness should be noted. This information is important in the planning stage. For example, if new utilities are to be provided, the estimator should know if he has to drill through 12" of concrete block or hand chisel through 54" of stone and mortar.

In cases of water or moisture problems, the plans and specifications may call for foundation waterproofing. Depending upon the amount and detail of information provided for the work, the estimator may have to determine if the method chosen is best for the solution of the problem. The solution can be as simple as repairing an undiscovered buried water pipe leak or as extensive as total exterior excavation and coating of the entire foundation. If possible, the source of the problem should be determined before work begins.

The inside surface of the foundation should be inspected. The condition of the masonry, mortar or concrete can tell much about subsurface conditions. Spalling or deteriorated mortar in only a small area suggests a localized problem. Inspect the exposed portion of the foundation's exterior. Downspout locations should be noted and examined for adequate runoff away from the foundation. Potential site drainage problems, low spots, standing water, clogged catch basins and sewer drains should be recognized. If the source of the water problem cannot be readily found, the estimator should consult the architect or owner to discuss the problem and possible solutions before starting the work.

The estimator should note cracks or any signs of settling at the foundation, interior bearing walls, or columns. If conditions suggest unusual amounts of settling, or if there are any questions about the foundation's structural integrity, an engineer should be consulted.

If specified work is to be performed on the foundation, the estimator must determine how to do the work and what equipment to use. If workers must excavate, is there adequate access for machinery or will the work be performed by hand? Concrete placement, too, could be difficult, and contractors may have to substitute a masonry wall. Workers must often create access for equipment and required materials. For exterior foundation work, this may call for the use of an adjoining property if the building is close to lot lines. There have been many cases where contractors have had to "rent" space in lots adjacent to renovation projects, whether for actual work access or material storage. This arrangement soon becomes an expensive item, one which may or may not have been included in the original estimate. For interior foundation work, where much of the work and delivery of materials must be performed manually, workers sometimes gain access by cutting holes in floors or walls. Expenses include not only the cost of opening the holes, but also the cost of labor and materials to patch the opening. In excavated areas, sheet piling (see Table I1.1) may be necessary to protect adjacent areas and to prevent the collapse of trenches. The estimator should think about the project in advance and envision the work to be done. This will help prevent omissions, cutting down unforeseen costs in the course of the renovation project.

When inspecting the foundation the estimator should take little for granted. Former methods of construction can be extremely dissimilar to methods used today. Above grade, the different types of construction can be seen. Below, they can be a mystery. Figure I1.2 shows a good example of where looks can be deceiving. Note how the basement slab, obviously added after the building was constructed, is actually below the base of the foundation (with no footing). Depending on the proposed use of the building, this condition could be a potential problem and a costly "extra" to rectify. Again, the estimator should consult an engineer if there is any question about structural integrity and how it affects the work or its proposed use.

2.3 Earthwork

	Description	CREW	MAN-HOURS	UNIT	MAT.	LABOR	EQUIP.	TOTAL	TOTAL INCL O&P
35-001	**MOBILIZATION AND DEMOBILIZATION** Dozer, 105 H.P.	B-34C	1.290	Ea.		21	61	82	99
090	Shovel, backhoe or dragline, 3/4 C.Y.		1.860			30	88	118	145
120	Tractor shovel or front end loader, 1 C.Y.		1.290			21	61	82	99
38-001	**SHEET PILING** Steel, not incl. wales, 15' excav., left in place	B-40	5.930	Ton	580	120	135	835	975
010	Pull & salvage, 22 psf, 15' excavation		8.890	"	145	175	205	525	660
120	15' deep excavation, 22 psf, left in place		.065	S.F.	6.40	1.29	1.49	9.18	10.70
130	Pull & salvage		.098	"	1.60	1.94	2.24	5.78	7.30
210	Rent sheet piling and wales, first month			Ton	150			150	165M
220	Per added month			"	14			14	15.40M
390	Wood, solid sheeting, incl. wales, braces and spacers,								
391	pull & salvage, 8' deep excavation	B-31	.121	S.F.	.80	2.03	.37	3.20	4.42
452	Left in place, 8' deep, 55 S.F./hr.		.091	"	1.55	1.52	.28	3.35	4.36
499	Minimum labor/equipment charge		20	Job		334	61	395	585
500	For creosoting add cost of treatment to lumber								
42-001	**SHORING** Existing building, with timber, no salvage allowance	B-51	21.820	M.F.B.M.	390	349	26	765	995
100	With 35 ton screw jacks, per box and jack		13.330	Jack	25	214.10	15.90	255	375
109	Minimum labor/equipment charge		24	Ea.		381	29	410	620
110	Masonry openings in walls, see div. 2.2-08								
50-001	**TERMITE PRETREATMENT**	1 Skwk	.005	S.F. Flr	.10	.11		.21	.27
010	Commercial, minimum		.003	"	.04	.06		.10	.14
020	Maximum		.005	"	.07	.10		.17	.23
039	Minimum labor/equipment charge		2	Job		40		40	62L
040	Insecticides for termite control, minimum			Gal.	10			10	11M
050	Maximum			"	15			15	16.50M
52-001	**UNDERPINNING FOUNDATIONS** Including excavation,								
002	forming, reinforcing, concrete and equipment								
010	5' to 16' below grade, up to 500 C.Y.	B-52	24.350	C.Y.	130	445	125	700	965
020	Over 1000 C.Y.		22.400		115	410	115	640	885
040	16' to 25' below grade, up to 500 C.Y.		28		140	510	145	795	1,100
050	Over 1000 C.Y.		26.670		125	485	140	750	1,050
070	26 ft. to 40 ft. below grade, up to 500 C.Y.		35		155	635	185	975	1,350
080	Over 1000 C.Y.		31.110		140	565	165	870	1,200
090	For under 50 C.Y., add				10%	40%			

NOTES

When calculating **SHEET PILING** costs, the area of toe-in must be added to the exposed area. Wood sheet piling can be economically used up to 20' where minimal ground water is encountered. Possible higher costs for excavation between sheet piling and the cost of dewatering should be considered.

Sheet Piling, Steel

Sheet Piling, Wood

Table I1.1

1.2
Substructure

The substructure consists of the basement floor or the slab on grade. Older buildings may not have concrete slabs but instead only soil floors. Basement floors were often constructed of brick. In some instances, wood floors were built directly on soil. Where concrete slabs do exist in older buildings, they may have been installed at some point after the building was constructed (as in Figure I1.2). Often no reinforcing exists. Modern compaction methods and specific materials used in subgrading today were not as widely used. Settling and cracking are thus more evident in older buildings. Cracks should be checked for excessive movement, and the general condition of the slab should be checked for level and for signs of deterioration. Any existing penetrations through the slab should be examined to attempt to determine the thickness. Remember, especially in older buildings, slab thickness may not be constant.

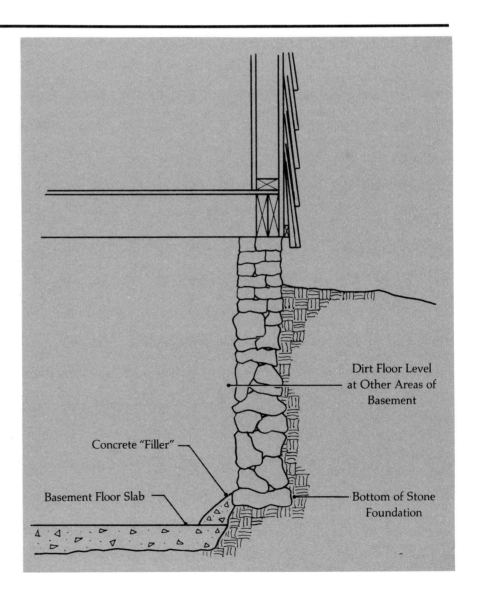

Dirt Floor Level at Other Areas of Basement

Concrete "Filler"

Basement Floor Slab

Bottom of Stone Foundation

Figure I1.2

As is the case with foundations, water seepage can be a problem at floor slabs. Placing a new reinforced slab with a vapor barrier is an effective but expensive, and not always feasible solution. If the instructions provided are not specific, the estimator may have to determine the source of the problem and how best to repair the existing slab for less cost. Cracks should be checked for moisture seepage. The estimator should note the time of year the site visit is conducted and the amount of precipitation over recent weeks. If there has been a dry spell, the potential water problems may not be evident. Any water marks should be noted. Any existing interior drainage should be checked for clogs or broken pipes. If a new drainage system is to be installed, the estimator should check the proposed path and ultimate outlet to assure that existing conditions will not inhibit the installation. Such drainage may be required by Building Codes for boilers and hot water heaters.

If the plans and specifications call for a new basement floor slab, or concrete pads for equipment, builders face the same problems of access for equipment and materials as they do when performing foundation work. Handwork is often the only way to excavate and compact the subgrade.

The estimator should be especially aware of new utility and mechanical installations. Clearances for the installation of new equipment should be verified. Presumably, a structural engineer has checked bearing capacities of existing slabs. If not, and there is any question regarding heavy equipment, an analysis should be done.

A new specified electrical service can pose many problems. In urban areas, space for exterior transformers is often not available and transformer vaults are required in basements. The contractor must provide the utility with access for the transformers. We all know how inflexible utility companies can be. Often, installation of utility equipment and service switch-overs must be performed at night or over weekends, especially when the building remains partially occupied during renovations. Overtime work must be anticipated.

Before beginning the estimate, the estimator must determine from his evaluation of the substructure how the specified work is to be performed. Particular attention should be given to access for materials and equipment.

If an architect or engineer has not thoroughly analyzed the building, the estimator should examine and check the location of existing structural elements as seen in the basement: columns, beams, interior bearing walls. This will become important when examining the structure above. On upper floors, the structural members may not be exposed or readily evident. Columns above may be buried in interior partitions. The plans may call for a large opening to be cut in a bearing wall that was thought to be non-bearing. In some cases, columns could have been removed in the past with no provisions for the structural consequences. Conversely, there may be existing structures on upper floors that appear to be columns but are not. They possibly can be eliminated. Even if this information is included in the plans and specifications, the estimator should have knowledge of the location of structural elements in the building.

1.3
Superstructure

The superstructure, floor systems, ceilings, and stairs should be thoroughly inspected and evaluated. The estimator should consult a structural engineer if there are any questions regarding structural integrity or bearing capacity that are not addressed in the plans and specifications. The plans and specifications may generally state that the contractor shall patch and repair floors to match existing conditions. This may be the only information provided. It is then the responsibility of the estimator to determine the type and extent of work involved. For example, in an old mill building, steam pipes are to be removed and the holes patched. It may be a simple operation to attach a plate to the underside of the floor and fill the hole with concrete. But if the ceiling below is to be sandblasted as the finished ceiling, or if the floor is to be sanded and refinished, much more work is involved. A wood plug may have to be custom fitted or possibly a whole flooring plank may have to be replaced with an original board that is to be removed from elsewhere in the building. Obviously, these options are more costly and must be taken into account in the estimate. At this point in the site visit, a hammer and wrecking bar may be the estimator's best friends. First, the materials in the floor systems must be identified as mill-type wood planking, wood joists, steel joist with concrete slab, or another material. It is often necessary to open holes in ceilings and to inspect under floor finishes. Often, different flooring systems may occur in the same building.

Floors in older buildings are often out of level, sometimes extremely. Settling is common in buildings built before modern engineering standards and Building Codes were established. The plans and specifications may call for the floors to be leveled with a lightweight "self-leveling" concrete. Not only is the placement of the concrete often difficult, but the determination of quantities involved can also be a problem. It often takes more concrete than originally thought, and if a large amount is required, a structural engineer may have to be consulted to determine whether or not the existing structure can support it.

The estimator should look for patched or repaired areas in the flooring and ceilings. This may be evidence of past damage or repair. Fire or water damage may possibly be covered up. Where possible, existing steel should be inspected for corrosion. Throughout the site evaluation, the estimator should recall the proposed renovations and how the existing conditions will affect the work.

When new floor systems are to be added in existing buildings, the estimator must be able to visualize the whole construction process. Depending on the floor system specified in the plans, placement of new structural members can be difficult at best. Figure I1.3 shows three typical floor systems that may be used in commercial renovation. Instead of installing larger pieces directly upon delivery, workers may have to handle materials two or three times before erecting the system. If the job calls for long structural members, some fabrication may be needed on-site because of restrictive existing conditions. Depending on the bearing capacity of existing structural members, the new structural support system may have to be carried down to new footings.

The whole process of adding new floors in commercial renovation can be very costly. Because of the great expense involved, which can be a significant percentage of a renovation project, the decision by the owner or architect of whether or not to add a new floor is often not assured until the estimator has determined the costs. Thus, it becomes the estimator's responsibility to be thorough and to include all costs that may result from such work.

Much commercial renovation performed before the relatively recent general acceptance of uniform Building Codes would not be acceptable under today's standards. Such poor quality work must be discovered. Openings in floors are often filled with materials of weaker structural capacity than the original surrounding floor system. These factors will all have an effect on the renovation to be performed, and the estimator should be aware of the consequences. The owner or architect should be notified immediately of any such conditions.

Particularly under today's Building Codes, stairways are an extremely important focus of commercial renovation. Often in older buildings only one unenclosed stairway exists where two enclosed stairways will be required. If

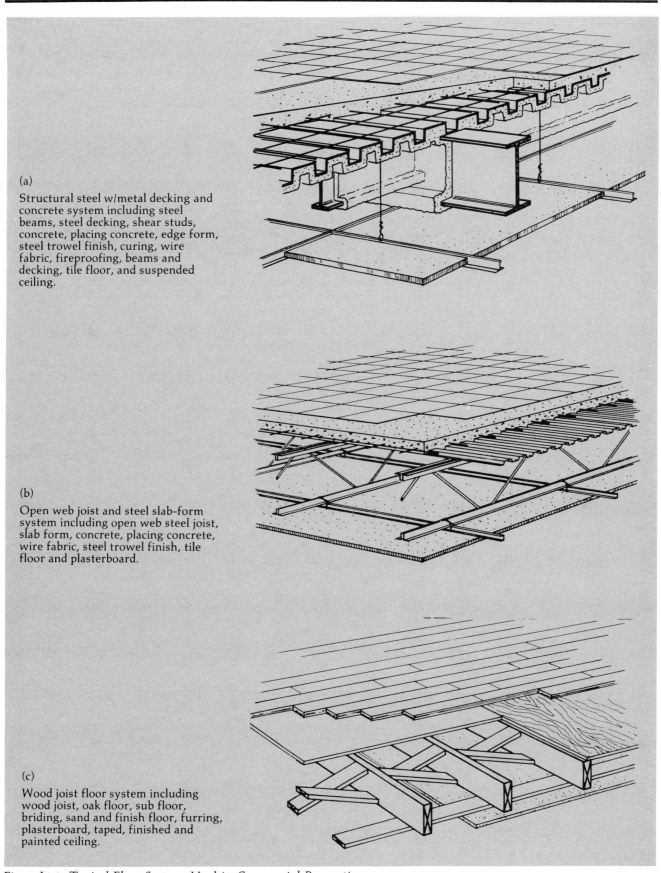

(a)

Structural steel w/metal decking and concrete system including steel beams, steel decking, shear studs, concrete, placing concrete, edge form, steel trowel finish, curing, wire fabric, fireproofing, beams and decking, tile floor, and suspended ceiling.

(b)

Open web joist and steel slab-form system including open web steel joist, slab form, concrete, placing concrete, wire fabric, steel trowel finish, tile floor and plasterboard.

(c)

Wood joist floor system including wood joist, oak floor, sub floor, briding, sand and finish floor, furring, plasterboard, taped, finished and painted ceiling.

Figure I1.3 Typical Floor Systems Used in Commercial Renovation

no architect is involved, local building inspectors should be consulted as early as possible to make sure the renovation complies with access and egress requirements. When new stairways are specified as part of the work, installation becomes a major factor. It is often impossible to preassemble large sections to be lowered into place. Workers must carry smaller pieces to the site and assemble them by hand. Railings often must be built in place. These factors require more labor, and obviously greater expense than does new construction. Existing stairways, as well as new, will most likely have to be enclosed in firewalls. It can be difficult for builders to achieve the required continuity of firewalls in existing buildings. Where the existing ceilings are suspended, made of plaster or another material, these ceilings must be cut. The firewall must then be constructed on the underside of the deck above, and the existing structure patched to meet the new work. These firewalls also must be extended through attic spaces to the underside of the roof deck. Again, estimators must anticipate the extra labor involved.

1.4 Exterior Closure

Upon determining the work to be performed, from the plans and specifications, the estimator must thoroughly inspect the entire exterior of a building. If the building is tall, the exterior should be checked from upper story windows. Much can be overlooked from a ground level inspection. For example, when the project calls for repointing of any deteriorated or loose masonry joints, the estimator must determine the area of wall surface where repointing is required. Without close inspection, areas of deteriorated mortar may go undetected until the work has begun. All sides of the building should be checked. Different weather exposures will exhibit varied amounts of deterioration. Conditions will also vary over a particular wall surface.

A great number of older commercial buildings have some form of masonry exterior, whether stone or brick. In addition, cast iron, copper, and bronze were often used for storefronts, cornices, and facades. These materials differ greatly from the concrete, manufactured brick, and aluminum that are so common in new construction. Therefore, a knowledge of the different materials and methods is important for both estimator and architect when renovating older buildings.

When inspecting the masonry, note the type of brick or stone, and if possible, the type of mortar used. Note the joint size and conditions, paying particular attention to the condition of joints between dissimilar materials (e.g. brick-stone, brick-wood). Due to differences in thermal expansion and contraction of different materials, this type of joint is most susceptible to deterioration. The information gathered from such an inspection will become important when determining the best way to perform the specified work and when calculating costs.

When the plans call for the exterior of a brick building to be cleaned (often before repair), the estimator must carefully read the specifications and not assume particular methods of work. Older brick is usually very porous and softer than modern brick. Sandblasting and harsh chemical washing can cause extensive damage. Architects and preservation officials often reject these methods for cleaning masonry. High pressure water with perhaps a mild chemical cleaner can be effective but is much more time consuming. Hand scrubbing may be necessary. Therefore, the estimator and architect alike must be aware of the materials involved and the appropriate methods of work.

When working on the exterior of an existing building, estimators must take factors other than actual labor and materials into account. Scaffolding often must be erected at the whole exterior. This in turn involves pedestrian protection, sidewalk permits and depending on the weather, tarpaulins to enclose the scaffolding (see Figure I1.4). If the exterior work is lengthy, the rental expense can be great. When possible, the estimator should determine if swing staging could be an adequate, less costly alternative.

When exterior repairs or replacement are specified, materials to match the existing surrounding conditions are often required. These materials may have to come from other parts of the exterior, whether demolished or borrowed. If existing materials must be reused elsewhere, the estimator should include extra labor expense for special handling to prevent damage to these materials.

When the project calls for new windows, the estimator should determine if the windows can be easily installed from the interior or if scaffolding is required. Some types of replacement windows require only the removal of the existing sash. This type is installed around or within the existing frames. If the existing frames are to be removed, more labor is involved in both demolition and installation.

In most renovation projects, doors and windows must be custom made to fit existing openings, or the openings must be altered to accept standard sizes. Often, both options take much time, work, and money. Figures I1.5 and I1.6 are two buildings with very different window types. The building in Figure I1.5 has a different size and shape of window at each floor. The windows in the building in Figure I1.6 are all rectangular and are of only two sizes. The estimator must remember that every job is different and must be evaluated carefully and independently.

Figure I1.4

Figure I1.5

Figure I1.6

Especially on older buildings, the exterior closure can be a significant factor in commercial renovation. Today, a heightened appreciation for fine old architecture and a rising interest in historical preservation present new considerations in dealing with older buildings. Not only should the exterior be thoroughly inspected, but if an architect is not involved, the estimator should determine whether local preservation officials have any jurisdiction over renovations to the exterior of the building. Renovation projects have been legally stopped because historic guidelines were not being met.

The building in Figure I1.5 was renovated according to required historic preservation guidelines. Under these guidelines the existing windows could have been replaced only by custom made wood windows exactly replicating the existing windows. The millwork subcontractor's estimate for this work was so great that the owner chose to have the existing windows repaired. The estimator bid the repair work at thirty percent of the replacement cost. When the repair work was completed, the eventual cost was over fifty percent of the cost of replacement. A more careful and thorough evaluation would have prevented this expensive error.

The estimator should carefully read and understand the drawings and specifications. Required methods of work and materials will vary from project to project and will be greatly affected by the age of the building and the role of historic preservation in the project. Older buildings often require more exterior work in commercial renovation than more recently constructed buildings, but the relative age of the existing building should not affect the the attention the estimator gives it or the importance of the site evaluation.

1.5 Roofing

In commercial renovation, the estimator will encounter many different roof types and combinations of roof types. Older houses may have two layers of asphalt shingles over cedar shingles. A flat built-up roof may have patches over patches. If the project includes roof work, the estimator must know what exists to make a proper estimate of the work. If access is possible, the estimator should closely examine the existing roof structure, roofing materials, flashing, and roof penetrations.

The roof structural system is often hidden by a ceiling. Inspection holes should be made or access gained to examine the structure. The structural members and especially the roof decking should be checked for water marks, damage, or deterioration. When older roofing materials are removed for replacement, portions of existing decking or sheathing, sometimes over the whole roof, often must be replaced. If possible, such conditions should be discovered before work starts.

When examining the roof structure, the estimator should note any existing insulation. The specifications may call for an R-value of 19, leaving the methods and materials up to the estimator. As seen in Table I1.2, 6" of glass fiber insulation and 3" of paperbacked urethane have approximately the same R-value, but differ greatly in cost. By evaluating related work to be performed, the estimator must choose which materials are appropriate. For example, many older commercial buildings have heavy timber trussed roof systems. Owners and architects today like to expose these trusses and wood plank roof decks for aesthetic reasons. There may be no attic space or access to spaces under the roof deck. Under these conditions (if the roofing materials are to be replaced) the more expensive foam insulation may be required. A wet sprinkler system in an attic space makes it necessary to install insulation above the piping to prevent freezing. If the architect has made no provisions, ventilation must be addressed. Without proper ventilation, adding insulation to a building where there was none can cause condensation problems.

05.9-300 Roofing & Ceiling Finish Selective Price Sheet

ROOFING / INSULATION

	DESCRIPTION		MAT.	INST.	TOTAL
ROOFING					
Built-up	Asphalt	3 ply mineral surfaces	.42	.63	1.05
	Roll roofing	4 ply type I.V.	.64	.66	1.30
	Cold applied	3 ply	.80	.20	1.00
	Coal tar pitch	4 ply asbestos felt	1.05	.80	1.85
	Mopped	3 ply glass fiber	.75	.90	1.65
		4 ply organic felt	.87	.78	1.65
Elastomeric	Hypalon	Neoprene unreinforced	1.49	1.47	2.96
		Polyester reinforced	1.50	1.74	3.24
		Neoprene 5 coats 60 mils	3.74	2.97	6.71
		Over 10,000 S.F.	3.50	2.49	5.99
	PVC	Traffic deck sprayed	1.21	2.67	3.88
		With neoprene	1.13	1.02	2.15
Shingles	Asbestos	Strip 14" x 30", 325#/sq.	1.10	.60	1.70
		12" x 24", 167#/sq.	.90	.70	1.60
		Shake 9.35"x16" 500#/sq.	1.62	1.08	2.70
	Asphalt	Strip 210-235 #/sq.	.31	.43	.74
		235-240 #/sq.	.31	.47	.78
		Class A laminated	.56	.54	1.10
		Class C laminated	.53	.57	1.10
	Slate	Buckingham 3/16" thick	6.27	1.38	7.65
		black 1/4" thick	6.27	1.38	7.65
	Wood	Shingles 16" No. 1, 5" exp	1.46	.99	2.43
		Red cedar 18" perfections	1.21	.89	2.10
		Shakes 24", 10" exposure	1.20	.95	2.15
		18", 8½" exposure	.92	1.23	2.15
INSULATION					
Ceiling Batts	Fiberglass	3-1/2" thick, R11	.20	.15	.35
		6" thick, R19	.33	.18	.51
		9" thick, R30	.53	.21	.74
		12" thick, R38	.72	.24	.96
	Mineral Fiber	3-1/2" thick, R13	.53	.15	.68
		6" thick, R19	.64	.15	.79
Roof Deck	Fiberboard	1" thick, R2.78	.28	.29	.57
	Mineral	2" thick, R5.26	.55	.30	.85
	Perlite boards	3/4" thick, R2.08	.22	.30	.52
		2" thick, R5.26	.59	.34	.93
	Polystyrene extruded	1" thick, R4	.31	.16	.47
		2" thick, R8	.61	.19	.80
	Urethane paperbacked	1" thick, R6.7	.45	.24	.69
		3" thick, R20	.97	.30	1.27
	Foamglass sheets	1-1/2" thick, R3.95	1.56	.30	1.86
		2" thick, R5.26	2.07	.30	2.37

CEILING

	DESCRIPTION		MAT.	INST.	TOTAL
CEILING					
Plaster	Gypsum	2 coats	.31	1.39	1.70
		3 coats	.43	1.64	2.07
	Perlite or Vermiculite	2 coats	.31	1.62	1.93
		3 coats	.48	2.07	2.55
	Lath Gypsum	Plain 3/8" thick	.24	.32	.56
		1/2" thick	.26	.33	.59
		Firestop 1/2" thick	.34	.38	.72
		5/8" thick	.35	.42	.77
	Metal	Rib 2.75#	.26	.36	.62
		3.40#	.28	.38	.66
		Diamond 2.50#	.19	.36	.55
		3.40#	.24	.45	.69
Drywall	Standard	1/2" thick	.23	.40	.63
		5/8" thick	.25	.44	.69
	Fire resistant	1/2" thick	.26	.41	.67
		5/8" thick	.29	.44	.73
	Water resist.	1/2" thick	.30	.40	.70
		5/8" thick	.33	.44	.77
	Finish	Taping & finishing, add	.01	.24	.25
		thin coat plaster, add	.08	.38	.46
		textured spray, add	.10	.33	.43
Ceiling Tile	Stapled or Glued	Mineral fiber 5/8" thick	.68	.61	1.29
		plastic coated 3/4" thick	.88	.61	1.49
		Wood fiber 1/2" thick	.57	.61	1.18
		3/4" thick	.86	.60	1.46
	Suspended	Fiberglass 5/8" thick	.34	.36	.70
		film faced 3" thick	.45	.49	.94
		Mineral fiber Standard	.36	.36	.72
		5/8" thick Aluminum	.75	.40	1.15
		Wood fiber 1" thick	1.32	.40	1.72
		Reveal edge 3" thick	2.88	.54	3.42
Suspension Systems	Ceiling Tile	"T" bar 2' x 4' grid	.40	.30	.70
		Class A 2' x 2' grid	.34	.36	.70
		Concealed "Z" 12" module	.51	.46	.97
	Plaster or Drywall	3/4" channels 16" O.C.	.25	.82	1.07
		24" O.C.	.19	.56	.75
		1-1/2" channels 16" O.C.	.32	.91	1.23
		24" O.C.	.24	.61	.81
		2" x 4" studs 16" O.C.	.25	.56	.81
		24" O.C.	.20	.45	.65

336

Table I1.2

The estimator should examine the ceiling under the roof structure and under any eaves for signs of water damage or leaks. Knowing the locations of problems at the underside of the roof will be helpful when inspecting above.

The estimator should try to gain access to the roof for close examination of the roofing materials. Built-up roofing should be inspected for visible cracks and bubbles. If the specifications call only for patching of the existing material, the estimator must determine the limits of the work. The work involved in patching may be extensive and the estimator may conclude that a new roof may cost little more than the repair. In this case, as with any in commercial renovation where the estimator can draw on experience, it may be in the client's best interests for the estimator to suggest alternatives to the proposed work. Not only might the client get a better job, but the estimator may get more work for providing better service.

Flashing, gutters and downspouts should be examined to determine materials and condition. If the roofing materials are to be replaced, but not the flashing, then it will take extra care and labor expense to protect the flashing. If the materials are very old, then disturbance may cause problems. When copper or lead gutters and flashing are to be repaired by soldering, the estimator must account for the additional cost of adequate fire protection. Caution is needed even to the point of hiring personnel to remain at the end of the day to assure that no smoldering materials ignite.

Even if no general roofing work is specified, the estimator should examine the plans to see if any existing plumbing vents or other penetrations are to be removed where incidental patching is needed. Conversely, new penetrations, vents, equipment curbs, smoke hatches, and skylights will require flashing and roofing work which may not be specifically shown on the drawings. In this case, the estimator must know what conditions exist and therefore what work is required.

Roofing repair and patching must be performed with extra care. One or two callbacks to repair leaks can severely erode profit margin. Knowing what is involved and what to expect before starting to work will help to eliminate future problems.

1.6 Interior Construction

It cannot be emphasized enough that every existing building is different and should be given thorough and independent examination. The restoration of existing interior features in older buildings, such as brick walls, plaster cornices, and wood floors, is becoming more popular as a design concept in commercial renovation. This new popularity must be accompanied by the expertise, in estimating as well as in construction, for repair, patching, and even duplication of existing features. If existing doors or moldings are to be matched, they may have to be custom milled. Plaster cornice work, almost unheard of in new construction, may have to be repaired or recreated.

Interior construction in commercial renovation can be more difficult than new construction, from initial delivery of materials to final installation. Existing windows may have to be removed to allow for delivery by lift truck. When the building is more than three stories high, workers must place material by crane or by hand, carrying it upstairs or in an elevator. When an existing elevator is used, materials such as sheets of drywall may have to be cut to fit in the elevator. This entails not only the extra costs for material handling but also the extra labor involved in taping more joints upon installation. Only in very large renovation projects will it be cost effective to install a temporary exterior construction elevator. During the site visit, the estimator should anticipate material handling problems and check clearances for large items which cannot be broken down, like large sheets of glass. The timing of deliveries is also critical. Large items must be on-site before construction restricts access.

Every building to be renovated is different, and the new interior construction must be built around existing conditions. Ceiling heights in older buildings are often higher than those found in new construction and can vary from floor to floor. The two foot module of modern materials was not a standard in the past. A 10'-3" high ceiling necessitates buying 12' studs and drywall for partitions. The estimator should check all existing ceiling heights if not clearly shown on the drawings.

The labor involved in constructing a relatively simple stud wall can almost double when working around existing conditions. The upper plate may have to be secured with mastic and toggle bolts to an existing hollow terra cotta ceiling. The new wall may have to be fitted around ceiling beams. If the floor is extremely out of level, each stud may have to be cut to a different length. Extra inside and outside corners are necessary when workers have to box existing piping. The estimator cannot assume that a wall is just a simple straight run without evaluating the existing conditions. Similarly, installation of ceilings, whether acoustical grid type, drywall, or plaster, may require soffits to conform to accommodate existing conditions or to enclose new mechanical and electrical systems.

Typical instructions in plans and specifications for commercial renovation are: "Prepare existing surfaces to receive new finishes" or "Refinish existing surfaces." When the existing surface is a plaster wall, the work may be as simple as light sanding or as extensive as complete replacement of the wall by hand-scraping and replastering. In this example, the estimator must determine the soundness of the existing conditions to be able to estimate the amount of work involved. When scraping loose plaster, what was thought to be a minor patching job can easily spread to include large areas that were not anticipated. If the condition of the existing surfaces is questionable or very deteriorated, the estimator may suggest alternatives to the architect or owner, such as covering an unsound plaster wall with drywall. Especially if the project is being competitively bid, it is in the estimator's best interest to use experience and ingenuity to suggest comparably good but less costly alternatives.

When sandblasting interior surfaces, the estimator must take many indirect factors into account. Extensive precautions must be taken because of the vast amounts of dust created. Large, high volume window fans are needed to exhaust the dust. This creates exterior problems, however, and pedestrian protection must be addressed. Often, sandblasting must be performed at night or on weekends and requires special permits. If the building is partially occupied, floors and ceilings must be covered or sealed to prevent dust dispersion. Adjacent surfaces must be masked or otherwise protected. Often, the costs involved in preparation can exceed the actual cost of the sandblasting.

Similarly, such preparation costs can become a major factor when refinishing wood floors. Repair of damaged areas or replacement of random individual boards can involve much handwork in the removal of the existing and the custom fitting of new pieces. If the original floor was installed with exposed nails, each nail must be hand set before sanding.

In order to conform to existing conditions, installation of required firewalls at stairways and tenant separation may involve additional expense. Most Building Codes require vertical continuity of firewalls and fireproofing of structural members that support the firewalls. Vertical continuity is not always possible and may involve fireproofing ceilings, beams, or columns outside of the stairway enclosure. While these conditions are almost always addressed in the plans and specifications, the estimator should pay particular attention to the existing conditions and the labor involved in constructing firewalls.

This discussion of the site evaluation for interior construction demonstrates the importance of thoroughly understanding the existing conditions and the work to be performed. The estimator must use every resource of experience and knowledge to prepare a complete and proper estimate.

1.7 Conveying Systems

For the installation of an elevator in commercial renovation, the best estimates are obviously competitive bids from elevator subcontractors. In other than budget pricing, such bids are necessary. The estimator should look closely at the elevator subcontractors' bids because they may involve more exclusions than inclusions. It is the estimator's responsibility to provide pricing for such items as construction and preparation of the shaft, structural supports for rails and equipment, access for drilling machinery if required, and construction of the machine room. In other words, the estimator may have to include all work other than the actual direct installation of the elevator equipment.

Often in older buildings there is no shaft, or the existing shaft for an old freight or passenger elevator does not conform to requirements for the proposed new elevator. Pre-engineered standard size elevators often must be altered or custom built to conform to existing conditions. In either case, the installing subcontractor should be consulted, and the costs included in the estimate. Where new floor openings are to be cut or existing openings altered, structural details in the plans and specifications are often general. The estimator should determine if the structural configuration is similar at all levels. As stated previously, floor systems and materials can vary in existing buildings. If there are questions regarding the structure, the estimator should consult an engineer.

During construction of an elevator shaft, and obviously throughout the entire renovation project, the estimator must plan for the requirements and costs of job safety. Temporary railings and toe boards must be securely erected and maintained at floor openings. When welding equipment or cutting torches are being used, an adequate number of fire extinguishers must be supplied and maintained. Time should be allotted to monitor fire safety during hazardous operations.

Unless adequate overhead structure and space exists for pulleys and machinery at the top of the shaft, hydraulic elevators are usually specified in commercial renovation (See Figure I1.7). Machinery for hydraulic elevators is usually placed adjacent to and at the base of the shaft. Standard hydraulic elevators do, however, require a piston shaft to be drilled, often to a depth equal to the height of elevator travel. In new construction, drilling is a relatively easy operation because it is usually performed before erection of the structure. The tailings, waste, and mud from drilling can often be disposed of at the site. In renovation, however, the drilling can become a difficult and expensive proposition. The drilling rig often must be dismantled and reassembled by hand within the existing structure. While this work is usually performed under the elevator subcontract, the estimator must be aware of the associated costs and include them in the estimate.

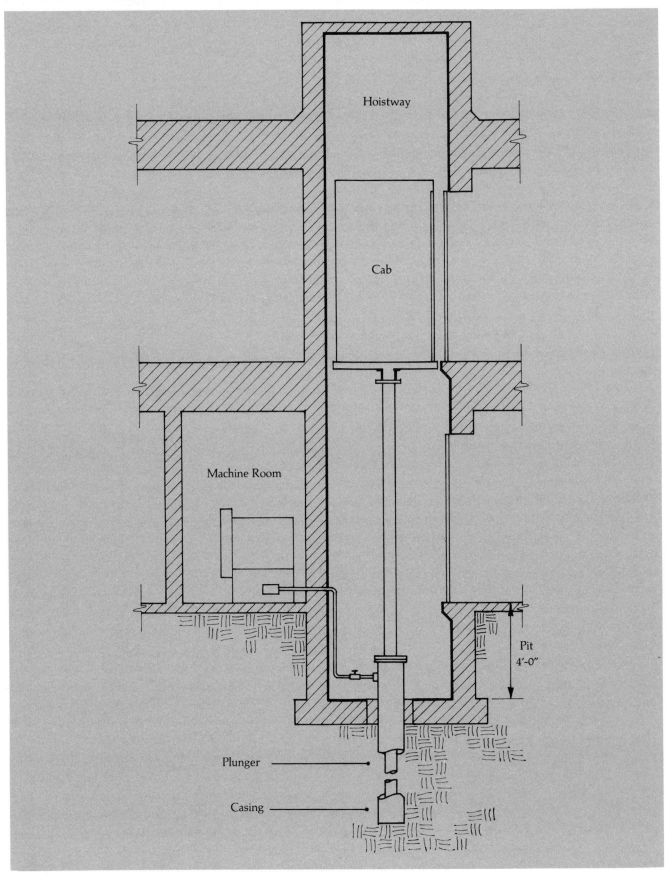

Hoistway

Cab

Machine Room

Pit
4'-0"

Plunger

Casing

Figure I1.7

20

The costs of collecting, draining, and removing drilling waste (usually 90% water, 10% solids) must also be included in the estimate. Especially in urban settings, the contractor is not allowed to dispose of this material in public sewers. The waste often must be somewhat filtered and hauled to an appropriate dumpsite.

The preparation and provisions required to install proposed elevators must be well planned and included in the estimate. In the building shown in Figure I1.9, an interesting problem occurred during the installation of a hydraulic elevator. An existing freight elevator shaft was to be used for the new passenger elevator. At the base of the shaft was a metal pan. The estimator had included the cost of cutting a hole in the pan for drilling as required by the elevator subcontract. After two hours of attempting to cut the metal with an acetylene torch, workers determined that the metal was cast iron and would not melt at the temperature of the torch. Attempts to break the brittle metal with a sledgehammer failed. After many telephone calls, project managers located a welding subcontractor with a high temperature heli-arc welder able to cut what was found to be 2-1/2" thick cast iron. The cost for the work of the welding subcontractor alone was $1,600.00. This does not include the cost of labor for the five hours of previous attempts to cut the hole. Determination of which party, the owner or the contractor, is responsible for assuming the extra expense still rests in litigation.

This is obviously an isolated and unique example, but it is appropriate to show how important the site evaluation can be. While every conceivable problem may not be discovered, the estimator's thorough inspection and evaluation can reduce the probability that such hidden problems will occur.

There are many other factors involved in preparing an existing building for elevators. Shaft enclosures are usually of fire-rated drywall, "shaftwall", masonry, or a combination of these. Elevator pits and roof top enclosures with smoke hatches are often required. When contractors dig pits, water may be encountered, calling for the installation of pumps. The estimator should carefully examine the plans and specifications, including the elevator subcontractor's requirements, to evaluate the existing conditions and to prepare a proper estimate.

Other conveying systems often encountered in commercial renovation are wheelchair lifts and pneumatic tube systems. While these are specialty items, usually installed by the supplier, the estimator still must anticipate the work involved in preparing the existing structure for such installations.

Until recent years, accessibility for the handicapped had not been addressed in building design and construction. Almost all Building Codes today require modifications for the handicapped when a building is renovated. When there is no room for exterior or sidewalk ramps, especially in urban locations, electric wheelchair lifts are often specified. The estimator should carefully evaluate the installation, which usually requires extensive cutting and patching.

The existing conditions at locations for pneumatic tube installation should also be closely inspected. Invariably, structural members will occur in places preventing straight run installations of the tubes, requiring offsets. Unless these problems are included in the estimate, the contractor may have to bear any extra costs for irregular installations.

Upon installation of conveying systems, the estimator should provide for protection of the finished work during the remainder of the construction period. In commercial renovation, where construction elevators are usually not provided, the brand new passenger elevator can be damaged and abused when workers use it to carry materials, equipment, and tools.

As stated above, the best estimates for conveying systems are competitive bids by installing subcontractors. But the estimator must be aware of and anticipate the work and costs involved.

1.8 Mechanical

When estimating mechanical systems, the estimator should read and study the architectural, structural, and mechanical plans and specifications before visiting the site. This way, the estimator is sure to include all items and is fully able to understand how the proposed work will be affected by existing conditions. The estimator should make as few assumptions as possible, and direct any questions to the architect or engineer. Symbols used on the plans should be checked to assure conformity with the estimator's interpretations. Mechanical plans are often prepared by consulting engineers hired by the architect. Plans prepared by different parties should be compared for possible variation of scale or inconsistencies regarding proposed locations for installation.

In new construction, the mechanical systems are incorporated and designed into the planning of the structure. Architectural consideration is given to make mechanical installations as practical and efficient as possible. In renovation, however, mechanical systems must be designed around existing systems and conform to them. The following description of the site visit may include items that would normally be included in a complete set of plans and specifications. But since much layout and design of mechanical work in commercial renovation is left to the contractor, these items are included.

The basement if there is one, is the best place to begin the inspection of the mechanical systems. The existing utility connections should be noted and located on a plan. The estimator should verify sizes of sewer connections and of water and gas services. If the building has sprinklers, check for two water services, domestic and fire protection. The estimator should also inspect the exterior of the building for shut-offs, man-holes, and any other indications of utility connections. Where new utilities are specified, closely examine the proposed locations and surrounding conditions. For example, a building with an individual sewage disposal system (septic tank and leaching field) is to be tied into a public sewer. The estimator should be aware of the location of the proposed connection, requirements of the local public works department, and the contractor responsible for trenching and backfilling. Many municipalities require that the existing septic or holding tanks be removed and backfilled. If no engineer is involved, the estimator should investigate such possibilities.

The estimator should inspect the general condition of existing piping to remain. Corrosion or pitting of the exposed piping may indicate similar conditions at those areas where piping is concealed in walls or ceilings. When old piping remains, the estimator should, if possible, try to inspect the inside of pipes for scaling. Often old pipes, especially galvanized steel, may be encrusted so that flow is severely restricted. When such conditions are found, the owner or architect should be notified to effect a solution before work begins.

Where existing plumbing fixtures are to remain, gaskets and seals should be checked for general condition. If existing fixtures are to be replaced, rough-in dimensions should be measured to assure compliance with the new fixtures.

The proposed plumbing installation should be visually followed up through the building. In renovation, the typical efficient "stacked bathrooms" of new construction are not always feasible, and piping may require many jogs, extra fittings, and substantially more labor for installation. If a tenant is occupying the space below a proposed plumbing installation, the estimator must be aware of the work required below the floor. If the ceiling below is concealed spline or plaster, large sections may have to be replaced. This may require overtime work and the protection of the existing finished spaces.

Proposed sprinkler installations require the same thorough preparation and evaluation. Existing sprinkler valves should be checked. If no regular maintenance has been performed, the valve may not be properly operable. If the existing sprinkler system is connected to a fire alarm system, the estimator may have to provide for extra labor to keep the system operational during renovations. Each morning, the fire alarm monitoring agency must be notified and the system drained. Similarly, at the end of each day, workers must notify the monitoring agency again to refill and activate the system. These necessary operations may require up to two hours or 25 percent of each working day.

When no engineer is involved, it may become the estimator's responsibility to bring an old sprinkler system into conformity with current codes and regulations. Along with local Fire and Building Code officials, the owner's insurance company should be consulted on sprinkler system requirements. Items that should be noted are: the age of the sprinkler heads (usually engraved on the fused link), location of the heads, sizes and condition of piping, and existing water pressure. A possible extreme example: If the existing water pressure is not sufficient to meet regulation, a supplementary electric fire pump may be required. The installation of a fire pump has many ramifications. The existing electrical service must be adequate to handle what is usually a large horsepower motor. Codes may call for an emergency power generator, which in turn includes many indirect costs. Obviously, when a job becomes this involved, an engineer should design the system. Building owners, however, often wish to avoid such costs and request that the contractor do the planning.

When an engineer designs and specifies a new sprinkler system, the estimator must compare the plans with the existing conditions. New plans are often prepared from old as-built plans which may not be accurate or current. What are shown as proposed straight pipe runs may in fact require many offsets, fittings, and more labor to conform to existing conditions. The estimator should walk through the space to be renovated with the proposed system in mind, anticipating any installation problems.

Similar design and installation problems can occur with heating and cooling systems. The engineer may provide system type and capacity, diffuser or register locations, with only line diagrams for piping or ductwork. The contractor is then usually required to furnish shop drawings showing the actual configuration of the installation. Especially with ductwork, the estimator should examine accompanying architectural and structure drawings to assure that there is adequate space for the proposed work. Equipment locations should be inspected. Any questions about bearing capacities for equipment—for example, roof top compressors—should be directed to the structural engineer.

The estimator should visualize all of the proposed mechanical installations as a whole. Even if one engineering firm has provided complete mechanical drawings and specifications, it is likely that different individuals designed each system, and conflicts may occur. Many times sprinkler pipes have run through ductwork. Such conflicts should be discovered and rectified as early as possible. When following the paths of the proposed work, the estimator must be aware of any obstacles that may restrict installation. Penetrations through masonry walls require much handwork, and penetrations of ductwork through firewalls, sometimes not allowed by local codes, require fire dampers.

Even if the specifications do not require shop drawings, the estimator may find that sketches or drawings of the proposed work, including all mechanical systems, will be helpful in preventing problems and in preparing a complete estimate.

Mechanical work in commercial renovation can be challenging and even fun, requiring ingenuity, innovation and the resources of the experienced estimator.

1.9 Electrical

As with mechanical systems, the electrical plans and specifications should be inspected thoroughly so that the estimator will understand the full extent of the work involved before the site visit.

The electrical estimator should have adequate knowledge of both national and local Electric Codes. Even when an engineer prepares the plans and specifications, there is often a clause included: "Perform all electrical work in compliance with applicable codes and ordinances, even when in conflict with the drawings and specifications." If inspectors reject work for non-compliance with codes, it may become the contractor's responsibility to rectify the condition. When analyzing the plans and specifications, the estimator should make notes on questionable installations and advise the architect or engineer as soon as possible.

The electrical drawings will show wiring layouts and circuiting but often not wire types. Different localities have various requirements regarding the uses of non-metallic sheathed cable ("Romex"), BX cable (flexible metallic), EMT (conduit) and galvanized steel conduit. Table I1.3 shows the differences in the cost of wiring similar devices using different materials. Note the cost of a duplex receptacle for each wiring type. The lowest to highest costs vary by over 100 percent. This demonstrates the importance of knowing what type of wiring is required in particular localities. Similarly, aluminum wiring was once widely used as a less expensive alternative to copper, but is now often disallowed as wiring material. And since copper prices have been fluctuating greatly in recent years, the estimator must keep abreast of suppliers' current prices for wiring.

The site evaluation should begin at the existing incoming electric service. The estimator should attempt to determine the size and condition of wiring, switches, meter trim, and other components. If the service is to be revamped or increased, the estimator may be required to determine what materials to reuse and what to replace. In older buildings, all electrical wiring and equipment often must be replaced. If the existing wiring is not very old, some equipment may be rebuilt or reused, saving costs. Local electrical inspectors should be consulted. These determinations require experience and ingenuity, attributes so necessary to the estimator in commercial renovation.

For a new electric service, the estimator should contact the electric utility company as soon as possible. Scheduling for new connections should be established. Often, adjacent buildings may be affected by an electric service switchover and the work must be performed at night or over weekends. If the existing service must be removed before connecting the new, the estimator may have to include the costs of a temporary generator in the estimate.

09.9-500 | Wiring Devices Selective Price Sheet

DESCRIPTION		COST EACH		TOTAL
		MAT.	INST.	
Using non metallic sheathed cable	Air conditioning receptacle	6.60	26.40	33.00
	Disposal wiring	5.50	29.50	35.00
	Dryer circuit	14.30	47.70	62.00
	Duplex receptacle	6.05	19.95	26.00
	Fire alarm or smoke detector	39.60	26.40	66.00
	Furnace circuit & switch	7.81	44.19	52.00
	Ground fault receptacle	39.60	32.40	72.00
	Heater circuit	5.50	32.50	38.00
	Lighting wiring	5.50	16.50	22.00
	Range circuit	33.00	66.00	99.00
	Switches, single pole	5.94	16.06	22.00
	3-way	7.70	22.30	30.00
	Water heater circuit	7.70	52.30	60.00
	Weatherproof receptacle	56.10	43.90	100.00
Using BX cable	Air conditioning receptacle	11.00	32.00	43.00
	Disposal wiring	8.80	35.20	44.00
	Dryer circuit	22.00	57.00	79.00
	Duplex receptacle	9.90	24.10	34.00
	Fire alarm or smoke detector	42.90	32.10	75.00
	Furnace circuit & switch	12.10	52.90	65.00
	Ground fault receptacle	45.10	39.90	85.00
	Heater circuit	8.80	40.20	49.00
	Lighting wiring	9.90	20.10	30.00
	Range circuit	46.20	78.80	125.00
	Switches, single pole	9.90	20.10	30.00
	3-way	13.20	25.80	39.00
	Water heater circuit	13.20	62.80	76.00
	Weatherproof receptacle	60.50	54.50	115.00
Using EMT conduit	Air conditioning receptacle	11.00	30.00	50.00
	Disposal wiring	8.80	44.20	53.00
	Dryer circuit	16.50	71.50	88.00
	Duplex receptacle	9.90	30.10	40.00
	Fire alarm or smoke detector	42.90	39.10	82.00
	Furnace circuit & switch	12.10	65.90	78.00
	Ground fault receptacle	45.10	48.90	94.00
	Heater circuit	8.80	48.20	57.00
	Lighting wiring	9.90	24.10	34.00
	Range circuit	28.60	96.40	125.00
	Switches, single pole	9.90	24.10	34.00
	3-way	13.20	32.80	46.00
	Water heater circuit	13.20	77.80	91.00
	Weatherproof receptacle	60.50	64.50	125.00

DESCRIPTION		COST EACH		TOTAL
		MAT.	INST.	
Using aluminum conduit	Air conditioning receptacle	19.14	52.86	72.00
	Disposal wiring	17.60	58.40	76.00
	Dryer circuit	25.30	94.70	120.00
	Duplex receptacle	18.70	40.30	59.00
	Fire alarm or smoke detector	50.60	54.40	105.00
	Furnace circuit & switch	20.46	89.54	110.00
	Ground fault receptacle	52.80	67.20	120.00
	Heater circuit	17.60	65.40	83.00
	Lighting wiring	18.70	33.30	52.00
	Range circuit	37.40	132.60	170.00
	Switches, single pole	18.70	33.30	52.00
	3-way	19.80	44.20	64.00
	Water heater circuit	19.80	105.20	125.00
	Weatherproof receptacle	68.20	86.80	155.00
Using galvanized steel conduit	Air conditioning receptacle	18.26	55.74	74.00
	Disposal wiring	16.50	62.50	79.00
	Dryer circuit	24.20	100.80	125.00
	Duplex receptacle	17.60	43.40	61.00
	Fire alarm or smoke detector	49.50	55.50	105.00
	Furnace circuit & switch	19.36	95.64	115.00
	Ground fault receptacle	51.70	68.30	120.00
	Heater circuit	16.50	69.50	86.00
	Lighting wiring	17.60	35.40	53.00
	Range circuit	36.30	138.70	175.00
	Switches, single pole	17.60	35.40	53.00
	3-way	18.70	45.30	64.00
	Water heater circuit	18.70	111.30	130.00
	Weatherproof receptacle	66.00	94.00	160.00

Table I1.3

The entire electrical installation should be visualized and kept in mind as the estimator walks through the building. If no engineer is involved, the estimator must determine the best distribution system. If the building is to have many separately metered areas, options are available. Some local electric utilities require that all meters be installed in one location. This requires expensive, and possibly long, individual feeders to each tenant. If remote meter locations are allowed, however, only one main feeder is required to each remote multiple meter location. Distribution feeders can be much shorter (see Figure I1.8). The latter example can be less expensive. The estimator should be able to analyze the options to determine the best system for each renovation project.

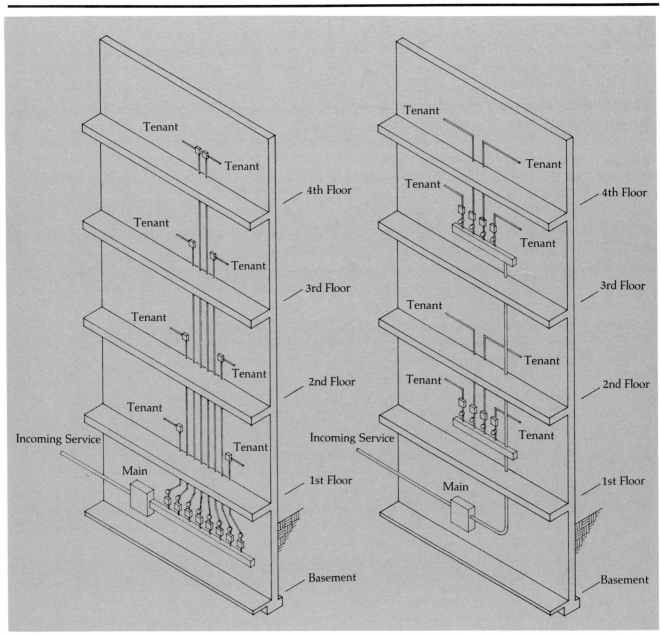

Figure I1.8 Electrical Distribution Alternatives

At some point in new construction, all spaces are open and accessible for the electrical installation. This can be before concrete slabs are poured or before walls and ceilings are closed. In the renovation of existing buildings, however, gaining access to spaces for wiring can be difficult, costly, and time-consuming. Cutting and patching can become a major expense. If existing walls and ceilings are to remain, access holes must be made to snake wiring, and then patched. Wiring often must be installed in circuitous routes to avoid obstacles. This involves both more labor and more material. In renovation wiring, the shortest route from point A to point B is not always a straight line. An example is when duplex receptacles are being installed in existing plaster walls. To wire horizontally from one outlet box to the next would involve removing large amounts of plaster, drilling each stud, and then patching. Instead, each box must be individually fed from a junction box, perhaps at the ceiling. When rigid conduit is needed for fire alarms or other purposes, many more offsets and bends may be necessary when adapting the wiring to existing conditions. Similarly, when wiring is to be exposed, rigid conduit or surface mounted raceway are often specified and must be run at right angles to the existing structure. A neat finished installation calls for extra care and work.

The estimate should also include temporary lighting and power. The estimator must thoroughly evaluate the plans, specifications, and site to assure that they contain all such requirements. If scaffolding is to be erected at the exterior, weatherproof temporary lighting is necessary for pedestrian protection. Certain construction equipment, like mortar mixers and welders, may have special temporary electrical needs.

With or without plans and specifications, the estimator must use imagination in visualizing the complete electrical installation in order to evaluate existing conditions and to complete a proper estimate.

1.10
General Conditions

The estimator must not only include all the "hard costs," the materials and labor to produce the actual finished project, but also the "soft costs," those indispensible items that are required for the performance of the work, must be determined. The following is a partial list of items that are included in the General Conditions, or General Requirements:

1. Overhead and Main Office Expenses
2. Profit
3. Sales and Employer's Taxes
4. Bonds
5. Insurance
6. Architectural and Engineering Fees
7. Testing & Borings
8. General Working Conditions
9. Temporary Requirement & Construction
10. Contractor Equipment

Added together, these items can become a large percentage of the cost of the proposed renovation project. How these items are incorporated into the estimating process will be discussed later in this book. This section will deal with how the estimator anticipates the cost of General Conditions while evaluating the site and analyzing the existing conditions.

The first seven items mentioned above are determined and included while preparing the actual estimate. Items 8 through 10, however, must be determined in part while inspecting the building to be renovated.

1.1 Overhead

No.	Description	CREW	MAN-HOURS	UNIT	MAT.	LABOR	EQUIP.	TOTAL	TOTAL INCL O&P
09-001	CONSTRUCTION MANAGEMENT FEES								
006	For work to $10,000			Project					10%
007	To $25,000								9%
009	To $100,000								6%
010	To $500,000								5%
011	To $1,000,000								4%
11-001	CONTINGENCIES Allowance to add at conceptual stage								20%
005	Schematic stage								15%
010	Preliminary working drawing stage								10%
015	Final working drawing stage								2%
15-001	ENGINEERING FEES Educational planning consultant, minimum			Contract					4.10%
010	Maximum								10.10%
040	Elevator & conveying systems, minimum								2.50%
050	Maximum								5%
100	Mechanical (plumbing & HVAC), minimum								4.10%
110	Maximum								10.10%
120	Structural, minimum			Project					1%
130	Maximum			"					2.50%
17-001	FACTORS To be added to construction costs for particular job requirements								
010									
050	[1] Cut & patch to match existing construction, add, minimum			Costs	2%	3%			
055	Maximum				5%	9%			
080	[2] Dust protection, add, minimum				1%	2%			
085	Maximum				4%	11%			
110	[3] Equipment usage curtailment, add, minimum				1%	1%			
115	Maximum				3%	10%			
140	[4] Material handling & storage limitation, add, minimum				1%	1%			
145	Maximum				6%	7%			
170	[5] Protection of existing work, add, minimum				2%	2%			
175	Maximum				5%	7%			
200	[6] Shift work requirements, add, minimum					5%			
205	Maximum					30%			
230	[7] Temporary shoring and bracing, add, minimum				2%	5%			
235	Maximum				5%	12%			
18-001	INSURANCE Builders risk, standard, minimum			Job Cost					.10%
005	Maximum								50%
020	All-risk type, minimum								12%
025	Maximum								68%
040	Contractor's equipment floater, minimum			Value					.90%
045	Maximum			"					1.60%
060	Public liability, average			Job Cost					82%
081	Workers compensation & employer's liability								
200	Range of 36 trades in 50 states, excl. wrecking, min.			Payroll		1.04%			
210	Average					9%			

NOTES

FACTORS: In planning and estimating repair and remodeling projects, there are many factors that can affect the project cost more than material and labor. The economics of scale usually associated with new construction often has no influence on the cost of repair and remodeling. Small quantities of components may have to be custom fabricated at great expense. Work schedule coordination between trades frequently becomes difficult and work area restrictions can lead to subcontractor quotations with start-up and shutdown costs which are in excess of the cost of actual work involved. Some of the more prominent factors affecting repair and remodeling projects include:

1. Cutting and patching to match the existing construction can often lead to an economical trade-off of removing entire walls rather than creating new door and window openings. Substitutions for materials which are no longer manufactured can be expensive. Piping and ductwork runs may not be as straight as in new construction and wiring may have to be snaked through walls and floors.

2. Dust and noise protection of adjoining nonconstruction areas can alter usual construction methods.

3. Equipment usage curtailment resulting from physical limitations of the project may force workmen to use slow hand-operated equipment instead of power tools.

4. The confines of an enclosed building have a costly influence on movement and material handling. Low capacity elevators and stairwells may be the only access to upper floors of a multi-story building.

5. On some repair or remodeling projects completed work must be secured or otherwise protected from possible damage during construction. In certain areas completed work must be guarded to prevent theft and vandalism. (cont.)

For expanded coverage of these items see *Building Construction Cost Data 1985*

Table I1.4

Table I1.4 shows a page from R.S. Means' *Repair and Remodeling Cost Data, 1985.* Please note section 17-001, Factors. The seven factors listed are those that most commonly increase the costs of a renovation project. The estimator must visualize the proposed work and keep in mind how existing conditions will affect the work.

Almost every renovation or remodeling job involves much cutting and patching to match existing conditions. Workers must open access holes in existing walls to install wire and pipe. Often, original components, moldings, and trim must be carefully removed and then replaced. Damaged pieces must be recreated or repaired at some expense. For example, a job calls for a new plumbing vent to be installed through an old slate shingle roof. A copper sleeve and flashing must be custom made to match the existing work. Cutting the hole for the pipe can be difficult. Undoubtedly, shingles at the hole and elsewhere near the work will break and need replacement. The scaffolding or roof jacks must be installed with extreme care to prevent such breakage. The cost of performing such work could be many times greater than that for similar work on an asphalt shingle roof. The estimator must be familiar with the materials to determine how the work is to be performed and what it will cost.

When a renovation project is to be performed in a partially occupied building, the estimator is often required to protect adjacent areas not involved in the project from dust, noise, and general disturbance. When the main lobby and only elevator are in constant use by tenants and must be used for materials and equipment, the estimator has to provide for constant cleaning of these areas. Door and window openings at the work site must be sealed to prevent dust dispersion. Workers must employ certain methods to prevent spreading dust while performing the work. This can slow production. If a dust problem occurs in adjacent areas, the contractor may be required to hire an outside cleaning contractor. Especially in urban areas, dumpsters have to be covered, and laborers must use trash chutes (Figure I1.9) instead of throwing materials out of a window. These requirements are not only for pedestrian protection but for the reduction of dust problems. Also, covering a dumpster may help to prevent the contractor from hauling the entire neighborhood's garbage, which mysteriously appears in dumpsters each morning.

In new construction, work is planned and scheduled to take full advantage of the most efficient and productive construction equipment. For example, hydraulic elevator piston shafts are drilled before erection of the superstructure to allow the mobile drilling rig free access. In commercial renovation, however, such access is often severely curtailed. Work must be performed with small, less effective equipment or even by hand. This can add substantially to the labor costs of the project. The use of equipment may also be restricted because of noise. In a partially occupied building, the specifications may state that the contractor must cease a noisy operation when a tenant disturbance results in a complaint. The options then available are to forego the use of the equipment for more time consuming, quieter methods or to perform the work during overtime hours when the building is not occupied. Both result in higher construction costs. The estimator must anticipate such restrictions and include the appropriate costs in the estimate.

Limitations regarding the delivery, storage, and handling of construction materials can also add to the cost of renovation projects. The specifications may impose a restriction that allows delivery and placement of materials only at certain off-peak times of the day. Local authorities may restrict the use of the street, or the building may limit the use of loading areas or elevators. All parties should be consulted before the estimate is prepared. If delivery and handling is restricted to certain times, it may be required that all personnel stop work to assist with unloading and placement of materials. This process can reduce productivity. Work must be stopped and started during the course of the day, and the project may require more deliveries than were anticipated.

Inside the building, there may be insufficient bearing capacities or lack of area for material storage. Materials stored outside must be adequately protected from the elements. Architects usually specify that materials be stored in the environment where they are to be used for a stated period of time before placement. This is necessary for proper installation. If interior storage areas are limited, this will require the placement of only small amounts of material at a time. Often, materials must be carried up stairs or cut to fit inside elevators.

Figure I1.9

When materials are delivered or work is performed in a building where certain areas are finished or occupied, contractors must protect finished work. The contractor may be responsible for providing temporary coverings, moving pads, or plywood for elevators, and floor runners for carpeted areas. The estimator must determine appropriate measures to protect areas adjacent to the location of the actual work, and must be sure to include the costs in the estimate.

In many of the instances described, shift work or overtime may be required. When such work is anticipated, the estimator should discuss the conditions involved with the architect and owner to be sure that all requirements are met and that such appropriate costs are included in the estimate. For smaller projects, even a minor amount of unanticipated overtime work can severely erode the profit margin.

When contractors perform structural work in an existing building, temporary shoring or bracing may be necessary. If bracing is not included in the plans and specifications, the estimator should consult the engineer on the structural requirements of such work.

Temporary requirements and construction can add substantially to the costs of renovation. A field office inside the building or in a trailer may be required. This may include a telephone, heat, and lighting for the duration of the project.

Barricades, scaffolding, temporary railings, and fences are temporary items that may not be directly specified. In new construction, these items may be included in the estimate as established costs or percentages determined from previous similar jobs. Each commercial renovation project is unique, however, and has particular requirements.

Hiring non-construction personnel may also be necessary. Local authorities in cities may call for a police officer to direct traffic or to protect pedestrians when work or material deliveries are performed at the street. Watchmen, sometimes with guard dogs, may be necessary to prevent theft and vandalism. It is helpful if estimators are familiar with the neighborhood of the renovation project. If so they can anticipate and include such indirect costs in the estimate.

Another intangible item that affects the costs of a commercial renovation is the coordination of subcontractors. Divisions of labor and responsibility are often unclear in commercial renovation. Existing conditions may inhibit the efficient coordination. The estimator must anticipate such problems by visualizing the complete renovation process including the appropriate supervision for each particular project. During the site visit, the estimator must determine how many workers will be needed and what equipment can and cannot be used.

Other appropriate items are shown in Table I1.5 from R.S. Means' *Repair and Remodeling Cost Data*. Section 19-001, Job Conditions, lists more general items that will affect the estimate. Please note that the items discussed in Tables I1.4 and I1.5 all involve percentages of project costs to be added or deducted. The estimator must use experience and constructive imagination to incorporate these figures into the estimate without losing accuracy.

1.1 Overhead	CREW	MAN-HOURS	UNIT	MAT.	LABOR	EQUIP.	TOTAL	TOTAL INCL O&P
220 Maximum			Payroll		54.13%			
19-001 JOB CONDITIONS Modifications to total								
002 project cost summaries								
010 Economic conditions, favorable, deduct			Project					2%
020 Unfavorable, add								5%
030 Hoisting conditions, favorable, deduct								1%
040 Unfavorable, add								5%
050 General Contractor management, experienced, deduct								2%
060 Inexperienced, add								10%
070 Labor availability, surplus, deduct								1%
080 Shortage, add								10%
090 Material storage area, available, deduct								1%
100 Not available, add								2%
110 Subcontractor availability, surplus, deduct								5%
120 Shortage, add								12%
130 Work space, available, deduct								1%
140 Not available, add								4%
22-001 MAIN OFFICE EXPENSE Average for General Contractors								
002 a percentage of their annual volume								
003 Annual volume to $50,000, minimum			% Vol.				20%	
004 Maximum							30%	
006 To $100,000, minimum							17%	
007 Maximum							22%	
008 To $250,000, minimum							16%	
009 Maximum							19%	
011 To $500,000, minimum							14%	
012 Maximum							16%	
013 To $1,000,000, minimum							10%	
014 Maximum							8%	
070 Project Manager, minimum	1 Skwk	38.100	Week		765		765	1.175L
075 Average		42.110			845		845	1.300L
080 Maximum		47.060			945		945	1.450L
100 Superintendent, minimum		34.780			700		700	1.075L
105 Average		38.100			765		765	1.175L
110 Maximum		44.440			895		895	1.375L
28-001 OVERHEAD As percent of direct costs, minimum			%				5%	
005 Average							15%	
010 Maximum							30%	
30-001 OVERHEAD & PROFIT Allowance to add to items in this								
002 book that do not include Subs O&P, average			%				30%	
010 Allowance to add to items in this book that								
011 do include Subs O&P, minimum								5%

NOTES

6. Work may have to be done on other than normal shifts and may have to be done around an existing production facility in operation during the repair and remodeling project.

7. Requirements for shoring and bracing to hold up the building while structural changes are being made and allowance for temporary storage of construction materials on above-grade floors will affect costs.

INSURANCE: Builders risk insurance generally includes fire insurance, extended coverage and vandalism. Rates are related to type of construction and amount of deductible. In dollars per $100 value for $1000 deductible for contracts less than $500,000, the range is from $.096 to $.652.

	RANGE	AVERAGE
FRAME	$.250 to $.500	$.40/$100
BRICK	$.150 to $.300	$.28/$100
FIRE-RESISTIVE	$.096 to $.254	$.21/$100

Blasting, collapse and underground insurance is additional. Floater policies for material delivered to the job runs from $1.00 to $1.50 per $100 value. Construction equipment insurance runs from $.50 to $2.50 per $100 value.

MAIN OFFICE EXPENSE consists of costs incurred in maintaining a business. These costs include salaries for managers, estimators and clerical personnel; profit sharing; pension and bonus plans; insurance; legal, accounting and data processing costs; auto and light truck expenses; office rent; utilities; office equipment maintenance and depreciation. [Usually main office expense declines, as a percentage of annual volume, with increased volume.]

For expanded coverage of these items see *Building Construction Cost Data 1985*

Table I1.5

1.11
Special

Special items usually included in renovation are kitchens, cabinets, toilet accessories, toilet partitions, wood or coal stoves, and fireplaces. These items are often clearly specified, and materials prices can be easily obtained. The estimator should inspect locations for installation. If the installation is to be on existing surfaces, the estimator must be sure that there is adequate backing or space for specified recessed equipment. The labor can become expensive when workers have to remove existing wall finishes, install backing, and patch the area.

When installing wood burning stoves or metal or masonry fireplaces, contractors should consult a structural engineer to determine if there is adequate bearing capacity or if the structure is to be modified. The estimator should examine the existing framing to be penetrated by the flue or chimney to determine the alterations needed. The inspection may show that the proposed location is at a bearing structural member that cannot be removed. Also, the estimator should be aware of local fire safety codes and ordinances regulating the installation of stoves and fireplaces. These codes are constantly being updated because of the increasing popularity of wood stove use. If there are any questions, an engineer or local fire official should be consulted. Again, the estimator must know exactly what is specified and how the existing conditions will affect the work.

1.12
Site Work and Demolition

Usually, site work in commercial renovation is relatively limited. The economy of scale used for new construction is often not applicable for renovation work. Trenching and excavation usually involve cutting and patching concrete or asphalt. If the particular job is small or if there is inadequate room for the use of large equipment, the work may have to be performed by hand. To prevent damage, workers must take extra care when digging near existing buried utilities or piping.

The estimator must try to gather as much information as possible when inspecting for proposed site work. Any holes or test pits should be examined for soil type and stability. Shutoffs and manholes for utilities should be located or verified on a site plan. If site work is to be performed on public sidewalks or in the street, the estimator should consult local authorities to determine what requirements must be met. For example, the renovation project calls for a new sewer connection in the street. After a visual examination, the estimator thought the job included only cutting and patching the concrete sidewalk and asphalt pavement, trenching, and backfilling. Upon investigation the estimator learns that the existing sidewalk contains metal reinforcing, that the street has a six-inch reinforced concrete base that must be cut and patched to match the existing work, and that under local regulations, a policeman must be hired for traffic control. Also, low overhead wires severely restrict the use of large equipment. As can be seen, the project can become much more involved than originally planned without proper investigation and evaluation.

Demolition can be the most challenging aspect of the estimating commercial renovation. When the job calls for extensive demolition, it may be best to obtain prices from local subcontractors who are familiar with local regulations, hauling requirements, and dumpsite locations. Also, local demolition subcontractors are most familiar with the values and procedures for disposing of salvageable materials, a condition that may reduce the costs of demolition. When asbestos or other hazardous materials are specified to be removed, the estimator should always consult with local authorities and a licensed subcontractor. Not only does asbestos present a health hazard, but EPA and OSHA regulations impose stiff fines and penalties if hazardous materials are improperly handled and discarded.

When the specified demolition is selective, the estimator must use all resources, experience, and knowledge to estimate the costs effectively. Demolition in commercial renovation can be divided into three phases:

1. The actual dismantling of the existing structures, including the labor and equipment necessary.
2. Handling the debris. This includes the transport of material to an on-site container or truck and may include the installation and rental of a trash chute and the rental of dumpsters.
3. Hauling the rubbish to an approved dumpsite.

It is very important to be correct when identifying the materials and determining the limits of the demolition. Table I1.6 shows a page from R.S. Means' *Repair and Remodeling Cost Data*. Note Section 68-001, Wall & Partition Demolition. Removal of gypsum plaster on metal lath ($.64 per square foot) is three times more costly than removal of nailed drywall ($.19 per square foot). If the estimator does not take the time to identify the material, expensive mistakes can occur.

Determining the limits of demolition is often the estimator's responsibility. Even if a demolition drawing is included in the plans and specifications, and often this is not the case, it may have been drawn from obsolete plans. Or the specifications may say "Contractor is to remove and dispose of all materials not to remain as part of the work." This is a vague statement that leaves all responsibility on the estimator. If there is a demolition plan, the estimator should walk through the renovation site to verify location and dimensions and to identify materials to be removed. To assist in determining quantities, the estimator should measure ceiling heights. If there is no plan, the estimator should make a sketch, using the proposed floor plan as a reference. Measurements should be taken and written on the sketch at the site. The estimator should leave as little as possible to memory when preparing the estimate.

When certain existing materials are to remain, the estimator must choose the method of work that offers them effective protection. Sometimes skilled labor may be necessary to remove items adjacent to materials that will remain.

The estimator may also have to determine when it is more economical to remove existing material completely and build new, or when it is cheaper to cut, patch, and alter existing work to conform to new specifications.

Once the materials marked for demolition have been dismantled, the estimator must decide upon the best method for moving the debris to a dumpster or truck for removal from the site. If the building is not tall, a covered slide may be constructed with relative ease. If the building is many stories above grade, however, alternatives must be examined. An existing freight elevator might be available but the process of transporting small loads may be very time consuming. Workers may have to erect a trash chute. Table I1.7 shows the costs involved. It should be noted that in addition to these costs, the estimator should include the costs of support scaffolding and the possibility that workers will need a crane to erect it.

2.2 Building Demolition

		CREW	MAN-HOURS	UNIT	MAT.	LABOR	EQUIP.	TOTAL	TOTAL INCL O&P
64	900 Minimum labor/equipment charge	1 Clab	4	Job		62		62	96L
68-001	**WALLS & PARTITIONS DEMOLITION**								
	002								
	100 Drywall, nailed	1 Clab	.008	S.F.		.12		.12	.19L
	102 Glued & nailed		.009			.14		.14	.21L
	150 Fiberboard, nailed		.009			.14		.14	.21L
	152 Glued & nailed		.010			.16		.16	.24L
	200 Movable walls, metal, 5' high		.027			.41		.41	.64L
	202 8' high		.020			.31		.31	.48L
	220 Metal studs, finish 2 sides, fiberboard	B-1	.046			.75		.75	1.15L
	225 Lath and plaster		.092			1.49		1.49	2.30L
	230 Plasterboard (drywall)		.046			.75		.75	1.15L
	235 Plywood		.053			.86		.86	1.33L
	300 Plaster, lime & horsehair, on wood lath	1 Clab	.020			.31		.31	.48L
	302 On metal lath		.024			.37		.37	.57L
	340 Gypsum or perlite, on gypsum lath		.020			.30		.30	.47L
	342 On metal lath		.027			.41		.41	.64L
	380 Toilet partitions, slate or marble		1.600	Ea.		25		25	38L
	382 Hollow metal		1	"		15.50		15.50	24L
	900 Minimum labor/equipment charge		2	Job		31		31	48L
72-001	**WINDOW DEMOLITION**								
	002								
	020 Aluminum, including trim, to 12 S.F.	A-1	.667	Ea.		10.35	2.93	13.28	19.20
	024 To 25 S.F.		1			15.50	4.40	19.90	29
	028 To 50 S.F.		2			31	8.80	39.80	58
	032 Storm windows, to 12 S.F.		.400			6.20	1.76	7.96	11.50
	036 To 25 S.F.		.500			7.75	2.20	9.95	14.40
	040 To 50 S.F.		.667			10.35	2.93	13.28	19.20
	060 Glass, minimum	1 Clab	.040	S.F.		.62		.62	.96L
	062 Maximum	"	.053	"		.83		.83	1.28L
	100 Steel, including trim, to 12 S.F.	A-1	.800	Ea.		12.40	3.52	15.92	23
	102 To 25 S.F.		1.140			17.70	5.05	22.75	33
	104 To 50 S.F.		2.670			41	11.75	52.75	77
	200 Wood, including trim, to 12 S.F.	1 Clab	.500			7.75		7.75	11.95L
	202 To 25 S.F.		.667			10.35		10.35	15.95L
	206 To 50 S.F.		1.330			21		21	32L
	502 Remove & reset window, minimum	1 Carp	1.330			26		26	40L
	504 Average		2			39		39	61L
	508 Maximum		4			78		78	120L
	900 Minimum labor/equipment charge	1 Clab	2	Job		31		31	48L
76-001	**MOVING BUILDINGS** One day move, up to 24' wide								
	002 Reset on new foundation, patch & hook-up, average move			Total					5,000

NOTES

GENERAL DEMOLITION A2.2-20 thru 72

When estimating demolition the authors recommend getting a bid from a local contractor, if possible. Variables including disposal sites, protection of adjacent structures, salvage, and economic conditions can affect costs by 100%.

In calculating the line item costs of this major classification, three preliminary qualifications are assumed:

1. The tools used for demolition are generally of the hand or pneumatic hand type (note crew size).

2. The cost of rubbish handling (removing rubbish to on-site containers or trucks) is not included.

3. The cost of hauling rubbish to an approved dumpsite is not included.

Therefore, for total general demolition cost, add rubbish handling (See Division 2.2-78) and hauling (See Division 2.3-30).

For expanded coverage of these items see *Means' Site Work Cost Data 1985*

32

Table I1.6

2-2 Building Demolition

		CREW	MAN-HOURS	UNIT	MAT.	LABOR	EQUIP.	TOTAL	TOTAL INCL O&P	NOTES
76	004 Wood or steel frame bldg., based on ground floor area	B-4	.259	S.F.		4.15	1.70	5.85	8.25	
	006 Masonry bldg., based on ground floor area	"	.350	↓		5.61	2.29	7.90	11.15	
	020 For 24' to 42' wide, add								1.40	
	022 For each additional day on road, add	B-4	48	Day		760	315	1,075	1,525	
	024 Construct new basement, move building, 1 day									
	030 move, patch & hook-up, based on ground floor area	B-3	.369	S.F.	7.95	6.20	8.80	22.95	28	
78-001	RUBBISH HANDLING The following are to be added to the									
	002 demolition prices									
	040 Chute, circular, prefabricated steel, 18" diameter	B-1	.600	L.F.	7.40	9.70		17.10	23	
	044 30" diameter	"	.800	"	14.75	12.95		27.70	36	
	060 Dumpster, (debris box container), 5 C.Y., rent per week			Ea.					85	
	070 10 C.Y.								110	
	080 30 C.Y. capacity								150	
	084 40 C.Y. capacity			↓					185	
	100 Dust partition, 6 mil polyethylene, 4' x 8' panels, 1" x 3" frame	1 Carp	.010	S.F.	.10	.20		.30	.41	
	108 2" x 4" frame	"	.008	"	.25	.16		.41	.52	
	200 Load, haul to chute & dumping into chute, 50' haul	B-6	.022	C.F.		.36	.14	.50	.71	
	204 100' haul		.027			.44	.17	.61	.87	
	208 Over 100' haul, add per 100 LF		.010			.16	.06	.22	.31	
	212 In elevators, per 10 floors, add	↓	.024	↓		.40	.15	.55	.78	
	300 Loading & trucking									
	304 Hand loaded	B-16	.800	C.Y.		12.90	7	19.90	28	
	308 Machine loaded	B-6	.480			8.01	3.04	11.05	15.65	
	312 Wheeled and ramp dump loaded	B-1	.750	↓		12.15		12.15	18.75L	
79-001	SAW CUTTING Asphalt over 1000 L.F., per inch of depth	A-1	.016	L.F.		.25	.07	.32	.46	
	002 Each additional inch of depth		.006			.10	.03	.13	.18	
	040 Concrete slabs, mesh reinforcing, per inch of depth		.026			.40	.12	.52	.76	
	042 Rod reinforcing, per inch of depth		.067			1.04	.29	1.33	1.92	
	080 Concrete walls, plain, per inch of depth		.100			1.55	.44	1.99	2.88	
	082 Rod reinforcing, per inch of depth		.131			2.03	.58	2.61	3.78	
	120 Masonry walls, brick, per inch of depth		.100			1.55	.44	1.99	2.88	
	122 Block, per inch of depth	↓	.084			1.31	.37	1.68	2.42	
	500 Wood sheathing to 1" thick on walls	1 Carp	.040			.78		.78	1.21L	
	502 On roof	"	.032	↓		.63		.63	.97L	
	900 Minimum labor/equipment charge	A-1	4	Job		62.40	17.60	80	115	
80-001	TORCH CUTTING Steel, 1" thick plate	A-1	.084	L.F.		1.31	.37	1.68	2.42	
	004 1" diameter bar	"	.038	Ea.		.59	.17	.76	1.10	
	100 Oxygen lance cutting, reinforced concrete walls									
	104 12" to 16" thick walls	1 Clab	.800	L.F.		12.40		12.40	19.15L	
	108 24" thick walls	"	1.330	"		21		21	32L	
	109 Minimum labor/equipment charge	A-1	8	Job		125	35	160	230	
	110 See division 5.1-41									

For expanded coverage of these items see *Means' Site Work Cost Data 1985*

Table I1.7

The estimator must also draw upon experience to determine the number of dumpsters or truckloads required. Most disposal contractors include landfill costs in the dumpster rental fees, but the estimator should verify this service. If the estimator decides that hauling by truck is the best alternative, he should contact local landfills to make sure that they will accept construction materials and to determine the cost of dumping.

Demolition and the removal of materials is rarely well defined in plans and specifications. It is a facet of commercial renovation where the estimator could easily underestimate the costs involved. The whole process of the work must be well thought out and planned.

The overriding point made throughout this discussion of the site evaluation is that the estimator must have a thorough understanding of the proposed work and must perform a detailed inspection of the site to determine how the work will be affected by the existing conditions. The size or age of an existing building should have no bearing on the importance of the site visit. In fact, with a smaller project, a particular error or oversight can have a larger percentage effect on the accuracy of the estimate than with a larger job.

The estimator should always verify dimensions and feasibility, and should be familiar with the types of construction and materials to be encountered. The estimator must use all the experience, knowledge, and resources available in order to prepare complete and accurate estimates for commercial renovation.

Chapter 2.
The Quantity Take-off and Determination of Costs

There are many helpful rules to follow when handling the numbers and measurements for the quantity take-off in estimating for commercial renovation. These rules are suggested as guidelines to assist the estimator to work logically and to be thorough. They are designed to prevent omissions or duplications and to provide a system that can be easily checked and analyzed. No quantity take-off method for commercial renovation is foolproof, and the estimator must use all information gathered from the site visit in conjunction with the plans and specifications to assure that all work is included. It should be noted that these guidelines are only suggestions. They do, however, represent tried and proven methods.

2.1
Working with the Plans and Specifications

It is very important to be consistent when examining and determining quantities from the plans and specifications. Inconsistency can easily lead to errors or omissions.

The estimator should develop the quantity take-off by starting at the foundation or lowest level, and should move up floor by floor. Even if a floor is a duplicate of another, each floor should be listed separately. Each drawing should be approached systematically. The estimator should determine the quantities by moving north to south or vice versa, clockwise or counterclockwise. The direction doesn't matter. The consistency does. If the building has wings or well defined sections, the approach again must be consistent: for example, move from the main section out to the wings.

When examining the plans and specifications, the estimator should always use printed dimensions. Multiple dimensions should be added to provide fewer but larger measurements. When dimensions must be measured, be careful and alert for notes such as N.T.S. (not to scale). Details, sections, and elevations are often drawn at different scales from the floor plans. If the drawings have been reduced, then the listed scales are probably not accurate. The estimator should also thoroughly read the specifications to find any discrepancies in the plans.

The estimator must measure and list not only every item shown on the plans, but those items not shown that are required to complete the work. This is

39

especially important in commercial renovation. The estimator must rely on the site evaluation and on experience to include items that are not directly specified.

As quantities are determined, the estimator should mark the drawings, perhaps with different colors, to avoid duplication and to assure inclusion of all items. The following is a list of materials and aids that may be helpful when determining quantities from the plans and specifications:

1. Architectural scale (1/8, 1/4, 1/2, 1" = 1'-0")
2. Engineering scale (10, 20, 30, 40, 50, 60 parts per inch)
3. Rotometer
4. Colored pencils
5. Pre-printed or custom-developed estimating forms

2.2
The Paperwork

Consistency should also be of primary emphasis when dealing with the paperwork. Preprinted forms should be used wherever possible. Figure I2.1 is an R.S. Means Consolidated Estimate Form which has been created to be most effective and efficient for commercial renovation. Figure I2.2 is an R.S. Means Quantity Sheet which is used to tabulate and calculate quantities before pricing. When transferring dimensions from the plans to such forms, be consistent. For example, always list length, width, and height in the same order. This will help to avoid confusion. And as stated before, always use printed dimensions where possible.

Measurements should be converted from feet and inches to decimal feet for multiplication purposes. Table I2.1, from the American Institute of Steel Construction, provides a conversion table for fractions to 1/32 of an inch. Decimal equivalents to .01 part of a foot should be memorized. It should always be remembered that every time a dimension is added, converted, or transferred, the possibility of error increases. The estimator should use care and concentration when performing these operations.

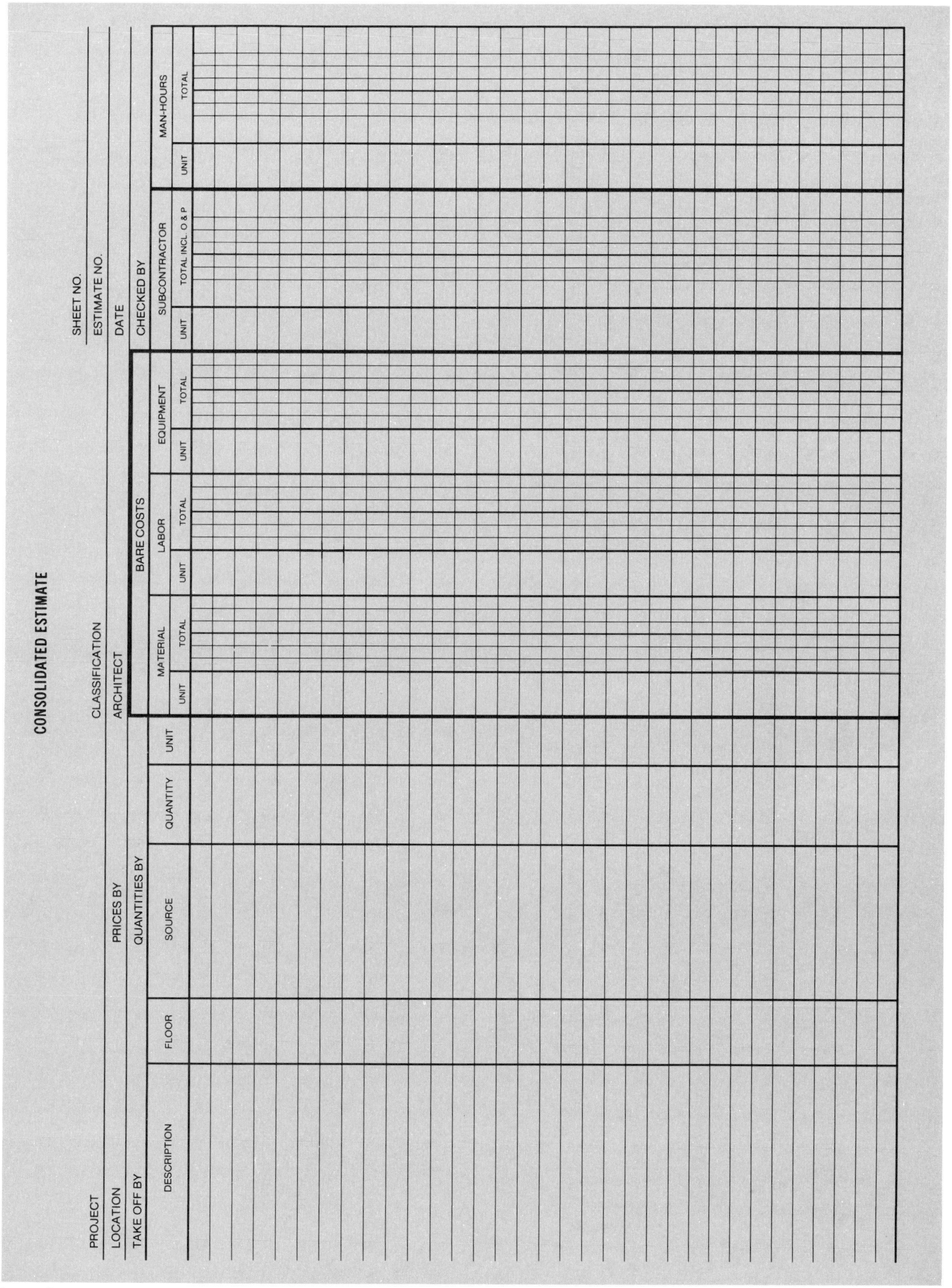
CONSOLIDATED ESTIMATE
PROJECT
LOCATION
TAKE OFF BY
CLASSIFICATION
PRICES BY
QUANTITIES BY
ARCHITECT
SHEET NO.
ESTIMATE NO.
DATE
CHECKED BY
DESCRIPTION
FLOOR
SOURCE
QUANTITY
UNIT
BARE COSTS
MATERIAL
LABOR
EQUIPMENT
UNIT
TOTAL
SUBCONTRACTOR
TOTAL INCL. O & P
MAN-HOURS

Figure 12.1

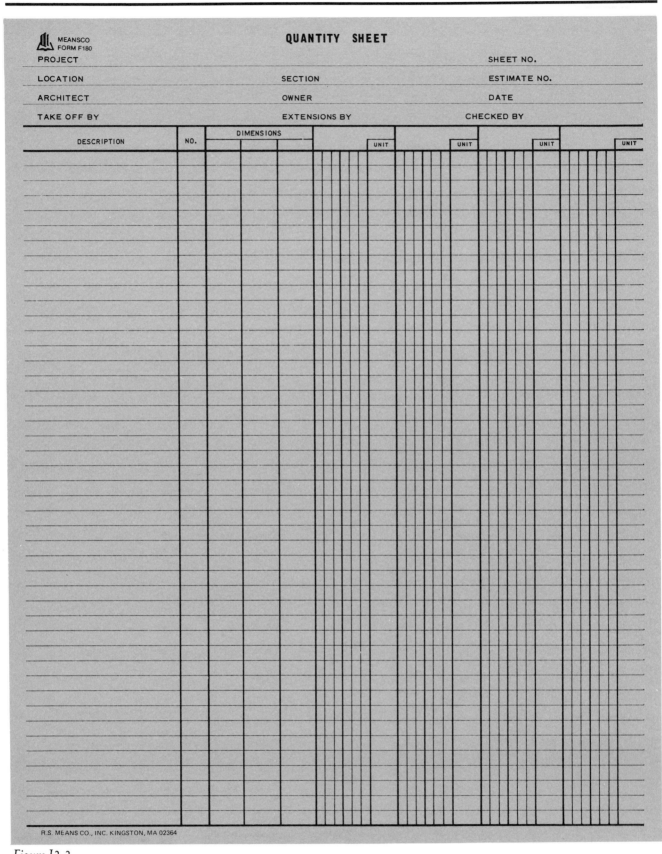

Figure I2.2

			Decimals of a Foot for Each 32nd of an Inch			
Inch	**0**	**1**	**2**	**3**	**4**	**5**
0	0	.0833	.1667	.2500	.3333	.4167
1/32	.0026	.0859	.1693	.2526	.3359	.4193
1/16	.0052	.0885	.1719	.2552	.3385	.4219
3/32	.0078	.0911	.1745	.2578	.3411	.4245
1/8	.0104	.0938	.1771	.2604	.3438	.4271
5/32	.0130	.0964	.1797	.2630	.3464	.4297
3/16	.0156	.0990	.1823	.2656	.3490	.4323
7/32	.0182	.1016	.1849	.2682	.3516	.4349
1/4	.0208	.1042	.1875	.2708	.3542	.4375
9/32	.0234	.1068	.1901	.2734	.3568	.4401
5/16	.0260	.1094	.1927	.2760	.3594	.4427
11/32	.0286	.1120	.1953	.2786	.3620	.4453
3/8	.0313	.1146	.1979	.2812	.3646	.4479
13/32	.0339	.1172	.2005	.2839	.3672	.4505
7/16	.0365	.1198	.2031	.2865	.3698	.4531
15/32	.0391	.1224	.2057	.2891	.3724	.4557
1/2	.0417	.1250	.2083	.2917	.3750	.4583
17/32	.0443	.1276	.2109	.2943	.3776	.4609
9/16	.0469	.1302	.2135	.2969	.3802	.4635
19/32	.0495	.1328	.2161	.2995	.3828	.4661
5/8	.0521	.1354	.2188	.3021	.3854	.4688
21/32	.0547	.1380	.2214	.3047	.3880	.4714
11/16	.0573	.1406	.2240	.3073	.3906	.4740
23/32	.0599	.1432	.2266	.3099	.3932	.4766
3/4	.0625	.1458	.2292	.3125	.3958	.4792
25/32	.0651	.1484	.2318	.3151	.3984	.4818
13/16	.0677	.1510	.2344	.3177	.4010	.4844
27/32	.0703	.1536	2370	.3203	.4036	.4870
7/8	.0729	.1563	.2396	.3229	.4063	.4896
29/32	.0755	.1589	.2422	.3255	.4089	.4922
15/16	.0781	.1615	.2448	.3281	.4115	.4948
31/32	.0807	.1641	.2474	.3307	.4141	.4974

Table 12.1

Inch	6	7	8	9	10	11
Decimals of a Foot for Each 32nd of an Inch						
0	.5000	.5833	.6667	.7500	.8333	.9167
1/32	.5026	.5859	.6693	.7526	.8359	.9193
1/16	.5052	.5885	.6719	.7552	.8385	.9219
3/32	.5078	.5911	.6745	.7578	.8411	.9245
1/8	.5104	.5938	.6771	.7604	.8438	.9271
5/32	.5130	.5964	.6797	.7630	.8464	.9297
3/16	.5156	.5990	.6823	.7656	.8490	.9323
7/32	.5182	.6016	.6849	.7682	.8516	.9349
1/4	.5208	.6042	.6875	.7708	.8542	.9375
9/32	.5234	.6068	.6901	.7734	.8563	.9401
5/16	.5260	.6094	.6927	.7760	.8594	.9427
11/32	.5286	.6120	.6953	.7786	.8620	.9453
3/8	.5313	.6146	.6979	.7813	.8646	.9479
13/32	.5339	.6172	.7005	.7839	.8672	.9505
7/16	.5365	.6198	.7031	.7865	.8698	.9531
15/32	.5391	.6224	.7057	.7891	.8724	.9557
1/2	.5417	.6250	.7083	.7917	.8750	.9583
17/32	.5443	.6276	.7109	.7943	.8776	.9609
9/16	.5469	.6302	.7135	.7969	.8802	.9635
19/32	.5495	.6328	.7161	.7995	.8828	.9661
5/8	.5521	.6354	.7188	.8021	.8854	.9688
21/32	.5547	.6380	.7214	.8047	.8880	.9714
11/16	.5573	.6406	.7240	.8073	.8906	.9740
23/32	.5599	.6432	.7266	.8099	.8932	.9766
3/4	.5625	.6458	.7292	.8125	.8958	.9792
25/32	.5651	.6484	.7318	.8151	.8984	.9818
13/16	.5677	.6510	.7344	.8177	.9010	.9844
27/32	.5703	.6536	.7370	.8203	.9036	.9870
7/8	.5729	.6563	.7396	.8229	.9063	9896
29/32	.5755	.6589	.7422	.8255	.9089	.9922
15/16	.5781	.6615	.7448	.8281	.9115	.9948
31/32	.5807	.6641	.7474	.8307	.9141	.9974

Table I2.1 (cont.)

Numbers should not be rounded off until the final summary of quantities. If dimensions are rounded when taken from the plans, large errors may result. Tables I2.2 and I2.3 show how such an error can occur. The 5.6% error that is demonstrated can have a significant effect if such practices are used throughout the estimate. In the particular example, the effect is to come up with an estimate that is too high. While some may look at this as a safety margin, this kind of error may make the estimator lose the job to a lower bidder. Conversely, such errors can occur on the low side and may cost the estimator a significant portion of the anticipated profit margin. Any adjusting or rounding should be done only at the final summary of the estimate.

The following short cuts can be used effectively when making a quantity take-off:

1. Abbreviate when possible.
2. List all gross dimensions that can be used again either for different quantities or as a rough-check of other quantities for approximate verifications. These include exterior perimeter, gross floor area, and individual floor areas.
3. Multiply the large numbers first to reduce rounding errors.
4. Do not convert units until the final answer is obtained. For example, when estimating concrete work, keep all answers to the nearest Cubic Foot, then summarize and convert to Cubic Yards.
5. Take advantage of design symmetry or repetition: Repetitive floors, Repetitive wings, Symmetrical design around a center line, and Similar room layouts.

Great care must be exercised; otherwise, entire wings or floors can be omitted rather easily. This is one area to keep checking as the estimate progresses. Refer back to total floor area listed on the plan's posted sheet or gross dimensions.

When figuring alternates, it is best to total all items that are involved in the basic system, then total all items that are involved in the alternates. Thus you work with positive numbers in all cases. When adds and deducts are used, it often gets confusing whether to add or subtract a given item, especially on a complicated or involved alternate. Read or list the alternates before starting the take-off. List items involved in the alternates to allow for easy quantity access. This helps prevent take-off duplication.

Effect of Rounding off Measurements at Quantity Take-off

Example: Metal stud, non-load bearing, drywall partition (see Table I2.3)

	Actual	Rounded Off	% Difference
Length of partition	96'-8"	100'	3.4%
Height of partition	11'-9"	12'	2.1%
Total S.F.	1135.87 S.F	1200 S.F	5.3%
Cost ($3.83/S.F.)	$4350.38	$4596.00	5.6%
+ 15% overhead	$5002.94	$5285.40	5.6%
+ 10% profit	$5503.23	$5813.94	5.6%
Total cost difference (incl. O & P)			$310.71

Table I2.2

INTERIOR CONSTRUCTION | 06.1-594 | Partitions, Metal Stud, Non-Load Bearing

This page illustrates and describes a non-load bearing metal stud partition system including metal studs with runners, gypsum plasterboard, taped and finished, insulation, baseboard and painting. Lines 06.1-594-04 thru 10 give the unit price and total price per square foot for this system. Prices for alternate non-load bearing metal stud partition systems are on Line Items 06.1-594-13 thru 23. Both material quantities and labor costs have been adjusted for the system listed.

Example: 20 ga., 2-1/2'' wide, 24'' O.C. as an alternate system: choose Line Item 06.1-594-18, $1.45 MAT., $2.49 INST., $3.94 TOTAL. This price includes all materials compatible with the original system. For alternatives not listed, use the selective price sheet for this section (pages 353, 354, 356). Substitute the new prices from the price sheet into the typical system and adjust the total to reflect each change.

Factors: To adjust for job conditions other than normal working situations use Lines 06.1-594-29 thru 40.

Example: You are to install the above system and cut and patch to match existing construction. Go to Line 06.1-594-30 and apply these percentages to the appropriate MAT. and INST. costs.

LINE NO.	DESCRIPTION	QUANTITY	COST PER S.F. MAT.	INST.	TOTAL
01	Non-load bearing metal studs, including top & bottom runners, 5/8'' drywall				
02	Taped, finished and painted 2 faces, insulation, painted baseboard.				
03					
04	Metal studs, 25 ga., 3-5/8'' wide, 24'' O.C.	1 S.F.	.23	.51	.74
05	Gypsum drywall, 5/8'' thick	2 S.F.	.51	.57	1.08
06	Taping & finishing	2 S.F.	.02	.48	.50
07	Insulation, 3-1/2'' fiberglass batts	1 S.F.	.22	.15	.37
08	Baseboard, painted	.2 L.F.	.14	.30	.44
09	Painting, roller work, 2 coats	2 S.F.	.20	.50	.70
10	TOTAL	S.F.	1.32	2.51	3.83
11					
12	For alternate metal stud systems:				
13	Non-load bearing, 25 ga., 24'' O.C., 2-1/2'' wide	S.F.	1.29	2.49	3.78
14	6'' wide		1.43	2.55	3.98
15	16'' O.C., 2-1/2'' wide		1.33	2.62	3.95
16	3-5/8'' wide		1.38	2.64	4.02
17	6'' wide		1.51	2.69	4.20
18	20 ga. 24'' O.C., 2-1/2'' wide		1.45	2.49	3.94
19	3-5/8'' wide		1.55	2.54	4.09
20	6'' wide		1.66	2.55	4.21
21	16'' O.C., 2-1/2'' wide		1.54	2.61	4.15
22	3-5/8'' wide		1.66	2.68	4.34
23	6'' wide		1.81	2.68	4.49
24					
25					
26					
27					
28					
29	Cut & patch to match existing construction, add, minimum		2%	3%	
30	Maximum		5%	9%	
31	Dust protection, add, minimum		1%	2%	
32	Maximum		4%	11%	
33	Material handling & storage limitation, add, minimum		1%	1%	
34	Maximum		6%	7%	
35	Protection of existing work, add, minimum		2%	2%	
36	Maximum		5%	7%	
37	Shift work requirements, add, minimum			5%	
38	Maximum			30%	
39	Temporary shoring and bracing, add, minimum		2%	5%	
40	Maximum		5%	12%	
41					
42					

Table I2.3

Once the dimensions are determined, the quantities must be calculated or extended. The estimator should perform this process and use it as a cross-check to prevent omission or duplication.

2.3
The Quantity Take-off

The following discussion describes certain items and methods that are helpful in assuring that all specification divisions are included in the estimate, and that all items are included in each division. One extremely useful method is to refer to a source book such as R.S. Means' *Repair and Remodeling Cost Data*, which systematically lists most items applicable to commercial renovation in its Table of Contents (Tables I2.4a and I2.4b). For example, Table I2.5 is a page in Division 1.1, Overhead, listing various types of temporary construction that may be required to perform the work, but may not be shown on the plans.

While completing the quantity take-off, the estimator should make note of any relevant factors (see Table I1.4) that will be used when pricing the estimate and could substantially affect the costs.

Division 1: General Requirements

The General Requirements of a commercial renovation project are those described in the General Conditions of the specifications, as well as those items required for the completion of the work but not necessarily included in the plans and specifications. (For example, see Table I2.5). The General Conditions section of a specification usually describes the manner and procedures required in the performance of the work. The content is intended to impose rules and guidelines on the contractor to assure compliance with construction industry standards and methods of work. Each set of General Conditions specifications is usually tailored to each project. The estimator should read it thoroughly to learn what indirect or "overhead" costs are to be included in the estimate. The items most often described are:

1. Definitions
2. Contract Documents
3. Contractor's Rights and Responsibilities
4. Architect/Engineer's Authority and Responsibilities
5. Owner's Rights and Responsibilities
6. Variation from Contract Provisions
7. Prices and Payments
8. Conduct of the Work
9. Insurance and Bonds
10. Job Conditions and Operation

A statement often included in the General Conditions portion of the specification may be: "Contractor shall supply all necessary labor, materials, tools, equipment, utilities, and other items that are required for the proper and timely performance of the work." This is a very general statement that covers a great deal. It often negates the possibility of change orders for work or indirect costs that the estimator may have overlooked when preparing the estimate.

TABLE OF CONTENTS

Table I2.4a

TABLE OF CONTENTS

Table I2.4b

	Overhead	CREW	MAN-HOURS	UNIT	MAT.	LABOR	EQUIP.	TOTAL	TOTAL INCL O&P	NOTES
035	Average			%	5.50%					
040	Maximum				6.50%					
58-001	TEMPORARY CONSTRUCTION See also Division 1.5-150									
030	Barricades, 5' high, 3 rail @ 2" x 8", fixed	2 Carp	.533	L.F.	8.50	10.45		18.95	25	
035	Movable	"	.800	"	9.10	15.70		24.80	34	
050	Stock units, 6' high, 8' wide, plain, buy			Ea.	340			340	375M	
055	With reflective tape, buy			"	435			435	480M	
060	Break-a-way 3" PVC pipe barricade									
061	with 3 ea. 1' x 4' reflectorized panels, buy			Ea.	240			240	265M	
150	Plywood with steel legs, 32" wide				40			40	44M	
170	Telescoping Christmas tree, 9' high, 5 flags, buy				83			83	91M	
190	Traffic cones, PVC, 18" high				5.55			5.55	6.10M	
195	28" high				9.70			9.70	10.65M	
197	Barrels, 55 gal, with flasher	1 Clab	.083		28	1.29		29.29	33	
210	Catwalks, no handrails, 3 joists, 2" x 4"	2 Carp	.291	L.F.	2.80	5.70		8.50	11.90	
215	3 joists, 3" x 6"	"	.400		5.25	7.85		13.10	17.90	
230	Fencing, chain link, 5' high	2 Sswk	.160		4.50	3.41		7.91	10.55	
235	6' high		.213		7.15	4.54		11.69	15.35	
250	Rented chain link, 6' high, to 500'		.160		1.75	3.41		5.16	7.50	
255	Over 1000' (up to 12 mo.)		.145		1.47	3.10		4.57	6.70	
270	Plywood, painted, 2" x 4" frame, 4' high	A-4	.178		3.18	3.44		6.62	8.80	
275	4" x 4" frame, 8' high	"	.218		5.50	4.22		9.72	12.55	
290	Wire mesh on 4" x 4" posts, 4' high	2 Carp	.160		3.60	3.14		6.74	8.80	
295	8' high		.200		5.40	3.92		9.32	12	
310	Guardrail, wooden, 3' high, 1" x 6", on 4" x 4" posts		.080		1.24	1.57		2.81	3.78	
315	2" x 6", on 4" x 4" posts		.097		2.08	1.90		3.98	5.20	
320	Portable metal with base pads, buy	2 Carp	.027		10.50			10.50	11.55M	
321	Typical installation, assume 10 reuses					1.22	.52	1.74	2.15	
330	Heat, incl. fuel and operation, per week, 12 hrs. per day	1 Skwk	.914	CSF Flr	13.75	18.40		32.15	43	
335	24 hrs. per day	"	1.780		18.25	36		54.25	75	
350	Lighting, incl. service lamps, wiring & outlets, minimum	1 Elec	.235		1.69	5.20		6.89	9.60	
355	Maximum	"	.471		3.90	10.40		14.30	19.75	
370	Power for temporary lighting only, per month, minimum/month							.82	.88	
375	Maximum/month							2.15	2.55	
390	Power for job duration incl. elevator, etc., minimum							41	49	
395	Maximum							84	100	
420	Office trailer, furnished, no hookups, 20' x 8', buy	2 Skwk	16	Ea.	3,300	320		3,620	4,125	
425	Rent per month				115			115	125M	
427	32' x 8', buy	2 Skwk	22.860		5,500	460		5,960	6,750	
428	Rent per month				165			165	180M	
430	50' x 10', buy	2 Skwk	26.670		9,100	535		9,635	10,800	
440	Rent per month				300			300	330M	
443	50' x 12', buy	2 Skwk	32		10,000	645		10,645	12,000	
444	Rent per month				330			330	365M	

NOTES — TAXES: State sales taxes on construction materials vary from 0% to 7.5%. Five states have no sales tax. Many states permit local jurisdictions to levy additional sales taxes. Some projects may be sales tax exempt.

Federal Unemployment tax is 3.5% of the first $7,000 of wages. This is reduced by a credit for payment to the state. The minimum Federal Unemployment tax is 0.8% after all credits. Rates may vary from state to state. For example, Massachusetts State Unemployment tax ranges from 1.5% to 5.7% plus an experience rating assessment the following year, on the first $7,000 of wages. Combined State and Federal rates in Massachusetts rates vary from 3.4% to 7.2% for the first $7,000 of wages.

For expanded coverage of these items see *Building Construction Cost Data 1985*

Table I2.5

Although the General Conditions are the first part of the specification and essentially set the stage for the rest of the project, the estimate usually includes them throughout or at the end of the remaining divisions. A standardized form, such as R.S. Means' Project Overhead Summary (see Figures I2.3a and I2.3b) can be useful in assuring that all such indirect costs are included. The estimator should refer to the form throughout the estimating process. For example, a project includes exterior masonry cleaning and repair. Indirect costs that might be necessary are: testing of areas for compatibility with cleaning solutions and methods, rental of special lift equipment for materials, temporary barricades, special permits, added insurance requirements, winter protection, and rental of scaffolding. While these items are not direct costs of the actual work to be performed, they can become a large percentage of total cost and must be included in the project overhead summary. Each division may have such indirect costs. The estimator must be constantly aware of what may be necessary, but not directly specified, for the completion of the work.

Division 2: Site Work (including Demolition)

In most commercial renovation projects, any site work involved is usually small relative to the amount of interior work. However small, the amount of site work involved should not be of less importance during the quantity take-off. Because most site work requires special tools or heavy equipment, its role in commercial renovation requires special attention. The estimator must determine the cost effectiveness of such equipment. Minimum charges may be in effect if the quantities of work are small. Table I2.6, from R.S. Means' *Repair and Remodeling Cost Data* shows costs for core drilling. The estimator has determined that only two six inch holes are required through a 4" concrete slab. (Please note that line 20-002 states "with water and power available." The costs for these items must be included elsewhere in the estimate.) Line 20-070 would suggest that the cost would be 2 x $48 or $96.00. Line 20-205, however, shows the minimum charge to be $120. Obviously the latter cost must be carried in the estimate. Not only must the estimator determine exact quantities involved, but must employ careful judgement and experience to anticipate consequences.

PROJECT OVERHEAD SUMMARY

MEANSCO FORM FME112

PROJECT										SHEET NO.	

LOCATION — ESTIMATE NO.

ARCHITECT — OWNER — DATE

QUANTITIES BY — PRICES BY — EXTENSIONS BY — CHECKED BY

DESCRIPTION	QUANTITY	UNIT	MATERIAL		LABOR		TOTAL COST	
			UNIT	TOTAL	UNIT	TOTAL	UNIT	TOTAL
Job Organization: Superintendent								
Accounting and bookkeeping								
Timekeeper and material clerk								
Clerical								
Shop								
Safety, watchman and first aid								
Engineering: Layout								
Quantities								
Inspection								
Shop drawings								
Drafting & extra prints								
Testing: Soil								
Materials								
Structural								
Supplies: Office								
Shop								
Utilities: Light and power								
Water								
Heating								
Equipment: Rental								
Light trucks								
Freight and hauling								
Loading, unloading, erecting, etc.								
Maintenance								
Travel Expense								
Main office personnel								
Freight and Express								
Demurrage								
Hauling, misc.								
Advertising								
Signs and Barricades								
Temporary fences								
Temporary stairs, ladders & floors								
Photos								
Page total								

Figure I2.3a

DESCRIPTION	QUANTITY	UNIT	MATERIAL		LABOR		TOTAL COST	
			UNIT	TOTAL	UNIT	TOTAL	UNIT	TOTAL
Total Brought Forward								
Legal								
Medical and Hospitalization								
Field Offices								
Office furniture and equipment								
Telephones								
Heat and Light								
Temporary toilets								
Storage areas and sheds								
Permits: Building								
Misc.								
Insurance								
Bonds								
Interest								
Taxes								
Cutting and Patching & Punch list								
Winter Protection								
Temporary heat								
Snow plowing								
Thawing materials								
Temporary Roads								
Repairs to adjacent property								
Pumping								
Scaffolding								
Small Tools								
Clean up								
Contingencies								
Main Office Expense								
Special Items								
Total: Transfer to Meansco Form 110 or 115								

Figure I2.3b

2.1 Exploration & Clearing

		CREW	MAN-HOURS	UNIT	BARE COSTS				TOTAL INCL O&P
					MAT.	LABOR	EQUIP.	TOTAL	
05 150	For inner city borings add, minimum								10%
151	Maximum								20%
20-001	**CORE DRILLING** Reinforced concrete slab, up to 6" thick slab								
002	with water and power available								
010	1" diameter core	A-1	.800	Ea		12.38	3.52	15.90	23
015	Each added inch thick, add		.075			1.16	.33	1.49	2.15
030	3" diameter core		1.010			15.54	4.46	20	29
035	Each added inch thick, add		.084			1.30	.37	1.67	2.42
050	4" diameter core		1.270			19.40	5.60	25	37
055	Each added inch thick, add		.112			1.74	.49	2.23	3.23
070	6" diameter core		1.680			26.60	7.40	34	48
075	Each added inch thick, add		.168			2.61	.74	3.35	4.84
090	8" diameter core		2			31.20	8.80	40	58
095	Each added inch thick, add		.261			4.05	1.15	5.20	7.55
110	10" diameter core		2.420			37.35	10.65	48	70
115	Each added inch thick, add		.449			6.97	1.98	8.95	12.95
130	12" diameter core		5			78	22	100	145
135	Each added inch thick, add		.559			8.69	2.46	11.15	16.10
150	14" diameter core		6.400			97	28	125	185
155	Each added inch thick, add		.635			9.86	2.79	12.65	18.30
170	18" diameter core		8			125	35	160	230
175	Each added inch thick, add		.825	▼		12.77	3.63	16.40	24
176	For horizontal holes, add to above								30%
177	Prestressed hollow core plank, 6" thick								
178	1" diameter core	A-1	.374	Ea		5.81	1.64	7.45	10.75
179	Each added inch thick, add		.019			.29	.08	.37	.54
180	3" diameter core		.559			8.69	2.46	11.15	16.10
181	Each added inch thick, add		.028			.44	.12	.56	.81
182	4" diameter core		.635			9.86	2.79	12.65	18.30
183	Each added inch thick, add		.028			.44	.12	.56	.81
184	6" diameter core		.825			12.77	3.63	16.40	24
185	Each added inch thick, add		.037			.58	.16	.74	1.07
186	8" diameter core		1.010			15.54	4.46	20	29
187	Each added inch thick, add		.066			1.01	.29	1.30	1.89
188	10" diameter core		1.310			20.25	5.75	26	38
189	Each added inch thick, add		.075			1.16	.33	1.49	2.15
190	12" diameter core		1.680			26.60	7.40	34	48
191	Each added inch thick, add		.093	▼		1.45	.41	1.86	2.69
195	Minimum charge for above, 3" diameter core		3.350	Total		52.25	14.75	67	96
200	4" diameter core		3.760			58.45	16.55	75	110
205	6" diameter core		4.170			64.65	18.35	83	120
210	8" diameter core		5.410			86	24	110	155
215	10" diameter core		7.690			121	34	155	220
220	12" diameter core		9.410			144	41	185	270

NOTES

BORINGS are the most common means of subsurface exploration. They are used to determine the depth and type of soil strata, the water table, and the depth to ledge.

CORE DRILLING may be required for the following:

1. Testing of concrete in place.
2. Investigating for strength, thickness, and reinforcing prior to remodeling, or demolition.
3. Installation of pipes and ducts in existing concrete walls or floors.

Before drilling, make sure the strength of the member being drilled remains sufficient. This is particularly important with large holes in prestressed and post-tensioned concrete.

For expanded coverage of these items see *Means' Site Work Cost Data 1985*

16

Table I2.6

Demolition may have to be carefully broken down into individual components that are not directly included in the plans and specifications. A review of Division 2.2, Building Demolition, in R.S. Means' *Repair and Remodeling Cost Data* may help the estimator to include all required work in the estimate. Unless the estimator has had extensive experience with selective demolition, or unless a local subcontractor can provide a bid, each item to be demolished should be listed separately. When performing the quantity take-off, requirements for handling, hauling, and dumping the debris must also be included.

When the contractor needs only a preliminary or budget cost for demolition, the estimator may have to determine only the size of the area (square feet or cubic feet) where the demolition is required. Table I2.7, Div. 2.2-24, lists costs for gutting that may be used for budgetary pricing. The estimator, however, must observe caution when using this technique. As emphasized, every renovation project is different and the amount of demolition whether selective or complete will vary from job to job.

When determining the quantities involved in all aspects of site work, the estimator must also keep in mind the methods that must be used and the restrictions involved to determine what equipment is appropriate. For example, plans specify a trench for a buried tank. The estimator, having determined the size of the trench, must decide upon the best, and the least expensive, method of work. The following data is taken from R.S. Means' "*Repair and Remodeling Cost Data*":

Trench: 10' length x 4' width x 6' depth = 240 cubic feet
8.89 cubic yards
(to be excavated)

Line Item	Unit Price	Cost
2.3-18-140 Excavation by hand	$24.00/CY	$213.36
2.3-03-001 Backfill by hand	$13.65/CY	$121.35
Actual cost by hand		$334.71
2.3-18-004 Backhoe excavation	$ 3.44/CY	$ 30.58
2.3-03-130 Backhoe backfill	$ 0.85/CY	$ 7.56
Actual cost by backhoe		$ 38.14
1.5-05-010 Minimum daily rental of backhoe		$480.00

When the estimator looks only at the actual cost of the excavating and backfilling, digging by hand is almost 10 times more expensive than using a backhoe. The daily rental, however (usually the minimum charge), makes the backhoe the more costly alternative. If this particular excavation is the only such work required on the project then it is more economical to work by hand. But if other excavation is required and can be performed during the same day, then the backhoe may become the less expensive alternative. When determining quantities, the estimator must also be aware of the consequences pertaining to the economy of scale.

2.2 Building Demolition

		CREW	MAN-HOURS	UNIT	BARE COSTS MAT.	LABOR	EQUIP.	TOTAL	TOTAL INCL O&P
20	320 Steel, welded connections, 4" diameter	B-6	.150	L.F.		2.50	.95	3.45	4.89
	324 10" diameter	↓	.300	"		5	1.90	6.90	9.75
	385 Minimum labor/equipment charge		8	Job		134	51	185	260
	387								
	400 Railroad track, ties and track	B-14	.436	L.F.		7.17	1.38	8.55	12.55
	402 Ballast		.096	C.Y.		1.58	.30	1.88	2.76
	420 Remove and reset ties & track with new bolts & spikes		.960	L.F.		15.76	3.04	18.80	28
	426 Turnouts with new bolts & spikes		48	Ea.		790	150	940	1,375
	485 Minimum labor/equipment charge	↓	9.600	Job		160	30	190	275
	490								
	500 Sidewalks, bituminous, 2-1/2" thick	B-6	.074	S.Y.		1.23	.47	1.70	2.41
	510 Brick, set in mortar		.130			2.17	.82	2.99	4.23
	540 Sidewalks, concrete, plain		.150			2.50	.95	3.45	4.89
	550 Mesh reinforced	↓	.160	↓		2.67	1.01	3.68	5.20
	600 Minimum labor/equipment charge	B-39	4	Job		65.20	11.80	77	115
24-001	GUTTING Building interior, including disposal								
	050 Residential building								
	056 Minimum	B-16	.080	S.F.Flr.		1.29	.70	1.99	2.76
	058 Maximum		.089			1.43	.78	2.21	3.07
	100 Commercial building, minimum		.091			1.48	.80	2.28	3.16
	102 Maximum	↓	.128	↓		2.07	1.12	3.19	4.42
	300 Minimum labor/equipment charge	↓	8	Job		130	70	200	275
32-001	DOOR DEMOLITION								
	002								
	020 Doors, exterior, 1-3/4" thick, single, 3' x 7' high	1 Clab	.500	Ea.		7.75		7.75	11.95L
	022 Double, 6' x 7' high		.667			10.35		10.35	15.95L
	050 Interior, 1-3/8" thick, single, 3' x 7' high		.400			6.20		6.20	9.55L
	052 Double, 6' x 7' high		.500			7.75		7.75	11.95L
	070 Bi-folding, 3' x 6'-8" high		.400			6.20		6.20	9.55L
	072 6' x 6'-8" high		.444			6.90		6.90	10.65L
	090 Bi-passing, 3' x 6'-8" high		.500			7.75		7.75	11.95L
	094 6' x 6'-8" high	↓	.571	↓		8.85		8.85	13.65L
	150 Remove and reset, minimum	1 Carp	1			19.60		19.60	30L
	152 Maximum	"	1.330			26		26	40L
	200 Frames, including trim, metal	A-1	1			15.50	4.40	19.90	29
	220 Wood	↓	.571	↓		8.85	2.51	11.36	16.45
	220 Alternate pricing method	1 Clab	.040	L.F.		.62	.18	.80	1.15
	295 Minimum labor/equipment charge		2	Job		31		31	48L
	298								
	300 Special doors, counter doors	F-2	2.670	Ea.		52	2.33	54.33	83
	310 Double acting		1.600			31	1.40	32.40	50
	320 Floor door (trap type)	↓	2	↓		39	1.75	40.75	62

NOTES

GENERAL DEMOLITION

When estimating demolition the authors recommend getting a bid from a local contractor, if possible. Variables including disposal sites, protection of adjacent structures, salvage, and economic conditions can affect costs by 100%.

In calculating the line item costs of this major classification, three preliminary qualifications are assumed:

1. The tools used for demolition are generally of the hand or pneumatic hand type (note crew size).

2. The cost of rubbish handling (removing rubbish to on-site containers or trucks) is not included.

3. The cost of hauling rubbish to an approved dumpsite is not included.

Therefore, for total general demolition cost, add rubbish handling (See Division 2.2-78) and hauling (See Division 2.3-30).

GUTTING: Prices given are a range for preliminary estimates. For a detailed cost, use Div. 2.2-32 thru 72.

For expanded coverage of these items see *Means' Site Work Cost Data 1985*

Table 12.7

2.4 Caissons & Piling

Line		CREW	MAN-HOURS	UNIT	MAT.	LABOR	EQUIP.	TOTAL	TOTAL INCL O&P
05-001	CAISSONS Incl. excav., concrete, 50 lbs. reinf. per C.Y., but not incl.								
002	mobilization, boulder removal, disposal or pre-drilling								
010	Open style, machine drilled, to 50' deep, in stable ground, no								
012	casings or ground water								
020	24" diameter, .116 C.Y./L.F.	B-43	.253	V.L.F.	13.55	4.28	2.87	20.70	25
021	4' bell diameter		2.400	Ea.	37	41	27	105	135
050	48" diameter, .465 C.Y./L.F.		.430	V.L.F.	54	8.15	5.45	67.60	78
051	9' bell diameter	→	24	Ea.	370	405	275	1,050	1,325
121	Open style, machine drilled, to 25' deep, in wet ground, pulled								
122	casing and pumping								
140	24" diameter, .116 C.Y./L.F.	B-48	.448	V.L.F.	13.55	7.75	5.05	26.35	32
141	4' bell diameter	"	2.830	Ea.	37	49	32	118	150
170	48" diameter, .465 C.Y./L.F.	B-49	1.600	V.L.F.	54	28.55	18.45	101	125
171	9' bell diameter	"	26.670	Ea.	370	480	310	1,160	1,475
231	Open style, machine drilled, to 25' deep, in soft rocks and								
232	medium hard shales								
250	24" diameter, .116 C.Y./L.F.	B-49	2.930	V.L.F.	13.55	53	34	100.55	135
251	4' bell diameter	"	8.070	Ea.	37	147	93	277	370
280	48" diameter, .465 C.Y./L.F.		8.800	V.L.F.	54	160	100	314	415
281	9' bell diameter		80	Ea.	370	1,450	925	2,745	3,650
360	For rock excavation, sockets, add, minimum		.733	C.F.		13.55	8.45	22	30
365	Average		.926	→		16.30	10.70	27	38
370	Maximum	→	1.830	V.L.F.		33	21	54	74
390	For 50' to 100' deep, add				7%	7%			
400	For 100' to 150' deep, add				25%	25%			
410	For 150 ft. to 200 ft. deep, add				30%	30%			
420	For casings left in place, add			Lb.	.45			.45	.49M
430	For other than 50 lb. reinf. per C.Y., add or deduct			"	.51			.51	.56M
440	For steel "I" beam cores, add	B-49	10.600	Ton	500	195	120	815	980
450	Load and haul excess excavation, 2 miles	B-34B	.045	C.Y.		.73	1.57	2.30	2.84
460	For mobilization, 50 mile radius, rig to 36"			Ea.					895
465	Rig to 84"								1,350
470	For low headroom, add					50%			
475	For lack of access, add					25%			
15-001	PILES, CONCRETE 200 piles, 60' long								
002	Unless specified otherwise, not incl. pile caps or mobilization								
080	Cast in place friction pile, 50' long, fluted,								
081	tapered steel, 4000 psi concrete, no reinforcing								
090	12" diameter, 7 ga.	B-19	.107	V.L.F.	10.65	2.12	1.62	14.39	16.85
120	18" diameter, 7 ga.	"	.133	"	16	2.65	2.03	20.68	24
130	End bearing, fluted, constant diameter,								
132	4000 psi concrete, no reinforcing								
134	12" diameter, 7 ga.	B-19	.107	V.L.F.	10.95	2.12	1.62	14.69	17.20
140	18" diameter, 7 ga.	"	.133	"	17.15	2.65	2.03	21.83	25

NOTES

The three principal types of CAISSONS and their uses are:

1. Straight Shaft caissons for light loads on good bearing soil.
2. Belled caissons when a greater bearing area is required than the most economical shaft area.
3. Keyed caissons when a heavy load is to be transmitted to underlaying ledge.

25' Type 1

25' Type 2

25' Type 3

For expanded coverage of these items see *Means' Site Work Cost Data 1985*

38

Table I2.8

Caissons and pilings are very seldom required in commercial renovation. When they are specified, however, they may become a very expensive portion of the work. Not only must the correct quantities (size and linear feet) be determined, but the estimator must be aware of restrictive conditions. As can be seen in Table I2.8, the labor involved increases significantly for lack of headroom or access.

Bituminous paving is taken off and priced by the square yard or ton. The quantity is also determined by the thickness. The average weight of bituminous concrete is 145 pounds per cubic foot. By quick calculation this can be converted to 12.08 pounds per square foot per inch thickness. This figure can be used when prices from a local supplier are by the ton. For renovation, in addition to the costs of paving, the estimator should determine the quantities involved in the removal of existing materials, subgrading, and subgrade material.

Division 3: Concrete

The quantity take-off for concrete should be very detailed. Many different items should be included such as formwork, reinforcing steel, expansion joints, and concrete placement. (Excavation and backfill, plus other related work, must also be included in the estimate.) The type of concrete should be identified, whether it is cast-in-place with formwork, cast-in-place slabs and special work, or precast. Different types may be used in different areas of commercial renovation. The estimator must also remember that in renovation, existing conditions may restrict the efficient installation of the concrete.

Concrete prices vary dramatically from place to place. The estimator should obtain a local price from a supplier near the job site. Minimum charges, as well as unloading time, are also important in figuring the material price of concrete. Four cubic yards of concrete may require the purchase of a complete eight-cubic-yard load. This doubles the material price.

Labor and equipment costs depend on productivity and will depend on existing conditions. For this reason, accurate job cost records of labor and equipment for a particular company should be developed. These should be coordinated with an estimating system and used in preparing future bids. Even if the estimator has developed such a system, or if a construction industry data source is used, the quantity take-off for renovation must be performed with extra care. Formwork may require custom construction and fitting. Forms that must be custom made are usually only good for one use. Table I2.9 shows prices for formwork. Most examples give prices for one use and for four uses. The prices for one use are 50% higher.

Having unit job cost records for similar items of work on several similar jobs and qualifying these for existing conditions, an estimator can estimate the costs for a renovation with the same degree of confidence and authority.

The three types of concrete work described above can be listed to include the following:

Cast-in-Place: Formwork
  1. Footings (continuous and spread)
  2. Piers
  3. Walls
  4. Columns
  5. Beams
  6. Underpinning

3.1 Formwork

	CREW	MAN-HOURS	UNIT	MAT.	LABOR	EQUIP.	TOTAL	TOTAL INCL O&P
55-001 FORMS IN PLACE, SLAB ON GRADE								
100 Bulkhead forms with keyway, 1 use, 2 piece	C-1	.063	L.F.	.34	1.17	.04	1.55	2.22
200 Curb forms, wood, 6" to 12" high, on grade, 1 use		.149	S.F.C.A.	1.10	2.76	.10	3.96	5.60
215 4 use		.116	"	.40	2.16	.08	2.64	3.86
300 Edge forms, to 6" high, 4 use, on grade		.053	L.F.	.16	.99	.04	1.19	1.74
305 7" to 12" high, 4 use, on grade		.074	S.F.C.A.	.51	1.36	.05	1.92	2.72
350 For depressed slabs, 4 use, to 12" high		.107	L.F.	.42	1.98	.07	2.47	3.60
355 To 24" high		.183		.50	3.40	.12	4.02	5.95
400 For slab blockouts, 1 use to 12" high		.160		.42	2.97	.11	3.50	5.15
405 To 24" high	↓	.267	↓	.50	4.97	.18	5.65	8.40
500 Screed, 24 ga. metal key joint, see division 3.1-10								
502 Wood, incl wood stakes, 1" x 3"	C-1	.036	L.F.	.26	.66	.02	.94	1.33
505 2" x 4"	"	.036	"	.79	.66	.02	1.47	1.91
510								
600 Trench forms in floor, 1 use	C-1	.200	S.F.C.A.	1.29	3.72	.13	5.14	7.30
615 4 use	"	.173	"	.41	3.22	.11	3.74	5.55
900 Minimum labor/equipment charge	F-1	4	Job		78.50	3.50	82	125
65-001 FORMS IN PLACE, WALLS								
010 Box out for wall openings, to 16" thick, to 10 S.F.	C-2	2	Ea.	12.20	38.83	1.17	52.20	74
015 Over 10 S.F. (use perimeter)	"	.171	L.F.	1.15	3.30	.10	4.55	6.45
025 Brick shelf, 4" wide, add to wall forms, use wall area								
026 above shelf, 1 use	C-2	.200	S.F.C.A.	1.20	3.85	.12	5.17	7.40
035 4 use		.160		.47	3.08	.09	3.64	5.35
050 Bulkhead forms for walls, with keyway, 1 use, 2 piece		.181	L.F.	1.40	3.48	.11	4.99	7.05
055 3 piece		.274		1.82	5.29	.16	7.27	10.35
070 Buttress forms, to 8' high, 1 use		.137	S.F.C.A.	1.35	2.64	.08	4.07	5.65
085 4 use		.100	"	.52	1.92	.06	2.50	3.61
100 Corbel (haunch) forms, up to 12" wide, add to wall forms, 1 use		.320	L.F.	1.41	6.16	.19	7.76	11.25
115 4 use		.267	"	.55	5.14	.16	5.85	8.70
200 Job built plyform wall forms, to 8' high, 1 use		.130	S.F.C.A.	127.65	2.49	.08	130.22	145
215 4 use		.095		.51	1.83	.06	2.40	3.45
240 Over 8' to 16' high, 1 use		.171		1.37	3.30	.10	4.77	6.70
255 4 use		.122		.57	2.34	.07	2.98	4.32
270 Over 16' high, 1 use		.204		1.55	3.93	.12	5.60	7.90
285 4 use		.145		.68	2.80	.08	3.56	5.15
300 For architectural finish, add		.026	↓	.30	.50	.02	.82	1.13
310 See also form liners, division 3.1-65-575								
330 For battered walls, 1 side battered, add			S.F.C.A.	10%	10%			
335 2 sides battered, add				15%	15%			
400 Radial wall forms, smooth curved, 1 use	C-2	.196		1.50	3.78	.11	5.39	7.60
415 4 use		.143		.66	2.76	.08	3.50	5.10
460 Retaining wall forms, battered, to 8' high, 1 use		.160		1.42	3.08	.09	4.59	6.40
475	↓	.123	↓	.58	2.37	.07	3.02	4.37

NOTES: **FORMS IN PLACE** for walls pertain to the formwork only. The costs are given in either cost per square foot of contact area (S.F.C.A.) or cost per lineal foot (L.F.). Concrete and reinforcing steel are not included.

Plyform Wall Form

For expanded coverage of these items see Means' Concrete & Masonry Cost Data 1985

Table 12.9

Cast-in-Place: Slabs and Specialties
1. Slabs on grade
2. Elevated slabs
3. Stairs
4. Curbs and gutters
5. Sidewalks

Precast Concrete (On-site and off-site precast)
1. Beams
2. Columns
3. Stairs
4. Slabs
5. Walls

Although the concrete and reinforcing material cost for a grade beam on the ground and interior beam of an upper floor may be the same, the forming, placing, stripping, and rubbing costs are not, especially in renovation work. This is one reason for the detailed breakdown stressed in the introduction to this section and a typical example for the importance placed on the site evaluation.

The cost of concrete formed in place is always a function of the area of forms or square foot of contact area required. Per cubic yard of concrete, an eight-inch foundation wall will require 50 percent more form material, form labor, stripping, rubbing, and waterproofing than a 12" wall. Still, many contractors continue to estimate cast-in-place concrete by the cubic yard without considering the wall thickness.

Estimators may prefer to compile and list the quantities for concrete work in different formats, but each of these quantities must be computed. It is important that once a format for compiling quantities is established that the same format be used throughout the estimate and all future estimates, establishing consistency and minimizing errors and omissions.

The following rules and suggestions may be helpful when determining the quantities for concrete work:

Spread Footings
Spread footings (column or fireplace footings) are square or rectangular footings designed for a point or column load.

Volume = Length (L) x Width (W) x Depth (D)
Form Area = (2L + 2W) x D
Finish Area = L x W

Continuous wall footings and grade beams
Wall footings transmit wall loads directly to the soil. (See Figure I2.4). Grade beams are structural members designed to support wall loads and may carry them across unacceptable soil to column footings, caissons, or support piles.

To accommodate changes in finished grade elevations, wall footings frequently are stepped. These steps will require an additional volume of concrete and forming material.

Proceed as follows:
1. Write down the location and dimension of each wall footing or grade beam shown on the plan.
2. Extend each of these lines as in the procedure for Spread Footings to obtain the Volume, Form Area, and Finish Area. VOLUME = L x W x D; FORM AREA = 2L x D; FINISH AREA = L x W
3. Total each column of figures.
4. Check off each wall footing and grade beam on the plans to assure none has been omitted.

Footings forms are usually figured with 2" stock and 2" x 4" stakes for minimum waste and maximum reuse. If you intend to use this system, allow 2.6 B.F. per SFCA and 10% waste for each reuse. See Figure 12.4.

When the location and dimensions of these footings have been determined, quantities for other items shown that incorporate these dimensions, reinforcing steel, keyways, anchor bolts, and underdrains should be taken off. To avoid errors and omissions, these should be computed and totaled on the same quantity sheets from which the dimensions were obtained.

No discussion of concrete footings would be complete without mentioning "pouring wild." This occurs when the concrete is placed directly into the excavated trench without forming. The quantity take-off procedure is the same as above except that an additional 5% to 10% extra volume of concrete should be added for waste.

Piers

Piers are used to extend the bearing of the superstructure down to the footing. They vary in length to accommodate subsurface conditions, original site grades, and frost penetration. The quantity take-off procedure for piers should be similar to that for spread footings.

Volume for round piers is computed from 3.1416 x the radius squared x height (depth). Columns and beams are estimated in a similar manner. Be sure to include inserts such as hangers.

Pile caps

Pile caps are basically a spread footing on piles. Their shape is not always rectangular so that the form area is determined by the perimeter times the depth. No concrete volume should be deducted for the protrusion of the piles into the cap.

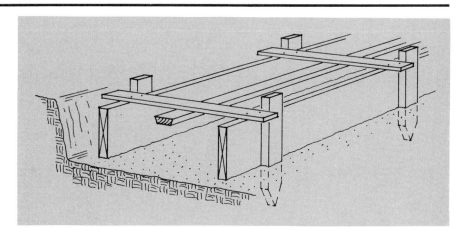

Figure 12.4

Walls and columns

The estimator should carefully examine the plans and specifications carefully to determine if there are any variations from standard wall construction. Otherwise the following calculations may be used:

Wall Volume = Length (L) x Height (H) x Thickness (T)
Wall Form Area = 2 x L x H
Wall Finish Area = 2 x L x H

See illustration in Table I2.9.

Column Volume = Horizontal Length (L) x Horizontal Width (W) x Height (H)
Column Form Area = (2L + 2W) x H
Column Finish Area = (2L + 2W) x H

Columns are formed just like piers except that the reuse of forms will depend upon the finish desired (See Figure I2.5). Good records of the system, time, and materials used are invaluable in pricing these items.

Beams

Quantities for concrete beams should be calculated as for columns. Beam forms can be divided into two categories: hung from encased structural steel and shored. The material is approximately the same: 1.15 Square Feet of plyform per SFCA and 2 B.F. framing per SFCA. Determine the number for reuses anticipated and allow 10% waste for each reuse. For shored beams and girders allow enough shores for reshoring after stripping.

Underpinning

Although underpinning is done with formed concrete, much of the cost involved is for excavation and shoring. Because of the unique features of each individual job, it is best to analyze the method, labor, and material that will probably be used. Major classification 2.3-52 of *Repair and Remodeling Cost Data,* 1985, provides some good ranges for checking your figures. Forming for underpinning is usually one-sided with the earth forming the other side. Allow 1.25 S.F. of plyform per SFCA and at least 5 B.F. per SFCA for framing and bracing.

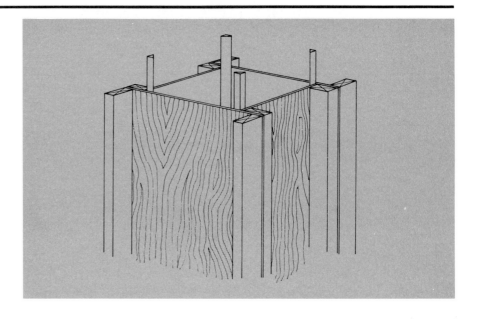

Figure I2.5

Quantities for reinforcing steel must also be determined for a complete estimate of concrete work. If requirements are not included in the plans and specifications, the estimator should consult with an engineer or the local building inspector. When taking off the quantities, the estimator should be aware of any special or existing conditions that may make the job more difficult than originally thought. Bars may have to be drilled and grouted into existing masonry at the new concrete joint. Tie wire and special commercial accessories should also be included in the quantity take-off. Reinforcing is usually priced by weight. When the lengths of the different specified reinforcing sizes have been computed, the estimator must convert the quantities to weight. Table I2.10 gives the conversion factors for the most commonly used sizes and types of reinforcing steel.

The site of concrete placement within the structure, sequence of pours, available equipment, and personal preference can all be factors used in determining the costs. The limiting factors in placing concrete are the quantities of materials (often small in commercial renovation), the forms available, and the productive capacity of the workers and equipment.

For concrete placed by direct chute or pump, the availability of forms generally determines the volume of concrete placed per hour. When estimating the number of forms and reuses for a job, be sure to remember the forming crew needs work during the curing period of the previous pour.

Estimate enough forms, if possible, to make it worthwhile to set up a crane and bucket, concrete pump, or conveyor. Usually the cost of any of these will have to be borne for the whole day regardless of the size of the pour. If the job is very small, and ready-mixed concrete can be bought only in large quantities, contractors may use a portable power mixer. See Figure I2.6.

The estimator should anticipate wheeled concrete placement when studying the plans or consulting with an experienced field superintendent. This method can be slow and expensive. When concrete is placed by crane and bucket into a hopper and then wheeled, these costs must be added together. If a hoisting elevator is used for the buggies, usually the hoisting rate determines the size of the pour. The more pours required, the higher the costs. The estimator must determine the number of pours that will be necessary.

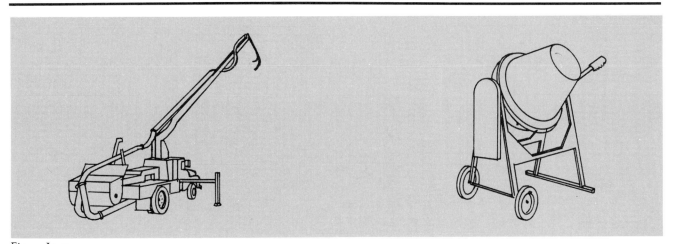

Figure I2.6

Reinforcing Bars				
		Nominal Dimensions - Round Sections		
Bar Size Designation	Weight Pounds Per Foot	Diameter Inches	Cross-Sectional Area-Sq. Inches	Perimeter Inches
#3	.376	.375	.11	1.178
#4	.668	.500	.20	1.571
#5	1.043	.625	.31	1.963
#6	1.502	.750	.44	2.356
#7	2.044	.875	.60	2.749
#8	2.670	1.000	.79	3.142
#9	3.400	1.128	1.00	3.544
#10	4.303	1.270	1.27	3.990
#11	5.313	1.410	1.56	4.430
#14	7.650	1.693	2.25	5.320
#18	13.600	2.257	4.00	7.090

Common Stock Styles of Welded Wire Fabric								
New Designation	Old Designation	Steel Area Per Foot				Approximate Weight Per 100 Sq Ft.		
Spacing - Cross Sectional Area (IN.)-(SQ. IN. 100)	Spacing Wire Gauge (IN.)-(AS & W)	Longitudinal		Transverse				
		IN.	CM	IN.	CM	LB	KG	
6 x 6-W1.4 x W1.4	6 x 6-10 x 10	0.028	0.071	0.028	0.071	21	9.53	
6 x 6-W2.0 x W2.0	6 x 6-8 x 8 (1)	0.040	0.102	0.040	0.102	29	13.15	
6 x 6-W2.9 x W2.9	6 x 6-6 x 6	0.058	0.147	0.053	0.147	42	19.05	
6 x 6-W4.0 x W4.0	6 x 6-4 x 4	0.080	0.203	0.080	0.203	58	26.31	
4 x 4-W1.4 x W1.4	4 x 4-10 x 10	0.042	0.107	0.042	0.107	31	14.06	
4 x 4-W2.0 x W2.0	4 x 4-8 x 8 (1)	0.060	0.152	0.060	0.152	43	19.50	
4 x 4-W2.9 x W2.9	4 x 4-6 x 6	0.087	0.221	0.087	0.221	62	28.12	
4 x 4-W4.0 x W4.0	4 x 4-4 x 4	0.120	0.305	0.120	0.305	85	38.56	
6 x 6-W2.9 x W2.9	6 x 6-6 x 6	0.058	0.147	0.058	0.147	42	19.05	
6 x 6-W4.0 x W4.0	6 x 6-4 x 4	0.080	0.203	0.080	0.203	58	26.31	
6 x 6-W5.5 x W5.5	6 x 6-2 x 2 (2)	0.110	0.279	0.110	0.279	80	36.29	
6 x 6-W4.0 x W4.0	4 x 4-4 x 4	0.120	0.305	0.120	0.305	85	38.56	

(Rolls: rows 1-8; Sheets: rows 9-12)

NOTES
1. Exact W-number size for 8 gauge is W2.1
2. Exact W-number size for 2 gauge is W5.4

Table 12.10

Cast in Place: Slabs and Specialties

When determining the quantities for this type of concrete, the estimator must consider many "auxiliary" items that may be part of the concrete work.

Granular Base	Screeds
Fine Grade	Concrete Material
Vapor Barrier	Finish and Topping
Edge Forms	Cure and Hardener
Expansion Joints	"Outs"
Contraction Joints	Haunches
Welded Wire Fabric and Reinforcing	Drops

The quantities for these items are derived from a few dimensions. The principal object is not to leave any of these items out of an estimate by oversight. Each item may not be incorporated in each slab to be estimated, but this provides a good check list.

Slab on grade

Some basic rules to remember when determining quantities for a slab on grade are:

1. Allow about 25% compaction for granular base.
2. Allow 10% overlap for vapor barrier and welded wire fabric.
3. Allow 5% extra concrete for slab on grade.
4. No deductions for columns or "outs" under 10 S.F.
5. If screeds are separated from forming and placing costs, allow 1 L.F. of screed per 10 S.F. of finish area.

Slabs on grade are separated on the estimate as follows:

1. Building: Enter on Quantity Sheet each of the quantities related to slab on grade. All the quantities, except for expansion joints around columns, are derived from the three basic dimensions, Length (L), Width (W) and Thickness (T), of the slab being estimated. When filling in quantities on the Quantity Sheet, fill in each line and draw a line through the space when there is no quantity. This helps eliminate omissions and duplications. Be sure to add the concrete volume, hand excavation, and reinforcing steel where haunches are shown on the plan.
2. Sidewalk and Paving: More edge forms and joints will be in sidewalk and paving concrete than in the building slab on grade. Other than this and the type of finish normally provided, the estimating procedure is the same.
3. Slab on grade forming consists mainly of edge forming. Pay particular attention to edge forms around "outs," changes in elevation, and changes in slab thickness. List edge forms by L.F. for each height.

The estimator should use imagination and experience when placing slabs and other types of concrete. For instance, is it possible to eliminate small-wheeled pours by using a particular sequence? When placing of formed concrete, the site, location within the structure, sequence of pours, available equipment, and personal preference are all used in determining the method of placement. Write the method of placement on the Quantity Sheet for reference when pricing the estimate.

Because no equipment is involved, placing slabs on grade by direct chute can be done in large or small pours without appreciably affecting the unit placing cost. Usually the only limit is the daily productive output of the finishing crew.

Elevated slab

When estimating elevated slabs, use the same basic dimensions (L, W and T) as in the slab on grade. The slab form area is usually figured straight across the beams, which makes it the same as the finish area. Pay close attention to edge forming around openings such as stairwells and elevator shafts. Also, these can contribute a significant "out" to the concrete volume and finish area.

When estimating the forming for elevated slabs, unless plyform is going to work out on exactly 4 x 8 modular size, allow 15% overrun on the first use and 10% waste on each reuse. The support lumber averages 2.1 B.F. per S.F. with shoring placed 4' center to center. The labor is less, but the framing lumber is not reduced appreciably.

The metal decking used to support elevated slabs is usually welded to the structural steel by the steel erector on the job. The formwork subcontractor usually does the edge forming. This important step has often stopped jobs, however, when the different parties involved try to determine responsibility. Forming that uses domes and pans for voids in a slab is identical to flat plate forming when the closed deck system is used.

Stairs

When taking off cast-in-place stairs, the estimator should investigate to be sure that all inserts such as railing anchors, nosings, and reinforcing steel have been included. The Quantity Sheet should also list any special tread finishes, which sometimes represent a considerable cost.

1. Stairs cast on fill are most easily estimated and recorded by the S.F. This is the slant length times the width. Because of the commonly used ratios adopted by the designers, this method works for high or low risers with wide or narrow treads.
2. Shored cast-in-place stairs can be estimated the same way-slant length times width.
3. Prefabricated metal stairs with poured concrete in pans should be identified on the take-off sheet and a price obtained from a local steel supplier or erector. To this price, the estimator must add the hand placing of the fill concrete.

Using the recommended method of estimating by slant length and width of stairs, the stringer, riser, and framing lumber figures to about 4.25 B.F. per S.F. The plyform can be figured with 10% waste. With careful stripping, four reuses may be anticipated.

Most elevated slabs and stairs are placed by crane and bucket, concrete pump, or conveyor (See Figure I2.6). Unless planning to price the estimate based on historical unit costs as in *Repair and Remodeling Cost Data*, 1985, estimate the number of days this equipment will be needed and write this on your Quantity Sheet: e.g., 10 days - 15 ton crane and bucket.

When estimating placement of slabs by wheeling, figure the maximum length for ramps required and the average length of ramps for time per round trip per buggy. For large pours you may have to figure on an extra buggy or two, which would not be used as the ramps get shorter. These buggies are either owned or rented for the duration of the job. Figure them from the start to finish of the slab pours.

Curbs and gutters

Concrete curbs and gutters should be identified (6" x 18", etc.) and the quantities measured on the site work sheets of the plans, then listed on the Quantity Sheets of the estimate. Check off each location on the plans as the quantity is listed on the Quantity Sheet.

Special metal curb and gutter forms can be purchased or rented. Except for special shapes or small quantities, these are more economical than building wooden forms and require less concrete finishing after stripping.

Precast concrete

Due to the special nature of precast concrete and the equipment and skills required for installation, it is best to obtain prices from precast contractors. Placement of precast concrete in commercial renovation is sometimes difficult.

Division 4: Masonry

There are a variety of masonry products and methods that can be used in commercial renovation. The method of installation can vary within the same project. The masonry should be broken down into exterior walls and interior partitions. Depending upon the structural design of masonry units, the reinforcement and grouting requirements vary considerably. The estimator must identify and list insulation, embedded items, special finishes, and scaffolding and shoring requirements.

Masonry is generally priced by the unit, by the piece, or per thousand units. The quantity of units is determined from measurements of the areas in square feet of walls and partitions. The areas are converted into number of units by appropriate multipliers. The multipliers are a function of size of the masonry unit, pattern or coursing of the masonry unit, thickness of mortar joints, and thickness of wall.

The number of units per square foot is calculated and multiplied by the area of the wall to determine the total quantity involved. For items installed in a course, the quantity per L.F. is calculated and multiplied by the length involved (items such as a cove base).

All items that are to be priced should be represented by an item or notation on the Quantity Sheet. Before starting the quantity take-off, the estimator should make notes based on the masonry specifications of all items that must be estimated. These notes will include the kind of masonry units, the bonds, the mortar type, joint reinforcement, grout, miscellaneous installed items, scaffolding, and cleaning.

The elevations show the exterior wall, door, and window openings. The plans show the number, area, and layout of interior walls. Sections, details and room-finish schedule serve to identify the masonry units and where they occur.

After the estimator has identified and analyzed the walls and partitions, each kind or combination of masonry unit is then measured and entered in the take-off sheets. The measurements are total areas with all openings over 2 square feet deducted and openings under 2 square feet ignored. The items may be grouped in the order that they would be constructed on the job:
1. Walls Below Grade
2. External Walls
3. Chimney
4. Partitions
5. Miscellaneous Brickwork

This allows the estimator to tackle one part of the work at a time. Once a consistent take-off pattern is established and followed, there is less chance an item will be overlooked or duplicated.

Walls below grade may be pointed on the exposed face and dampproofed or waterproofed on the earth side. The calculated area can also be used as a measurement of the dampproofing or waterproofing. Scaffolding is required for walls over 4' high. Partitions below grade are no different from other partitions, so they do not have to be kept separate.

External wall areas are the product of the wall length times the actual wall height taken from the section detail. A small scale sketch of the building can be an important visual aid for future reference.

It should be remembered that exterior measurements of a building's perimeter give an overlap of the thickness of the walls for every outside corner. This is accepted accuracy and should be included, since corners tend to require more cutting and waste.

When measuring exterior dimensions at inside corners, however, the estimator must add to the actual dimensions to account for the extra material and labor involved to construct the inside corners.

The estimator will often have no choice in determining the mortar proportions since the specifications set forth exactly which type is to be used. The mortar is very important to the structural integrity of the wall. It is false economy to alter a specification to save money on a mortar mix. See Table I2.11.

Especially in commercial renovation, the estimator will encounter all types and bonding methods of brickwork. Figures I2.7 and I2.8 show examples of brick coursing, joint types and bonding patterns. Structural bonds may be accomplished in three ways: by the overlapping (interlocking) of the masonry units, by the use of metal ties embedded in connecting joints of a backing wall,

			Brick Mortar Mixes*		
Type	Portland Cement	Hydrated Lime	Sand** (Maximum)	Strength	Use
M	1	1/4	3-3/4	High	General use where high strength is required, especially good compressive strength; work that is below grade and in contact with earth.
S	1	1/2	4-1/2	High	Okay for general use, especially good where high lateral strength is desired.
N	1	1	6	Medium	General use when masonry is exposed above grade; best to use when high compressive and lateral strengths are not required.
0	1	2	9	Low	Do not use when masonry is exposed to severe weathering; acceptable for non-loadbearing walls of solid units and interior non-loadbearing partitions of hollow units.

*The water used should be of the quality of drinking water. Use as much water as is needed to bring the mix to a suitably plastic and workable state.

**The sand should be damp and loose. A general rule for sand content is that it should not be less than 2-1/4 or more than 3 times the sum of the cement and lime volumes.

Table I2.11

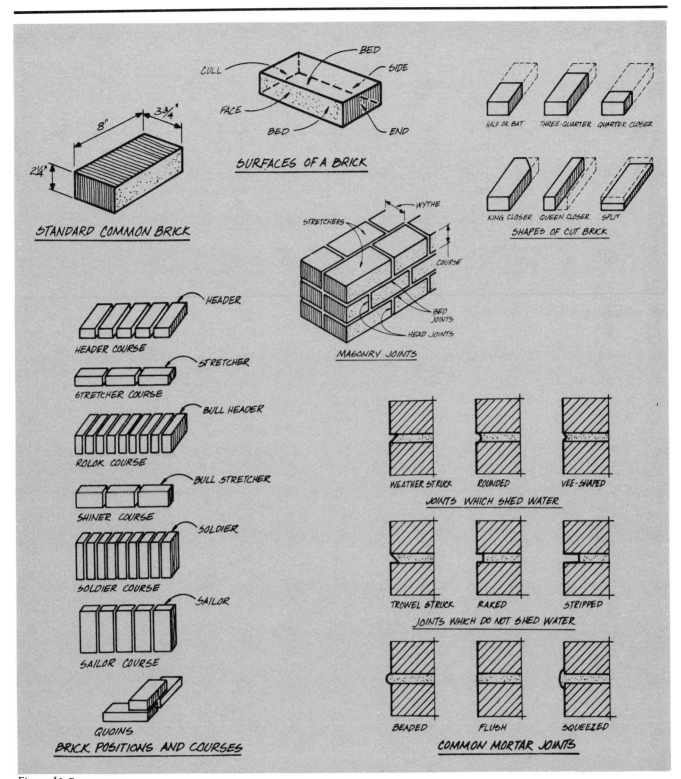

SURFACES OF A BRICK

STANDARD COMMON BRICK

SHAPES OF CUT BRICK

MAGONRY JOINTS

BRICK POSITIONS AND COURSES

COMMON MORTAR JOINTS

JOINTS WHICH SHED WATER

JOINTS WHICH DO NOT SHED WATER

Figure 12.7

69

Running or Stretcher Bond	The face brick are all stretchers and are tied to the backing by metal or reinforcing. Waste - 5%.
Common or American Bond	Every sixth course of stretcher bond is usually a header course. Waste - 4%.
Flemish Bond	Each course has alternate headers and stretchers with the alternate headers centered over the stretcher. Waste - 3 to 5%.
English Bond	Consists of alternate headers and stretchers with the vertical joints in the header and stretcher aligning or breaking over each other. Waste - 8 to 15%.
Stack Bond	Has no overlapping of units since all vertical joints are aligned. Usually this pattern is bonded to the backing with rigid steel ties. Waste - 3%.
English Cross or Dutch Bond	Built up of interlocking crosses. This wall consists of two headers and a stretcher forming a cross. Waste - 8%.

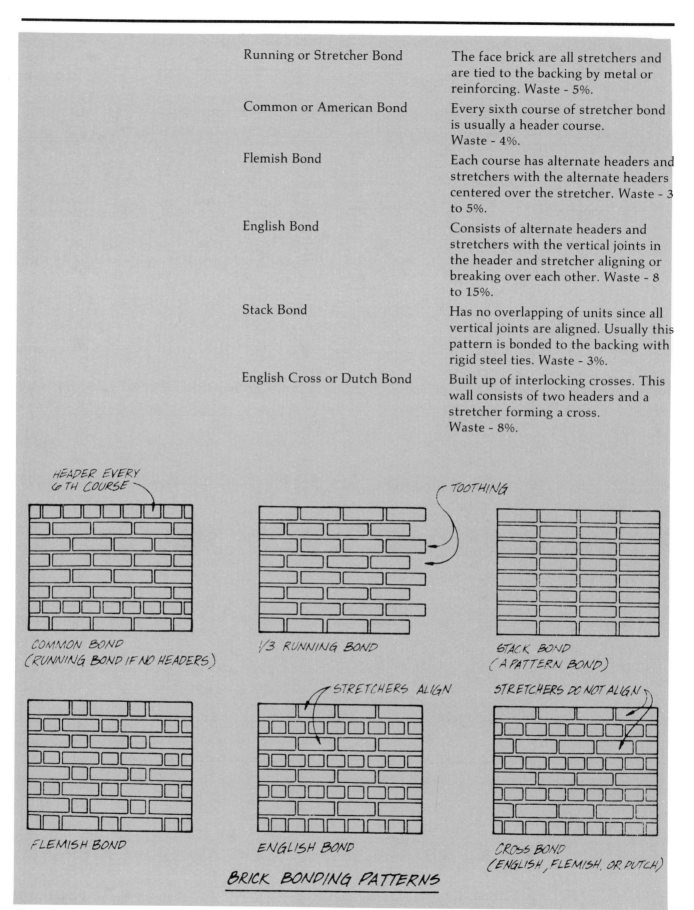

BRICK BONDING PATTERNS

Figure 12.8

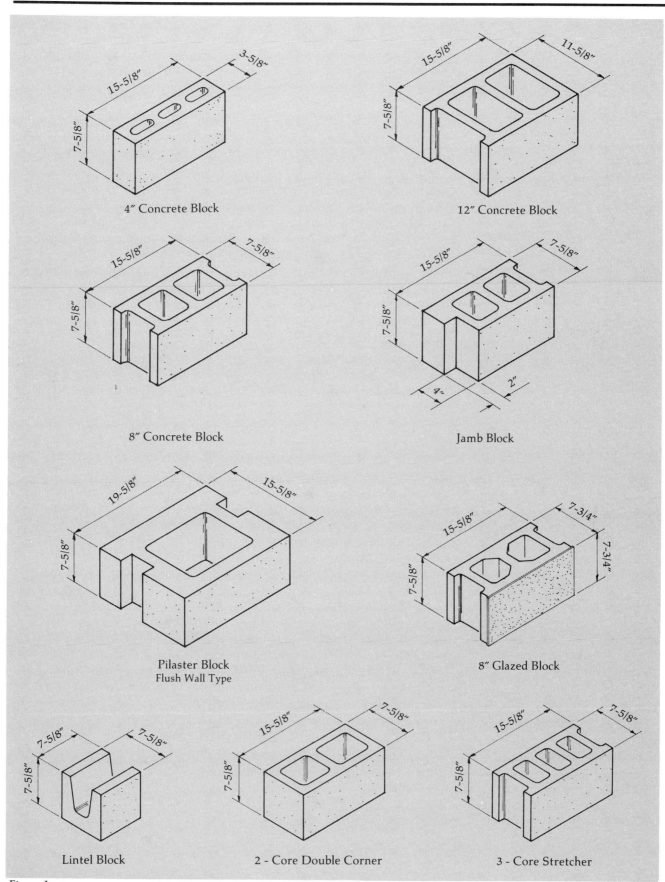

4" Concrete Block

12" Concrete Block

8" Concrete Block

Jamb Block

Pilaster Block
Flush Wall Type

8" Glazed Block

Lintel Block

2 - Core Double Corner

3 - Core Stretcher

Figure 12.9

71

and by the adhesion of grout to adjacent wythes of masonry. Frequently, structural bonds are used to create decorative patterns on the face of the wall. When using any of these patterns, an adjustment in the total number of face brick must be taken into account if the bricks have lengths of twice their bed depths.

Sizes of brick manufactured in one locality vary from the sizes produced in other areas. Often, too, the dimensions of brick shown on a plan may not be locally available. Brick removal may require toothing to make invisible jointing and needling work to temporarily support an opening in load-bearing masonry walls. Toothing involves tying new masonry work into the course pattern of existing masonry. Needling is required to support masonry when the underlying bearing structure must be removed or repaired. Structural members, usually steel, are inserted in a perpendicular direction through openings in the masonry wall and supported independently.

When determining the quantities for concrete block, it is important for the estimator to be aware of special conditions, bond beams, change in thickness with height, decorative and specialty blocks, and lintels. Each of these conditions will affect the costs appreciably. Figure I2.9 shows various sizes and shapes of commonly used concrete blocks.

When estimating interior partition heights, the estimator should check to see whether the partition stops just above the suspended ceiling line or goes to the underside of the floor slab above. This is also the time to see if cores must be filled and reinforced.

When partitions are the same height but of different thicknesses, the most efficient take-off method is to measure all the partitions in groups of the same thickness before multiplying by height. This ensures accuracy and helps prevent waste of materials later in the renovation.

When estimating solid or hollow masonry units, the estimator must give consideration to and include items such as anchor bolts, ledgers, fasteners, waterproofing, solid grouting, continuous reinforcing, metal frames, vents, sealants, reglets and flashing, insulation, and slurry coating. The miscellaneous items associated with masonry are often F.O.B. items by a fabricator with installation the responsibility of the mason or the general contractor.

In commercial renovation, the quantities of masonry work may be small and might involve localized areas of new work and varying amounts of repair and restoration. When the amount of new work is small the estimator must remember that the economy of scale may not be applicable. The cost of mobilization for the work may be more than the actual cost of installation. Masonry restoration, however, can often be a large project. The estimator must be very careful during the quantity take-off to assure that all areas requiring work are included. Photographs, notes, and sketches from the site visit will be particularly useful. Stringent controls are often placed on masonry restoration and must be considered in the estimate.

When interior masonry work is involved, the estimator should be aware of material delivery, storage, and handling restrictions.

Division 5: Metals
The amount of metals used in renovation is usually minimal. It is often mostly miscellaneous and ornamental work, unless a floor or roof is added or replaced.

Structural steel
The structural steel required to repair, modify and remodel buildings very

often is limited to small quantities of columns and beams purchased from local warehouses. Because warehouses sell structural steel shapes such as wide flange, channel, square, and rectangular tubing, and round pipe sections in mill lengths, it is necessary to include the weight of the cut-off material in the estimate, as well as fabrication and cutting costs.

Temporary shoring, jacking, safety nets, work platforms, and needling of the steel into position are items to think about. Thought must also be given to the requirements for fire lookout personnel, extinguishers, and fire curtains when cutting and welding torches are used for the dismantling or erection of structural steel.

When drawings are available for a proposed renovation project, they may include: special notes, lintel schedules, size, weight and location of each piece of steel, anchor bolt locations, special fabrication details, and special weldment. These must all be included on the Quantity Sheet.

When making a structural steel take-off, the estimator must consider the following items: the grade of steel, method of connection, cleaning, painting (type and number of coats), and the number of pieces. Investigation of required fireproofing is essential. Field inspection of existing fireproofing methods and materials is often the only source for quick estimating.

The estimator must give consideration to warehouse availability, type of fabrication required, fabricator capability and availability. Of equal importance are delivery dates, sequence of deliveries, size of pieces to be delivered, storage area, and access. Engineering and detailing, underwriter labels, and field dimensions are all items that must be included in the estimated cost.

Steel joists

By site inspection the estimator often times must determine the size and type of steel joists from visual inspection of existing joists. If specifications and drawings are available, they will include type of joists, size and length, end bearing conditions, tie joist locations, bridging type and size, headers required, header size, top and bottom chord extensions, and ceiling extensions.

The estimator must consider various types and sizes, special attachments, special paint and surface preparation, deliveries, site storage and access, and other variables that must be included in the estimate but not called out.

Existing floor and roof systems framed with steel joists are designed to support specified live and dead loads. When a given space is remodeled, the loads may be exceeded; therefore, added joists may be specified and must be taken off. The joists must be identified by type, size, and length. Special end bearings may also be required. Jacking or temporary shoring may be required to erect the joists.

Steel deck

In commercial renovation, metal decking is usually found in floor or roof systems added horizontally to an existing building. Steel-framed mezzanines are an example of a system that normally would include a metal deck. The type, depth, gauge, closures, finish, and attachment method of steel deck must be determined and listed.

Again, it is important to consider the quantity, availability, and delivery schedule of the types of deck specified, as well as site storage and access, special requirements and miscellaneous items necessary to complete the work.

Miscellaneous Metals

Because miscellaneous metals are difficult to identify, the estimator should carefully examine the existing conditions and add those items which are neither specified nor shown in sketches and drawings, but are necessary to complete the work.

Determine the type of finish required. Is the metal furnished and erected or is it furnished only? When required for installation, the field measurements, shop drawings, method of installation, and equipment required to erect must all be noted and given consideration.

Ornamental Metals

Stairs (type of construction, rails, nosing, number of risers and landings), railings (materials, type construction, finishes, protection), gratings (types, sizes, finishes), and attachments must be thought of in the same way as miscellaneous metals.

Consider the material availability, finishes required, protection of finished products, installation procedures, coordination with other trades, and finally, items not obvious or called out but needed to complete the installation.

While making the take-off, list equipment that can be used to erect fabricated materials. Erection costs cannot be determined without giving consideration to site storage, site access, type and size of equipment required, delivery schedules, and erection sequence. This is one area where the estimator must pay particular attention to minimum labor and equipment charges.

Providing that the estimator applies the information discussed in this chapter, the sub-bids received for Division 5 can be evaluated more closely. From the evaluation and comparison with subcontract proposals, items that were omitted can be identified and quickly quantified using a reference source such as R.S Means' *Repair and Remodeling Cost Data*, 1985.

Division 6: Wood and Plastics

Carpentry work can be broken down into rough carpentry, laminated framing and decking, plus finish carpentry and millwork. The rough and laminated materials can be sticks of lumber and sheets of plywood, job site fabricated and installed, or prefabricated laminated beams and decks, trusses and truss joists, and panelized roof systems all delivered to the job site and erected.

Rough carpentry

1. Lumber is usually estimated in board feet and purchased in 1000 board feet quantities, a board foot being 1" x 12" x 12" (nominal) or actual 3/4" x 11-1/2" x 12" milled. The Quantity Sheet should indicate species, grade, and any type of wood preservative or fire retardant specified or required by code.
2. Sills, Posts, and Girders used in subfloor framing should be taken off by length and quantity. The standard lengths available vary by species and dimensions and cut-offs often are used for blocking. Careful selection of lengths will decrease the waste factor required.
3. Floor Joists, shown or specified by size and spacing, should be taken off by nominal length and quantity required. Do not forget double joists under partitions, headers at openings, overhangs, laps at bearings, and blocking or bridging.
4. Ceiling Joists are similar to floor joists but may vary in direction. One must be alert for soffits and suspended ceilings. Ledgers may be a part of the ceiling joists system. In a flat roof system the rafters are called joists and are usually shown as a ceiling system.
5. Studs required are noted on the drawings by certain spacing, usually 16" O.C. or 24" O.C., with the size of stud given. Taking the linear feet of partitions that are similar in stud size, height and spacing, and dividing the linear feet by the spacing will give the estimator the number of studs required. Added studs required for openings, corners, double top plates, sole plates, and intersecting partitions must be taken off separately.

6. Number and Size of Openings are important. Even though there are no studs in these areas, the estimator must take off headers, subsills, king studs, trimmers, cripples, and knee studs. Where bracing and fire blocking are noted, indicate the type and quantity.

7. Roof Rafters vary with different types of roofs. A hip and valley, because of its complexity, has a greater material waste factor than most other roof types. Although straight gable, gambrel, and mansard roofs are not as complicated, care should be taken to ensure a good material take-off. Roof pitches, overhangs, and soffit framing all affect the quantity of material and costs. Do not scale rafters from the plan; always use the elevations.

8. Roof Trusses are usually furnished and delivered to the job site by the truss fabricator. Make certain that the fabricator furnishes shop drawings, and find out if erection is included in the cost. Architecturally exposed trusses are usually more expensive to fabricate and erect.

9. Tongue and Groove Roof Decks of various woods, solid planks, or laminated construction are usually 2" to 4" thick and used mostly with glued laminated beams or heavy timber. The square foot method is used to determine quantities with consideration given to roof pitches and non-modular areas for waste. The materials are purchased by board foot measurement, and the conversion from square foot to board must allow for net sizes as opposed to board measure, and loss of coverage because of the tongue and groove and mill lengths available.

10. Sheathing on walls can be plywood of different grades and thicknesses, wallboard, or solid boards nailed directly to the studs. Plywood can be applied with the grain vertical, horizontal, or diagonal to the studding. Solid boards are usually nailed diagonally, but can be applied horizontally when lateral forces are not present. Wallboard can be installed either horizontally or vertically, depending upon wall height and board dimensions. When estimating quantities of plywood or wallboard sheathing, the estimator calculates the number of sheets required by measuring the square feet of area to be covered and dividing by sheet size. Diagonal or non-module areas will create waste and must be considered in the estimate. For solid board sheathing, add 15% to 20% more material to the take-off when using tongue and groove sheathing as opposed to square edge. For diagonal application of boards, plywood, or wallboard, include an additional 10% to 15% material waste factor.

11. Subfloors can be CDX type plywood (with the thickness dependent on the load and span), solid boards laid diagonally or perpendicular to the joists, or tongue and groove planks. The quantity take-off is similar to solid board sheathing (noted above).

12. Stressed Skin Plywood includes prefabricated roof panels, with or without bottom skin or tie rods, and folded plate roof with intermediate rafters, all requiring the square foot quantity method.

13. Structural Joists are prefabricated type wood flanges with plywood or tubular steel webs. This type joist is spaced in accordance with the load and requires bridging and blocking supplied by the fabricator. Quantity take-off should include the following: type, number required, length, spacing, end-bearing conditions, number of rows, length of bridging, and blocking.

14. Grounds are normally 1" x 2" wood strips used for case work or plaster and the quantities are estimated in L.F.

15. Furring (1" x 2" or 1" x 3") wood strips generally are fastened to masonry or concrete walls so that wall coverings may be attached thereto. Furring is also used on underside of ceiling joists to fasten ceiling finishes. Quantities are estimated by L.F.

16. Plans and specifications should be carefully checked for lumber and plywood treatments used to inhibit decay, warping, fire, and insects. Depending upon the treatment, the cost of the material can sometimes double. Some of the most common wood treatments and current prices are listed in 6.1-57 and 6.1-60 of *Repair and Remodeling Cost Data, 1985*.

17. Tables I2.12 to I2.25 are several guides to assist in making a quantity take-off of rough carpentry. The estimator must remember that all items of rough carpentry are not listed or noted. One should be acquainted with the other divisions and realize where these items are required. An example would be temporary wood treads at steel pan stairs, or temporary wood rails at concrete stairs.

Finish carpentry and laminated construction

With the ever-increasing cost of job site labor and the improved technology of mass production, an entire room or half of a house is sometimes hoisted into place with no finish carpentry required. One of the results of this trend is the almost universal use of prefabricated cabinets, counter tops, and shelves.

1. Most cabinets, countertops, and shelves can be taken off in items of stated dimensions. Those which obviously cannot be preassembled should be taken off separately. Counter cutouts and radiator or air conditioner cutouts should be shown as labor items. This is the time to take off the valance board and moldings of these cabinets.

2. Carefully check the plans for nonstructural decorative beams and columns that were not included in the rough carpentry.

3. Millwork frequently has similar dimensions for two to four items. It is safer to list each item separately on your Quantity Sheet. All of these, except door and window trim, are listed by the linear foot. Standard door and window trim are listed per set. The common use of pre-hung doors and windows makes it convenient to take off this trim with the doors and windows. Exterior trim, other than door and window trim, should be taken off with the siding, since the details and dimensions are interrelated.

4. Paneling is taken off by the type, finish, and square foot (converted to full sheets). Be sure to list any millwork that would show up on the details. Also include a percentage for waste. Panel siding and associated trim are taken off by the square foot and linear foot, respectively. Be sure to provide an allowance for waste.

5. There are as many ways of taking off stairs as there are different types of stairs. The important thing is to be complete and thorough. Division 6.2-79 of *Repair and Remodeling Cost Data*, 1985, lists many combinations of stairs and stair parts that should fit almost any detail and specification.

6. Laminated construction can be listed and defined separately as it is frequently supplied and erected by a special subcontractor. Sometimes the beams are supplied and erected by one subcontractor and the decking done by the general contractor or another subcontractor. Since the members are factory fabricated, the plans and specifications must be submitted to a fabricator for take-off and pricing.

The estimator should consider the equipment required to erect or install the carpentry materials. Carpentry materials can arrive at the job assembled or partially assembled. Therefore, the man-hours expended to handle, cut, and install the finish materials will vary greatly.

Flat Roof Framing			
Joist Size	Inches on Center	Board Feet per Square Feet of Roof Area	Nails Lbs. per MBM
2" x 6"	12"	1.17	10
	16"	.91	10
	20"	.76	10
	24"	.65	10
2" x 8"	12"	1.56	8
	16"	1.21	8
	20"	1.01	8
	24"	.86	8
2" x 10"	12"	1.96	6
	16"	1.51	6
	20"	1.27	6
	24"	1.08	6
2" x 12"	12"	2.35	5
	16"	1.82	5
	20"	1.52	5
	24"	1.30	5
3" x 8"	12"	1.82	5
	16"	1.82	5
	20"	1.52	5
	24"	1.30	5
3" x 10"	12"	2.94	4
	16"	2.27	4
	20"	1.90	4
	24"	1.62	4

Table I2.12

Pitched Roof Framing

Rafters Including Collar Ties, Hip and Valley Rafters, Ridge Poles

Rafter Size	Spacing Center to Center							
	12"		16"		20"		24"	
	Board Feet per Square Feet of Roof Area	Nails Lbs. per MBM	Board Feet per Square Feet of Roof Area	Nails Lbs. per MBM	Board Feet per Square Feet of Roof Area	Nails Lbs. per MBM	Board Feet per Square Feet of Roof Area	Nails Lbs. per MBM
2" x 4"	.89	17	.71	17	.59	17	.53	17
2" x 6"	1.29	12	1.02	12	.85	12	.75	12
2" x 8"	1.71	9	1.34	9	1.12	9	.98	9
2" x 10"	2.12	7	1.66	7	1.38	7	1.21	7
2" x 12"	2.52	6	1.97	6	1.64	6	1.43	6
3" x 8"	2.52	6	1.97	6	1.64	6	1.43	6
3" x 10"	3.13	5	2.45	5	2.02	5	1.78	5

Table 12.13

Hip and Valley Rafter Ratios

Ratios of Hip or Valley Length to Run of Common Rafter for Various Slopes

Roof Slope			Roof Slope		
Rise	Run	Ratio	Rise	Run	Ratio
3	12	1.4361	9	12	1.6008
4	12	1.4530	10	12	1.6415
4.5	12	1.4631	11	12	1.6853
5	12	1.4743	12	12	1.7321
6	12	1.5000	13	12	1.7815
7	12	1.5298	14	12	1.8333
8	12	1.5635	15	12	1.8875

Table 12.14

Roof Slope Ratios

Ratios of Rafter Length to Run for Various Slopes

Rise	Run	Ratio	Rise	Run	Ratio
3	12	1.0308	9	12	1.2500
4	12	1.0541	10	12	1.3017
4.5	12	1.0680	11	12	1.3566
5	12	1.0833	12	12	1.4142
6	12	1.1180	13	12	1.5366
7	12	1.1577	14	12	1.5366
8	12	1.2019	15	12	1.6008

Table 12.15

Cross Bridging

Cross Bridging - Board Feet per Square Feet of Floors, Ceiling or Flat Roof Area
Nails - Pounds per MBM of Bridging

Joist Size	Spacing	1" x 3"		1" x 4"		2" x 3"	
		Bd. Ft.	Nails	Bd. Ft.	Nails	Bd. Ft.	Nails
2" x 8"	12"	.04	147	.05	112	.08	77
	16"	.04	120	.05	91	.08	61
	20"	.04	102	.05	77	.08	52
	24"	.04	83	.05	63	.08	42
2" x 10"	12"	.04	.36	.05	103	.08	71
	16"	.04	114	.05	87	108	58
	20"	.04	98	.05	74	.08	50
	24"	.04	80	.05	61	.08	41
2" x 12"	12"	.04	127	.05	96	.08	67
	16"	.04	108	.05	82	.08	55
	20"	.04	94	.05	71	.08	48
	24"	.04	78	.05	59	.08	39
3" x 8"	12"	.04	160	.05	122	.08	84
	16"	.04	127	.05	96	.08	66
	20"	.04	107	.05	81	.08	54
	24"	.04	86	.05	65	.08	44
3" x 10"	12"	.04	146	.05	111	.08	77
	16"	.04	120	.05	91	.08	62
	20"	.04	.02	.05	78	.08	52
	24"	.04	83	.05	63	.08	42

Table I2.16

				Lbs. Nails per MBM of Siding		
				Stud Spacing		
Type of Siding	Size	Exposure	Board Feet per Square Feet of Wall Area	16"	20"	24"
Plain Bevel Siding	1/2" x 4"	2-1/2"	1.60	17	13	11
		2-3/4"	1.45			
	1/2" x 6"	4-1/2"	1.33	11	9	7
		4-3/4"	1.26			
		5"	1.20			
	1/2" x 8"	6-1/2"	1.23	8	7	6
		7"	1.14			
Plain Bevel Bungalow Siding	5/8" x 8"	6-1/2"	1.23	14	11	9
		7"	1.14			
	5/8" x 10"	8-1/2"	1.18	16	13	11
		9"	1.11			
	3/4" x 8"	6-1/2"	1.23	14	11	9
		7"	1.14			
	3/4" x 10"	8-1/2"	1.18	16	13	11
		9"	1.11			
	3/4" x 12"	10-1/2"	1.14	14	11	9
		11"	1.09			
Drop or Rustic Siding	3/4" x 4"	3-1/4"	1.23	27	22	18
	3/4" x 6"	5-1/16"	1.19	18	15	12
		5-3/16"	1.17			

Siding

Table I2.17

	Furring					
	Board Feet Per Square Feet of Wall Area					Lbs. Nails per MBM of Furring
	Spacing Center to Center					
Size	12″	16″	20″	24″		
1″ x 2″	.18	.14	.11	.10		55
1″ x 3″	.28	.21	.17	.14		37

Table I2.18

Wallboard					
Includes Fiber Board, Gypsum Board and Plywood, Used as Underflooring, Sheathing, Plaster Base, or as Drywall Finish					
Factors		Nail			
Used for Underflooring, Sheathing and Plaster Base	Used for Exposed Dry Wall Finish	Pounds of Nails per 1000 Sq. Ft. of Wallboard			
		Joist, Stud of Rafter Spacing			
		12″	16″	20″	24″
1.05	1.10	7	6	5	4

Table I2.19

Floor Framing				
Floor Joists			Blocking Over Main Bearing	
Joist Size	Inches on Center	Board Feet per Square Feet of Floor Area	Nails Lbs. per MBM	Board Feet per Square Feet of Floor Area	Nails Lbs. per MBM Blocking
2″ x 6″	12″	1.28	10	.16	133
	16″	1.02	10	.03	95
	20″	.88	10	.03	77
	24″	.78	10	.03	57
2″ x 8″	12″	1.71	8	.04	100
	16″	1.36	8	.04	72
	20″	1.17	8	.04	57
	24″	1.03	8	.05	43
2″ x 10″	12″	2.14	6	.05	79
	16″	1.71	6	.05	57
	20″	1.48	6	.06	46
	24″	1.30	6	.06	34
2″ x 12″	12″	2.56	5	.06	66
	16″	2.05	5	.06	47
	20″	1.77	5	.07	39
	24″	1.56	5	.07	29
3″ x 8″	12″	2.56	5	.04	39
	16″	2.05	5	.05	57
	20″	1.77	5	.06	45
	24″	1.56	5	.06	33
3″ x 10″	12″	3.20	4	.05	72
	16″	2.56	4	.07	46
	20″	2.21	4	.07	36
	24″	1.95	4	.08	26

Table I2.20

Board Sheathing and Subflooring						
			Diagonal			
			Lbs. Nails per MBM Lumber			
		Board Feet per Square Foot of Area	Joist, Stud or Rafter Spacing			
Type	Size		12"	16"	20"	24"
Surface 4 Sides (S4S)	1" x 4"	1.22	58	46	39	32
	1" x 6"	1.18	39	31	25	21
	1" x 8"	1.18	30	23	19	16
	1" x 10"	1.17	35	27	23	19
Tongue and Groove (T&G)	1" x 4"	1.36	65	51	43	36
	1" x 6"	1.26	42	33	27	23
	1" x 8"	1.22	31	24	20	17
	1" x 10"	1.20	36	28	24	19
Shiplap	1" x 4"	1.41	67	53	45	37
	1" x 6"	1.29	43	33	28	23
	1" x 8"	1.24	31	24	20	17
	1" x 10"	1.21	36	28	24	19

Table I2.21

Board Sheathing and Subflooring						
			Right Angles			
			Lbs. Nails per MBM Lumber			
		Board Feet per Square Foot of Area	Joist, Stud or Rafter Spacing			
Type	Size		12"	16"	20"	24"
Surface 4 Sides (S4S)	1" x 4"	1.19	60	47	40	33
	1" x 6"	1.15	40	31	26	22
	1" x 8"	1.15	30	23	20	17
	1" x 10"	1.14	36	28	24	19
Tongue and Groove (T & G)	1" x 4"	1.32	66	52	44	36
	1" x 6"	1.23	43	33	28	23
	1" x 8"	1.19	32	24	21	17
	1" x 10"	1.17	37	29	24	20
Shiplap	1" x 4"	1.38	69	55	46	38
	1" x 6"	1.26	44	34	29	24
	1" x 8"	1.21	32	25	21	17
	1" x 10"	1.18	37	29	25	20

Table I2.22

Ceiling Joists			
Joist Size	Inches on Center	Board Feet per Square Feet of Ceiling Area	Nails Lbs. per MBM
2" x 4"	12"	.78	17
	16"	.59	19
	20"	.48	19
2" x 6"	12"	1.15	11
	16"	.88	13
	20"	.72	13
	24"	.63	13
2" x 8"	12"	1.53	9
	16"	1.17	9
	20"	.96	9
	24"	.84	9
2" x 10"	12"	1.94	7
	16"	1.47	7
	20"	1.21	7
	24"	1.04	7
3" x 8"	12"	2.32	6
	16"	1.76	6
	20"	1.44	6
	24"	1.25	6

Table 12.23

Exterior Wall Stud Framing					
		Studs Includings Corner Bracing		Horizontal Bracing Midway Between Plates	
Stud Size	Inches on Center	Board Feet per Square Feet of Ext. Wall Area	Lbs. Nails per MBM of Stud Framing	Board Feet per Square Feet of Ext. Wall Area	Lbs. Nails per MBM of Bracing
2" x 3"	16"	.78	30	.03	117
	20"	.74	30	.03	97
	24"	.71	30	.03	85
2" x 4"	16"	1.05	22	.04	87
	20"	.98	22	.04	72
	24"	.94	22	.04	64
2" x 6"	16"	1.51	15	.06	59
	20"	1.44	15	.06	48
	24"	1.38	15	.06	43

Table 12.24

Partition Stud Framing

Stud Size	Inches on Center	Studs Including Sole and Cap Plates — Board Feet per Square Feet of Partition Area	Lbs. Nails per MBM of Stud Framing	Horizontal Bracing in All Partitions — Board Feet per Square Feet of Partition Area	Lbs. Nails per MBM of Bracing	Horizontal Bracing in Bearing Partitions Only — Board Feet per Square Feet of Partition Area	Lbs. Nails per MBM of Bracing
2" x 3"	12"	.91	25	.04	145	.01	145
	16"	.83	25	.04	111	.01	111
	20"	.78	25	.04	90	.01	90
	24"	.76	25	.04	79	.01	79
2" x 4"	12"	1.22	19	.05	108	.02	108
	16"	1.12	19	.05	87	.02	87
	20"	1.05	19	.05	72	.02	72
	24"	1.02	19	.05	64	.02	64
2" x 6"	16"	1.02	19			.04	59
	20"	1.29	16			.04	48
	24"	1.22	16			.04	43
2" x 4" Staggered	8"	1.69	22				
3" x 4"	16"	1.35	17				
2" x 4" 2" Way	16"	1.08	19				

Table 12.25

Division 7: Moisture and Thermal Protection

This division includes all types of materials for sealing the outside of a building against moisture and air infiltration, plus the insulation and accessories used in connection with them. The principal concern is to determine the most probable places where these materials will be found, in or on a building. The estimator must also determine the best methods of taking off quantities, and the easiest, most accurate way of estimating the installed cost of each material.

Waterproofing
1. Dampproofing
2. Vapor Barriers
3. Caulking and Sealants
4. Sheet and Membrane
5. Integral Cement Coatings

Dampproofing usually consists of one or two bituminous coatings applied to foundation walls from about the finished grade line to the bottom of the footings. The areas involved are calculated from the total height of the dampproofing and the length of the wall. After separate areas are figured and added together to provide a total square foot area, a unit cost per square foot can be selected for the type of material, the number of coats, and the method of application specified for the building.

Waterproofing at or below grade with elastomeric sheets or membranes is estimated on the same basis as dampproofing, with two basic exceptions. First, the installed unit costs for the elastomeric sheets do not include bonding adhesive or splicing tape, which must be figured as an additional cost. Second, the membrane waterproofing on slabs must be estimated separately from the higher cost installation on walls. In all cases, unit costs are per square foot of covered surface.

Metallic coating material is applied to floors or walls, usually on the interior or dry side, after the masonry surface has been prepared by chipping or backing for bonding to the new material. The unit cost per square foot for these materials depends on the thickness of the material, the position of the area to be covered and the preparation required. In many places where these materials are applied, access may be difficult and under the control of others. The estimator should make an allowance for delays caused by this problem.

Caulking and sealants are usually applied on the exterior of the building except for special conditions on the interior. In most cases caulking and sealing is done to prevent water and/or air from entering a building. Therefore, at door and window frames and in other places where different materials meet, caulking and sealing are usually specified. To estimate the installed cost of this type of material, two things must be determined. From the specifications the estimator must note the kind of material to be used for each caulking or sealing job. On the plans, the dimensions of the joint to be caulked or sealed must be measured, with attention to any requirements for backer rods. With this information, the estimator can select the applicable cost per linear foot and multiply it by the total length in feet to provide an estimated cost for each kind of caulking or sealing on the job.

Insulation
1. Batt or Roll
2. Blown-in
3. Board (Rigid and Semi-rigid)
4. Cavity Masonry
5. Perimeter Foundation
6. Poured in Place
7. Reflective

8. Roof

9. Sprayed

Insulation is used to reduce heat transfer through the exterior enclosure of the building. The type and form of this insulation will vary according to its location in the structure and the accessibility of the space it occupies. Major insulation types include mineral granules, fibers and foams, vegetable fibers and solids, and plastic foams. These materials may be required around foundations, on or inside walls, and under roofing. The cost of insulation depends on the type of material, its form (loose, granular, batt or boards), its thickness in inches, the method of installation, and the total area in square feet.

It is becoming popular to specify insulation by "R" value. The estimator may have to do some shopping around to find the most inexpensive material for the specified "R" value. Installation costs may vary from one material to another. Also, wood blocking and/or nailers are often required to match the insulation thickness in some instances.

Working with the above data, the estimator can accurately select the installed cost per square foot and estimate the total cost. It should be noted that most unit insulation costs are per square foot. Exceptions are reflective aluminum foil, which is per hundred square feet (C.S.F.), and cellulose fiber, which is per board foot (B.F.). The estimate for insulation should also include associated costs, such as cutting and patching for installation, or requirements for air vents.

Factors for Converting Inclined to Horizontal					
Roof Slope	Approx. Angle	Factor	Roof Slope	Approx. Angle	Factor
Flat	0	1.000	12 in 12	45.0	1.414
1 in 12	4.8	1.003	13 in 12	47.3	1.474
2 in 12	9.5	1.014	14 in 12	49.4	1.537
3 in 12	14.0	1.031	15 in 12	51.3	1.601
4 in 12	18.4	1.054	16 in 12	53.1	1.667
5 in 12	22.6	1.083	17 in 12	54.8	1.734
6 in 12	26.6	1.118	18 in 12	56.3	1.803
7 in 12	30.3	1.158	19 in 12	57.7	1.873
8 in 12	33.7	1.202	20 in 12	59.0	1.943
9 in 12	36.9	1.250	21 in 12	60.3	2.015
10 in 12	39.8	1.302	22 in 12	61.4	2.088
11 in 12	42.5	1.357	23 in 12	62.4	2.162

Example:

[20' (1.302) 90'] 2 = 4,687.2 S.F. = 46.9 Sq.

OR

[40' (1.302) 90'] = 4,687.2 S.F. = 46.9 Sq.

Table 12.26

Shingles

Most residences and many other types of buildings have sloping roofs covered with some form of shingle. The materials used in shingles vary from the more common granular-covered asphalt and fiberglass units to wood, metal, clay, concrete, or slate.

The first step in estimating the cost of a shingle roof is to determine the material type specified, shingle size and weight, and installation method. This information will permit the estimator to select the accurate installed cost of the roofing material.

In a sloping roof deck, the ridge and eaves lengths, as well as the ridge to eaves dimension, must be known or measured before the actual roof area can be calculated. When the plan dimensions of the roof are known and the sloping dimensions are not, the actual roof area can be estimated if the approximate slope of the roof is known. Table I2.26 is a table of multipliers. The roof slope is given in both inches of rise per foot of horizontal run and degree of slope, which allows direct conversion of the horizontal plan dimension into the dimension on the slope.

After the roof area has been estimated in square feet, it must be divided by 100 to convert it into roofing squares. To determine the quantity of shingles required for hips or ridges, add one square for each 100 linear feet of hips and/or ridges.

When the total squares of roofing have been calculated, the estimator should make an allowance for waste due to the design of the roof. A minimum allowance of 3 to 5 percent is needed if the roof has two straight sides with two gable ends and no breaks. At the other extreme, any roof with several valleys, hips, and ridges many need a waste allowance of 15% or more to cover the excess cutting required.

Accessories that are part of a shingle roof include drip edges, flashings at chimneys, dormers, skylights, valleys, and walls. These are necessary to complete the roof and should be included in the estimate for the shingles.

Roofing and Siding

In addition to shingles, many types of roofing and siding are used on commercial and industrial buildings. These are made of several kinds of material and come in many forms for both roofing and siding.

The materials used in roofing and siding panels include: aluminum, mineral fiber-cement, epoxy, fibrous glass, steel, vinyl, coal tar, asphalt felt, tar felt, and asphalt asbestos felt and base sheets. Most of the latter materials are used in job-fabricated, built-up roofs and as backing for other materials such as shingles.

The basic data required for estimating either roofing or siding includes the specification for the material, the supporting structure, the method of installation, and the area to be covered. When selecting the correct unit price for these materials, the estimator must remember that basic installed unit costs are per square foot for siding and per square (100 square feet) for roofing. The major exceptions to this general rule are prefabricated roofing panels and single-ply roofing, which are priced per square foot.

Single-ply roofs

1. Chlorinated Polyethylene (CPE)
2. Chlorosulfonated Polyethylene
3. Ethylene Propylene Diene Monomer (EPDM)
4. Polychloroprene (Neoprene)
5. Polyisobutylene (PIB)
6. Polyvinyl Chloride (PVC)

7. Modified Bitumen

Since the early 1970s the use of single-ply roofing membranes in the construction industry has been on the rise. Market surveys recently have shown that of all the single-ply systems being installed, about one in three is on new construction. Materially, these roofs are more expensive than other, more conventional roofs; however, labor costs are much lower because of a faster installation. Re-roofing represents the largest market for single-ply roof today. Single-ply roof systems are normally installed in one of the following ways:

1. **Loose-laid and ballasted:** Generally this is the easiest type of single-ply roof to install. Some special consideration must be given, however, when flashing is attached to the roof. The membrane is typically fused together at the seams, stretched out flat, and then ballasted with stone (1-1/2" @ 10-12 PSF) to prevent wind blow-off. This extra dead load must be considered during design stages. It is particularly important if re-roofing over an existing built-up roof that already weighs 10-15 PSF. A slip-sheet or vapor barrier is sometimes required to separate the new roof from the old.

2. **Partially-adhered:** This method of installation uses a series of bar or point attachments, which adhere the membrane to a substrate. The membrane manufacturer typically specifies the method to be used based on the material and substrate. Partially-adhered systems do not use ballast material. A slip-sheet may be required.

3. **Fully-adhered:** This is generally the most time-consuming of the single-plies to install, because these roofs employ a contact cement, cold adhesive, or hot bitumen to adhere the membrane uniformly to the substrate. Only manufacturer-approved insulation board should be used to receive the membrane. No ballast is required. A slip sheet may be necessary.

The materials available can be broken down into three categories:

1. Thermo-Setting: EPDM, Neoprene, and PIB
2. Thermo-Plastic: Hypalon, PVC, and CPE
3. Composites: Modified Bitumen

Each has its own unique requirements and performance characteristics. Most are available in all three installation methods. See Table I2.27.

Single-ply roof systems are available from many sources. Most if not all manufacturers, however, sell their materials only to franchised installers. As a result, there may be only one source for a price in any given area. Finally, read the specifications carefully. Estimate the system required, not a suitable substitute. If the specifications call for a reinforced PVC, do not go looking for an EPDM, and be aware of the appropriate installation methods.

Sheet Metal Work

1. Copper and Stainless Steel
2. Gutters and Downspouts
3. Edge Cleats and Gravel Stops
4. Flashings
5. Trim
6. Miscellaneous

Sheet metal work included in this division is limited to that used on roofs or sidewalls of buildings, and usually, on the exterior exposed to the weather. Many of the items covered are wholly or partially prefabricated with labor added for installation. Several are materials with labor added for on-site fabrication.

Single-Ply Roofing Membrane Installation Guide

		EPDM (Ethylene, propylene diene monomer)	Neoprene (Synthetic rubber)	PIB (Polyisobutylene)	CSPE (Chlorosulfenated polyethyene)	CPE (Chlorinated polyethylene)	PVC (Polyvinyl chloride)	Glass reinforced EPDM/neoprene	Modified bitumen/polyester	Modified bitumen/polyethylene & aluminum	Modified bitumen/polyethylene sheet	Modified CPE	Non-woven glass reinforced PVC	Nylon reinforced PVC	Nylon reinforced/butyl or neoprene	Polyester reinforced CPE	Polyester reinforced PVC	Rubber asphalt/plastic sheet
Sealing Method	Torch Heating	X							X	X	X							
	Solvent	X		X			X							X	X		X	
	Self-Sealing																	X
	Hot Air Gun	X		X	X	X	X		X		X	X		X	X	X	X	
	Adhesive	X	X	X	X			X	X	X			X	X		X	X	
Attachment Method	Partially-Adhered	X			X	X	X									X	X	
	Loose Laid/Ballast		X	X	X	X	X	X			X			X	X	X	X	
	Fully Adhered	X	X		X	X					X	X		X	X		X	X
	Adhesive	X	X	X	X							X		X				
Compatible Substrates	Spray Urethane Foam	X		X	X		X	X									X	X
	Plywood	X	X	X	X	X	X	X	X	X	X		X			X	X	X
	Insulation Board	X	X	X	X	X	X	X	X	X	X		X			X	X	X
	Exist. Asphalt Memb.	X		X		X			X							X		X
	Concrete	X	X	X	X	X	X	X				X				X	X	X
	Slip-Sheet Req'd.	X	X	X	X	X	X	X	X	X	X		X			X	X	X

	Thermo Setting	Thermo Plastic	Composites

Table I2.27

Pricing shop-made items such as downspouts, drip edges, expansion joints, gravel stops, gutters, reglets, and termite shields requires that the estimator determine the material type, size, and shape of the fabricated section, and the linear feet of the item. From this data an accurate unit can be selected and multiplied by the linear footage to obtain a total cost.

Some roofing systems, particularly single-ply, require flashing materials unique for only that roofing system.

The cost of items like copper roofing and metal flashing is estimated in a similar manner, except that unit costs are per square foot.

Roofing materials like monel, stainless steel, and zinc copper alloy are also estimated by the same method, except the unit costs are per square (100 square feet). Prefabricated items like strainers and louvers are priced on a cost-per-unit basis. Adhesives are priced by the gallon. The cost of roofing adhesives installed depends on the cost per gallon and coverage per gallon.

With trowel grade adhesives the coverage will vary from a light coating at 25 S.F. per gallon to a heavy covering at 10 S.F. per gallon. With most flashing work, the asphalt adhesive will cover an average of 15 S.F. for each layer or course. In many specifications the coverage of special materials like adhesives will be stated and should be used as the basis for the estimate.

Roof Accessories
1. Hatches
2. Skylights
3. Vents
4. Snow Guards

Roof accessories are items that may not be a part of the weatherproofing system but are there for another purpose. All accessories that are a standard size are priced per installed unit. These include ceiling, roof and smoke vents, and snow guards.

Skylight costs are listed by the square foot with unit costs varying in steps as the nominal size of individual units increases.

Skyroofs are priced on the same basis, but due to the many variations in the shape of these units, costs are per square foot of horizontal area. These costs will vary as the size and type of the unit changes, and in many cases maximum and minimum costs give the estimator a range of prices for various design variations. Due to the number of types and styles of these skyroofs, the estimator must determine the exact specifications for the one being priced. The accuracy of the total cost figure will depend entirely on the selection of the proper unit cost and calculation of the skyroof area. Anyone estimating the installed cost of materials listed in Division 7 should always use an estimating form or forms that provide space for dimensions, areas, item identification, unit costs, extensions, and total costs. A form gives the estimator a guide to follow when taking off quantities and a means of identifying each item as it is listed. Once all unit costs, calculations, and total costs are noted on the estimate, the estimator or another person can check the estimate and verify its accuracy.

Division 8: Doors, Windows, and Glass

In commercial renovation, the specifications for replacement fenestration are dictated not only by the need for increased thermal efficiency but by requirements for historical accuracy. The doors and windows may have to be custom made to fit odd and different sized openings.

Most architectural plans and specifications include door, window, and hardware schedules. The estimator should use these schedules, in conjunction with the plans, to avoid duplication or omission of units when determining the quantities. The schedules should identify the location, size, and type of each unit. Schedules should also include information regarding the frame, fire-rating, hardware, and special notes. If no such schedules are included, the estimator should prepare them in order to provide an accurate quantity take-off. Figure I2.10 is an example of a schedule that may be prepared by the estimator.

Metal Doors and Frames

A proper door schedule on the architectural drawings identifies each opening in detail. Define each opening in accordance with the items in the schedule and any other pertinent data. Installation information should be carefully reviewed in the specifications.

For the quantity survey, combine all similar doors and frames, checking each off as you go to ensure none has been left out. An easy and obvious check is to count the total number of openings, making certain that two doors and only one frame have been included where double doors are used. Important details to check for both door and frame are:

1. Material
2. Gauge
3. Size
4. Core Material
5. Fire Rating Label
6. Finish
7. Style

Leave a space in the tabulation on the Quantity Sheet for casings, stops, grounds, and hardware. This can be done either on the same sheet or on separate sheets.

Wood and Plastic Doors

The quantity survey for wood and plastic laminated doors is identical to that of metal doors. Where local work rules permit, prehung doors and windows are becoming prevalent in the industry. For these, locksets and interior casings are not included. As these are usually standard for a number of doors in any particular building, they need only be counted. Remember that exterior prehung doors need casings on the interior.

Special Doors

There are many types of specialty doors that may be included in commercial renovation, including sliding glass doors, overhead garage doors and bulkhead doors. These items should be taken off individually. The estimator should thoroughly examine the plans and specifications to be sure to include all hardware, operating mechanisms, fireratings, finishes, and any special installation requirements.

Fire Doors

The estimator must pay particular attention to fire doors when performing the quantity take-off. It is important to determine the exact type of door required. Table I2.28 is a table describing various types of fire doors. Please note that a "B" label door can be one of four types.

DOOR AND FRAME SCHEDULE

PROJECT _____ ARCHITECT _____ PAGE _____ of _____
LOCATION _____ OWNER _____ DATE _____

LOCATION	DOOR NO.	DOOR									FRAME					FIRE RATING		HARDWARE		REMARKS
		SIZE			MAT.	TYPE	GLASS	LOUVER		MAT.	TYPE	DETAILS			LAB	CON	SET NO.	KEYSIDE ROOM NO.		
		W	H	T				W	H			JAMB	HEAD	SILL						

Figure I2.10

94

	Fire Door		
Classification	Time Rating (as Shown on Label)	Temperature Rise (as Shown on Label)	Maximum Glass Area
3 Hour fire doors (A) are for use in openings in walls separating buildings or dividing a single building into the areas.	3 Hr. (A) 3 Hr. (A) 3 Hr. (A) 3 Hr. (A)	30 Min. 250°F Max 30 Min. 450°F Max 30 Min. 650°F Max *	None
1-1/2 Hour fire doors (B) and (D) are for use in openings in 2 Hour enclosures of vertical communication through buildings (stairs, elevators, etc.) or in exterior walls which are subject to servere fire exposure from outside of the building. 1 Hour fire doors (B) are for use in openings in 1 Hour enclosures of vertical communication through buildings (stairs, elevators, etc.)	1-1/2 Hr. (B) 1-1/2 Hr. (B) 1-1/2 Hr. (B) 1-1/2 Hr. (B) 1 Hr. 1-1/2 Hr. (D) 1-1/2 Hr. (D) 1-1/2 Hr. (D) 1-1/2 Hr. (D)	30 Min. 250°F Max 30 Min. 450°F Max 30 Min. 650°F Max * 30 Min. 250°F Max 30 Min. 250°F Max 30 Min. 450°F Max 30 Min. 650°F Max *	100 square inches per door None
3/4 Hour fire doors (C) and (E) are for use in openings in corridor and room partitions or in exterior walls which are subject to moderate fire exposure from outside of the building.	3/4 Hr. (C) 3/4 Hr. (E)	** **	1296 square 720 square inches per light
1/2 Hour fire doors and 1/3 Hour fire doors are for use where smoke controls is a primary consideration and are for the protection of openings in partitions between a habitable room and a corridor when the wall has a fire-resistance rating of not more than one hour.	1/2 Hr. 1/3 Hr.	** **	No limit

*The labels do not record any temperature rise limits. This means that the temperature rise on the unexposed face of the door at the end of 30 minutes of test is in excess of 650°F.
**Temperature rise is not recorded.

Table 12.28

If the plans or door schedule do not specify exactly which type is required, the estimator should consult the architect or local building inspector. Many building and fire codes also require that frames and hardware at fire doors be fire rated and labelled as such. When determining quantities, the estimator must also include any glass (usually wired) or special inserts to be installed in doors.

Entrances and Storefronts

Entrances, storefronts, and large custom skylights are almost all special designs and combinations of unit items to fit a unique situation. The estimator should submit the plans and specifications to a specialty installer for take-off and pricing.

The general procedure for the installer's take-off is:
1. Stationary Units
   a. Determine height and width of each like unit.
   b. Determine linear feet of intermediate, horizontal, and vertical members rounded to next higher foot.
   c. Determine number of joints.
2. Entrance Units
   a. Determine number of joints.
   b. Determine special frame hardware per unit.
   c. Determine special door hardware per unit.
   d. Determine thresholds and closers.

Windows

As with doors, a window schedule should be found on the architectural drawings. Items to pay particular attention to are:
1. Material
2. Gauge/Thickness
3. Screens
4. Glazing (type of glass and setting specifications)
5. Trim
6. Hardware
7. Special installation requirements

When using pre-hung units, be sure to add interior trim and stools.

Finish Hardware and Specialties

The estimator should list the hardware separately or on the door and window schedule. Remember that most pre-hung doors and windows do not include locksets. Some casement, awning, and jalousie windows include cranks and locks.

Be certain to check the specifications for:
1. Base Metal
2. Finish
3. Service (Heavy, Light, Medium)
4. Any other special detail

Check the specifications and code for panic devices and handicap devices. Metal thresholds and astragals are also included in this division. Weatherstripping may or may not be included with pre-hung doors and windows.

Glass and Glazing

Glazing quantities are a function of material, method, and length to be glazed. Therefore, quantities are measured in united inches or united feet (length + width). Many installers, however, figure all glass and glazing by the square foot. Be certain to read the specifications carefully, as there are many different grades, thicknesses, and other variables in glass.

Different types of glass include tempered, plate, safety, insulated, tinted, and various combinations thereof.

Division 9: Finishes

Lathing and Plastering

For this section, proceed in the normal erection sequence of furring, lath, and accessories. Lath is estimated by the square yard for both gypsum and metal lath, plus a usual 5% allowance for waste. Furring, channels, and accessories are measured by the linear foot. An extra foot should be allowed for each accessory miter or stop.

Plaster is also estimated by the square yard. Deductions for openings vary by preference from zero deduction to 50% of all openings over 2 feet in width. Some estimators deduct a percentage of the total yardage for openings. The estimator should allow one extra square foot for each linear foot of horizontal interior or exterior angle located below the ceiling level. Also, double the areas of small radius work.

In pricing the work, the estimator should consider its quality. Basically, there are two categories:

1. Ordinary or commercial with waves 1/8" to 3/16" in 10 feet, angles and corners fairly true.
2. First quality with variations less than 1/16" in 10 feet.

Labor for first quality work is approximately 20% more than for ordinary plastering.

Each room should be measured, perimeter times maximum wall height. Ceiling areas equal length times width.

Although wood plaster grounds are usually installed by carpenters, they should be measured when taking off the plaster requirements.

Drywall

Accessories, studs, track, and acoustical caulking are all measured by the linear foot. Drywall taping is figured by the square foot. Gypsum wallboard comes in thicknesses of 1/4" to 5/8" and lengths of 6' to 20'. No material deduction should be made for door or window openings under 32 S.F. Coreboard can be obtained in 1" thicknesses for solid wall and shaft work. Additions should be made to price out the inside or outside corners.

Different types of partition construction should be listed separately on the Quantity Sheets. There may be walls with studs of various widths, double studded, and similar or dissimilar surface materials. Acoustical requirements vary, and different wall systems should be tallied separately. Shaft work is usually of different construction from surrounding partitions requiring separate quantities and pricing of the work.

Acoustical Treatment

Acoustical systems fall into several categories. For example, sound barriers may be specified with soft dense metals or with fibrous material of either batt or board type. Ceiling tiles are applied directly to a backer or hung in a suspension system. Tile and board materials can be mineral, fibrous glass, wood fibers, or metal pans with sound-absorbing pads. The take-off of these materials is by the square foot of area with a 5% allowance for waste. Laying patterns in other than regular bond require approximately 20% more installation time for diagonal and 50% more time for mixed ashlar work. Do not forget about scaffolding.

Tile and Terrazzo

Tile and terrazzo areas are taken off on a square-foot basis. Trim and base are measured by the linear foot. Accent tiles are listed per each. Two basic methods of installation are used. One is called "mud" set and the other "thin" or adhesive set. Mud set is about 30% more expensive than the thin set. In terrazzo work be sure to include the linear footage of embedded decorative strips, grounds, machine rubbing, and power cleanup.

Flooring

This section covers the following items: carpeting, composition, resilient and wood flooring, stair treads, and risers. Carpeting and pads are estimated by the square yard. Carpet is available in roll widths of 9, 12, and 15 feet. Some types are available in 18" or 24" square carpet tiles. Consideration should be given to use the most economical width, as waste must be figured into the total quantity. Consider also the installation methods available, direct glue-down or stretched. Composition flooring is a specialty product usually supplied and installed by a subcontractor. The estimator may take it off on a square-foot basis to analyze the bids received if quoted as a lump sum. Resilient flooring is also measured by the square foot for all types. Base is estimated by the linear foot. If adhesive materials are to be quantified, they are estimated at a specified coverage rate by the gallon depending upon the specified type and manufacturer's recommendations.

Wood floor is available in strip, parquet, or block configuration. The latter two types are set in adhesives with quantities estimated by the square foot. There are three basic grades of wood flooring: first, second, and third, plus combination grades of "second and better" and "third and better." There are also color grades and special grade labels for different kinds of lumber, such as oak, maple, pecan, or beech. The estimator should be acquainted with these and the associated price differences. The laying pattern will influence labor costs and material waste. In addition to the material and labor for laying wood floors, the estimator must make allowances for sanding and finishing these areas unless the flooring is prefinished.

During the site visit, the estimator should determine the amount of preparation that existing surfaces will need before they can receive new floor finishes. This will ensure a more accurate estimate and prevent costly delays later in the renovation process.

Painting

Painting is one area where bids vary to a greater extent than almost any other section of the renovation project. This arises from the many methods of measuring surfaces to be painted. We recommend that each estimator obtain a copy of *Estimating Guide*, published by Painting and Decorating Contractors of America.

The estimator should check the plans and specifications carefully to be sure of the required number of coats. Each area should be compared to a flat wall surface by increasing the area with a predetermined percentage on a square-foot basis as follows:

Balustrades:		1 Side x 4
Blinds:	Plain	Actual area x 2
	Slotted	Actual area x 4
Cabinets:		Front area x 5
Clapboards and Drop Siding:		Actual area x 1.1
Cornices:	1 Story	Actual area x 2
	2 Story	Actual area x 3
	1 Story Ornamental	Actual area x 4
	2 Story Ornamental	Actual area x 6
Doors:	Flush	150% per side
	Two Panel	175% per side
	Four Panel	200% per side
	Six Panel	225% per side
Door Trim:		LF = 50% per side
Fences:	Chain Link	1 side x 3 for both sides
	Picket	1 side x 4 for both sides
Gratings:		1 side x 4/6
Grilles:	Plain	1 side x 200%
	Lattice	Area x 2 per side
	Moldings Under 12" Wide	1 SF/LF
Open Trusses:		Length x Depth x 2.5
Pipes:	Up to 4"	1 SF per LF
	4" to 8"	2 SF per LF
	8" to 12"	3 SF per LF
	12" to 16"	4 SF pr LF
	Hangers Extra	
Radiator:		Face area x 7
Shingle Siding:		Area x 1.5
Stairs:		Number of risers x 8 widths
Tie Rods:		2 SF per LF
Wainscoting, Paneled:		Actual area x 2
Walls and Ceilings:		Length x Width, no deducts for less than 100 SF
Sanding and Puttying:		
	Quality Work	Actual area x 2
	Average Work	Actual area x 50%
	Industrial	Actual area x 25%
Downspouts and Gutters:		Actual area x 2
Window Sash: (See Figure I2.11)		1 LF of part = 1 SF

Wall Coverings

Wall coverings are estimated by the roll or by the linear yard. Single rolls contain approximately 36 S.F., which forms the basis of determining the number of rolls required. Yard goods are stocked in various widths.

The area to be covered is measured, length by height of wall above baseboards, to get the square footage of each wall. This figure is divided by 30 to obtain the number of single rolls, allowing 6 S.F. of waste per roll. Deduct one roll for every two door openings. Two pounds of dry paste makes about three gallons of ready-to-use adhesive and hangs about 35 single rolls of light to medium weight paper or 14 rolls of heavyweight paper. Application labor costs vary with the quality, pattern, and type of joint required.

With vinyls and grass cloths requiring no pattern match, a waste allowance of 10% is normal, 3 S.F./roll. Wall coverings requiring a pattern match need about 25-30% waste, 9-11 S.F./roll. Waste can run as high as 50-60% on wall coverings with a large, bold or intricate pattern repeat.

As with any printed goods, make certain that all materials used on the job have the same batch run number. If not, be prepared for colors and patterns that don't precisely match up. Architects, interior designers, and owners will reject work when these highly visible, and expensive, finish materials don't match.

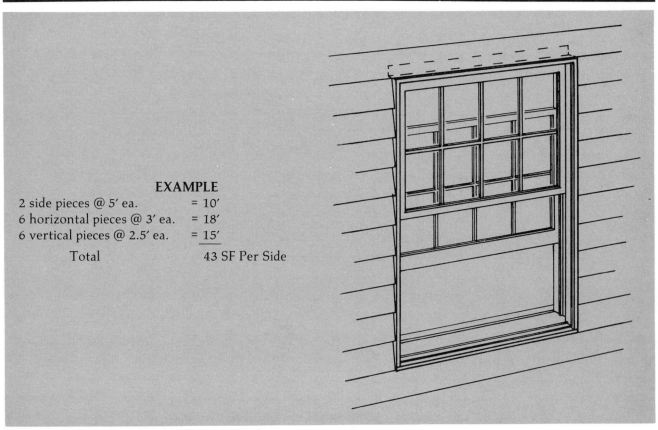

EXAMPLE

2 side pieces @ 5' ea.	= 10'
6 horizontal pieces @ 3' ea.	= 18'
6 vertical pieces @ 2.5' ea.	= 15'
Total	43 SF Per Side

Figure 12.11 Quantity Take-off for Painting Window

Division 10: Specialties

The specialty items included in this division are taken off by each, by square foot area, per linear foot, per opening, per station, or per floor. The boldface listings in R.S. Means' *Repair and Remodeling Cost Data* serve as a handy check list for items normally included. See Tables I2.4a and I2.4b.

The first step in making a take-off is to make a list of all materials and the accepted manufacturers of each. Next, the estimator makes a take-off for each of these items on the list. Most of these items are included in *Sweet's Catalog* but it is best to telephone the local supplier or specialty contractor for an up-to-date price quotation.

Industry source data is second only to locally obtained prices because the material prices shown at the date of the publication are based on national averages and can vary significantly between different geographic regions. Shipping costs may be determined by distance from the manufacturer. The labor is estimated to install the item completely from initial receiving to the final installation. In remodeling work where the specialty item is of sufficient size, and/or access is limited or restricted, the estimator must analyze the job to determine whether or not additional equipment is required for installation.

Division 11: Architectural Equipment

Architectural equipment, when installed, includes permanent fixtures that cause the space to function as designed. A challenge for the remodeling contractor can be the ability to locate and purchase architectural equipment that matches the existing design. Rather than take time to chase down suppliers, the estimator can use the average costs shown in *Repair and Remodeling Cost Data* 1985, for pricing purposes when completing the estimate for the division. Often the owner will purchase this equipment directly through the architect, and the contractor will install it. In this case, the man-hours shown in the cost book are used to complete the estimate for this division.

If architectural equipment is furnished by the owner, it is not a bad idea to add about 10% of the materials cost into the estimate. This protects the contractor from the risks and handling costs associated with the materials. Often the contractor must pick up these items and store them until ready for use.

Similar to Division 10, this is a counting type of measurement system and the boldface listings in *Repair and Remodeling Cost Data* can serve as a check list to ensure that items have not been omitted.

It is necessary to evaluate this equipment to determine what is required from other divisions for successful installation, such as:

1. Concrete
2. Miscellaneous Metals
3. Rough Carpentry
4. Mechanical Coordination
5. Electrical Requirements

This division includes equipment that can be packaged and delivered completely or partially factory assembled. Also, some items can or must be purchased and installed by an authorized factory representative. The estimator must investigate these variables.

Division 12: Furnishings

Furnishings are best defined as special types of furniture designed for use in dormitories, hospitals, hotels, offices, and restaurants. These important furnishings may be included in the budget estimate to help determine the total financial investment but are usually not a part of the renovation contract.

If the furnishings are built-in, then additional man-hours for unpacking, installing, and clean-up are necessary and must be calculated.

Division 13: Special Construction

The items found in this division are specialized subsystems that are usually manufactured or constructed and installed by specialty subcontractors. The costs shown are for budget purposes only. The final cost figure should be furnished by the specialty contractor after the exact requirements of the project have been specified.

It is a good idea to review this portion of the work with the subcontractor to determine the exact scope of work and to determine those items not covered by the quotation. If the subcontractor requires services such as excavation, unloading, and temporary services to perform the work, then these excluded items must be included in the Prime Contractor's bid.

The specialty contractor will have more detailed information at hand concerning the system. The more detailed the estimator's knowledge of a system, the easier it will be to subdivide the system into cost components. Each component can be further subdivided into material, labor, and equipment costs that will fully identify the direct cost of the specialty item.

Division 14: Conveying Systems

The following systems are included in this section:
1. Correspondence Lifts
2. Dumbwaiters
3. Elevators
4. Pneumatic Tube Systems
5. Handicapped Lifts

Because of the specialized construction of the above units, it is almost impossible for the general estimator to price most of this equipment, except in a budgetary capacity. Sometimes plans specify package units that carry standard prices. For general budget pricing, refer to R.S. Means' *Repair and Remodeling Cost Data* 1985. Quotations on specific equipment should be checked against the specifications to verify that all requirements are met. All required inspections, tests, permits, and responsibility for payment of these should be included in the installed price of the particular system.

Wherever possible, current prices should be obtained for each and every item. If items are installed by the Prime Contractor, installation costs should be developed from historical data. If this is not available, the man-hour figures in R.S. Means' *Repair and Remodeling Cost Data* 1985, may be used to develop installation costs.

Division 15: Mechanical

The amount of information supplied to the estimator for mechanical work in commercial renovation can vary greatly. When there are no plans and specifications, the estimator should prepare sketches or shop drawings, not only for quantity take-off but also for substantiation of the work to be performed for the benefit of the owner. Such drawings may also help to assure that all required items are included in the estimate.

When a complete set of mechanical plans and specifications are available, then the first step in preparing an estimate is to review the information provided, making notes on any special or unique requirements. Also, while it is not unusual to see something shown on the plans that is not reflected in the specifications, or vice versa, the estimator should make careful note of any contradictions, because these will require resolution before a meaningful estimate can be put together. It is also advisable to look at the other drawings for information concerning site plan, orientation, elevations, and access. During this review the drawing scales should be compared. Plumbing and HVAC designs are frequently prepared by a consulting engineer not associated with the architects, which sometimes leads to inconsistencies in scale, location, and terminology.

One feature that seems to be basic in nearly all mechanical designs is the ability to separate different elements into systems: hot water, cold water, fire protection, heating, cooling. Some of these systems may be interconnected or have some common parts, but they are nevertheless distinct. The majority of systems also have a source, a conductor or connector, and a terminal unit. Some of the examples of these are: source—water supply valve with meter; conductor—pipe; and terminal—sink faucet, fire department connection, standpipe, fire hose or sprinkler, boiler, pipe, radiator, air conditioner, duct, or diffuser. Note that while the sink with faucet or a water closet may be a terminal unit for the cold water system, it is the source for the "drain-waste-vent" system.

Pre-printed forms are a very useful tool in the preparation of estimates. This is especially true for the mechanical trades, which include a wide variety of items and materials. Careful measurements and a count of components cannot compensate for an oversight such as forgetting to include pipe insulation. A well-designed form acts as a check list, a guide for standardization, and a permanent record.

Plumbing

The first step in preparing a plumbing estimate is to visualize the scope of the job by scanning all the drawings and specifications. The next step is to complete a material take-off summary sheet. Leaf through the plumbing section of the specifications, listing each of the item headings on a summary sheet. This will help in remembering various components as they are located on the drawings and, for major items, can serve as a quantity check-off list. Include required labor-only items such as cleaning, adjusting, purifying, testing, and balancing, since these will not show up on the drawings and have little, if any, material costs.

The easiest way to make a material "quantity count" is by system, as most of the pipe components of a system will tend to be related as a group: same material, class weight, grade. For example, a waste system could consist of pipe varying from 3" to 8" in diameter but would probably be all service weight cast iron DWV copper, or PVC up to a specified size, and then heavy cast iron for the larger size.

Pipe and Fittings

Pipe runs for any type of system consist of straight sections and fittings of various shapes, styles, and purposes. Depending on personal preference, the estimator may use separate forms for pipe and fittings, or combine them on one sheet. The estimator will start at one end of each system, and using a tape, ruler, or wheeled indicator at the corresponding scale, will measure and record the straight lengths of each size of pipe. On passing a fitting, record this with a check in the appropriate column. The use of colored pencils may be an aid to mark runs that have been completed or termination points on the main line where measurements are stopped so that a branch may be taken off. Take care that all changes in material are noted. This would occur only at a joint fitting, so it should become an automatic habit to see that the material of piping going into a joint is the same as that leaving the joint.

Fixtures

Fixture take-off is usually nothing more than counting the various types, sizes, and styles and entering them on a fixture form. It is important, however, that each fixture be fully identified. A common source of error is to overlook what does or does not come with the fixture, such as faucets, tailpiece, or flush valve. Equipment such as pumps, water heaters, water softeners, and all items not previously counted are listed at this time. The order of proceeding is not as important as the development of a consistent method, which will help the estimator work quickly while minimizing the chances of overlooking any item or class of items. The various counts should then be totaled and transferred to the summary sheet. Miscellaneous items that add to the plumbing contract should also be listed. Many of these will be identified during the preliminary review of the plans and specifications. The estimator should also note necessary subcontractors, such as insulation specialists.

Fire Protection

The take-off of fire protection systems is very much like that of plumbing— the estimator measures the pipe loops and counts fittings, valves, sprinkler heads, alarms, and other components. The estimator then makes note of special requirements, as well as conditions that would affect job performance and cost.

Heating, Ventilation, and Air Conditioning

Heating, ventilation, and air conditioning sheet metal (ducts, plenums, etc.) are usually estimated by weight. The lengths of the various sizes are measured and recorded on a worksheet. The weight per foot of length is then determined. The estimator must also count all the duct-associated accessories such as fire dampers, diffusers, and registers. This may be done during the duct take-off; however, it is usually less confusing to make a separate count.

It is important to count items of equipment. Note sizes, capacities, controls, special characteristics and features. Weight and size may be important if the unit is especially large or is going into comparatively close quarters. The estimator must use personal judgement to evaluate the need for an increase in rigging allowances.

The take-off of heating, ventilation, and air conditioning pipe and fittings is accomplished in a manner similar to that used for plumbing, as is the fuel oil system.

In addition to the general miscellaneous items noted from the review of the plans and specifications, the heating, ventilation, and air conditioning estimate may also include several subcontractors. The more common of these are:
1. Rigging
2. Controls
3. Insulation
4. Balancing
5. Water Treatment
6. Sheet Metal
7. Core Drilling

Again, pre-printed forms help the estimator to assure that all required work is included in the complete estimate.

Division 16: Electrical

A good estimator must be able to form a mental image of the proposed electrical system from source (service) to end use (fixtures or devices). Visualize each component needed to make the system work. When the take-off is done, examine each item from source to end use to ensure that every component is included. Each item has to be handled and has some cost for material or labor, and therefore, it must be quantified. When plans and specifications for a renovation project are complete, the estimator should follow a consistent procedure.

1. Read the electrical specifications thoroughly.
2. Scan the electrical plan; check other sections of the specifications for effect on electrical work (in particular, mechanical and site work).
3. Check the architectural and structural plans to get an idea of how to install the electrical work.
4. Check the fixture and power symbols.
5. Clarify with the architects or engineers any gray areas, making sure that the scope of work is understood. Addenda may be necessary to clarify certain items of work so that the responsibility for the performance of all work is defined.
6. Evaluate the existing conditions, review the original electrical plans and as-builts, if any, and compare with the drawings proposed for the renovation.
7. Immediately contact suppliers, manufacturers, and subsystems specialty contractors to get their quotations, sub-bids, and drawings.

Fixture take-off can be the easiest way to become familiar with the plans. Try to take off one bay, section, or floor at a time. Mark each fixture with colored pencils and list them as you proceed, carefully measuring lengths of fixtures. Check the site plans for exterior fixtures. Next, take off switches, receptacles, telephone, fire alarm, sound and television outlets, plus any other system outlets.

While making a take-off of the above work, identify all other components of systems required and determine the amount of take-off necessary as opposed to the materials that will be included in a quotation or sub-bid from a supplier.

A separate Quantity Sheet should be used for each of the major categories. By keeping systems on separate sheets, the estimator finds it is easy to isolate various costs. This helps when the owner wants to know where to cut costs. It also provides a breakdown for submittal to the general contractor when billing.

Switchboards, panels and transformers can normally be entered directly onto the Quantity Sheet as they are counted. Some panels and transformers require a steel frame support from floor to ceiling; these should be added at this time.

Feeder conduit and wire should be carefully taken off using a scale, not a rotometer. This is more accurate. Large conduit and wire are expensive and require a large amount of labor. Switchboard locations should be marked on each floor using column lines; this makes horizontal runs easier to take off. Distance between floors should be marked on riser plans and added to the horizontal for a complete feeder run. Conduits should be measured at right angles unless it has been determined they can be installed in floors. Elbows, terminations, bends, or expansion joints should be taken off at this time and marked in proper columns on feeder take-off sheets.

If standard feeder take-off sheets are used, the wire column will reflect longer lengths than conduit. This is because of added amounts of wire used in the panels and switchboard to make connections. If the added length is not shown on the plans, it can be determined by checking a manufacturer's catalog. Conduit, cable supports, and expansion joints should be totaled at this time.

Branch circuits may be taken off using a rotometer. The estimator should take care to start and stop accurately on outlets. Start with two wire circuits and mark with colored pencil as you take off. Add about 5% to conduit quantities for normal waste. On wire, add 10% to 12% waste to make connections. Add conduit fittings such as locknuts, bushings, couplings, expansion joints, and fasteners. Two conduit terminations per box are average.

Wiring devices should be entered with plates, boxes, and plaster rings. Calculate stub ups or drops for wiring devices. Switches should be counted and multiplied by distance from switch to ceiling.

Receptacles are handled similarly, depending on whether they are wired from the ceiling or floor. In many cases there are two conduits going to a receptacle box as you feed in and out to next outlet. Some estimators let rotometers overrun outlets purposely as an adjustment for vertical runs; this can lead to inaccuracies.

The methods just described apply to most concrete and fireproof construction. In some metal stud partitions it is allowable to go horizontally from receptacle to receptacle. In wood partitions it is usual practice to make horizontal runs. In hung ceilings the specifications should be checked to see if straight runs are allowed.

Motors, safety switches, starters, controls, and supports each should include power lines, junction boxes, supports, wiring troughs, and wire connectors, including tape or connector covers. Add short runs of Greenfield, Sealtite, connectors, and wire for motor connections.

Fixtures should have outlet boxes, plaster rings, Greenfield with connectors, and fixture wire if needed. Fixture wire should be included for connections in long runs of fluorescent fixtures. Include fixture supports as needed and wirenuts or other connectors.

Service should be taken off from plans. Be careful to add all miscellaneous fittings not shown but needed to make a complete system.

Other systems should be handled in the same way, adding miscellaneous boxes, devices, conduit, and wire.
1. Sound Systems
2. TV Systems
3. Fire Alarm Systems
4. Security Systems

Chapter 3.
Pricing the Estimate

When the quantities for all work in a commercial renovation project have been determined the estimator must obtain prices for the unit items in order to calculate the costs. The estimator has different sources available from which to choose the most accurate and reliable prices. The best source is current, detailed costs from completed recent projects. These are useful only if the contractor keeps accurate records. Such record keeping can prove to be invaluable and is well worth the time invested. When a project is completed the contractor should compile and break down the actual costs in such a way as to be used for future estimating purposes. These costs should be compared to those of other recent projects. Any differences should be analyzed and the reasons for such differences determined and incorporated into the contractor's cost data. Obviously, these costs must be updated to reflect material and labor price changes.

Firm quotations from responsible subcontractors are another source of reliable costs, as are current material price quotations from competitive vendors. Even when subcontractor prices are used, the estimator should be aware of the extent of the work and the units and costs involved in the quotations. The estimator should use this information as a cross-check to be sure that quotes are competitive and to avoid omissions or duplications.

Up-to-date construction industry source books such as R.S. Means' *Repair and Remodeling Cost Data* provide another source of unit prices to the estimator. Such information is calculated as national averages and must be adjusted to local conditions.

When obtaining, analyzing, and tabulating costs, the estimator should use the same rules with the pricing paperwork as with the quantity take-off, and should work with the same diligence and consistency. Use only one side of the forms or tabulation sheets. Using two sides can easily increase confusion and lead to omissions. Mark each piece of paper with the appropriate Uniform Construction Index (UCI) division number and always number sheets with: [Page number] of [Total number of pages], e.g. Page 2 of 12.

A telephone quotation form should be used to assure consistency and completeness when prices are verbal. Figure I3.1 is such a form. It includes spaces for information that may not normally be communicated when prices are obtained by telephone. When the corresponding written quotations are received, they should be compared with and attached to the telephone form.

The estimator should note and write down the source of all information, data and prices and the date obtained. This information will be useful for updating and comparison purposes.

Each type of document (Quantity Sheets, material quotes, subcontractor bids)

TELEPHONE QUOTATION

MEANSCO
FORM 140

DATE _____

FIRM QUOTING _____ BY _____ TITLE _____

ADDRESS _____ PHONE _____
(Area Code)

PROJECT _____

LOCATION _____ ESTIMATE NO. _____

ITEM QUOTED _____ RECEIVED BY _____

WORK INCLUDED	AMOUNT OF QUOTATION

DELIVERY _____ **TOTAL BID**

DOES QUOTATION INCLUDE THE FOLLOWING:

IF ☐ NO IS CHECKED,
DETERMINE THE FOLLOWING:

STATE & LOCAL SALES TAXES	☐ YES ☐ NO	MATERIAL VALUE	
DELIVERY TO THE JOB SITE	☐ YES ☐ NO	WEIGHT	
COMPLETE ERECTION	☐ YES ☐ NO	QUANTITY	
COMPLETE SECTION AS PER SPECIFICATIONS	☐ YES ☐ NO	DESCRIBE BELOW	

EXCLUSIONS AND QUALIFICATIONS

ADDENDA ACKNOWLEDGEMENT _____ **TOTAL ADJUSTMENT**

ADJUSTED TOTAL

R.S. MEANS CO., INC. KINGSTON, MA 02364

Figure 13.1

should be kept separate. And even though it may seem repetitive, each piece of paper should have the project name or number written on it. The entire estimate and associated material for each project should be kept together. Without these precautions, major errors can occur. For example, if the estimator is working on more than one project at a time, the concrete estimate or quantities from one project could easily work its way into another.

3.1
Direct Job Costs

Direct job costs consist of the following:

1. Material
2. Labor
3. Equipment
4. Subcontractors

Material Costs

When the estimator has accurately determined and double-checked quantities of materials, prices can then be obtained from vendors, catalogues, previous project records, or industry source cost data books. Next, using appropriate unit prices, the estimator then extends the costs to arrive at a fixed total cost for materials. Or is it fixed? There are many factors, easily overlooked, that can have a significant impact on the cost of materials. The estimator must check with each vendor to determine how long the prices are guaranteed and when any price increases will go into effect. Sales tax can also be an important factor, as much as 8% of material costs in some states. If the project being estimated is out-of-state, the estimator must be familiar with the appropriate regulations. On the other hand, some forms of municipal or federal financing provide that materials on a project are tax exempt. Again, the estimator must be aware of the conditions for each project.

When obtaining material prices, especially by word of mouth, the estimator should be assured that the prices are for materials as specified. A vendor, not having the correct price list right at hand, may give prices for similar but slightly different materials. Catalogue numbers and reference data should always be used where possible. The estimator must also make sure that contractor prices, where applicable, are quoted along with retail prices.

Delivery times should also be obtained, preferably in writing, before orders are given. The estimator may choose to order from the vendor with the bargain basement price only to find out, too late, that the material will not arrive until after the proposed project completion date. Also, if an unfamiliar vendor is being used, payment terms should be discussed up front. The contractor's cash flow could be severely affected if payment is to be C.O.D. rather than net 30 days. If the plans and specifications give accepted alternates for material, the estimator should obtain prices. Possible savings could make a difference in competitive bidding.

Labor Costs

For the contractor with reliable and easily accessible cost records, the best way to start is to price the labor from the company cost records of previous jobs, adjusted for the conditions expected on the new project. If no labor cost records are available, the estimator has three alternative methods to determine the labor figures.

Annually updated and published industry source books, such as R.S. Means' *Repair and Remodeling Cost Data* are a reliable source of labor costs. These books usually include costs for all trades, crew sizes for all work, and the average man-hours involved per unit of work. The costs included in such books are based on national averages of union rates. *Repair and Remodeling Cost Data* includes charts and factors to be used to adjust the costs in each of 16 UCI divisions for 162 markets throughout the United States and Canada.

The estimator also has access to many estimating reference books from which crew sizes and man-hours can be synthesized. As a last resort, the estimator can use experience and a thorough understanding of the work to be performed to visualize, evaluate, and determine the required crews and time necessary for the labor component.

Any historical labor costs, either from the contractor's records or from any of the cost books, should be factored for environment of the new project. This factoring, or adjusting, may be done three ways:

1. As each individual price is written. (Most accurate, most time consuming.)
2. By division and subdivision totals. (Fairly accurate, fairly quick.)
3. By adjusting the total labor figure for the job. (Least accurate, quickest.)

Labor costs contain the highest degree of unpredictability of all the costs for a building project. For jobs running more than a few months, some allowance for labor rate escalation is normally included.

For union jurisdictions, the timing of the new rate increases is determined by the contract expiration date. Union contracts are normally negotiated for one-, two-or three-year periods, many with more than one step increase per year. The cost impact on the job must be calculated either trade-by-trade or by blanket consideration of the "average" effect throughout the course of the job. The sources of labor information listed in order of reliability are as follows:

1. From the local trade unions having jurisdiction over the area.
2. From employer bargaining groups in the location.
3. From annual labor rate publications such as *Labor Rates for the Construction Industry*.

The wage rates for nonunion workers are negotiated directly with the larger nonunion contractors within each area. For contractors bidding in their own backyard, their historical payroll records will best determine the wage rates.

For nonunion contractors bidding in out-of-town locations, the prevailing wage rates may require some guesswork unless contractors can establish communication with other nonunion contractors in the new location. Nonunion wage rates may be similar to or lower than the equivalent union wage rate, but worker productivity tends to be higher when there are fewer craft restrictions.

As with all labor rates, productivity must be considered. When using a cost data book such as *Repair and Remodeling Cost Data* the estimator should check the productivity that has been used to determine the costs, and check this against the job conditions and anticipated productivity. Variations can significantly alter the costs.

Equipment

For most building renovation projects, the total equipment costs are a small percentage of the total costs as compared with heavy construction.

There are two methods of figuring equipment costs. The first is to include the costs directly in each line item as a separate and identifiable price, totalling up at the end of the estimate after all the prices have been extended. This approach works well for some items but may not cover major equipment utilization, such as a personnel and material hoist and tower that may be used throughout the job. The second is to include the cost of all equipment as an overhead item and charge to the total job for the estimated time the equipment will be on the job. This approach is desirable if equipment has limited use.

Whichever method is used, the important thing is to make the estimating assumptions and the cost accounting feedback consistent. The estimator can then properly identify historical equipment costs when developing figures for future jobs.

Mobilization costs for equipment must also be included in the estimate. The costs to get a piece of equipment to and from the job is known as mobilization. To the inexperienced estimator this can be a lesson well remembered if mobilization is overlooked in the estimate. Some equipment has a relatively inexpensive mobilization cost, usually a day's rental. Others, however, such as cranes, may cost several thousand dollars just to mobilize to and from the job site. If a significant piece of equipment is to be used on the job, then take the time to determine and include mobilization allowances in the estimate.

Subcontractors

The estimator should thoroughly examine prices and bids from subcontractors, review the plans, and read the specifications for all work to be subcontracted. Because the ultimate responsibility for the subcontracted work is upon the general contractor, the estimator must be sure that all items are included as specified and as required. If the bid is not detailed, the estimator should determine whether any applicable sales tax is included or whether there are any exclusions for which the subcontractor may have made incorrect assumptions. For major subcontract items such as mechanical, electrical, conveying, and specialties, it may be necessary to make up spread sheets to tabulate inclusions and omissions. This ensures that all cost considerations are included in the "adjusted" quotation.

The estimator should note how long the subcontract bid will be honored. This usually varies from 30 to 90 days and is often included as a condition in complete bids. The general contractor may have to define the time limits of the prime bid based upon certain subcontractors. The estimator must also note any escalation clauses that may be included in subcontractor bids.

Reliability is another consideration that must be addressed when soliciting and evaluating subcontractors. This is a factor that cannot be quantified or priced until the project is under construction. Most general contractors often stay with the same subcontractors for just this reason. A certain unspoken communication exists, which is usually beneficial in the performance of the work. Such familiarity, however, can often erode the competitive nature of bidding. To be competitive with the prime bid, the estimator should always have a comparison price, whether from another subcontractor or prepared by the estimator.

Time permitting, the estimator should make a take-off and price major subcontract items to compare with the sub-bids. If time does not permit a detailed take-off, the estimator can at least budget the work. A Systems estimate is ideal for this.

If it happens that the estimator has made a detailed take-off, but the job is located "out of town," recommended sources of cost information are as follows:
1. The most reliable of the annual cost books such as *Repair and Remodeling Cost Data*.
2. Prices from a familiar subcontractor close enough to the location who could do the work if required to do so.
3. Prices from a familiar subcontractor who would not be in position to do the work even if the prime contractor landed the job.

When unfamiliar subcontractors are to be used, the estimator should determine if they are bondable. The estimator should also verify that the subcontractor has had sufficient experience in the type of work to be performed.

3.2
Completing the Cost Analysis

After the quantity take-off has been completed, the item descriptions and quantities should be neatly hand-printed on the cost analysis sheets. Figure I3.2 is an example of such a pre-printed form. Several blank lines should be included with each subdivision so that omitted items can be inserted later on without having to squeeze them in half of the line. Begin each division on a new page. At this stage all items in the estimate should be included on the Cost Analysis sheets even though there may be no quantities. For instance, all subcontract items should be listed so there will be a space to write in the dollar amount of the subcontracted item. The estimator may also write in gross subcontract quantities. A rough idea of the probable subcontractor prices may be established to get a preliminary total price for the job.

After all quantities, subcontract items, allowances, and owner-purchased, contractor-installed items have been listed, the estimator must price the estimate using the appropriate unit costs from sources discussed earlier.

Each estimator has methods of pricing sequence but a fairly common sequence is as follows:

1. All material, equipment and labor items from the estimator's own cost records.
2. All material and/or equipment from vendor quotes, together with labor from estimator's cost records.
3. All subcontract quotations.
4. All material, equipment, and subcontract items from cost books when cost records and vendor quotes are questionable or not available.
5. All labor and/or man-hour costs from cost data books when not available from cost records and productivity reports.

The reason for the above sequence is that the costs from the most reliable sources will be used first. The result is that an accurate price will not be replaced later on with a less accurate figure.

All subcontract costs should be circled or highlighted in some fashion to call attention to the fact that they contain all subcontractor mark-ups, since these will be treated differently when the estimator calculates the contractor's fee and contingency allowance.

After all the unit prices, subcontractor prices, and allowances have been entered on the Cost Analysis sheets, the estimate is extended. In making the extensions, ignore the cents column and round all totals to the nearest dollar. In a column of figures, the cents will average out and be of no consequence. Indeed, for budget-type estimates, the final figures could be rounded to the nearest 10, or even 100 dollars, with the loss of only a small amount of precision. Each subdivision is added and the results checked, preferably by someone other than the one doing the extensions.

It is important to check the larger items for order-of-magnitude errors. If the total subdivision costs are divided by the building area, the resultant square foot cost figures can be used to quickly pinpoint areas that are out of line with expected S.F. costs.

The purpose of the take-off and pricing method as discussed has been to utilize a Quantity Sheet for the material take-off (see Figure I3.3), and to transfer the data to a Cost Analysis form for pricing the material, labor, subcontractor, and/or equipment items (see Figure I3.2).

COST ANALYSIS

PROJECT _____ SHEET NO. _____

LOCATION _____ ESTIMATE NO. _____

ARCHITECT _____ OWNER _____ DATE _____

QUANTITIES BY _____ PRICES BY _____ EXTENSIONS BY _____ CHECKED BY _____

DESCRIPTION	QUANTITY	UNIT	MATERIAL		LABOR		TOTAL COST	
			UNIT	TOTAL	UNIT	TOTAL	UNIT	TOTAL

Figure 13.2

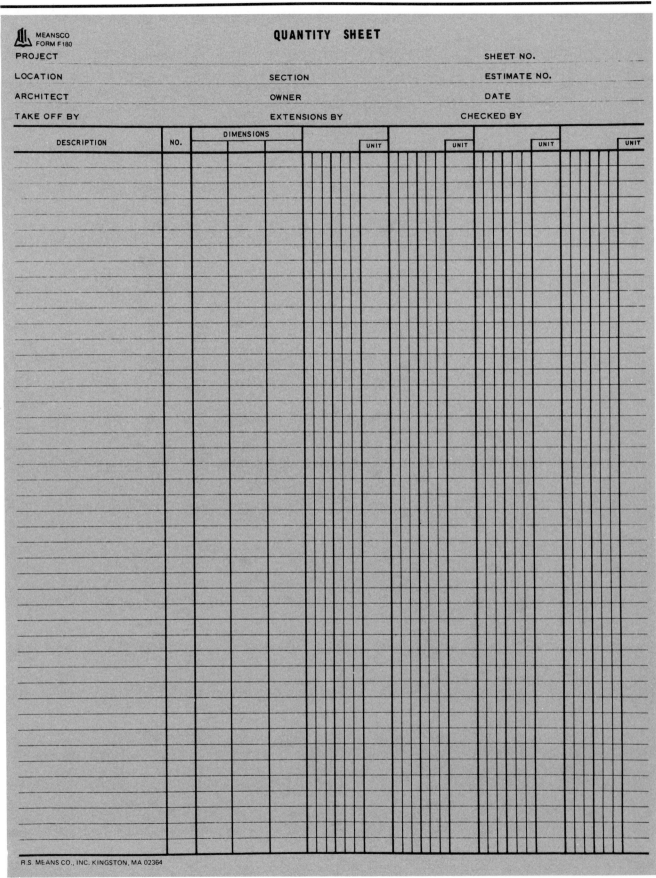

Figure 13.3

An accepted alternative to this method is a consolidation of the take-off task and pricing on a single form. This might be called the Consolidated Estimate form, which has been modified for use in estimating renovation projects. The same sequences and recommendations for completing the Quantity Sheet and Cost Analysis form are to be followed when using the Consolidated Estimate form to price the estimate. See Figure I3.4.

3.3 Completing the Estimate Summary

At this point the estimator has two choices: all further price changes can be made on the Cost Analysis or Consolidated Estimate sheets, or the total prices of each subdivision can be transferred to an estimate summary sheet so that all further price changes, until bid time, will be done on one sheet.

Except for estimates with a limited number of items, it is recommended that the costs be transferred to an estimate summary sheet. This step should be double-checked since an error of transposition may easily occur. Pre-printed forms can be useful. A plain columnar form, however, may suffice.

If a company has certain standard listings that are used repeatedly, it would save valuable time to have a custom estimate summary sheet printed with the items that need to be listed. The Condensed Estimate Summary form in Figure I3.5 is an example of a commonly used form. Appropriate column headings or categories for any estimate summary form are:
1. Material
2. Labor
3. Equipment
4. Subcontractor
5. Total

By listing items in their proper columns, the estimator makes it mathematically simple to arrive at the sum for each column and to apply appropriate markups to the total dollar values in each category. In other words, the sum of each column would normally have different percentages added near the end of the estimate for:
1. Insurance, Taxes, Fringe Benefits
2. Equipment and Tools (if equipment is added as an overhead item)
3. Profit and Contingencies

When the total direct costs and overhead have been calculated, the appropriate fee and contingency allowance must be added to the estimate.

The last figure on the Estimate Summary is the total bid or estimate, which will usually commit the general contractor if it is accepted by the owner. The figure had better be correct.

CONSOLIDATED ESTIMATE

PROJECT

LOCATION

TAKE OFF BY

CLASSIFICATION

PRICES BY

QUANTITIES BY

ARCHITECT

SHEET NO.

ESTIMATE NO.

DATE

CHECKED BY

DESCRIPTION	FLOOR	SOURCE	QUANTITY	UNIT	BARE COSTS							SUBCONTRACTOR		MAN-HOURS	
					MATERIAL		LABOR		EQUIPMENT						
					UNIT	TOTAL	UNIT	TOTAL	UNIT	TOTAL	UNIT	TOTAL INCL. O & P	UNIT	TOTAL

Figure 13.4

CONDENSED ESTIMATE SUMMARY

PROJECT	TOTAL AREA	SHEET NO.
LOCATION	TOTAL VOLUME	ESTIMATE NO.
ARCHITECT	COST PER S.F.	DATE
OWNER	COST PER C.F.	NO. OF STORIES
QUANTITIES BY PRICES BY		CHECKED BY

NO.	DESCRIPTION	MATERIAL	LABOR	EQUIPMENT	SUBCONTRACTOR	TOTAL
	SITE WORK					
	Excavation					
	CONCRETE					
	MASONRY					
	METALS					
	CARPENTRY					
	MOISTURE PROTECTION					
	DOORS, WINDOWS, GLASS					
	FINISHES					
	SPECIALTIES					
	EQUIPMENT					
	FURNISHINGS					
	SPECIAL CONSTRUCTION					
	CONVEYING SYSTEMS					
	MECHANICAL					
	Plumbing					
	Heating, Ventilating, Air Conditioning					
	ELECTRICAL					
	TOTAL DIRECT COSTS					
	CONTRACTORS OVERHEAD					
	Performance Bond					
	Profit & Contingencies					
	TOTAL BID					

Figure I3.5

Chapter 4.
Using R.S. Means' Repair and Remodeling Cost Data

Estimators use *Repair and Remodeling Cost Data* to develop fast, accurate costs for repair, remodeling, and renovation estimates. Two groups of data provide costs for the two most accurate estimating methods: "Unit Price" and "Systems."

As an estimating guide, *Repair and Remodeling Cost Data* can help overcome cost estimating problems for construction industry professionals. When used carefully, it will help to eliminate guesswork when estimating man-hours, labor charges, and material prices. Updated every year, *Repair and Remodeling Cost Data* helps to eliminate using out-of-date prices. More important, it contains data for over 10,000 construction items, which will help the estimator locate all components when estimating a renovation project.

4.1 The Unit Price Section

The Unit Price data is divided into the sixteen divisions of the Uniform Construction Index (UCI) classification. A visual depiction of these divisions is shown in Figure I4.1 from a page in *Repair and Remodeling Cost Data* 1985.

The Unit Price section presents the data as shown in Figure I4.2. The pages list construction items with up to nine components of information. To use the data effectively, the estimator must understand how this information is presented.

Line Numbering System

The major UCI subdivisions are shown in reverse type at the top left corner of each page. The description of each subdivision is adjacent in large bold letters.

The major classifications within each subdivision are numbered (1 to 99) in boldface type, and the boldface descriptions are listed alphabetically.

The individual line items (numbered 001 to 999) describe the units of construction for which costs are provided.

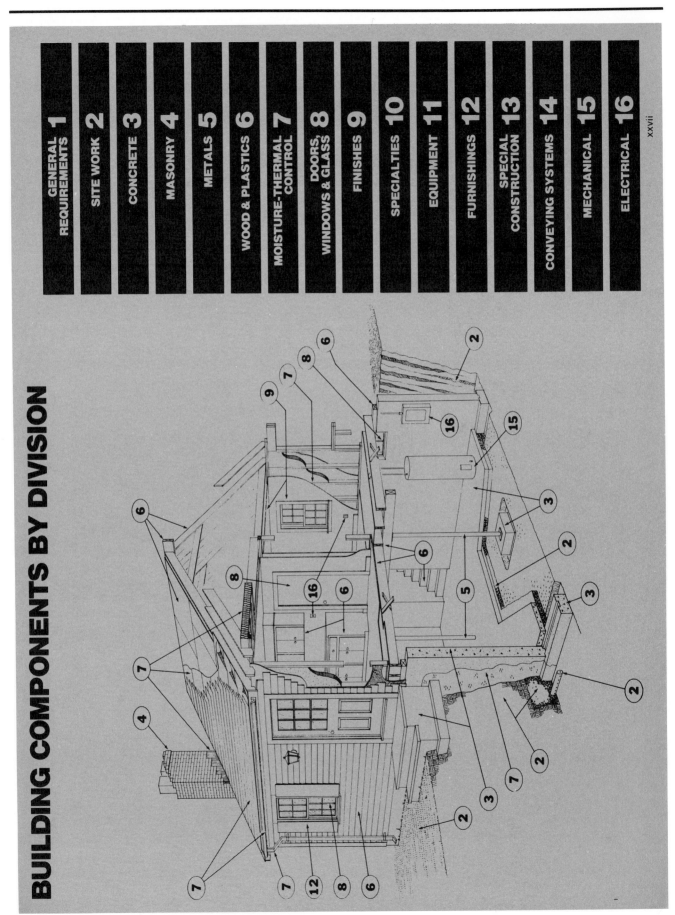

Figure I4.1

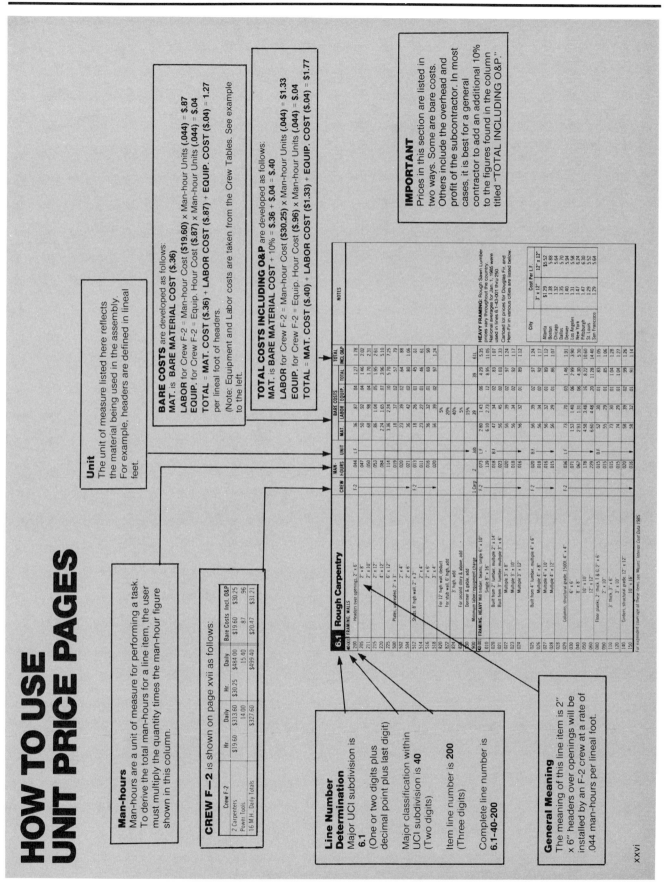

Figure I4.2

Crew

This column indicates the trade or trades (including workers and equipment) required to install the described item. If an individual trade installs the item using only hand tools, the smallest efficient number of tradesmen will be indicated (1 Carp, 2 Carp, etc.). If more than one trade is required to install the item or if powered equipment is needed, a crew number will be designated (B-5, D-3, etc.).

A complete listing of crews is presented in the Foreword pages of *Repair and Remodeling Cost Data*. Each crew breakdown contains the following components:

1. Number and type of tradesmen required.
2. Number, size, and type of any equipment required.
3. Hourly labor costs listed two ways: base (base rate including fringe benefits) and hourly cost including installing contractor's overhead and profit (billing rate).
4. Daily equipment costs, based on the weekly equipment cost divided by 5, plus the hourly operating cost times 8 hours. This cost is listed two ways: bare cost and with a 10% markup to cover the installing contractor's overhead and profit.
5. Labor and equipment are broken down further: cost per man-hour for designated crew and cost per equipment-hour for the crew.
6. The total daily labor man-hours for the crew.
7. The total bare costs per day for the crew, including equipment.
8. The total daily costs of the crew including the installing contractor's overhead and profit.

The total daily "bare" cost of the craftsmen involved or the total daily "bare" cost of the crew indicated is used to calculate the installation cost for each item.

Man-Hours

The figures in this column represent how many hours it takes one worker to do one unit of work (see "Units" below). This does not mean, however, that the man-hour figures reflect the labor of only one worker. For example, a unit of work takes six man-hours to complete. Depending on the crew size this can be interpreted as: one worker for six hours, two workers for three hours, six workers for one hour. In other words, the total man-hours to complete a task is the product of the number of workers multiplied by the hours required.

Total man-hours, calculated for each portion of a renovation project, are an invaluable scheduling tool. When figures from the "Man-Hours" column are used in conjunction with the crew size and the total number of units of work, the estimator can determine how much actual time is needed to complete each activity and the total man-hours to complete the project.

Units

This column indicates how the individual line items are measured and priced. The abbreviations used are listed in the back of *Repair and Remodeling Cost Data*. The units are derived from standard estimating and quantity take-off procedures.

Bare Costs

The four columns under "Bare Costs," material, labor, equipment, and total, represent the cost of items *not* including the overhead and profit of the installing contractor.

Material costs are listed based on average contractor purchase price. The costs include delivery to the job site, unless otherwise noted. Sales taxes, because they vary from state to state, are not included.

Labor costs are calculated by multiplying the "Bare Labor Cost" per man-hour times the number of man-hours, from the "Man-Hours" column. The "Bare" labor rate is determined by adding the base rate plus fringe benefits. The base rate is the actual hourly wage of a worker used in figuring payroll. It is from this figure that employee deductions are taken (Federal withholding, FICA, State withholding). Fringe benefits include all employer-paid benefits, above and beyond the payroll amount (employer-paid health, vacation pay, pension, profit sharing). The "Bare Labor Cost" is, therefore, the actual amount that the contractor must pay directly for construction workers. Table I4.1 shows labor rates for the 35 standard construction trades plus skilled worker, helper, and foreman averages. These rates are the averages of union wage agreements effective January 1 of the current year from 30 major cities in the United States. The "Bare Labor Cost" for each trade, as used in *Remodeling and Repair Cost Data*, is shown in column "A" as the base rate including fringes.

Refer to the "Crew" column to determine what rate is used to calculate the "Bare Labor Cost" for a particular line item.

Equipment costs are calculated by multiplying the "Bare Equipment Cost" per man-hour, from the appropriate "Crew" listing, times the man-hours in the "Man-Hours" column.

Total Bare Costs are the arithmetical sum of the "Bare Material Cost," "Bare Labor Cost," and "Bare Equipment Cost" columns. The "Total Bare Cost" of any particular line item is the amount that a contractor will directly pay for that item. This is, in effect, the contractor's wholesale price.

Total Including Overhead and Profit

This column represents the total cost of an item including the installing contractor's overhead and profit. The installing contractor could be either the general contractor or a subcontractor. If these costs are used for an item to be installed by a subcontractor, the general contractor should include an additional percentage (usually 10%-20%) to cover the expenses of supervision and management.

The costs in the "Total Including Overhead and Profit" column are the arithmetical sum of the following three calculations:
1. Bare Material Cost plus 10%.
2. Labor Cost, including overhead and profit, per man-hour times the number of man-hours.
3. Equipment Cost, including overhead and profit, per man-hour times the number of man-hours.

The Labor and Equipment Costs, including overhead and profit are found in the appropriate crew listings. The overhead and profit percentage factor for Labor is obtained from Column F in Table I4.1. The overhead and profit for Equipment is 10% of "Bare" cost.

If the "Total Bare Costs" can be thought of as the contractor's wholesale price, then the "Total Including Overhead and Profit" is the retail price.

CONTRACTOR'S OVERHEAD AND PROFIT

To the left are the average subcontractor's percentage mark-ups that should be applied directly to all labor rates in order to arrive at typical billing rates for subcontractors.

Column A:
Base rates including fringe benefits are described in Column A in hourly and daily terms. These figures are the sum of the base rate, employer-paid fringe benefits such as vacation pay, employer-paid health and welfare costs, pension costs, plus appropriate training and industry advancement funds costs.

Column B:
National average Workmen's Compensation rate by trade.

Column C:
Column C lists the average fixed overhead figures for all trades. In particular, Federal and State Unemployment costs are set at 5.5%; Social Security Taxes (FICA) are set at 7.05%; Builder's Risk Insurance costs are set at 0.38%; and Public Liability costs are set at 0.82%. These overhead costs are analyzed below. All the percentages except those for Social Security Taxes vary from state to state as well as from company to company.

Columns D & E:
Percentages in Columns D & E are based on the presumption that the subcontractor being used in any given project has an annual billing rate of $250,000. Smaller subcontractors' percentages for overhead are usually higher.
The overhead percentages for a subcontractor vary greatly and depend on a number of factors: the subcontractor's annual volume; his engineering and logistical support costs, his staff requirements, and the size of the equipment he is required to use on a particular construction project. The figures for overhead and profit will vary depending on the type of job, the job location, and the prevailing economic conditions. These factors should be examined very carefully for each job. For the purpose of estimating the cost of a project, it is reasonable to assume a 16% cost for the subcontractor's overhead, and a 15% cost for the subcontractor's profit.

Column F:
Column F lists the total of columns B, C, D, and E.

Column G:
Column G is Column A (hourly base labor rate) multiplied by the percentage in Column F (Sub's O&P percentage).

Column H:
Column H is the total of Column A (hourly base labor rate) plus Column G (Sub's O&P hourly rate).

Column I:
Column I is Column H multiplied by eight hours.

Mass. State Unemployment Tax ranges from 1.5% to 5.7% plus a small experience rating assessment the following year on the first $7,000. Federal Unemployment tax is 3.5% of the first $7,000 of wages. This is reduced by a credit for payment to the state. The minimum Federal Unemployment tax is 0.8% after all credits.

Combined rates in Mass. vary from 2.3% to 6.5% of the first $7,000 of wages. The combined average U.S. rate is about 5.5% of the first $7,000. Contractors with permanent workers will pay less, since the theoretical annual wage for skilled worker is $20.10 X 2,000 hours, or about $40,200 per year. The average combined rate for the U.S. would therefore be 5.50% x 7,000 ÷ 40,200 = 0.96% of total wages.

Abbr.	Trade	A Base Rate incl. fringes Hourly	A Daily	B Workers' Comp. Ins.	C Average Fixed Overhead	D Subs Overhead	E Subs Profit	F Subs Total O&H %	G Amount	H Rate with Subs O.&P. Hourly	I Daily
Skwk	Skilled Workers Average (35 trades)	$20.10	$160.80	9.0%	13.8%	16%	15%	53.8%	$10.80	$30.90	$247.20
	Helpers Average (5 trades)	15.20	121.60	9.3				54.1	8.20	23.40	187.20
	Foremen Average, Inside (50¢ over trade)	20.60	164.80	9.0				53.8	11.10	31.70	253.60
	Foremen Average, Outside ($2.00 over trade)	22.10	176.80	9.0				53.8	11.90	34.00	272.00
Clab	Common Building Laborers	15.50	124.00	9.6				54.4	8.45	23.95	191.60
Asbe	Asbestos Workers	22.20	177.60	7.4				52.2	11.60	33.80	270.40
Boil	Boilermakers	22.30	178.40	6.7				51.5	11.50	33.80	270.40
Brc	Bricklayers	20.05	160.40	7.2				52.0	10.45	30.50	244.00
Brhe	Bricklayer Helpers	15.65	125.20	7.2				52.0	8.15	23.80	190.40
Carp	Carpenters	19.60	156.80	9.6				54.4	10.65	30.25	242.00
Cefi	Cement Finishers	18.80	150.40	5.5				50.3	9.45	28.25	226.00
Elec	Electricians	22.10	176.80	3.9				48.7	10.75	32.85	262.80
Elev	Elevator Constructors	22.15	177.20	5.3				50.1	11.10	33.25	266.00
Eqhv	Equipment Operators, Crane or Shovel	20.65	165.20	6.9				51.7	10.70	31.35	250.80
Eqmd	Equipment Operators, Medium Equipment	20.20	161.60	6.9				51.7	10.45	30.65	245.20
Eqlt	Equipment Operators, Light Equipment	19.05	152.40	6.9				51.7	9.85	28.90	231.20
Eqol	Equipment Operators, Oilers	17.10	136.80	6.9				51.7	8.85	25.95	207.60
Eqmm	Equipment Operators, Master Mechanics	21.45	171.60	6.9				51.7	11.10	32.55	260.40
Glaz	Glaziers	19.85	158.80	7.6				52.4	10.40	30.25	242.00
Lath	Lathers	19.75	158.00	5.8				50.6	10.00	29.75	238.00
Marb	Marble Setters	19.55	156.40	7.2				52.0	10.15	29.70	237.60
Mill	Millwrights	20.35	162.80	6.4				51.2	10.40	30.75	246.00
Mstz	Mosaic and Terrazzo Workers	19.35	154.80	5.2				50.0	9.70	29.05	232.40
Pord	Painters, Ordinary	18.85	150.80	7.2				52.0	9.80	28.65	229.20
Psst	Painters, Structural Steel	19.60	156.80	26.0				70.8	13.90	33.50	268.00
Pape	Paper Hangers	19.15	153.20	7.2				52.0	9.95	29.10	232.80
Pile	Pile Drivers	19.70	157.60	16.6				61.4	12.10	31.80	254.40
Plas	Plasterers	19.60	156.80	7.2				52.0	10.20	29.80	238.40
Plah	Plasterer Helpers	16.15	129.20	7.2				52.0	8.40	24.55	196.40
Plum	Plumbers	22.20	177.60	4.7				49.5	11.00	33.20	265.60
Rodm	Rodmen (Reinforcing)	21.30	170.40	15.9				60.7	12.95	34.25	274.00
Rofc	Roofers, Composition	18.35	146.80	17.1				61.9	11.35	29.70	237.60
Rots	Roofers, Tile & Slate	18.50	148.00	17.1				61.9	11.45	29.95	239.60
Rohe	Roofer Helpers (Composition)	13.45	107.60	17.1				61.9	8.35	21.80	174.40
Shee	Sheet Metal Workers	22.20	177.60	6.0				50.8	11.30	33.50	268.00
Spri	Sprinkler Installers	22.60	180.80	5.6				50.4	11.40	34.00	272.00
Stpi	Steamfitters or Pipefitters	22.30	178.40	4.7				49.5	11.05	33.35	266.80
Ston	Stone Masons	19.85	158.80	7.2				52.0	10.30	30.15	241.20
Sswk	Structural Steel Workers	21.30	170.40	19.5				64.3	13.70	35.00	280.00
Tilf	Tile Layers (Floor)	19.25	154.00	5.1				49.9	9.60	28.85	230.80
Tilh	Tile Layer Helpers	15.25	122.00	5.1				49.9	7.60	22.85	182.80
Trlt	Truck Drivers, Light	16.00	128.00	8.4				53.2	8.50	24.50	196.00
Trhv	Truck Drivers, Heavy	16.20	129.60	8.4				53.2	8.60	24.80	198.40
Sswl	Welders, Structural Steel	21.30	170.40	19.5				64.3	13.70	35.00	280.00
Wrck	*Wrecking	15.50	124.00	20.7				65.5	10.15	25.65	205.20

*Not included in Averages.

Table I4.1

4.2
The Systems Section

The systems data are divided into twelve "uniformat" divisions, which reorganize the components of construction into logical groupings. The Systems approach was devised to provide quick and easy methods for estimating even when only preliminary design data are available. Figure I4.3 is a visual depiction of the twelve Systems Divisions.

The groupings, or systems, are presented in such a way so that the estimator can easily vary components within the systems as well as substituting one system for another. This is extremely useful when adapting to budget, design, or other considerations. Figure I4.4 shows how the data are presented in the Systems section.

Each system is illustrated and is accompanied by a detailed description. The book lists the components and sizes of each system, usually in the order of construction. Alternates for the most commonly variable components are also listed. Each individual component is found in the Unit Price Section. If an alternate that is not listed is required, it can easily be substituted.

Quantity
A unit of measure is established for each system. For example, floor systems are measured by the square foot; bathrooms are measured by "each"; stairs are measured by flight. Within each system, the components are measured by industry standard, using the same units as in the Unit Price section.

Material
The cost of each component in the Material column is the "Base Material Cost," plus 10% handling, for the unit and quantity as defined in the "Quantity" column.

Installation
Installation costs as listed in the Systems pages contain both labor and equipment costs. The labor rate includes the "Bare Labor Cost" plus the installing contractor's overhead and profit. These rates are shown in Table I4.1, columns H and I. The equipment rate is the "Base Equipment Cost" plus 10%.

Factors
Each Systems page lists "Factors" that should be taken into consideration when estimating for commercial renovation. These "Factors" are discussed in Chapter 1, 1.10 and shown in Table I1.4. The estimator must use experience and sound judgement when applying the "Factors" in the estimate.

4.3
Installing Contractor's Overhead and Profit

There are three labor rates for each trade that should be examined by the estimator and updated as changes in rates occur or are anticipated:
1. "Base Labor Rate" (i.e., hourly wage)
2. "Bare Labor Cost" (Base rate plus fringe benefits)
3. "Total Labor Cost", including installing contractor's overhead and profit (i.e., billing rate)

To calculate the Total Labor Cost, the "Bare Labor Cost" is adjusted to include all direct and indirect expenses assumed by the contractor. The following is a list of overhead expenses, which must be addressed to determine the correct adjustments.

Workers' Compensation and Employer's Liability
Workers' Compensation and Employer's Liability Insurance rates vary from state to state relative to the safety record in construction in that particular state. Rates also vary by trade according to the hazard involved. The proper authorities will most likely keep the contractor well informed of the rates and obligations.

125

BUILDING COMPONENTS BY DIVISION

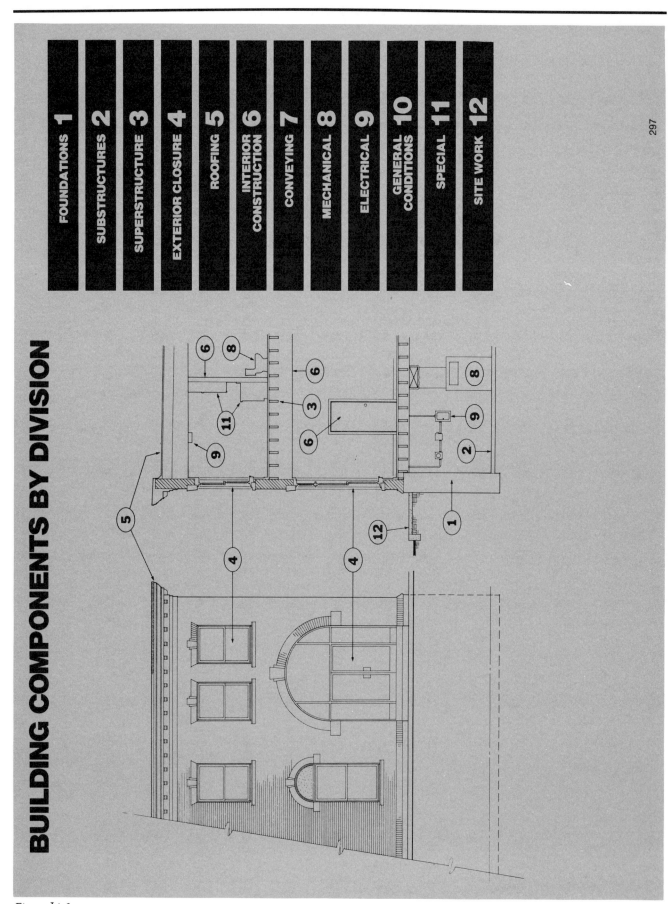

FOUNDATIONS **1**

SUBSTRUCTURES **2**

SUPERSTRUCTURE **3**

EXTERIOR CLOSURE **4**

ROOFING **5**

INTERIOR CONSTRUCTION **6**

CONVEYING **7**

MECHANICAL **8**

ELECTRICAL **9**

GENERAL CONDITIONS **10**

SPECIAL **11**

SITE WORK **12**

297

Figure 14.3

126

HOW TO USE
SYSTEMS PAGES

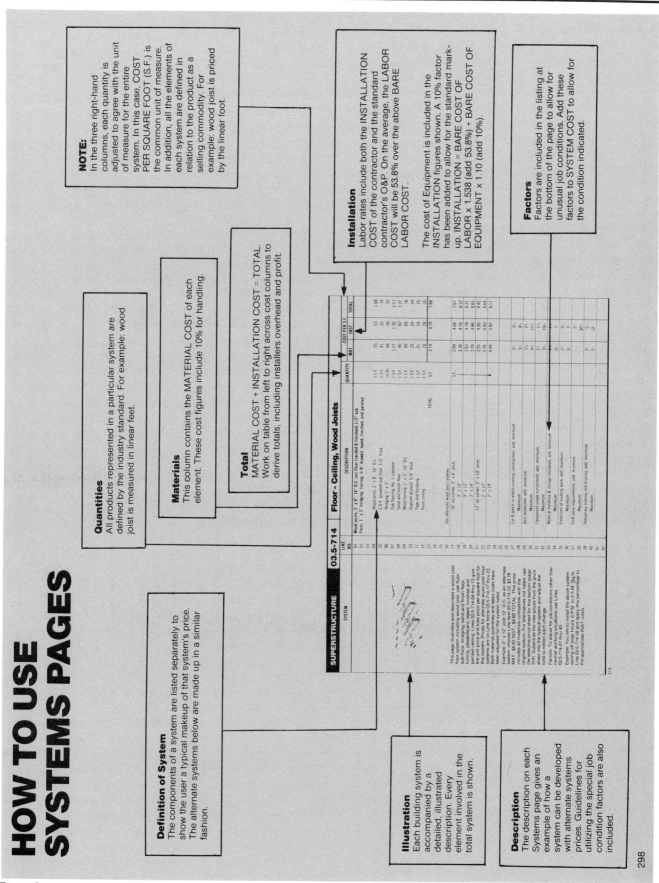

Definition of System
The components of a system are listed separately to show the user a typical makeup of that system's price. The alternate systems below are made up in a similar fashion.

Quantities
All products represented in a particular system are defined by the industry standard. For example: wood joist is measured in linear feet.

Materials
This column contains the MATERIAL COST of each element. These cost figures include 10% for handling.

Total
MATERIAL COST + INSTALLATION COST = TOTAL. Work on table from left to right across cost columns to derive totals, including installers overhead and profit.

NOTE:
In the three right-hand columns, each quantity is adjusted to agree with the unit of measure for the entire system. In this case, COST PER SQUARE FOOT (S.F.) is the common unit of measure. In addition, all the elements of each system are defined in relation to the product as a selling commodity. For example: wood joist is priced by the linear foot.

Installation
Labor rates include both the INSTALLATION COST of the contractor and the standard contractor's O&P. On the average, the LABOR COST will be 53.8% over the above BARE LABOR COST.

The cost of Equipment is included in the INSTALLATION figures shown. A 10% factor has been added to allow for the standard mark-up. INSTALLATION = BARE COST OF LABOR x 1.538 (add 53.8%) + BARE COST OF EQUIPMENT x 1.10 (add 10%).

Factors
Factors are included in the listing at the bottom of the page to allow for unusual job conditions. Add these factors to SYSTEM COST to allow for the condition indicated.

Illustration
Each building system is accompanied by a detailed, illustrated description. Every element involved in the total system is shown.

Description
The description on each Systems page gives an example of how a system can be developed with alternate systems prices. Guidelines for utilizing the special job condition factors are also included.

127

State and Federal Unemployment Insurance

The employer's tax rate is adjusted by a merit-rating system according to the number of former employees applying for benefits. Contractors who find it possible to offer a maximum of steady employment can enjoy a substantial reduction in unemployment tax rate.

Employer-Paid Social Security (FICA)

This tax rate is adjusted annually by the federal government. It is a percentage of an employee's salary up to a maximum annual contribution.

Builder's Risk and Public Liability

These insurance rates vary according to the trades involved and the state in which the work is done. Because of the varying rates, many contractors carry this insurance on the applicable trade.

Operating Overhead

The cost of maintaining a business, or operating overhead, is often overlooked, underestimated, or improperly allocated. Since this operating overhead must be recovered during the year, some planning and budgeting is needed. The contractor must anticipate this overhead and also should have an estimate of the expected volume of business that will be billed during the year. The operating overhead can be calculated as a percentage of job cost or as a percentage of labor. Other methods for allocating operating overhead can be adopted.

Overhead and profit for contractors will vary greatly. For estimating purposes, *Repair and Remodeling Cost Data* 1985, assumes 16% for overhead and 15% for profit. Overhead in this case accounts for those expenses that a business must incur to operate. It includes selling expenses, advertising, rental costs, vehicles and equipment, plus other costs that cannot be directly allocated to a specific project. These overhead expenses are generally based on budgeted annual volume and anticipated economic condition. The example below is typical of the operating overhead for a building contractor.

Owner's Salary (Salesman/Supervisor)	$ 50,000
Secretary ($300/wk)	15,600
Office Rental ($500/mo)	6,000
Telephone Answering Service ($75/mo)	900
Office Equipment ($100/mo)	1,200
Accountant	3,000
Legal	3,000
Medical, Workers' Comp. (office personnel)	9,200
Advertising (phone book, etc.)	3,600
Auto & Truck Expenses	9,000
Association Dues	500
Seminars, Travel	3,000
Entertainment	5,200
Bad Debts, 1% of gross	6,000
Total Overhead	$116,200

For a contractor who anticipates $600,000 in Total Billings for the coming year, with direct labor costs of $250,000, an allocation of 47% of labor costs for operating overhead would be more appropriate than the 16% allowed in *Repair and Remodeling Cost Data* 1985. If the contractor in this case were using the overhead data from *Repair and Remodeling Cost Data* an adjustment should be made to account for the increased cost of doing business versus that shown in the book.

Installing Contractor's Profit and Contingency

This percentage is the fee added by the contractor that will offer a return on an investment, plus an allowance covering the risk involved in the type of construction being bid. The profit percentage may vary from 4% on large straightforward projects to as much as 25% on small high-risk jobs. Profit percentages are directly affected by economic conditions, the expected number of bidders, and the estimated risk involved in the project. For estimating purposes, *Repair and Remodeling Cost Data* 1985, assumes 15% to be a reasonable profit and contingency factor.

4.4
Cost Adjustments

City Cost Index

Prices in different parts of the country vary. For the sake of clarity, the data in *Repair and Remodeling Cost Data* are based on national averages. The City Cost Index in *Repair and Remodeling Cost Data* provides a method to adjust estimates to various locations. One hundred sixty-two U.S. and Canadian cities are listed. Each UCI division is included and is broken down by material and installation. The index figures are based on a 30 major city average of 100. When using the index, the estimator should be aware of adjustments that may be peculiar to a particular renovation project:

1. Labor productivity
2. Contractor managerial efficiency
3. Competitive conditions
4. Automation
5. Restrictive union practices
6. Owner's unique requirements
7. Excessive material or labor

Historical Cost Index

A Historical Cost Index number is a percentage ratio of a given project's cost at any stated time compared to that same project's cost at a base period.

The Historical Index in Table I4.2 lists both the Means City Cost Index based on Jan. 1, 1975 = 100 as well as the computed value of an index based on January 1, 1985 costs. Since the Jan. 1, 1985 figure is estimated, space is left to write in the actual index figures as they become available through either the quarterly *Means Construction Cost Indexes* or as printed in the *Engineering News-Record*. To compute the actual index based on Jan. 1, 1985 = 100, divide the Quarterly City Cost Index for a particular year by the actual Jan. 1, 1985 Quarterly City Cost Index. For example, the Historical Cost Indexes for July 1, 1976 and January 1, 1985 are 107.3 and 190.0 respectively. By dividing, we see that construction costs in 1985 are 1.77 times the construction costs in 1976, or stated otherwise, there has been a 77% increase in construction costs from 1977 to 1985.

Historical Cost Indexes				
		"Quarterly City Cost Index" Jan. 1, 1975 = 100		Current Index Based on Jan. 1, 1985 = 100
Year	Est.	Actual	Est.	Actual
Oct. 1985				
July 1985				
April 1985				
Jan. 1985	190.0		100.0	100.0
July 1984		187.6	98.7	
1983		183.5	96.6	
1982		174.3	91.7	
1981		160.2	84.3	
1980		144.0	75.8	
1979		132.3	69.6	
1978		122.4	64.4	
1977		113.3	59.6	
1976		107.3	56.5	
1975		102.6	54.0	
1974		94.7	49.8	
1973		86.3	45.4	
1972		79.7	41.9	
1971		73.5	38.7	
1970		65.8	34.6	
1969		61.6	32.4	
1968		56.9	29.9	
1967		53.9	28.4	
1966		51.9	27.3	
1965		49.7	26.2	
1964		48.6	25.6	
1963		47.3	24.9	
1962		46.2	24.3	
1961		45.4	23.9	
1960		45.0	23.7	
1959		44.2	23.3	
1958		43.0	22.6	
1957		42.2	22.2	
1956		40.4	21.3	
1955		38.1	20.1	
1954		36.7	19.3	
1953		36.2	19.1	
1952		35.3	18.6	
1951		34.4	18.1	
1950		31.4	16.5	
1949		30.4	16.0	
1948		30.4	16.0	
1947		27.6	14.5	
1946		23.2	12.2	
1945		20.2	10.6	
1944		19.3	10.2	
1943		18.6	9.8	
1942		18.0	9.5	
1941		16.8	8.8	

Table I4.2

130

Part II: Unit Price Estimating Example

Part II
Introduction

The Unit Price Estimate is the most detailed and most accurate type of estimate. The estimator should have working drawings and specifications to provide sufficient information to complete the estimate effectively. In commercial renovation, however, the plans and specifications are not enough. The estimator must perform a thorough evaluation of the site in order to understand how the existing conditions will affect the work.

The following example is a Unit Price Estimate for a hypothetical commercial renovation project. A description of the project is included at the beginning of the estimating example. The site evaluation and discussion of the existing conditions is included in each division. The individual items in the estimate may not represent every item that will be found in a renovation project. But the example will provide a basis for understanding, evaluating, and estimating commercial renovation as a whole. If the reader uses this example as a guideline for actual projects, consideration must be given to all building, fire, health, and safety codes and regulations effective in a given locality.

Prices and costs used in this example are from R.S. Means' *Repair and Remodeling Cost Data*. The example assumes that working drawings and specifications have been provided, and reference will be made to them throughout the estimating example.

Project Description

The sample project is the renovation of a turn-of-the-century mill building into retail and commercial office space. The building is located in the downtown area of a small city. The exterior walls are brick and the floor systems are cast steel columns and wood beams with heavy wood decking. The roof structure is heavy timber trusses.

The building was originally used for manufacturing and has recently been used primarily for warehousing. The building has not been well maintained and is in a general state of disrepair. A retail tenant currently occupying the premises is to remain in operation throughout the renovation.

Figures II.1 through II.7 are plans, a section, and an elevation of the existing conditions of the building. Figures II.8 through II.13 are plans, a section, and an elevation of the proposed renovations. The owner has secured one office tenant for half of the third floor. Because the owner must know the costs for pricing future tenant renovations, the costs for the tenant improvements are estimated separately in each appropriate division.

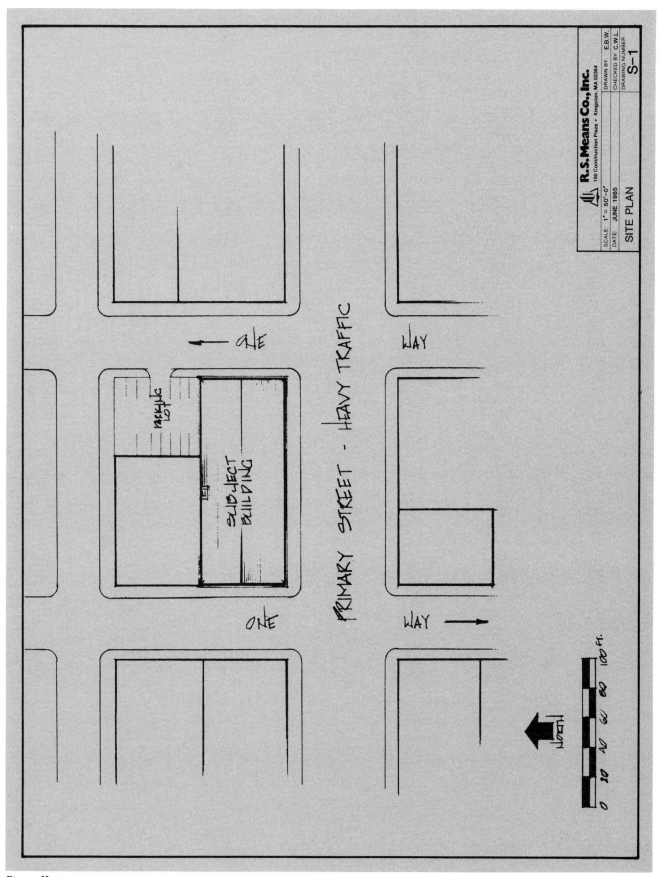

Figure II.1

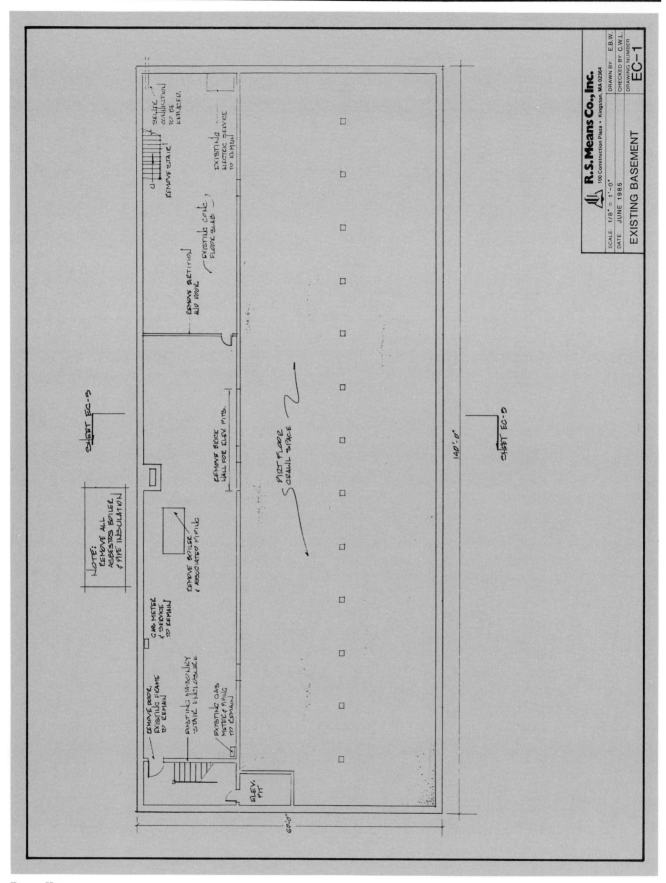

Figure II.2

134

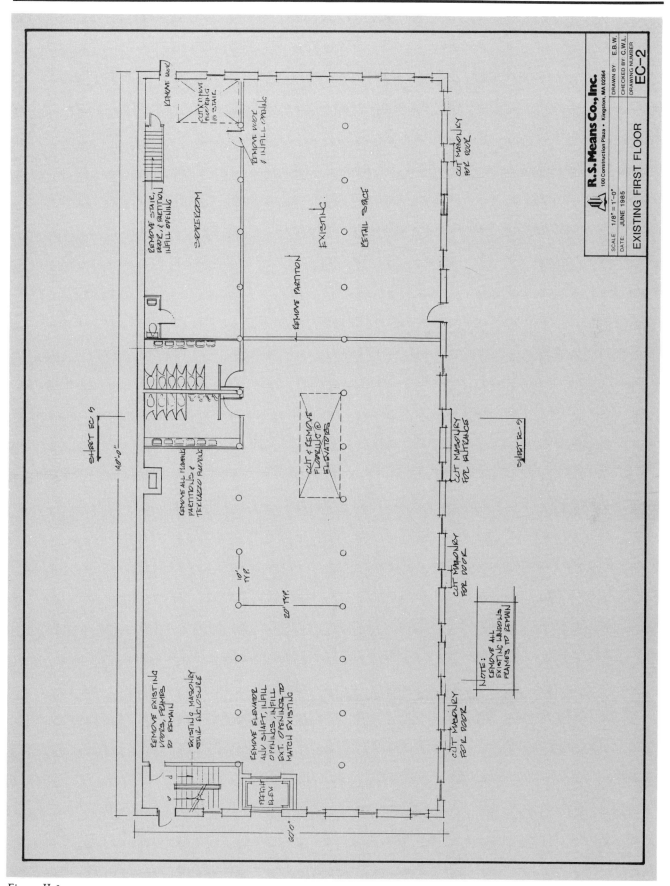

Figure II.3

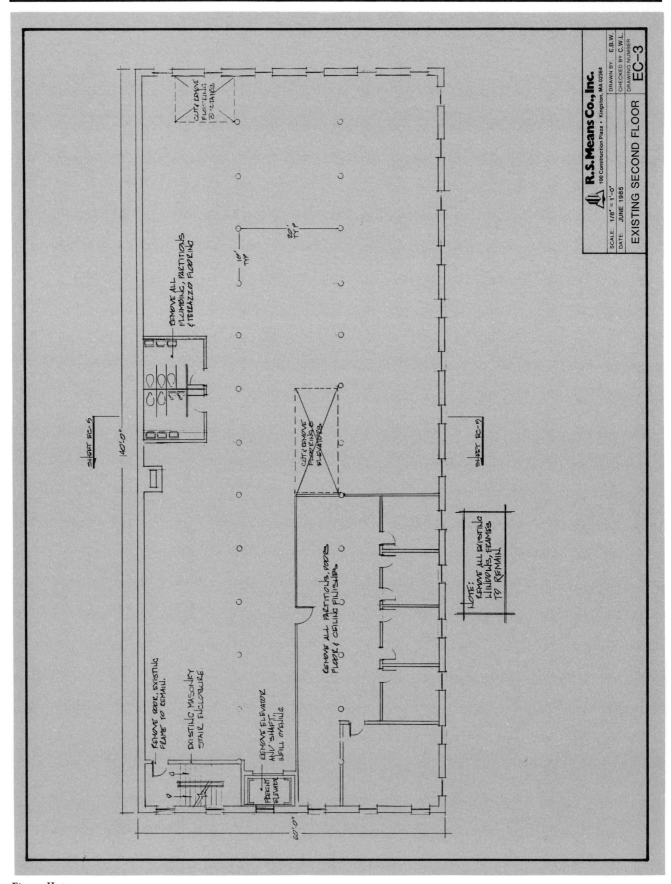

Figure II.4

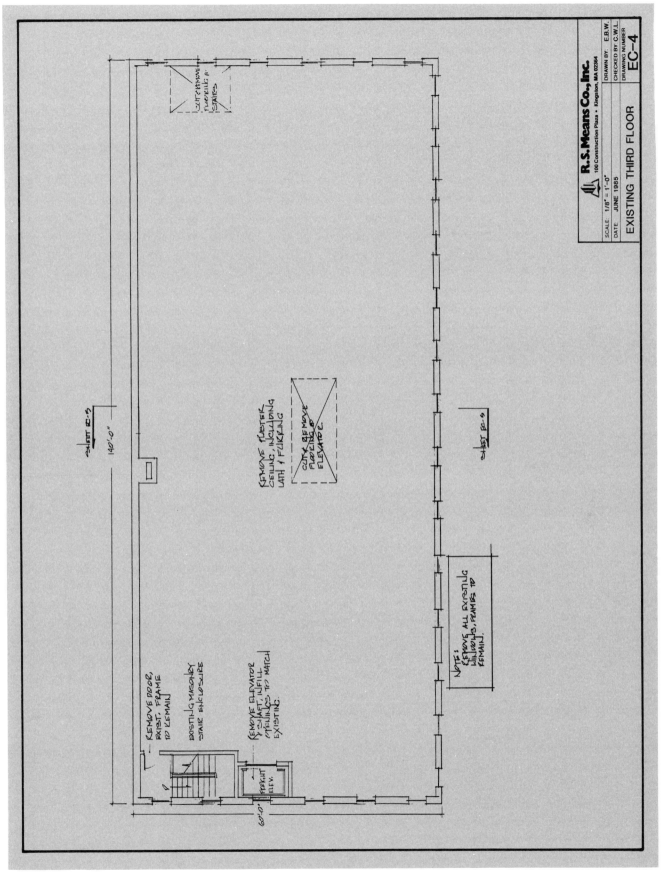

Figure II.5

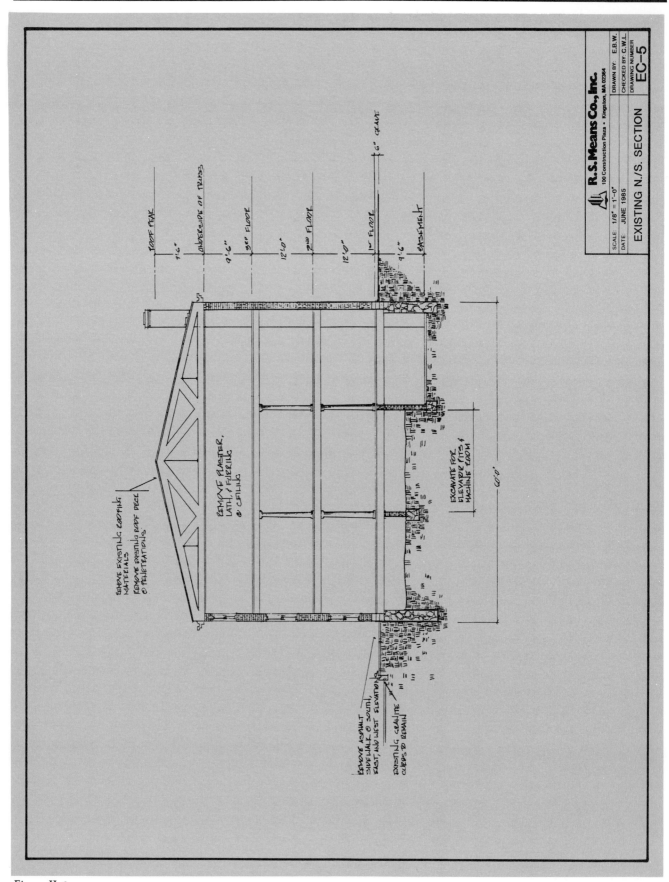

Figure II.6

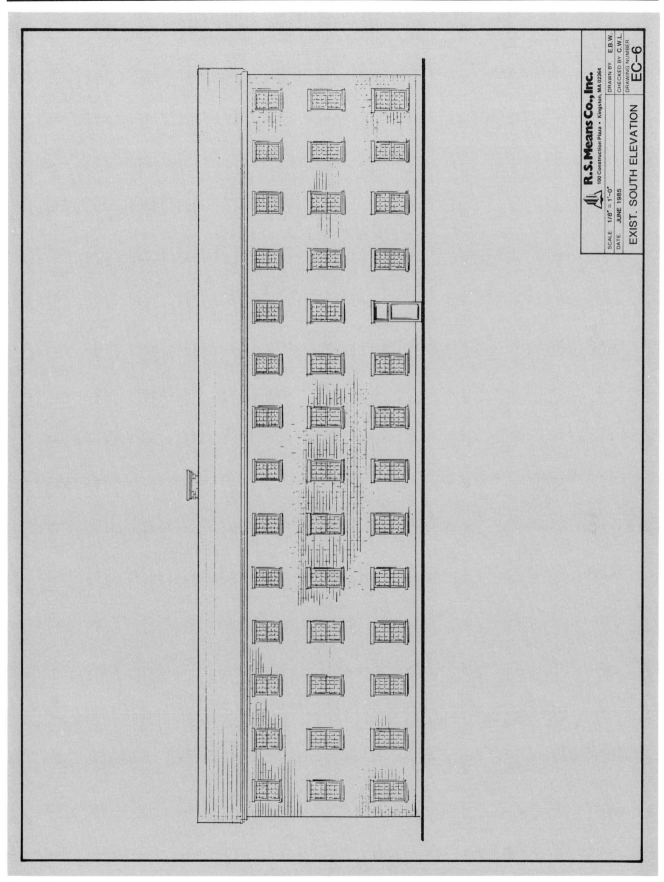

R.S. Means Co., Inc.
100 Construction Plaza • Kingston, MA 02364
SCALE 1/8" = 1'-0"
DATE: JUNE 1985
DRAWN BY   E.B.W.
CHECKED BY C.W.L.
DRAWING NUMBER
EC-6
EXIST. SOUTH ELEVATION

Figure II.7

139

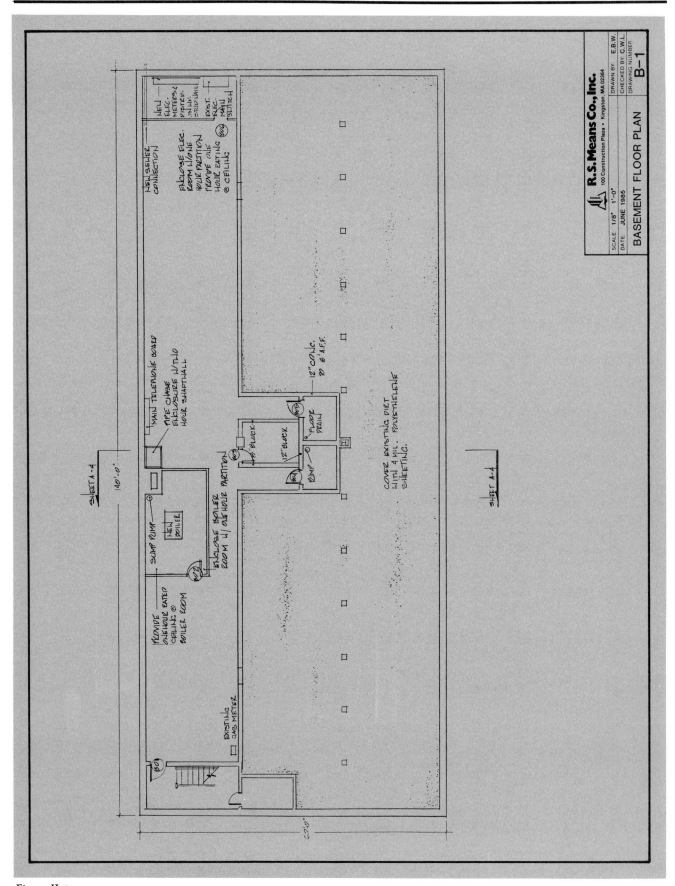

Figure II.8

140

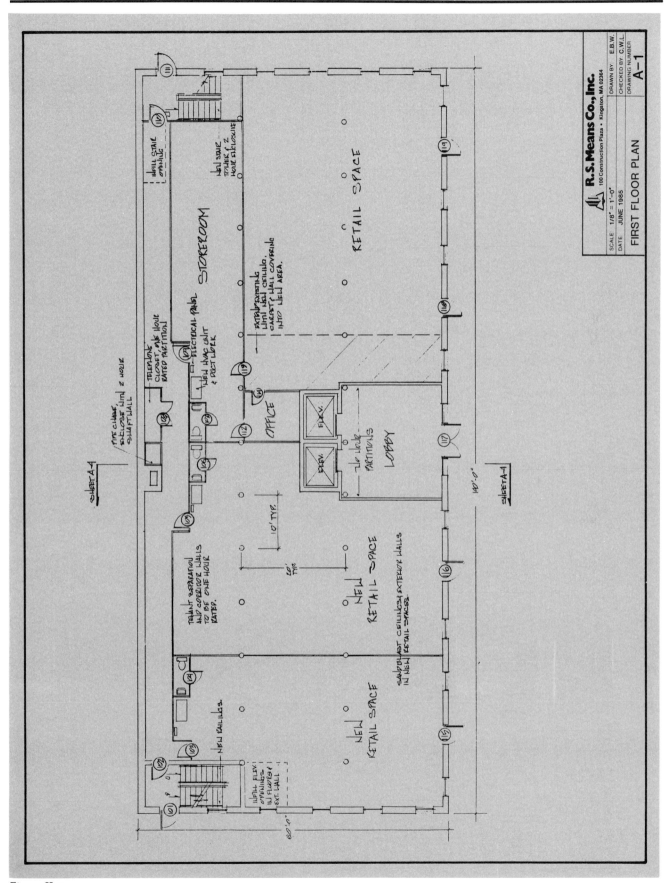

Figure II.9

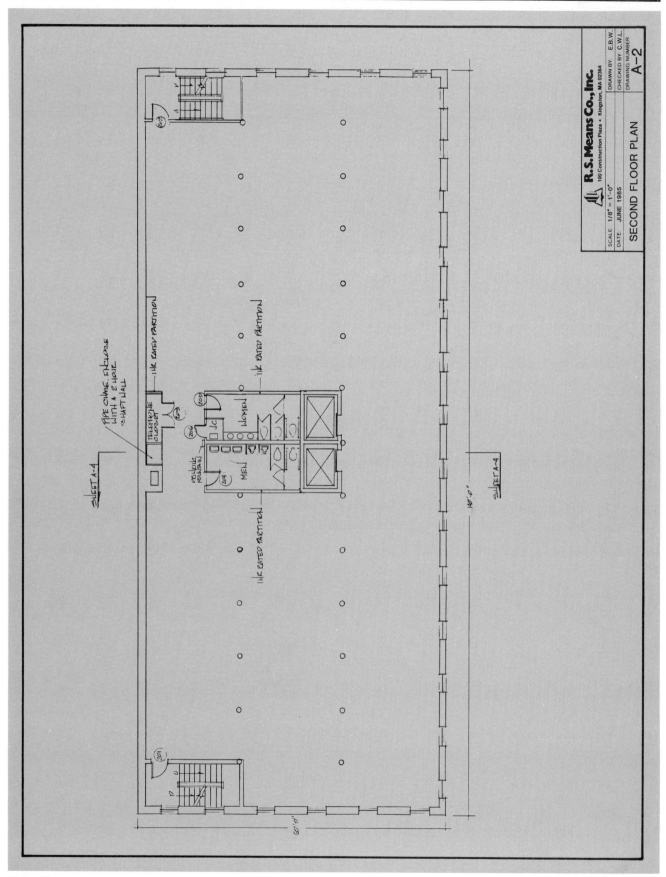

Figure II.10

142

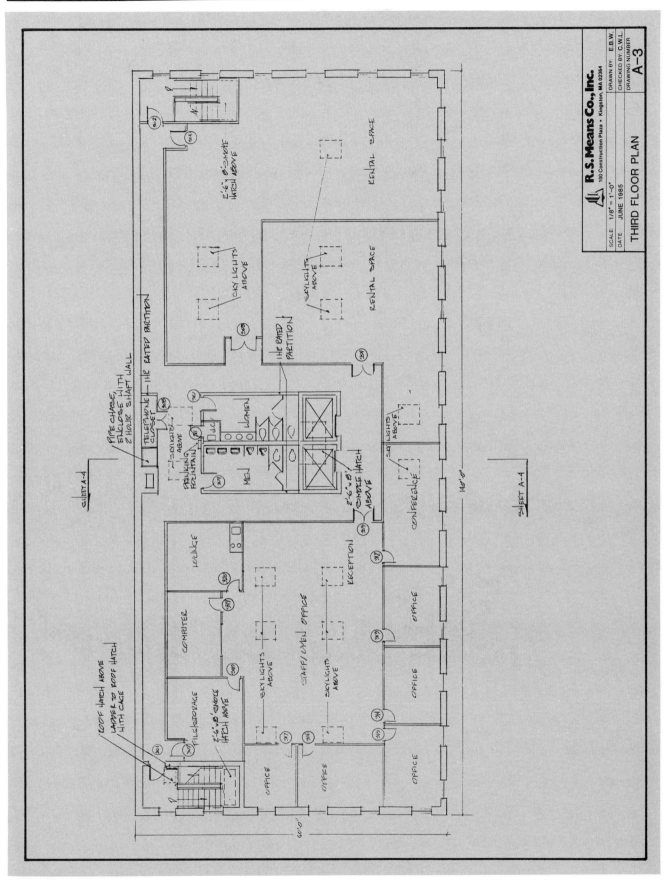

Figure II.11

143

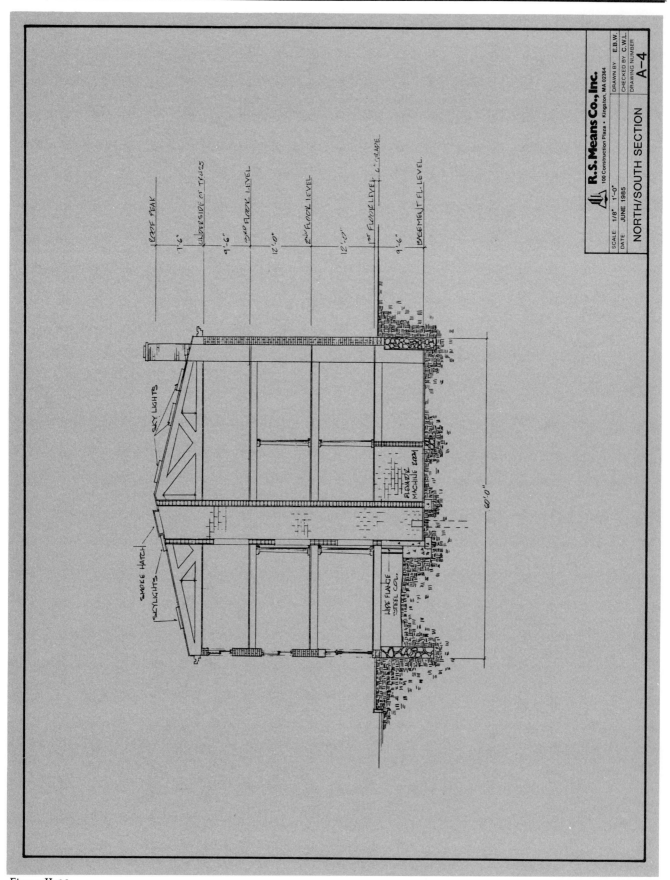

Figure II.12

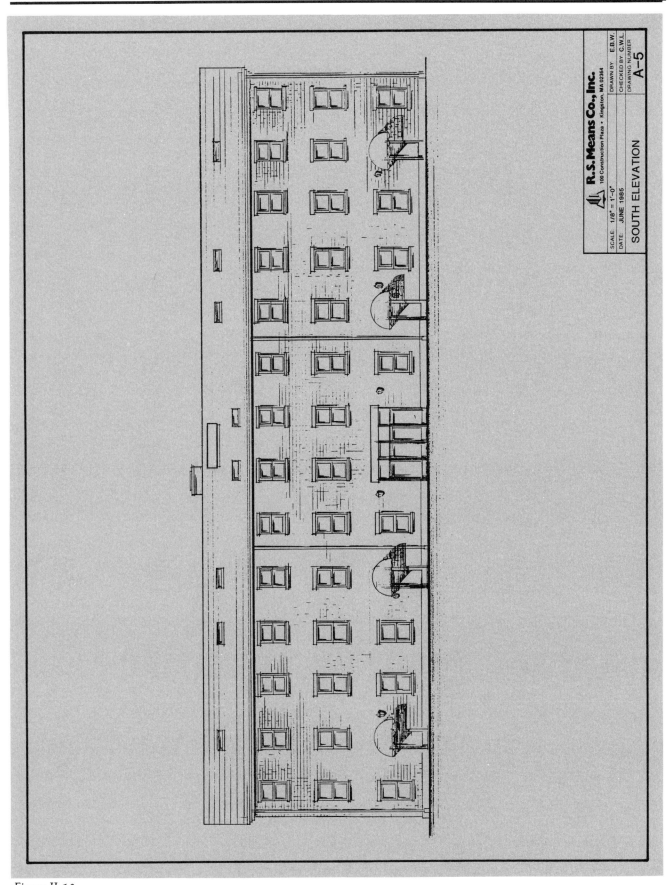

Figure II.13

Division 1: General Requirements

The General Requirements of a renovation estimate should include the costs for all items that are not directly part of the physical construction (permits, insurance, bonds) as well as those direct costs that cannot be allocated to a particular division (clean-up, temporary construction, scaffolding used by many trades).

Many of the items to be included in the General Requirements are dependent upon the total cost and/or the time duration of the project, and therefore cannot be quantified or priced until the Estimate Summary.

Figures II.14a and II.14b are of a Project Overhead Summary form, which lists most items to be included in General Requirements. This form will be used throughout the appropriate divisions of the sample estimate wherever such items are to be included.

Please note that "Contingencies" and "Main Office Expense" are among the final items of Figure II.14b. Some contractors include pro-rated costs for these items as indirect job costs within the estimate. Most contractors, however, include these costs as part of the overhead and profit percentages added at the Estimate Summary. The latter method is used in this sample estimate.

Included in one column are the costs for equipment, fees, rentals, and other items that are not labor or purchased material costs. All such costs receive the same mark-up in the estimate summary, usually 10% for supervision and handling. The material costs also receive a 10% mark-up as well as added sales tax. These percentages may vary depending upon local practice.

"Factors" that affect the costs are included in each division and are discussed in Part I, Chapter 1.10 of this book (see Table II.1). The application of these factors is crucial to effective estimating for commercial renovation. They help to determine added costs caused by existing conditions and the restrictions placed on the project because of them.

Division 2: Site Work

After a quick glance of the floor plans of existing conditions, the estimator concludes that site work and demolition costs are minimal. But upon investigation of the proposed plans and specifications, and upon evaluation of the site, it is determined that these costs are significant. Please refer to Tables II.2 to II.5 throughout the following discussion.

Asbestos removal has become a job only for licensed and experienced companies. A quotation is required and is shown in Table II.6. When the quotation is by telephone, the estimator must be sure to obtain all pertinent information. In this case, the estimator must determine what work required by the general contractor is not included in the quote. A factor for dust protection must be added to the costs. Table II.2 shows how the costs are included in the estimate. It is also important for the estimator to determine how long the work will take since other workers will not be allowed in the area during the asbestos removal. This will affect the Project Schedule.

Even when specific items are not listed as an individual line item in *Repair and Remodeling Cost Data,* the costs can be derived. In Table II.2, the costs for cutting the mill-type wood flooring for the elevator, stair, and roof openings have been calculated by estimating the time required and determining the crew (F-2) that will perform the work. Referring to the Crew Lists in *Repair and Remodeling Cost Data* provides the labor and equipment costs to be used. The estimator should make a note that the flooring that is removed should be saved to fill in the openings where the freight elevator is to be removed.

PROJECT OVERHEAD SUMMARY

MEANSCO
FORM FME112

PROJECT								SHEET NO.			
LOCATION								ESTIMATE NO.			
ARCHITECT			OWNER					DATE			
QUANTITIES BY		PRICES BY			EXTENSIONS BY			CHECKED BY			

DESCRIPTION	QUANTITY	UNIT	MATERIAL		LABOR		EQUIPMENT	
			UNIT	TOTAL	UNIT	TOTAL	UNIT	TOTAL
Job Organization: Superintendent								
Accounting and bookkeeping								
Timekeeper and material clerk								
Clerical								
Shop								
Safety, watchman and first aid								
Engineering: Layout								
Quantities								
Inspection								
Shop drawings								
Drafting & extra prints								
Testing: Soil								
Materials								
Structural								
Supplies: Office								
Shop								
Utilities: Light and power								
Water								
Heating								
Equipment: Rental								
Light trucks								
Freight and hauling								
Loading, unloading, erecting, etc.								
Maintenance								
Travel Expense								
Main office personnel								
Freight and Express								
Demurrage								
Hauling, misc.								
Advertising								
Signs and Barricades								
Temporary fences								
Temporary stairs, ladders & floors								
Photos								
Page total								

R. S. MEANS CO., INC., KINGSTON, MA 02364

Figure II.14a

DESCRIPTION	QUANTITY	UNIT	MATERIAL		LABOR		EQUIPMENT	
			UNIT	TOTAL	UNIT	TOTAL	UNIT	TOTAL
Total Brought Forward								
Legal								
Medical and Hospitalization								
Field Offices								
Office furniture and equipment								
Telephones								
Heat and Light								
Temporary toilets								
Storage areas and sheds								
Permits: Building								
Misc.								
Insurance								
Bonds								
Interest								
Taxes								
Cutting and Patching & Punch list								
Winter Protection								
Temporary heat								
Snow plowing								
Thawing materials								
Temporary Roads								
Repairs to adjacent property								
Pumping								
Scaffolding								
Small Tools								
Clean up								
Contingencies								
Main Office Expense								
Special Items								
Total: Transfer to Meansco Form 110 or 115								

Figure II.14b

11 Overhead

	CREW	MAN-HOURS	UNIT	MAT.	LABOR	EQUIP.	TOTAL	TOTAL INCL O&P
09-001 CONSTRUCTION MANAGEMENT FEES								
006 For work to $10,000			Project					10%
007 To $25,000								9%
009 To $100,000								6%
010 To $500,000								5%
011 To $1,000,000								4%
11-001 CONTINGENCIES Allowance to add at conceptual stage								20%
005 Schematic stage								15%
010 Preliminary working drawing stage								10%
015 Final working drawing stage								2%
15-001 ENGINEERING FEES Educational planning consultant, minimum			Contract					4.10%
010 Maximum								10.10%
040 Elevator & conveying systems, minimum								2.50%
050 Maximum								5%
100 Mechanical (plumbing & HVAC), minimum								4.10%
110 Maximum								10.10%
120 Structural, minimum			Project					1%
130 Maximum			"					2.50%
17-001 FACTORS To be added to construction costs for particular job requirements								
010								
[1] 050 Cut & patch to match existing construction, add, minimum			Costs	2%	3%			
055 Maximum				5%	9%			
[2] 080 Dust protection, add, minimum				1%	2%			
085 Maximum				4%	11%			
[3] 110 Equipment usage curtailment, add, minimum				1%	1%			
115 Maximum				3%	10%			
[4] 140 Material handling & storage limitation, add, minimum				1%	1%			
145 Maximum				6%	7%			
[5] 170 Protection of existing work, add, minimum				2%	2%			
175 Maximum				5%	7%			
[6] 200 Shift work requirements, add, minimum					5%			
205 Maximum					30%			
[7] 230 Temporary shoring and bracing, add, minimum			↓	2%	5%			
235 Maximum				5%	12%			
18-001 INSURANCE Builders risk, standard, minimum			Job Cost					.10%
005 Maximum								.50%
020 All-risk type, minimum								.12%
025 Maximum								.68%
040 Contractor's equipment floater, minimum			Value					.90%
045 Maximum			"					1.60%
060 Public liability, average			Job Cost					82%
081 Workers compensation & employer's liability								
200 Range of 36 trades in 50 states, excl. wrecking, min.			Payroll		1.04%			
210 Average					9%			

NOTES

FACTORS: In planning and estimating repair and remodeling projects, there are many factors that can affect the project cost more than material and labor. The economics of scale usually associated with new construction often has no influence on the cost of repair and remodeling. Small quantities of components may have to be custom fabricated at great expense. Work schedule coordination between trades frequently becomes difficult and work area restrictions can lead to subcontractor quotations with start-up and shutdown costs which are in excess of the cost of actual work involved. Some of the more prominent factors affecting repair and remodeling projects include:

1. Cutting and patching to match the existing construction can often lead to an economical trade-off of removing entire walls rather than creating new door and window openings. Substitutions for materials which are no longer manufactured can be expensive. Piping and ductwork runs may not be as straight as in new construction and wiring may have to be snaked through walls and floors.

2. Dust and noise protection of adjoining nonconstruction areas can alter usual construction methods.

3. Equipment usage curtailment resulting from physical limitations of the project may force workmen to use slow hand-operated equipment instead of power tools.

4. The confines of an enclosed building have a costly influence on movement and material handling. Low capacity elevators and stairwells may be the only access to upper floors of a multi-story building.

5. On some repair or remodeling projects completed work must be secured or otherwise protected from possible damage during construction. In certain areas completed work must be guarded to prevent theft and vandalism. (cont.)

For expanded coverage of these items see *Building Construction Cost Data 1985*

Table II.1

CONSOLIDATED ESTIMATE

Division 2

SHEET NO. 1 of 4
ESTIMATE NO. 85-1
DATE 1985
CHECKED BY

PROJECT Commercial Renovation
LOCATION
PRICES BY RSM
TAKE OFF BY EBW
QUANTITIES BY EBW
CLASSIFICATION
ARCHITECT

DESCRIPTION	FLOOR	SOURCE	QUANTITY	UNIT	MATERIAL UNIT	MATERIAL TOTAL	LABOR UNIT	LABOR TOTAL	EQUIP. UNIT	EQUIP. TOTAL	SUBCONTRACTOR UNIT	TOTAL INCL O&P	MAN-HOURS UNIT	MAN-HOURS TOTAL
Division 2: Site Work Demolition														
Asbestos Removal Factor [2]+	B	Telephone Quote			SUBCONTRACT						11%	3400	11%	48
												374		5
Remove wood deck @ Elev, Stair & Skylights		Crew F-2	2	Day			313.60	627	14	28			16	32
Brick Wall @ Pits	B	2.2-20-128	180	C.F.			1.25	225	.81	146			.071	13
Brick Walls @ Ext Openings Factors [5][7]+	1	2.2-20-128	314	C.F.			1.25	392	.81	254			.071	22
19% Labor							19%	74					19%	4
Remove Elev. & Machinery		Written Quote			SUBCONTRACT							800		80
Elevator Shaft [2][5]+		2.2-20-128 18% Labor	1040	C.F.			1.25	1300	.81	842			.071	74
							18%	234					18%	13
Roofing (Compensate SF for slope)		2.2-64-300	8660	SF			.40	3464					.025	217
Page Subtotals								(6316)		(1270)		(4574)		(508)

Table II.2

150

CONSOLIDATED ESTIMATE

					SHEET NO. 2 of 4
PROJECT Commercial Renovation					ESTIMATE NO. 85-1
LOCATION	PRICES BY RSM		CLASSIFICATION		DATE 1985
TAKE OFF BY EBW	QUANTITIES BY EBW		ARCHITECT		CHECKED BY

DESCRIPTION	FLOOR	SOURCE	QUANTITY	UNIT	MATERIAL UNIT	MATERIAL TOTAL	LABOR UNIT	LABOR TOTAL	EQUIPMENT UNIT	EQUIPMENT TOTAL	SUBCONTRACTOR UNIT	TOTAL INCL. O & P	MAN-HOURS UNIT	MAN-HOURS TOTAL
Division 2: Sitework Demolition (cont'd)														
Ceilings: Suspended	2	2.2-06-158	2440	SF			33	805					.021	51
Plaster	3	2.2-06-100	8400	SF			35	2940					.023	193
Doors:														
Exterior	3	2.2-32-020	3	Ea.			7.75	23					.5	2
Interior	1&2	2.2-32-050	15	Ea.			6.20	93					.4	6
Stair	All	2.2-32-020	4	Ea.			7.75	31					.5	2
Walls:														
Drywall	1	2.2-68-100	400	SF			.12	48					.008	3
Studs	1	2.2-44-660	680	LF			.12	82					.008	5
⑦ ⑤ ④		43% Labor					43%	56					13%	1
Drywall	2	2.2-68-100	1920	SF			.12	230					.008	15
Plaster	1&2	2.2-68-300	1560	SF			.31	484					.02	31
Studs	2	2.2-44-660	3300	LF			.12	397					.008	26
Carpet	2	2.2-36-040	1800	SF			.12	216					.008	14
Terrazzo	1&2	2.2-36-264	640	SF			.71	454					.040	29
Stair	1	2.2-44-620	15	Ris			6.20	93	22	128			4.	4
Page Subtotals								5952		128				384

Table II.3

Division 2

CONSOLIDATED ESTIMATE

PROJECT: Commercial Renovation
LOCATION:
TAKE OFF BY: EBW
PRICES BY: RSM
QUANTITIES BY: EBW
CLASSIFICATION:
ARCHITECT:
SHEET NO. 3 of 4
ESTIMATE NO. 85-1
DATE 1985
CHECKED BY:

DESCRIPTION	FLOOR	SOURCE	QUANTITY	UNIT	MATERIAL UNIT	MATERIAL TOTAL	LABOR UNIT	LABOR TOTAL	EQUIPMENT UNIT	EQUIPMENT TOTAL	SUBCONTRACTOR UNIT	SUBCONTRACTOR TOTAL INCL O&P	MAN-HOURS UNIT	MAN-HOURS TOTAL
Division 2: Sitework Demolition (Cont'd)														
Windows	All	2.2-72-202	75	Ea.			10.35	776					.67	50
Plumbing:														
Water Closet		2.2-60-140	16	Ea.			22	352					1	16
Lavatories		2.2-60-120	19	Ea.			17.75	337					.8	15
Urinals		2.2-60-152	6	Ea.			25	150					1.14	7
Toilet Partitions		2.2-68-380	19	Ea.			25	475					1.6	30
Trash Chute		2.2-78-044	30	LF	14.75	442	12.95	388					.8	24
Load & Haul (6 Loads)		2.2-18-204	4860	CF			.44	2138	.17	826			.027	131
Asphalt Sidewalk		2.2-20-500	249	SY			1.23	306	.47	117			.074	18
HVAC: Boiler Radiators Piping	Removed By Salvage Co. at no cost													
Plumb: Piping														
Elec														
Page Subtotals						442		4922		943				291

Table II.4

152

Division 2

CONSOLIDATED ESTIMATE

PROJECT **Commercial Renovation**
LOCATION
TAKE OFF BY: EBW PRICES BY: RSM QUANTITIES BY: EBW
CLASSIFICATION ARCHITECT
SHEET NO. 4 of 4
ESTIMATE NO. 85-1
DATE 1985
CHECKED BY

DESCRIPTION	FLOOR	SOURCE	QUANTITY	UNIT	BARE COSTS — MATERIAL UNIT	MATERIAL TOTAL	LABOR UNIT	LABOR TOTAL	EQUIPMENT UNIT	EQUIPMENT TOTAL	SUBCONTRACTOR UNIT	TOTAL INCL. O & P	MAN-HOURS UNIT	MAN-HOURS TOTAL
Division 2: Sitework														
Sidewalk		2.6-40-031	2241	SF	.79	1770	.72	1614					.04	90
Sewer Connection														
Excav.		2.3-17-010	4	CY			31	124					2	8
Backfill		2.3-03-810	4	CY			14.00	56					.902	4
Pipe	B	2.5-27-625	10	LF	2.20	22	1.48	15					.072	1
Factors [6]+		30% Labor					30%	5						
Excavation @ Elev. Shaft	B	2.3-17-001	60	CY			15.50	930					1	60
[7]+		12% Labor					12%	112					12%	7
Page Subtotals						(1792)		(2856)						(170)
Sheet 1								6316		1270		4574		508
Sheet 2								5952		128				384
Sheet 3						442		4922		943				291
Demolition Subtotal						442		17190		2341		4574		1183
Sheet 4						1792		2856						170
Division 2 Totals						22234		20046		2341		4574		1353

Table II.5

153

TELEPHONE QUOTATION

MEANSCO FORM 140	DATE
FIRM QUOTING Asbestos Removal Co.	BY _____ TITLE _____
ADDRESS	PHONE (Area Code)
PROJECT Office Renovation	
LOCATION	ESTIMATE NO.
ITEM QUOTED	RECEIVED BY EBW

WORK INCLUDED	AMOUNT OF QUOTATION
Removal of asbestos pipe & boiler insulation in basement (Includes required permits) Lump Sum	3400
Job requires 3 workers /2 days	
DELIVERY TOTAL BID	3400

DOES QUOTATION INCLUDE THE FOLLOWING:

IF ☐ NO IS CHECKED, DETERMINE THE FOLLOWING:

	YES	NO		
STATE & LOCAL SALES TAXES	☐	☐ N|A	MATERIAL VALUE	
DELIVERY TO THE JOB SITE	☐	☐ N|A	WEIGHT	
COMPLETE ERECTION	☐	☐ N|A	QUANTITY	
COMPLETE SECTION AS PER SPECIFICATIONS	☐	☒ NO	DESCRIBE BELOW	

EXCLUSIONS AND QUALIFICATIONS

Does not include dust protection of existing Tenant
Add factor to quote   [2] 11%
                        +

ADDENDA ACKNOWLEDGEMENT	TOTAL ADJUSTMENT
	ADJUSTED TOTAL

R.S.MEANS CO.,INC. KINGSTON,MA. 02364

Table II.6

2.2 Building Demolition

20		CREW	MAN-HOURS	UNIT	BARE COSTS MAT.	LABOR	EQUIP.	TOTAL	TOTAL INCL. O&P	NOTES
040	Fencing, barbed wire, 3 strand	2 Clab	.037	L.F.		.58		.58	.89L	**GENERAL DEMOLITION**
042	5 strand		.057			.89		.89	1.37L	When estimating demolition the authors recommend getting a bid from a local
050	Chain link, remove only		.052			.80		.80	1.24L	contractor, if possible. Variables including
052	Remove and reset		.320			4.96		4.96	7.65L	disposal sites, protection of adjacent
080	Guard rail, remove only		.188			2.92		2.92	4.50L	structures, salvage, and economic
084	Remove and reset		.457	↓		7.10		7.10	10.95L	conditions can affect costs by 100%.
090	Minimum labor/equipment charge	↓	4	Job		62		62	96L	In calculating the line item costs of this
095										major classification, three preliminary
100	Hydrants, fire, remove only	2 Plum	3.400	Ea.		76		76	115L	qualifications are assumed:
104	Remove and reset		11.430	"		255		255	380L	1. The tools used for demolition are
110	Minimum labor/equipment charge	↓	8	Job		180		180	265L	generally of the hand or pneumatic
115										hand type (note crew size).
120	Masonry walls, block or tile, solid	B-5	.036	C.F.		.63	.40	1.03	1.41	2. The cost of rubbish handling
122	Cavity		.029			.51	.33	.84	1.15	(removing rubbish to on-site
128	Brick, solid		.071			1.25	.81	2.06	2.81	containers or trucks) is not included.
130	With block		.057			1	.64	1.64	2.24	3. The cost of hauling rubbish to an
132	Stone, with mortar		.071			1.25	.81	2.06	2.81	approved dumpsite is not included.
134	Dry set	↓	.043	↓		.76	.48	1.24	1.69	Therefore, for total general demolition
180	Minimum labor/equipment charge	A-1	2	Job		31.20	8.80	40	58	cost, add rubbish handling (See Division
190										2.2-78) and hauling (See Division 2.3-30).
200	Pavement, with power equipment, bituminous roads	B-38	.035	S.Y.		.58	.52	1.10	1.47	
204	Bituminous driveways		.035			.59	.53	1.12	1.49	
208	Concrete to 6" thick, mesh reinforced		.094			1.57	1.42	2.99	3.97	
212	Rod reinforced		.120			2	1.81	3.81	5.05	
216	Concrete, 7" to 24" thick, plain		1.830	C.Y.		30	28	58	77	
218	Reinforced	↓	2.530	"		42	38	80	105	
220	Minimum labor/equipment charge	B-38	4	Job		65	60	125	170	
230										
240	With hand held air equipment, bituminous	B-39	.025	S.F.		.42	.07	.49	.72	
242	Concrete to 6" thick, no reinforcing		.040			.65	.12	.77	1.14	
244	Mesh reinforced		.058			.95	.17	1.12	1.65	
246	Rod reinforced	↓	.063	↓		1.04	.18	1.22	1.79	
248	Minimum labor/equipment charge	B-38	4	Job		65	60	125	170	
249										
250	Curbs, concrete, plain	B-6	.074	L.F.		1.23	.47	1.70	2.41	
252	Reinforced		.109			1.82	.69	2.51	3.55	
260	Granite curbs		.068			1.13	.43	1.56	2.20	
262	Bituminous curbs	↓	.029	↓		.49	.18	.67	.94	
290	Minimum labor/equipment charge	B-38	4	Job		67	25	92	130	
295										
300	Pipe, concrete, not incl. excavation, 12" diameter	B-6	.137	L.F.		2.29	.87	3.16	4.47	
304	15" diameter		.160			2.67	1.01	3.68	5.20	
308	24" diameter		.200			3.34	1.27	4.61	6.50	
312	36" diameter	↓	.267	↓		4.46	1.69	6.15	8.70	

For expanded coverage of these items see *Means' Site Work Cost Data 1985*

Table II.7

The estimator must use experience and good judgement when applying the "Factors" to the estimate. The project includes openings to be cut in the exterior masonry walls for the lobby entrance and retail doorways, as shown in Table II.2. Table II.7 contains the appropriate line item. The estimator knows that this masonry removal will have to be performed carefully because the edges of the openings will have to be rebuilt as finished surfaces. The estimator chooses the appropriate factors as shown in Table II.8, and records them in Table II.2.

The existing freight elevator is to be used for hauling materials and is to remain in operation for as long as possible. This forces a delay of the demolition of the shaft and elevator as well as the construction of the third floor office. Since the new windows and other work will be in place when the shaft is demolished, factors are applied for the protection of existing work and for dust protection. The estimator should also note for scheduling purposes that workers should place all materials on the upper floors before removal of the elevator.

The removal of the wall at the existing retail space will also entail extra labor expense to protect existing work, and the work must be performed after business hours. Note on Table II.3 that the total factors (43% for labor) are added only to the labor cost. The 30% added for overtime effects only the cost and is not used as a factor in determining the man-hours.

Other work, from other divisions, is required when the masonry is removed at the openings. For example, needling will be necessary at the wall above the entrance opening, and all opening jambs require toothing and rebuilding, using existing brick that has been removed. When items such as these are encountered the estimator should make notes on separate sheets, as in Table II.9, so that items will not be omitted.

Salvaged materials can help to reduce the costs of demolition. In this case, a wrecking subcontractor is to remove all piping, wiring, radiators, and the boiler at no cost. Ingenuity and legwork by the estimator can result in lower costs for the client and lower prices for competitive bids.

17-001 010	FACTORS To be added to construction costs for particular job requirements								
050	1	Cut & patch to match existing construction, add, minimum			Costs	2%	3%		
055		Maximum				5%	9%		
080	2	Dust protection, add, minimum				1%	2%		
085		Maximum				4%	11%		
110	3	Equipment usage curtailment, add, minimum				1%	1%		
115		Maximum				3%	10%		
140	4	Material handling & storage limitation, add, minimum				1%	1%		
145		Maximum				6%	7%		
170	5	Protection of existing work, add, minimum				2%	2%		
175		Maximum				5%	7%		
200	6	Shift work requirements, add, minimum					5%		
205		Maximum					30%		
230	7	Temporary shoring and bracing, add, minimum				2%	5%		
235		Maximum				5%	12%		

Table II.8 Factors for Brick Demolition (Division 2) from Division 1.1: Overhead

When all items in Division 2 have been entered, the estimator should review the division to note and include all related items to be entered on the Project Overhead Summary as shown in Tables II.10a and II.10b. The costs for a dumpster and the scaffolding, for example, are included in Division 1 in this estimate because they are to be used by different trades throughout the job, not just for demolition. Note that quantities only have been listed for these and other items. The total costs are dependent on the time extent of the project and will be entered when the Project Schedule has been completed.

Division 3: Concrete

The cast-in-place concrete for the project is limited to the footings, walls, and slab in the basement for the new elevator shafts. These items can be estimated in two ways using *Repair and Remodeling Cost Data.*

The individual components, forms, reinforcing, labor, and concrete can be priced separately. The costs for the floor slab in the basement were derived from the line items in Table II.11. Entry in the estimate is shown in Table II.12. No forms are required because the new floor slab is to be placed flush with the existing basement floor. The "out" for the sump pump is too small to be deducted. (At this point, the sump pumps and associated floor drain should be listed on a sheet for Division 15: Mechanical, Table II.13.) For small pours, the estimator should be aware of minimum concrete costs.

The second method for pricing the cast-in-place concrete is shown in Table II.14. *Repair and Remodeling Cost Data* provides costs for complete concrete installations, including forms, reinforcing, concrete and placement. This method is used for the footings and walls in Table II.12.

The precast concrete beam that will serve as the lintel at the lobby entrance cannot be lowered into place with a crane. The beam must be slid into place by hand and winch. A factor for the added labor is included in the estimate. The specifications call for the beam to receive a special stucco finish to match the existing limestone window lintels. This is included in Division 9: Finishes.

During the estimate, the owner asks for an alternate price to lower the basement dirt floor to create area for tenant storage. While the estimator knows from experience that such a project would not be cost effective, the owner needs to know the costs. In a short period of time, the estimator can calculate fairly accurate costs, without plans and specifications, by visualizing the work to be performed. The costs for the alternate are shown in Table II.15. This price does not include the costs for continuing the new stairway to the basement (required by code for basement occupancy) or the resulting costs for relocating the electrical service. After a phone call to the owner, the estimator does not have to waste any more time.

CONSOLIDATED ESTIMATE

PROJECT Commercial Renovation					CLASSIFICATION				SHEET NO. 1 of 1
LOCATION		PRICES BY RSM							ESTIMATE NO. 85-1
TAKE OFF BY EBW		QUANTITIES BY EBW			ARCHITECT				DATE 1985
									CHECKED BY

| DESCRIPTION | FLOOR | SOURCE | QUANTITY | UNIT | MATERIAL | | LABOR | | EQUIPMENT | | SUBCONTRACTOR | | TOTAL INCL. O & P | MAN-HOURS | |
					UNIT	TOTAL	UNIT	TOTAL	UNIT	TOTAL	UNIT	TOTAL INCL. O & P		UNIT	TOTAL
Division 4: Masonry															
Needling Extra Floors @ Entrance	1	4.5-32-108 4.5-32-200													
Toothing @ Ext. Openings	1	4.5-60-052													

Table II.9

PROJECT OVERHEAD SUMMARY

Division 1

PROJECT	Commercial Renovation			SHEET NO. 1 of 2
LOCATION				ESTIMATE NO. 85-1
ARCHITECT		OWNER		DATE 1985
QUANTITIES BY EBW	PRICES BY RSM	EXTENSIONS BY		CHECKED BY

DESCRIPTION	man-Hours	QUANTITY	UNIT	MATERIAL UNIT	MATERIAL TOTAL	LABOR UNIT	LABOR TOTAL	EQUIP., FEES, RENTAL UNIT	EQUIP., FEES, RENTAL TOTAL
Job Organization: Superintendent									
Accounting and bookkeeping									
Timekeeper and material clerk									
Clerical									
Shop									
Safety, watchman and first aid									
Engineering: Layout									
Quantities									
Inspection									
Shop drawings									
Drafting & extra prints									
Testing: Soil									
Materials									
Structural									
Supplies: Office									
Shop									
Utilities: ~~Light and~~ power		28	MSF					84	2352
Water									
Heating									
Lighting 1.1-58-350	(66)	280	CSF	1^{69}	473	5^{20}	1456		
Equipment: Rental									
Light trucks									
Freight and hauling									
Loading, unloading, erecting, etc.									
Maintenance									
Dumpster 2.2-78-080			WK					150	
Travel Expense									
Main office personnel									
Freight and Express									
Demurrage									
Hauling, misc.									
Advertising Job Sign		1	Ea.		250				
Signs and Barricades									
Temporary fences									
Temporary stairs, ladders & floors									
Rails @ Stairs & Elev.	(22)	270	LF	1^{24}	335	1^{57}	424		
~~Photos~~ 1.1-58-310									
Page total									

Table II.10a

Division 1 Sheet 2 of 2 DESCRIPTION	QUANTITY	UNIT	MATERIAL		LABOR		EQUIP., FEES, RENTAL	
			UNIT	TOTAL	UNIT	TOTAL	UNIT	TOTAL
Total Brought Forward								
Legal								
Medical and Hospitalization								
Field Offices								
Office furniture and equipment								
Telephones		Mo.					100	
Heat and Light								
Temporary toilets								
Storage areas and sheds								
Permits: Building								
Misc. Street Use	1	Ea.					50	50
Insurance								
Bonds								
Interest								
Taxes								
Cutting and Patching & Punch list								
Winter Protection								
Temporary heat								
Snow plowing								
Thawing materials								
Temporary Roads								
Rent 6 Parking Spaces		Mo.					300	
Repairs to adjacent property								
Pumping								
Scaffolding 1.1-44-010 (170)	119	CSF			28	3332		
Rental - 381 Frames - $2³⁵/mo		Mo.						
Small Tools								
Clean up								
Contingencies								
Main Office Expense								
Special Items								
Total:								

Table II.10b

3.2 Reinforcing Steel

		CREW	MAN-HOURS	UNIT	BARE COSTS MAT.	BARE COSTS LABOR	BARE COSTS EQUIP.	BARE COSTS TOTAL	TOTAL INCL O&P
06-001	WELDED WIRE FABRIC Rolls, 6 x 6 = #10/10 (W1.4/W1.4) 21 lb.	2 Rodm	.457	C.S.F.	7.65	9.75		17.40	24
030	6 x 6 = #6/6 (W2.9/W2.9) 42 lb. per C.S.F.		.552		14.80	11.75		26.55	35
050	4 x 4 = #10/10 (W1.4/W1.4) 31 lb. per C.S.F.		.516		10.25	11		21.25	29
090	2 x 2 = #12 galv. for gunite reinforcing	↓	2.460	↓	16.10	52		68.10	100

3.3 Cast in Place Concrete

		CREW	MAN-HOURS	UNIT	BARE COSTS MAT.	BARE COSTS LABOR	BARE COSTS EQUIP.	BARE COSTS TOTAL	TOTAL INCL O&P
12-001	CONCRETE, READY MIX Regular weight, 2000 psi			C.Y.	43			43	47M
010	2500 psi				44			44	48M
015	3000 psi				46.15			46.15	51M
020	3500 psi				47			47	52M
025	3750 psi				48.60			48.60	53M
030	4000 psi				49.25			49.25	54M
035	4500 psi				51.10			51.10	56M
040	5000 psi				52.05			52.05	57M
100	For high early strength cement, add				10%				
200	For all lightweight aggregate, add			↓	50%				
300	For integral colors, 2500 psi, 5 bag mix								
310	Red, yellow or brown, 1.8 lb. per bag, add			C.Y.	12.60			12.60	13.85M
320	9.4 lb. per bag, add				66			66	73M
340	Black, 1.8 lb. per bag, add				13.10			13.10	14.40M
350	7.5 lb. per bag, add				55			55	61M
370	Green, 1.8 lb. per bag, add				27			27	30M
380	7.5 lb. per bag, add			↓	115			115	125M
38-001	PLACING CONCRETE and vibrating, including labor & equipment								
002									
370	Pile caps, under 5 C.Y., direct chute	C-6	.533			8.75	.59	9.34	14.05
375	Pumped	C-20	.753			12.60	6.50	19.10	26
380	With crane and bucket	C-7	.800			13.40	7.45	20.85	29
430	Slab on grade, 4" thick, direct chute	C-6	.436			7.15	.48	7.63	11.50
435	Pumped	C-20	.533			8.95	4.59	13.54	18.75
440	With crane and bucket	C-7	.582			9.75	5.40	15.15	21
460	Slab over 6" thick, direct chute	C-6	.291			4.77	.32	5.09	7.70
465	Pumped	C-20	.388			6.50	3.34	9.84	13.65
470	With crane and bucket	C-7	.441			7.40	4.10	11.50	15.85
490	Walls, 8" thick, direct chute	C-6	.533			8.75	.59	9.34	14.05
495	Pumped	C-20	.753			12.60	6.50	19.10	26
500	With crane and bucket	C-7	.800			13.40	7.45	20.85	29
505	12" thick, direct chute	C-6	.480			7.85	.53	8.38	12.65
510	Pumped	C-20	.674			11.30	5.80	17.10	24
520	With crane and bucket	C-7	.711	↓		11.90	6.60	18.50	26
521	Minimum labor/equipment charge	C-6	48	Job		787	53	840	1,275
532									
560	Wheeled concrete dumping, add to placing costs above								
561	Walking cart, 50' haul, add	A-1	.258	C.Y.		4.00	1.14	5.14	7.45
562	150' haul, add		.296			4.59	1.30	5.89	8.55
570	250' haul, add	↓	.348			5.40	1.53	6.93	10
580	Riding cart, 50' haul, add	B-9	.125			1.99	.44	2.43	3.56
581	150' haul, add		.174			2.77	.62	3.39	4.95
590	250' haul, add	↓	.200	↓		3.18	.71	3.89	5.70
900	Minimum labor/equipment charge	A-1	4	Job		62.40	17.60	80	115

Table II.11

CONSOLIDATED ESTIMATE

PROJECT	Commercial Renovation					
LOCATION		PRICES BY RSM		CLASSIFICATION		
TAKE OFF BY EBW	QUANTITIES BY EBW			ARCHITECT		

SHEET NO. 1 of 1
ESTIMATE NO. 85-1
DATE 1985
CHECKED BY

DESCRIPTION	FLOOR	SOURCE	QUANTITY	UNIT	MATERIAL UNIT	MATERIAL TOTAL	LABOR UNIT	LABOR TOTAL	EQUIPMENT UNIT	EQUIPMENT TOTAL	SUBCONTRACTOR UNIT	TOTAL INCL. O & P	MAN-HOURS UNIT	MAN-HOURS TOTAL
Division 3: Concrete														
Footings	B	3.3-14-385	12	CY	64	768	22.53	270	4.47	54			1.08	13
Walls	B	3.3-14-426	18	CY	105	1890	121.60	2189	8.40	151			5.93	107
3 Both Above					5%		5%	123					5%	6
Slab:	B													
Reinforcing		3.2-06-001	4	CSF	7.65	31	9.75	39					.457	2
Labor		3.3-38-430	6	CY			6.57	33	.45	2			.436	2
Concrete (8CY min)		3.3-12-015	8	CY	46.15	369								
wheeled		3.3-38-900	5	CY	Min.		Min.	62	Min.	18			Min.	4
Precast Beam @ Entrance	1	3.4-01-005	16	LF	125	2000	6.29	101	4.26	68			.3	5
[3]+		10% Labor			10%		10%	10					10%	1
Division 3: Totals						5058		2827		293				140

Table II.12

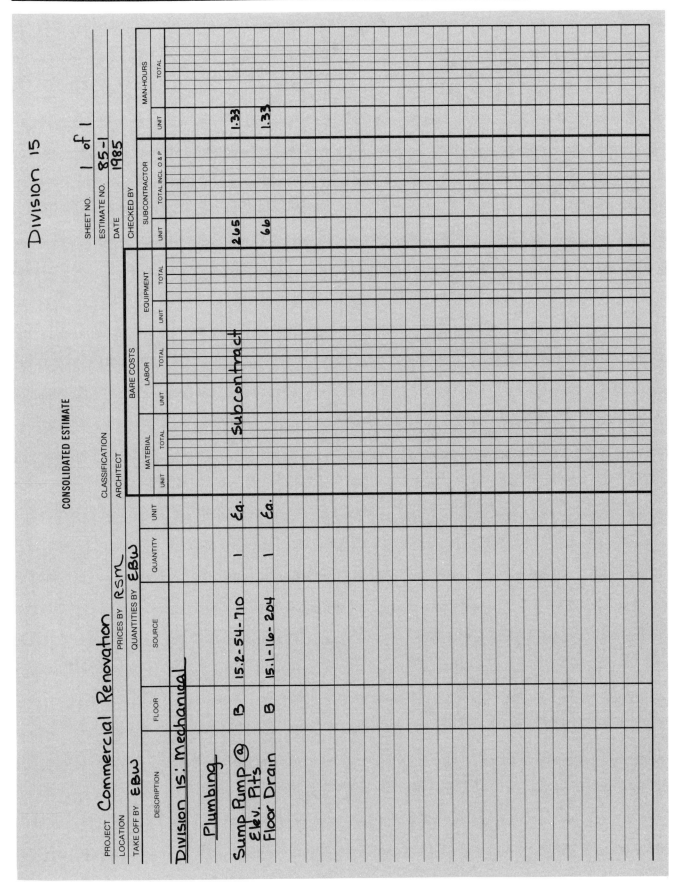

Table II.13

	Cast in Place Concrete	CREW	MAN-HOURS	UNIT	BARE COSTS				TOTAL INCL O&P
					MAT.	LABOR	EQUIP.	TOTAL	
14-001	CONCRETE IN PLACE Including forms (4 use), reinforcing								
005	steel, including finishing unless otherwise indicated								
010	Average for concrete framed building,								
011	including finishing	C-17B	4.850	C.Y.	94.05	101.80	13.20	209.05	270
013	Average for substructure only, simple design, incl. finishing	↓	2.700	↓	66.15	55.65	7.35	129.15	165
015	Average for superstructure only, including finishing	↓	5.900	↓	103	118.95	16.05	238	315
020	Base, granolithic, 1" x 5" high, straight	C-10	.137	L.F.	.10	2.43	.31	2.84	4.13
022	Cove	"	.171	"	.10	3.03	.39	3.52	5.15
030	Beams, 5 kip per L.F., 10' span	C-17A	11.480	C.Y.	165	233.75	16.25	415	560
035	25' span		9.650		145	196.35	13.65	355	480
050	Chimney foundations, minimum		3		77.50	61.76	4.24	143.50	185
051	Maximum		4.060		88.90	83.25	5.75	177.90	230
070	Columns, square, 12" x 12", minimum reinforcing		17.390		160	355	25	540	750
072	Average reinforcing	↓	19.510		255	402	28	685	925
074	Maximum reinforcing	C-17B	20.830		345	428	57	830	1,100
080	16" x 16", minimum reinforcing	C-17A	13.330		140	271.15	18.85	430	595
082	Average reinforcing	"	16.100		250	332	23	605	805
084	Maximum reinforcing	C-17B	9.590		366	199	26	591	735
120	Columns, round, tied, 16" diameter, minimum reinforcing		6.140		196	128.30	16.70	341	430
122	Average reinforcing		9.640		315	199	26	540	680
124	Maximum reinforcing		13.220		444	269	36	749	945
130	20" diameter, minimum reinforcing		4.610		185	92.45	12.55	290	365
132	Average reinforcing		7.670		295	159	21	475	590
134	Maximum reinforcing	↓	10.710	↓	410	221	29	660	820
170	Curbs, formed in place, 6" x 18", straight,	C-15	.180	L.F.	2.75	3.33	.10	6.18	8.25
175	Curb and gutter	"	.424	"	4.45	7.81	.24	12.50	17.25
380	Footings, spread under 1 C.Y.	C-17B	2.230	C.Y.	57	45.95	6.05	109	140
385	Over 5 C.Y.	C-17C	1.080		64	22.53	4.47	91	110
390	Footings, strip, 18" x 9", plain	C-17B	2.740		58	56.55	7.45	122	160
395	36" x 12", reinforced		1.560		53	31.77	4.23	89	110
400	Foundation mat, under 10 C.Y.		2.480		98	50.25	6.75	155	195
405	Over 20 C.Y.	↓	1.690		87	34.41	4.59	126	155
420	Grade walls, 8" thick, 8' high	C-17A	8.420		103	173.10	11.90	288	390
425	14' high	C-20	8.770		130	145	75	350	450
426	12" thick, 8' high	C-17A	5.930		105	121.60	8.40	235	310
427	14' high	C-20	5.520		98	92	48	238	300
430	15" thick, 8' high	C-17B	4.350		80	88.20	11.80	180	240
435	12' high	C-20	4.320	↓	83	73	37	193	245
475	Ground slab, incl. troweled finish, not incl. forms								
476	or reinforcing, over 10,000 S.F., 4" thick slab	C-8	.016	S.F.	.62	.28	.14	1.04	1.26
482	6" thick slab		.016		.91	.27	.14	1.32	1.56
484	8" thick slab		.017		1.25	.30	.15	1.70	2
490	12" thick slab		.019		1.87	.34	.17	2.38	2.77
495	15" thick slab	↓	.022	↓	2.35	.39	.19	2.93	3.38
520	Lift slab in place above the foundation, incl. forms,								
521	reinforcing, concrete and columns, minimum	C-17E	.107	S.F.	1.63	2.20	.06	3.89	5.25
525	Average		.122		2.60	2.51	.07	5.18	6.80
530	Maximum	↓	.186	↓	2.83	3.81	.11	6.75	9.10
590	Pile caps, incl. forms and reinf., square or rectangular, under 5 C.Y.	C-17C	1.640	C.Y.	66	33.20	6.80	106	130
595	Over 10 C.Y.		.949		65	19.08	3.92	88	105
600	Triangular or hexagonal, under 5 C.Y.		1.670		62	34.10	6.90	103	130
605	Over 10 C.Y.	↓	1.030		66	20.75	4.25	91	110
620	Retaining walls, gravity, 4' high (see also division 2.7-32)	C-17B	4.190		70	85.60	11.40	167	220
625	10' high		2.950		62	60.95	8.05	131	170
630	Cantilever, level backfill loading, 8' high		4.910		83	101.65	13.35	198	260
635	16' high	↓	4.710	↓	89	97.20	12.80	199	260
680	Stairs, not including safety treads, free standing	C-15	.600	L.F.Nose	4.34	11.06	.34	15.74	22
685	Cast on ground	↓	.400	"	3.25	7.37	.23	10.85	15.20
700	Stair landings, free standing		.253	S.F.	1.76	4.67	.14	6.57	9.30
705	Cast on ground	↓	.105	"	1.03	1.94	.06	3.03	4.19

Table II.14

Basement Alternate

CONSOLIDATED ESTIMATE

PROJECT Office Renovation
LOCATION
TAKE OFF BY EBW
PRICES BY RSM
QUANTITIES BY EBW
CLASSIFICATION
ARCHITECT

DESCRIPTION	FLOOR	SOURCE	QUANTITY	UNIT	MATERIAL UNIT	MATERIAL TOTAL	LABOR UNIT	LABOR TOTAL	EQUIPMENT UNIT	EQUIPMENT TOTAL	SUBCONTRACTOR UNIT	SUBCONTRACTOR TOTAL INCL. O&P	MAN-HOURS UNIT	MAN-HOURS TOTAL
Underpinning @ Columns	B	2.3-52-010	13	CY	130	1690	445	5785	125	1625			24.39	317
Under 50 CY		2.3-52-090			10%	169	40%	2314					40%	127
Factors [3][7] +					8%	149	22%	1782					22%	98
Excavating	B	2.3-11-001	700	CY			15.50	10850					1	700
Factors [3][7] +							22%	2389					22%	154
Conveyor		1.5-10-090	2	wk					425	850				
Reinforcing	B	3.2-06-001	56	CSF	7.65	428	9.75	546					.457	26
Floor Slab wheeled [1][3] -	B	3.3-38-430	69	CY			6.67	460	48	33			.436	30
		3.3-38-561	69	CY			2%	197	14	79			.258	18
		4% Labor					4%	26					4%	2
Concrete	B	3.3-12-015	69	CY	46.15	3184								
Subtotals (Bare Costs)						5620		24347		2581				1472
Overhead 10% mat. & Equip. 53.8% Labor						562		13099		259				
						6182		37446		2846				
Profit 10%						618		3745		285				
Total								51122						

Table II.15

Division 4: Masonry

In commercial renovation, new masonry work is usually limited compared to the extent of repair and restoration of existing masonry, which takes extensive time and labor. Normal methods of work must be altered to accommodate existing conditions. Table II.2, in Division 2 lists costs for removing the brick at the new exterior openings. The demolition of the brick for the lobby entrance cannot occur until the structure above is supported by needles as in Figure II.15. Such an operation should always be planned and supervised by a structural engineer. The costs are included in Table II.17

Included in the costs for removing the exterior brick is a factor for protection of existing work (Table II.2). This factor is applied, not only for protection of adjacent surfaces to remain, but also because the existing brick must be removed carefully to be reused to construct the jambs at the new exterior openings. Brick in older buildings usually cannot be matched with new brick. Since the old brick is to be used, there are no material costs for the specified brick masonry. There is no specific line item for rebuilding jambs to match existing conditions at new openings, using existing materials. The estimator must use good judgement to determine the most accurate costs. The work is similar to constructing brick columns, so line 4.2-09-030 in Table II.16 is chosen. Since the work requires care to match existing conditions, a factor is included as shown in Table II.17. Tables II.17 to II.19 are the estimate sheets for Division 4: Masonry.

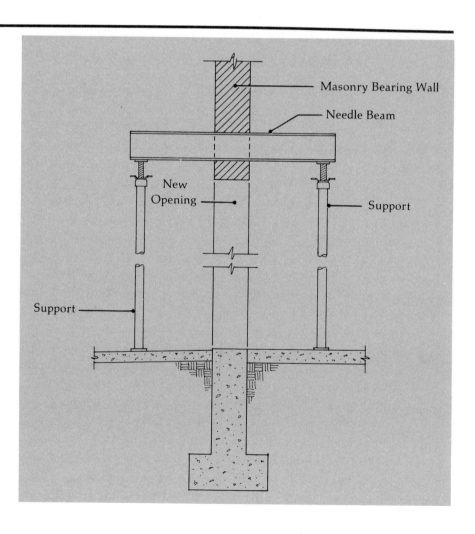

Figure II.15

4.2 Brick Masonry

Item	CREW	MAN-HOURS	UNIT	MAT.	LABOR	EQUIP.	TOTAL	TOTAL INCL O&P
06-001 CHIMNEY Standard bricks @ $208 per M, 16" x 16" with one 8" x 8" flue	D-1	.889	V.L.F.	9.20	15.85		25.05	34
005 16" x 20" with one 8" x 12" flue		1		11.30	17.85		29.15	40
010 16" x 24" with two 8" x 8" flues		1.140		13.60	20		33.60	46
015 20" x 20" with one 12" x 12" flue		1.140		13.35	20		33.35	46
020 20" x 24" with two 8" x 12" flues		1.330		17.60	24		41.60	56
025 20" x 32" with two 12" x 12" flues		1.600		22	29		51	68
900 Minimum labor/equipment charge	↓	8	Job		145		145	215L
09-001 COLUMNS Standard bricks @ $208 per M, 8" x 8", 9 brick	D-1	.286	V.L.F.	2.15	5.10		7.25	10.10
010 12" x 8", 13.5 brick		.432		3.25	7.70		10.95	15.30
020 12" x 12", 20.3 brick		.640		4.90	11.40		16.30	23
030 16" x 12", 27 brick		.842		6.50	15.05		21.55	30
040 16" x 16", 36 brick		1.140		8.65	20		28.65	41
050 20" x 16", 45 brick		1.450		10.80	26		36.80	51
060 20" x 20", 56.3 brick		1.780		13.55	32		45.55	63
070 24" x 20", 67.5 brick		2.290		16.20	41		57.20	80
080 24" x 24", 81 brick		2.670		19.45	48		67.45	94
100 36" x 36", 182.3 brick		5.330		44	95		139	195
900 Minimum labor/equipment charge	↓	8	Job		145		145	215L
10-001 COMMON BRICK Standard size, material only, minimum			M	180			180	200M
005 Average			"	200			200	220M
12-001 COPING For 12" wall, stock units, aluminum	D-1	.200	L.F.	5.50	3.57		9.07	11.50
005 Precast concrete, stock units, 6" wide		.160		3.50	2.86		6.36	8.20
010 10" wide		.178		4.70	3.17		7.87	10
015 14" wide		.200		5.10	3.57		8.67	11.05
030 Limestone for 12" wall, 4" thick		.178		8.25	3.17		11.42	13.90
035 6" thick		.200		11.50	3.57		15.07	18.10
050 Marble to 4" thick, no wash, 9" wide		.173		14.85	3.17		18.02	21
055 12" wide		.200		19.80	3.57		23.37	27
070 Terra cotta, 9" wide		.178		2.90	3.17		6.07	8
075 12" wide		.200		4.75	3.57		8.32	10.65
900 Minimum labor/equipment charge	↓	8	Job		145		145	215L
15-001 CORNICES Brick cornice on existing building								
002 Standard bricks @ $215 per M, minimum	D-1	.533	S.F.Face	3.35	9.50		12.85	18.15
011 Maximum		.696	"	3.35	12.40		15.75	23
900 Minimum labor/equipment charge	↓	10.670	Job		190		190	290L

18-001 FACE BRICK Prices Jan. 1985, C.L. lots, material only, not including truck delivery
002

		COLORS		
UNIT	RED	BUFF	GRAY	

NOTES

20" x 20" CHIMNEY Total per L.F. $34.65

37 bricks @ $200 per M	$ 7.40
.6 CF Type M mortar @ $2.20 per CF	1.30
12" x 12" Flue tile	4.65
.57 hr. 1 bricklayer @ $20.05 per Hr.	11.45
Scaffold rental	.95
.57 hr. 1 brick layer helper @ $15.65 per Hr.	8.90
TOTAL per L.F. high	$34.65

Note: For Foundation see Div. 3.3-14-050 & 051.

Chimney

For expanded coverage of these items see Means' *Concrete & Masonry Cost Data 1985*

Table II.16

CONSOLIDATED ESTIMATE

PROJECT **Commercial Renovation**

LOCATION

TAKE OFF BY **EBW**   PRICES BY **RSM**   QUANTITIES BY **EBW**

CLASSIFICATION

ARCHITECT

SHEET NO. **1 of 3**
ESTIMATE NO. **85-1**
DATE **1985**
CHECKED BY

DESCRIPTION	FLOOR	SOURCE	QUANTITY	UNIT	MATERIAL UNIT	MATERIAL TOTAL	LABOR UNIT	LABOR TOTAL	EQUIPMENT UNIT	EQUIPMENT TOTAL	SUBCONTRACTOR TOTAL INCL O&P UNIT	MAN-HOURS UNIT	MAN-HOURS TOTAL
Division 4: Masonry													
Needling Extra Floors @ Entrance	1	4.5-32-108	4	Ea.	32	128	144	576	31	124		8.89	36
		4.5-32-200	(2×4) 8	Ea.	32	256	65	520				4	32
Toothing @ Ext. Openings	1	4.5-60-052	80	VLF			4.^{13}	330				.267	21
Stone Lintel & Sill @ Elevator	1	4.4-25-210	5	CF	45	225	38	190	11	55		2	10
Brick @ Door Jambs (No material-Use exist'g) ☐+	1	4.2-09-030 9% Labor	80	VLF			15.^{05} 9%	1204 108				.842 9%	67 6
Brick Wall @ Ext. Elevator (No material-Use exist'g) ☐+	1	4.2-60-105 9% Labor	42	SF			10.^{30} 9%	432 39				.56 9%	24 2
Page Subtotals						609		3399		179			198

Table II.17

CONSOLIDATED ESTIMATE

PROJECT	Commercial Renovation				CLASSIFICATION		SHEET NO.	2 of 3
LOCATION		PRICES BY RSM					ESTIMATE NO.	85-1
TAKE OFF BY EBW		QUANTITIES BY EBW			ARCHITECT		DATE	1985
							CHECKED BY	

DESCRIPTION	FLOOR	SOURCE	QUANTITY	UNIT	MATERIAL UNIT	MATERIAL TOTAL	LABOR UNIT	LABOR TOTAL	EQUIPMENT UNIT	EQUIPMENT TOTAL	SUBCONTRACTOR UNIT	SUBCONTRACTOR TOTAL INCL O&P	MAN-HOURS UNIT	MAN-HOURS TOTAL
Division 4: Masonry														
High Pressure H2O Cleaning Ext.		4.5-12-044	11,900	SF			64	7616	14	1666			.04	476
Pedestrian Protection		4.5-12-420	10%	Job	10%		10%	761	10%	167			10%	48
Tarpaulins		1.1-68-020	1000	SF	10	100	17	170					.011	11
Move 6 Times		2 Laborers	6	Ea.			31	186					2	12
Cut & Repoint @ Exterior Walls		4.5-52-032	6000	SF	13	780	2.08	12480					.104	624
Cut & Repoint @ Store Foundation	1	4.5-52-090	370	LF	20	74	1.15	425					.057	21
Caulk @ Sills & Lintels		4.5-22-110	780	LF	36	281	1.28	998					.064	50
Cut & Repoint @ Chimney		4.5-52-032	140	SF	13	18	2.08	291					.104	15
Page Subtotals						1253		22927		1833				1257

Table II.18

Division 4

CONSOLIDATED ESTIMATE

PROJECT: Commercial Renovation
LOCATION:
PRICES BY: RSM
QUANTITIES BY: EBW
TAKE OFF BY: EBW
CLASSIFICATION:
ARCHITECT:
CHECKED BY:

DESCRIPTION	FLOOR	SOURCE	QUANTITY	UNIT	MATERIAL UNIT	MATERIAL TOTAL	LABOR UNIT	LABOR TOTAL	EQUIP. UNIT	EQUIP. TOTAL	SUBCONTRACTOR UNIT	TOTAL INCL. O&P	MAN-HOURS UNIT	MAN-HOURS TOTAL
Division 4: Masonry														
Concrete Block 8"	B	4.3-52-420	288	SF	1.17	337	1.95	562					.107	31
Lintels @ 3'×6' Doors		4.1-45-025	6	Ea.	9.25	74	3.54	28					.178	1
Concrete Block 12" (Elev. Shafts)		4.3-52-430	2696	SF	1.76	4745	2.52	6794					.141	380
Lintels @ Elev. Doors		4.1-45-040	12	Ea.	11.80	142	4.01	48					.2	2
Sandblast Int. Brick 2.5.6 +	1&3	4.5-12-142	2100	SF	(Add to Sub's Total)		TO BE SUBCONTRACTED →				.76	1596	.023	48
		43% Labor									.23	483	13%	6
Sandblast Int. Wood	1&2	4.5-12-142	11,800	SF							.76	8968	.023	271
Corn Chips 2.5.6 +		4.5-12-182	11,800	SF	(Add to Sub's Total)						.25	2950		
		43% Labor									.23	2714	13%	35
Page Subtotals						5298		7432		—		16711		774
Sheet 1						609		3399		179				198
Sheet 2 (Restoration)						1253		22927		1853				1257
Sheet 3						5298		7432				16711		774
Division 4 Totals						7160		33758		2012		16711		2229

Table II.19

Unless the contractor has a great deal of experience in masonry restoration, it is recommended that a knowledgeable architect or a historic preservationist be consulted regarding masonry cleaning and repair in older buildings. It is very easy to damage existing masonry if the wrong methods and materials are used. In this example the work is very clearly specified. High pressure water with no chemical cleaners is required (see Table II.18). The cleaning is to be performed during normal working hours. Pedestrian protection and tarpaulins are included (although not directly specified) to prevent the high volumes of water and mist from causing complaints or damage. Also, the type of mortar should be defined in detail. Modern mortars have different strengths and expansion/contraction properties from former types and can cause damage to old brick.

Sandblasting is often rejected as a method of cleaning exterior masonry because it destroys the weatherproof integrity of the masonry surface. For interior surfaces, however, it is widely used. In the sample project, the perimeter walls and wood ceiling of the new retail spaces, the entire second floor ceiling, and the perimeter walls of the third floor tenant space are to be sandblasted. A subcontractor will perform the work, but since the estimator has not yet received quotations, the costs must be calculated. Because the building is occupied by the existing retail tenant and is located in an active urban area, worker must take precautionary measures and perform the job after business hours. The appropriate factors are added to the costs. The factors (43%) are applied to labor costs only (see Tables II.19 and II.20). Since the work is to be subcontracted, the increase must be figured to include overhead and profit for the subcontractor. The calculations are shown in Table II.21. The 53.8% increase for subcontractor overhead and profit is the average for skilled labor as shown in Table II.22. The resulting costs are included in the estimate in Table II.19. Note that a factor of only 13% is added to the man-hours. This is because the overtime factor (30%) does not entail more time expended, only greater expense.

1.1 Overhead			CREW	MAN-HOURS	UNIT	BARE COSTS				TOTAL INCL O&P
						MAT.	LABOR	EQUIP.	TOTAL	
17-001 010	**FACTORS** To be added to construction costs for particular job requirements									
050 055	1	Cut & patch to match existing construction, add, minimum			Costs	2%	3%			
		Maximum				5%	9%			
080 085	2	Dust protection, add, minimum				1%	2%			
		Maximum				4%	11%			
110 115	3	Equipment usage curtailment, add, minimum				1%	1%			
		Maximum				3%	10%			
140 145	4	Material handling & storage limitation, add, minimum				1%	1%			
		Maximum				6%	7%			
170 175	5	Protection of existing work, add, minimum				2%	2%			
		Maximum				5%	7%			
200 205	6	Shift work requirements, add, minimum					5%			
		Maximum					30%			
230 235	7	Temporary shoring and bracing, add, minimum				2%	5%			
		Maximum				5%	12%			

Table II.20 Factors for Sandblasting (Division 4) from Division 1.1: Overhead

4.5 Masonry Restoration

No.	Description	CREW	MAN-HOURS	UNIT	MAT.	LABOR	EQUIP.	TOTAL	TOTAL INCL O&P
12-001	CLEANING MASONRY, no staging included								
020	Chemical cleaning, brush and wash, minimum	D-1	.020	S.F.	.02	.36		.38	.57
022	Average		.040		.03	.71		.74	1.12
024	Maximum		.048		.04	.87		.91	1.36
040	High pressure water only, minimum	B-9	.020			.32	.07	.39	.57
042	Average		.027			.43	.09	.52	.76
044	Maximum		.040			.64	.14	.78	1.14
080	High pressure water and chemical, minimum		.022		.02	.35	.08	.45	.65
082	Average		.033		.03	.53	.12	.68	.98
084	Maximum		.050		.04	.79	.18	1.01	1.47
120	Sandblast wet system, minimum		.023		.08	.36	.08	.52	.74
122	Average		.036		.10	.58	.13	.81	1.14
124	Maximum		.057		.12	.91	.20	1.23	1.76
140	Dry system, minimum		.016		.08	.25	.06	.39	.54
142	Average	▼	.023		.10	(.36)	.08	.54	.76
144	Maximum		.040		.12	.64	.14	.90	1.27
180	For walnut shells, add				.30			.30	.33M
182	For corn chips, add				.23			.23	.25M
200	Steam cleaning, minimum	B-9	.013			.21	.05	.26	.38
202	Average	▼	.016			.25	.06	.31	.46
204	Maximum		.027	▼		.43	.09	.52	.76
206									
400	Add for masking doors and windows			S.F.					.80
420	Add for pedestrian protection			Job					10%
440	Add for wire cut face brick			S.F.					.28
900	Minimum labor/equipment charge	D-4	16	Job		282	73	355	510
22-001	CAULKING MASONRY, no staging included								
005	Re-caulk only, oil base	1 Bric	.036	L.F.	.19	.71		.90	1.29
010	Butyl		.039		.37	.78		1.15	1.60
020	Polysulfide		.040		.36	.80		1.16	1.61
030	Silicone	▼	.041	▼	.89	.82		1.71	2.23
035									
100	Cut out and re-caulk, oil base	1 Bric	.055	L.F.	.19	1.11		1.30	1.89
105	Butyl		.062		.37	1.23		1.60	2.28
110	Polysulfide		.064		.36	1.28		1.64	2.35
115	Silicone	▼	.064	▼	.89	1.28		2.17	2.93
900	Minimum labor/equipment charge		2	Job		40		40	61L
32-001	NEEDLE MASONRY, includes shoring								
002									
040	Block, concrete, 8" thick	B-9	5.630	Ea.	32	90.05	19.95	142	195
042	12" thick		5.970		32	94	21	147	205
080	Brick, 4" thick with 8" backup block	▼	7.020	▼	32	110	25	167	235
081									

NOTES

Great care is needed in cleaning masonry surfaces. Consultation with the architect or client and a sample cleaning area are suggested for desired results.

(handwritten annotations)

Factors- [2] [5] [6] + − +

43% Labor Only

Bare Labor Cost .36

Bare Labor Increase (43%) .15

Labor O&P (53.8%) .08

Total Increase (incl. O&P) .23

BRICKWORK NEEDLE prices are for needling and shoring a masonry wall to install a new door or opening. The engineer on the project must specify how many needles are needed to support a given opening.

For expanded coverage of these items see Means' Concrete & Masonry Cost Data 1985

76

Table II.21

Table II.22

Abbr.	Trade	A Base Rate incl. fringes Hourly	A Daily	B Workers' Comp. Ins.	C Average Fixed Overhead	D Subs Overhead	E Subs Profit	F Subs Total Overhead & Profit %	G Amount	H Rate with Subs O. & P. Hourly	I Daily
					13.8%	16%	15%				
Skwk	Skilled Workers Average (35 trades)	$20.10	$160.80	9.0%				53.8%	$10.80	$30.90	$247.20
	Helpers Average (5 trades)	15.20	121.60	9.3				54.1	8.20	23.40	187.20
	Foremen Average, Inside (50¢ over trade)	20.60	164.80	9.0				53.8	11.10	31.70	253.60
	Foremen Average, Outside ($2.00 over trade)	22.10	176.80	9.0				53.8	11.90	34.00	272.00
Clab	Common Building Laborers	15.50	124.00	9.6				54.4	8.45	23.95	191.60
Asbe	Asbestos Workers	22.20	177.60	7.4				52.2	11.60	33.80	270.40
Boil	Boilermakers	22.30	178.40	6.7				51.5	11.50	33.80	270.40
Bric	Bricklayers	20.05	160.40	7.2				52.0	10.45	30.50	244.00
Brhe	Bricklayer Helpers	15.65	125.20	7.2				52.0	8.15	23.80	190.40
Carp	Carpenters	19.60	156.80	9.6				54.4	10.65	30.25	242.00
Cefi	Cement Finishers	18.80	150.40	5.5				50.3	9.45	28.25	226.00
Elec	Electricians	22.10	176.80	3.9				48.7	10.75	32.85	262.80
Elev	Elevator Constructors	22.15	177.20	5.3				50.1	11.10	33.25	266.00
Eqhv	Equipment Operators, Crane or Shovel	20.65	165.20	6.9				51.7	10.70	31.35	250.80
Eqmd	Equipment Operators, Medium Equipment	20.20	161.60	6.9				51.7	10.45	30.65	245.20
Eqlt	Equipment Operators, Light Equipment	19.05	152.40	6.9				51.7	9.85	28.90	231.20
Eqol	Equipment Operators, Oilers	17.10	136.80	6.9				51.7	8.85	25.95	207.60
Eqmm	Equipment Operators, Master Mechanics	21.45	171.60	6.9				51.7	11.10	32.55	260.40
Glaz	Glaziers	19.85	158.80	7.6				52.4	10.40	30.25	242.00
Lath	Lathers	19.75	158.00	5.8				50.6	10.00	29.75	238.00
Marb	Marble Setters	19.55	156.40	7.2				52.0	10.15	29.70	237.60
Mill	Millwrights	20.35	162.80	6.4				51.2	10.40	30.75	246.00
Mstz	Mosaic and Terrazzo Workers	19.35	154.80	5.2				50.0	9.70	29.05	232.40
Pord	Painters, Ordinary	18.85	150.80	7.2				52.0	9.80	28.65	229.20
Psst	Painters, Structural Steel	19.60	156.80	26.0				70.8	13.90	33.50	268.00
Pape	Paper Hangers	19.15	153.20	7.2				52.0	9.95	29.10	232.80
Pile	Pile Drivers	19.70	157.60	16.6				61.4	12.10	31.80	254.40
Plas	Plasterers	19.60	156.80	7.2				52.0	10.20	29.80	238.40
Plah	Plasterer Helpers	16.15	129.20	7.2				52.0	8.40	24.55	196.40
Plum	Plumbers	22.20	177.60	4.7				49.5	11.00	33.20	265.60
Rodm	Rodmen (Reinforcing)	21.30	170.40	15.9				60.7	12.95	34.25	274.00
Rofc	Roofers, Composition	18.35	146.80	17.1				61.9	11.35	29.70	237.60
Rots	Roofers, Tile & Slate	18.50	148.00	17.1				61.9	11.45	29.95	239.60
Rohe	Roofer Helpers (Composition)	13.45	107.60	17.1				61.9	8.35	21.80	174.40
Shee	Sheet Metal Workers	22.20	177.60	6.0				50.8	11.30	33.50	268.00
Spri	Sprinkler Installers	22.60	180.80	5.6				50.4	11.40	34.00	272.00
Stpi	Steamfitters or Pipefitters	22.30	178.40	4.7				49.5	11.05	33.35	266.80
Ston	Stone Masons	19.85	158.80	7.2				52.0	10.30	30.15	241.20
Sswk	Structural Steel Workers	21.30	170.40	19.5				64.3	13.70	35.00	280.00
Tilf	Tile Layers (Floor)	19.25	154.00	5.1				49.9	9.60	28.85	230.80
Tilh	Tile Layer Helpers	15.25	122.00	5.1				49.9	7.60	22.85	182.80
Trlt	Truck Drivers, Light	16.00	128.00	8.4				53.2	8.50	24.50	196.00
Trhv	Truck Drivers, Heavy	16.20	129.60	8.4				53.2	8.60	24.80	198.40
Sswl	Welders, Structural Steel	21.30	170.40	19.5				64.3	13.70	35.00	280.00
Wrck	*Wrecking	15.50	124.00	20.7				65.5	10.15	25.65	205.20

*Not included in Averages.

CONTRACTOR'S OVERHEAD AND PROFIT

To the left are the average subcontractor's percentage mark-ups that should be applied directly to all labor rates in order to arrive at typical billing rates for subcontractors.

Column A:
Base rates including fringe benefits are described in Column A in hourly and daily terms. These figures are the sum of the base rate, employer-paid fringe benefits such as vacation pay, employer-paid health and welfare costs, pension costs, plus appropriate training and industry advancement funds costs.

Column B:
National average Workmen's Compensation rate by trade.

Column C:
Column C lists the average fixed overhead figures for all trades. In particular, Federal and State Unemployment costs are set at 5.5%, Social Security Taxes (FICA) are set at 7.05%, Builder's Risk Insurance costs are set at 0.38%; and Public Liability costs are set at 0.82%. These overhead costs are analyzed below. All the percentages except those for Social Security Taxes vary from state to state as well as from company to company.

Columns D & E:
Percentages in Columns D & E are based on the presumption that the subcontractor being used in any given project has an annual billing rate of $250,000. Smaller subcontractors' percentages for overhead are usually higher.
The overhead percentages for a subcontractor vary greatly and depend on a number of factors: the subcontractor's annual volume; his engineering and logistical support costs, his staff requirements, and the size of the equipment he is required to use on a particular construction project. The figures for overhead and profit will vary depending on the type of job, the job location, and the prevailing economic conditions. These factors should be examined very carefully for each job. For the purpose of estimating the cost of a project, it is reasonable to assume a 16% cost for the subcontractor's overhead, and a 15% cost for the subcontractor's profit.

Column F:
Column F lists the total of columns B, C, D, and E.

Column G:
Column G is Column A (hourly base labor rate) multiplied by the percentage in Column F (Sub's O&P percentage).

Column H:
Column H is the total of Column A (hourly base labor rate) plus Column G (Sub's O&P hourly rate).

Column I:
Column I is Column H multiplied by eight hours.

Mass. State Unemployment Tax ranges from 1.5% to 5.7% plus a small experience rating assessment the following year on the first $7,000. Federal Unemployment tax is 3.5% of the first $7,000 of wages. This is reduced by a credit for payment to the state. The minimum Federal Unemployment tax is 0.8% after all credits.

Combined rates in Mass. vary from 2.3% to 6.5% of the first $7,000 of wages. The combined average U.S. rate is about 5.5% of the first $7,000. Contractors with permanent workers will pay less, since the theoretical annual wage for skilled worker is $20.10 X 2,000 hours, or about $40,200 per year. The average combined rate for the U.S. would therefore be 5.50% x 7,000 ÷ 40,200 = 0.96% of total wages.

173

CONSOLIDATED ESTIMATE

PROJECT Commercial Renovation
LOCATION
TAKE OFF BY EBW PRICES BY RSM QUANTITIES BY EBW
CLASSIFICATION
ARCHITECT

SHEET NO. 1 of 2
ESTIMATE NO. 85-1
DATE 1985
CHECKED BY

Division 5: metals

DESCRIPTION	FLOOR	SOURCE	QUANTITY	UNIT	MATERIAL UNIT	MATERIAL TOTAL	LABOR UNIT	LABOR TOTAL	EQUIP. UNIT	EQUIP. TOTAL	SUBCONTR. UNIT	SUBCONTR. TOTAL INCL O & P	MAN-HOURS UNIT	MAN-HOURS TOTAL
Steel Col.	B	Quote (mat. Only)	1	Ea.	150	150								
Expansion Anchors		5.8-12-120	4	Ea.	8.10	32	Min	39					.123	1
Lag Bolts		5.8-17-030	4	Ea.	75	3	1.84	7					.094	1
Drill-Concrete		5.8-03-060	4	Ea.	61	1	7.45	30					.381	2
Drill-Timber		5.8-35-080	12	In.			35	4					.018	1
Ladder To Roof	3	5.4-44-001	12	VLF							74	888	.64	8
Wall Railings:														
Exist'g Stair		5.4-58-350	78	LF							13.55	1057	.125	10
New Stair		5.4-58-350	52	LF							13.55	705	.125	6
New metal Stair		5.4-64-020	36	Ris.							191.45	6892	.711	26
4'-0" wide		5.4-64-110									57.6			2
Landings		5.4-64-150	72	SF							30	2160	.20	14
Subcontract Total												11702		
Page Subtotals						(186)		(80)				(11702)		(71)

SUB CONTRACT →

Table II.23

CONSOLIDATED ESTIMATE

PROJECT	Commercial Renovation		SHEET NO.	2 of 2
LOCATION		CLASSIFICATION	ESTIMATE NO.	85-1
TAKE OFF BY EBW	PRICES BY RSM	ARCHITECT	DATE	1985
	QUANTITIES BY EBW		CHECKED BY	

DESCRIPTION	FLOOR	SOURCE	QUANTITY	UNIT	BARE COSTS						SUBCONTRACTOR		MAN-HOURS	
					MATERIAL		LABOR		EQUIPMENT					
					UNIT	TOTAL	UNIT	TOTAL	UNIT	TOTAL	UNIT	TOTAL INCL. O & P	UNIT	TOTAL
Division 5: Metals														
Beam Hangers @ Roof Openings	R	5.8-35-180 (19 Openings - 4 Ea.)	76	Ea	1.05	80	1.01	77					.052	4
Stud Driver:														
Chargers		5.8-32-030	3	C	12.25	37								
Studs		5.8-32-060	3	C	30	90								
Page Subtotals						207		77						4
Sheet 1						186		80				11702		71
Sheet 2						207		77						4
Division 5 Totals						393		157				11702		75

Table II.24

Division 5: Metals

The specified wide flange steel column at the elevator pit is 4' high with special bearing plates. This is a unique item and requires a quotation from a steel fabricator for the material cost. The quotation would most likely come from the subcontractor who will be installing the new stairs. Since this is a single, odd item, the installation must be visualized in order to estimate it properly. Tables II.23 and II.24 are the estimate sheets for Division 5.

Table II.25 lists costs for structural steel. Note on line 52-900 that the minimum labor and equipment charges are $585 and $395, respectively. If the estimator does not use common sense, the total installation costs for this single, small column could be $980. When using *Repair and Remodeling Cost Data* or any other data source, the estimator must be aware of the crew and equipment necessary for installation. The crew listed for the minimum labor and equipment charges in Table II.25, is E-2, shown in Table II.26. The minimum charge is for a half day. Obviously this kind of crew and equipment is not required for the column installation in the sample estimate. The specifications call for expansion bolts into the concrete footing and lag bolts into the wood beam above. These are easily priced as shown in Table II.23. Note that drilling the holes is a separate item. The crew used for these prices is one carpenter. There is a minimum charge of $39 for the expansion anchors, substantially less than $980. A little extra time and sound judgement can help to prevent expensive mistakes. The temporary shoring and bracing is included in Division 2, Table II.5.

5.1 Structural Metals	CREW	MAN-HOURS	UNIT	MAT.	LABOR	EQUIP.	TOTAL	TOTAL INCL O&P
52-001 STRUCTURAL STEEL Bolted, including fabrication								
005 Beams, 6 WF 9	E-2	.078	L.F.	4.50	1.62	1.10	7.22	8.75
010 8 WF 10		.078		5	1.62	1.10	7.72	9.30
015 10 WF 15		.078		7.50	1.62	1.10	10.22	12.05
020 Columns, 6 WF 15.5		.104		7.75	2.17	1.46	11.38	13.60
025 8 WF 31		.104		15.50	2.17	1.46	19.13	22
050 Girders, 12 WF 22		.062		11	1.30	.88	13.18	15.15
055 14 WF 26		.062		13	1.30	.88	15.18	17.35
060 16 WF 31	▼	.062	▼	16.50	1.30	.88	18.68	21
070 Joists (bar joists, H series), span to 30'	E-7	.003	Lb.	.30	.06	.03	.39	.45
075 Span to 50'	E-7	.004	Lb.	.28	.08	.05	.41	.50
080 Not including trucking								
900 Minimum labor/equipment charge	E-2	28	Job		585	395	980	1,375

Table II.25

Crew E-2	Hr.	Daily	Hr.	Daily	Bare Costs	Incl. O&P
1 Struc. Steel Foreman	$23.30	$186.40	$38.30	$306.40	$20.89	$33.65
4 Struc. Steel Workers	21.30	681.60	35.00	1120.00		
1 Equip. Oper. (crane)	20.65	165.20	31.35	250.80		
1 Equip. Oper. Oiler	17.10	136.80	25.95	207.60		
1 Crane, 90 Ton		790.00		869.00	14.10	15.51
56 M.H., Daily Totals		$1960.00		$2753.80	$34.99	$49.16

Table II.26

5.4 Misc. & Ornamental Metals

		CREW	MAN-HOURS	UNIT	MAT.	LABOR	EQUIP.	TOTAL	TOTAL INCL O&P
63					BARE COSTS				
030	Stock, no supports or frames incl. alum. extrusions, minimum			S.F.	3.50			3.50	3.85M
050	Maximum				12			12	13.20M
070	Slotted aluminum sheets, minimum				1.20			1.20	1.32M
080	Maximum				3			3	3.30M
900	Minimum labor/equipment charge	1 Sswk	4	Job		85		85	140L
64-001	STAIR Steel, 3'-6" wide, grating tread, safety nosing, steel								
002	stringers and pipe railing, stock units	E-4	.711	Riser	100	15.50	1.25	116.75	135
020	Cement fill metal pan and picket rail	"	.711		135	15.50	1.25	151.75	175
060	For isolated stairs, add					100%			
080	Custom steel stairs, minimum	E-4	.711		135	15.50	1.25	151.75	175
081	Average		.914		170	20.39	1.61	192	220
090	Maximum		1.280		200	27.74	2.26	230	270
110	For 4' wide stairs, add				10%	5%			
130	For 5' wide stairs, add				20%	10%			
150	Landing, steel pan, conventional	E-4	.200	S.F.	20	4.36	.35	24.71	30
181	Spiral aluminum, 5'-0" diameter, stock units		.711	Riser	135	15.50	1.25	151.75	175
182	Custom units		.711		200	15.50	1.25	216.75	245
183	Stock units, 4'-0" diameter, safety treads		.640		135	13.97	1.13	150.10	175
184	Oak treads		.640		85	13.97	1.13	100.10	120
185	5'-0" diameter, safety treads		.711		150	15.50	1.25	166.75	190
186	Oak treads		.711		100	15.50	1.25	116.75	135
187	6'-0" diameter, safety treads		.800		175	17.44	1.41	193.85	225
188	Oak treads		.800		125	17.44	1.41	143.85	170
190	Spiral, cast iron, 4'-0" diameter, ornamental, minimum		.711		125	15.50	1.25	141.75	165
192	Maximum		1.280		185	27.74	2.26	215	250
200	Spiral, steel, industrial checkered plate, 4'-6" diameter		.711		90	15.50	1.25	106.75	125
220	Stock units, 6'-0" diameter		.800		105	17.44	1.41	123.85	145
240	Custom units, 4' to 6' diameter, minimum		.711		50	15.50	1.25	66.75	82
250	Maximum		1.070		225	23.12	1.88	250	290
390	Inclined ladder type, 3' wide, steel		.320	V.L.F.	75	6.99	.56	82.55	95
400	Aluminum		.320	"	150	6.99	.56	157.55	175
900	Minimum labor/equipment charge		16	Job		347	28	375	605
72-001	WEATHERVANES Residential types, minimum	1 Carp	1	Ea.	15	19.60	.16	34.60	47
010	Maximum		4	"	550	78	.19	628	725
900	Minimum labor/equipment charge		2	Job		39		39	61L
74-001	WINDOW GUARDS Expanded metal, steel angle frame, permanent	E-4	.091	S.F.	10	1.99	.16	12.15	14.45
002	Steel bars, 1/2" x 1/2", spaced 5" O.C.	"	.110	"	5.50	2.41	.19	8.10	10.20
003	Hinge mounted, add			Opng.	15.75			15.75	17.30M
004	Removable type, add			"	10			10	11M
005	For galvanized guards, add			S.F.	35%				
007	For pivoted or projected type, add			"	110%	40%			

NOTES

STAIR design is affected by story height and building occupancy. There are a variety of code requirements and general rules including:

- Maximum height between landings is 12'

- Usual stair angle is 20° to 50° with 30° to 35° best.

- Usual relation of riser to tread is:
  Riser + tread = 17.5
  2 x (Riser) + tread = 25
  Riser x tread = 70 or 75.

- Maximum riser height is 7-1/2" for commercial, 8" for residential.

- Usual riser height is 6-1/2" to 7-1/4".

- Minimum tread width is 9".

Table II.27

It should be noted that there is relatively little structural metal work in this sample project or in any efficiently designed commercial renovation. This keeps the costs down and makes renovation a favorable alternative, in terms of cost, to new construction. Whether the work is planned by an architect or by the contractor, the designer should try to work with and around the existing structural elements.

The new stairway, ladder, and railings are to be subcontracted to a steel fabricator. The estimator has received quotations but feels that they are not quite right, either too high or too low, based upon past experience. The costs are included in the estimate as a crosscheck in Table II.23. These costs are subtotaled so that the quotation can easily be substituted in the Estimate Summary. The costs are obtained from Table II.27. The added percentages for 4' width must be incorporated into the total including overhead and profit. The calculations are shown in Table II.28. The 64.3% figure for labor overhead and profit is obtained by noting the crew (E-4, comprised of steel workers and referring to Table II.22, Column F, for "Welders, Structural Steel."

The specifications (and building codes) require that the contractor place fire extinguishers at every level when welding. Since the extinguishers will be in place throughout the project for all trades, they are included in Division 1. Tables II.29a and II.29b show the Project Overhead Summary as items are added throughout the estimate. The purchase of a powder-actuated stud driver is also listed as project overhead because it will be used for future jobs. The charges and studs to be used only for this job are included in Table II.24.

	Bare Costs			
Line Item	Material	Labor	Equipment	Total Including O&P
5.4-64-020	$135.00	$15.50	$1.25	
5.4-64-110	(10%) 13.50	(5%) .77		
	148.50	16.27	1.25	
Overhead and Profit	(10%) 14.85	(64.3%) 10.46	(10%) .12	
	$163.35	$26.73	$1.37	$191.45

Adding Bare Cost Percentages to Total Including Overhead and Profit

Table II.28

178

PROJECT	Commercial Renovation			SHEET NO.	1 of 2
LOCATION				ESTIMATE NO.	85-1
ARCHITECT		OWNER		DATE	1985
QUANTITIES BY EBW	PRICES BY RSM	EXTENSIONS BY		CHECKED BY	

DESCRIPTION	man-Hours	QUANTITY	UNIT	MATERIAL		LABOR		EQUIP., FEES, RENTAL	
				UNIT	TOTAL	UNIT	TOTAL	UNIT	TOTAL
Job Organization: (Superintendent)									
Accounting and bookkeeping									
Timekeeper and material clerk									
Clerical									
Shop									
Safety, watchman and first aid									
1.1-22-105			WK			765			
Engineering: Layout									
Quantities									
Inspection									
Shop drawings									
Drafting & extra prints									
Testing: Soil									
Materials									
Structural									
Supplies: Office									
Shop									
Utilities: ~~Light and~~ power		28	MSF					84	2352
Water									
Heating									
Lighting 1.1-58-350	(66)	280	CSF	1⁶⁹	473	5²⁰	1456		
Equipment: Rental									
Light trucks									
Freight and hauling									
Loading, unloading, erecting, etc.									
Maintenance									
Dumpster 2.2-78-080			WK					150	
Travel Expense									
Main office personnel									
Freight and Express									
Demurrage									
Hauling, misc.									
Advertising Job Sign		1	Ea.		250				
Signs and Barricades									
Temporary fences									
Temporary stairs, ladders & floors									
Rails @ Stairs & Elev.	(22)	270	LF	1²⁴	335	1⁵⁷	424		
~~Photos~~ 1.1-58-310									
Page total									

Table II.29a

Division 1 Sheet 2 of 2 DESCRIPTION	QUANTITY	UNIT	MATERIAL		LABOR		EQUIP., FEES, RENTAL	
			UNIT	TOTAL	UNIT	TOTAL	UNIT	TOTAL
Total Brought Forward								
Legal Contract Review							100	100
Medical and Hospitalization								
Field Offices								
Office furniture and equipment								
Telephones		mo.					100	
Heat and Light								
Temporary toilets								
Storage areas and sheds								
Permits: Building								
Misc. Street Use	1	Ea.					50	50
Sewer Connection	1	Ea.					300	300
Insurance								
Bonds								
Interest								
Taxes								
Cutting and Patching & Punch list								
Winter Protection								
Temporary heat								
Snow plowing								
Thawing materials								
Temporary Roads								
Rent 6 Parking Spaces		mo.					300	
Repairs to adjacent property								
Pumping								
Scaffolding 1.1-44-010 (170)	119	CSF			28	3332		
Rental -381 Frames - #2$\frac{35}{}$/mo.		Mo.						
Small Tools								
Stud Driver 5.8-32-001	1	Ea.	285	285				
Clean up								
Final 1.1-04-010								
Contingencies (44)	28	mSF	1$\frac{52}{}$	43	24$\frac{76}{}$	693	1$\frac{24}{}$	35
Main Office Expense								
Special Items								
Fire Exting. 15.4-20-208	4	Ea.	41	164				
Total: Transfer to meansco Form 110 or 115								

Table II.29b

Division 6: Wood and Plastics

The use of wood in commercial renovation is often dependent upon two factors: the type of existing construction and the local building code requirements for fire-resistance. When the use of wood (whether structural, rough, or finish) is permitted in buildings of fire-resistant construction, fire-retardant treatment is usually specified. Because the interior structure of the sample project is wood, such treatment is not required. Light gauge metal studs are becoming more common in commercial renovation because they are lightweight and easy to install. It is easier for a carpenter, with a pair of tin snips and a screw gun, to cut and install metal studs to conform to existing conditions than to do the same with wood. Also, with the wide use of materials such as metal door frames and vinyl base, wood is becoming less prevalent as a primary material in commercial renovation as well as new construction. On some projects, it is not unusual for a carpenter never to work with wood at all.

In this example, metal studs are specified for all interior, non-load bearing partitions. Wood is specified only to match existing work, and for blocking and framing for fixtures and equipment. Tables II.30, II.31 and II.32 are the estimate sheets for Division 6.

To frame the floor openings at the freight elevator, contractors use planking that has been removed from other areas, so no material costs are included. The planks must be cut to match existing conditions. This work will occur in the late stages of the renovation, so a factor for protection of existing work must be applied.

The roof openings for hatches and skylights are also framed, using existing materials (see Figure II.16). In Division 2, the costs for cutting the openings were calculated by determining the crew size and time required. The same method and crew are used to price the framing because the two will be done together.

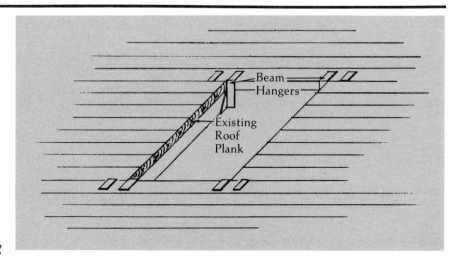

Figure II.16 Framing and Roof Opening

Division 6

CONSOLIDATED ESTIMATE

PROJECT: Commercial Renovation
PRICES BY: RSM
QUANTITIES BY: EBW
TAKE OFF BY: EBW
CLASSIFICATION
ARCHITECT
CHECKED BY

Division 6: Wood & Plastics — Rough Carpentry

Description	Floor	Source	Quantity	Unit	Material Unit	Material Total	Labor Unit	Labor Total	Equip. Unit	Equip. Total	Man-Hours Unit	Man-Hours Total
Blocking - 2x8	All	6.1-02-246	.125	MBF	335	42	579	72	26	3	29.6	4
Blocking - 2x4 @ Door Frames	All	6.1-02-262	.314	MBF	315	99	924	290	41	13	47.06	15
Stud Wall @ Elec. Meters	B	6.1-58-038	10	LF	397	40	3.92	39	18	2	.20	2
Plywood @ Elec. & Telephone		6.1-90-070	196	SF	41	80 min		78	9	2	.015	3
Infill Elev. Openings (Use existing material) 10% Labor		6.1-43-110	639	BF	32			192	9	6	.010	10
10% Labor					10%		10%	19			10%	1
Frame Roof Openings		Crew F-2	1.5	Day			313.60	470	14	21	16	24
9% Labor		9% Labor					9%	42	9%		9%	2
Underlayment	1	6.1-86-001	390	SF	34	133	5	82	1		.011	4
	2&3	6.1-86-001	2060	SF	34	707	5	437	1	21	.011	23
Page Subtotals						(1011)		(1721)		(72)		(88)

Table II.30

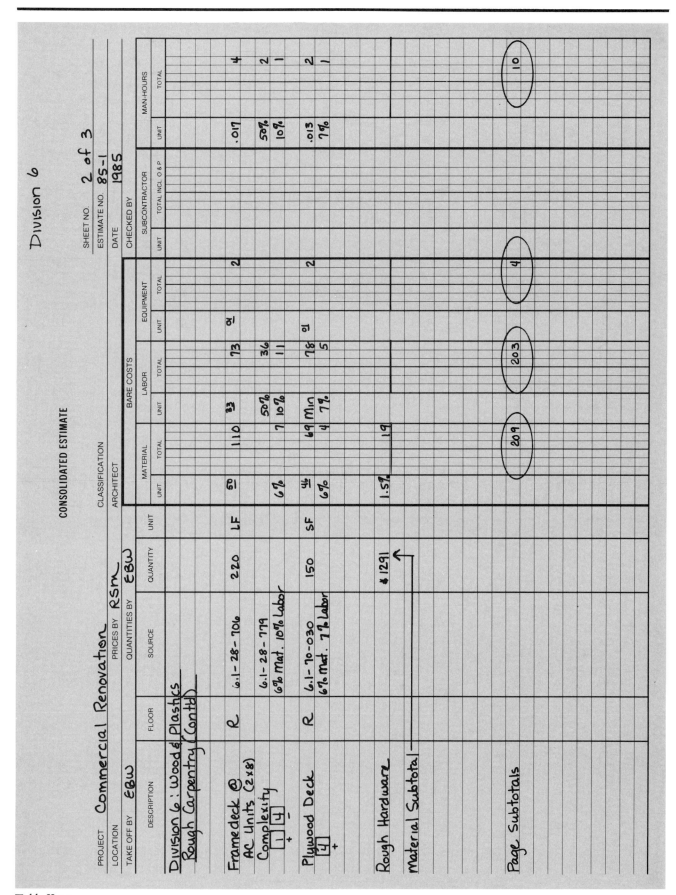

CONSOLIDATED ESTIMATE

SHEET NO.	2 of 3					
ESTIMATE NO.	85-1					
DATE	1985					
CHECKED BY						

PROJECT Commercial Renovation
LOCATION   PRICES BY RSM
TAKE OFF BY EBW   QUANTITIES BY EBW
CLASSIFICATION
ARCHITECT

DESCRIPTION	FLOOR	SOURCE	QUANTITY	UNIT	MATERIAL UNIT	MATERIAL TOTAL	LABOR UNIT	LABOR TOTAL	EQUIP. UNIT	EQUIP. TOTAL	SUBCONTR. UNIT	SUBCONTR. TOTAL INCL. O&P	MAN-HOURS UNIT	MAN-HOURS TOTAL
Division 6: Wood & Plastics														
Rough Carpentry (Cont'd)														
Frame deck @														
AC Units (2×8)	R	6.1-28-706	220	LF	50	110	33	73	9	2			.017	4
Complexity [1][4] + -		6.1-28-779			6%	7	50%	36					50%	2
		6% Mat. 10% Labor					10%	11					10%	1
Plywood Deck	R	6.1-70-030	150	SF	44	49 Min	18	78	9	2			.013	2
[4] +		6% Mat. 7% Labor			6%	4	7%	5					7%	1
Rough Hardware			$1291		1.5%	19								
Material Subtotal														
Page Subtotals						209		203		4				10

Table II.31

CONSOLIDATED ESTIMATE

PROJECT	Commercial Renovation													
LOCATION		PRICES BY RSM							SHEET NO. 3 of 3					
QUANTITIES BY EBW									ESTIMATE NO. 85-1					
TAKE OFF BY EBW					CLASSIFICATION				DATE 1985					
					ARCHITECT				CHECKED BY					

DESCRIPTION	FLOOR	SOURCE	QUANTITY	UNIT	MATERIAL UNIT	MATERIAL TOTAL	LABOR UNIT	LABOR TOTAL	EQUIPMENT UNIT	EQUIPMENT TOTAL	SUBCONTRACTOR UNIT	SUBCONTRACTOR TOTAL INCL O&P	MAN-HOURS UNIT	MAN-HOURS TOTAL
Division 6: Wood & Plastics														
Finish Carpentry														
Shelves @ Jan. Closets	2&3	6.2-64-060	30	LF	94	28	2 09	63	09	3			.107	3
Vanities: Base	2&3	6.2-88-810	4	Ea.	140	560	39	166					2	8
Top	"	6.4-80-150	12	LF	2 25	27	6 25	75					.32	4
Backsplash	"	6.4-80-260	12	LF	65	8	4 36	52					.222	3
Cutouts	"	6.4-80-390	6	Ea.			13 05	78					.667	4
Window Sills	2&3													
material		Quotation (Incl. Milling)	116	LF	1 50	174								
Installation		6.2-51-510	116	LF			1 05	122					.053	6
3% Labor							3%	4					3%	1
Grounds (@ sills, headers, & jambs)		6.1-54-010	606	LF	7	42	55	333					.028	17
Page Subtotals						839		883		3				46
Rough: Sheet 1						1101		1721		12				88
Sheet 2						209		203		4				10
Subtotal						1310		1924		76				98
Finish: Sheet 3						839		883		3				46
Division 6 Totals						2149		2807		79				144

Table II.32

The exterior walls of older masonry buildings are usually very thick. Oversized window sills are required. The plans specify solid oak for the sills as shown in Figure II.17. A material price is obtained from a local supplier. Note that 1 x 10 (nominal) boards are needed, cut to 8" wide and surfaced 3 sides. Installation is similar to that of normal window stools, so line item 6.2-51-510, in Table II.33, is used for labor only. A factor is added for cutting to conform to the variations in wall thickness and window installation.

In Table II.32, the quantities for the sills and grounds are 116 L.F. and 606 L.F., respectively. It is important to record how these, and all quantities, are derived for cross-checking and future reference. A Quantity Sheet, as shown in Table II.34, is useful to keep track of this information. Sketches are helpful to show how dimensions are obtained.

The first floor windows receive no sills or grounds because the windows at the existing retail space are already finished and trimmed, and the exterior walls in the new retail spaces will be sandblasted. The existing stone sills will remain exposed.

All windows on the second floor, except in the stairways, will receive grounds and sills. On the third floor, the walls in the tenant space will be sandblasted, so only the remaining eleven windows are included. Walls in the stairways will also be sandblasted.

In order to price rough hardware for the project, the material costs for rough carpentry must be totalled, as shown in Table II.32. The costs for rough hardware are shown in Table II.35 as a minimum and a maximum. The maximum percentage is used because material costs are slightly low due to the use of existing materials for some of the work.

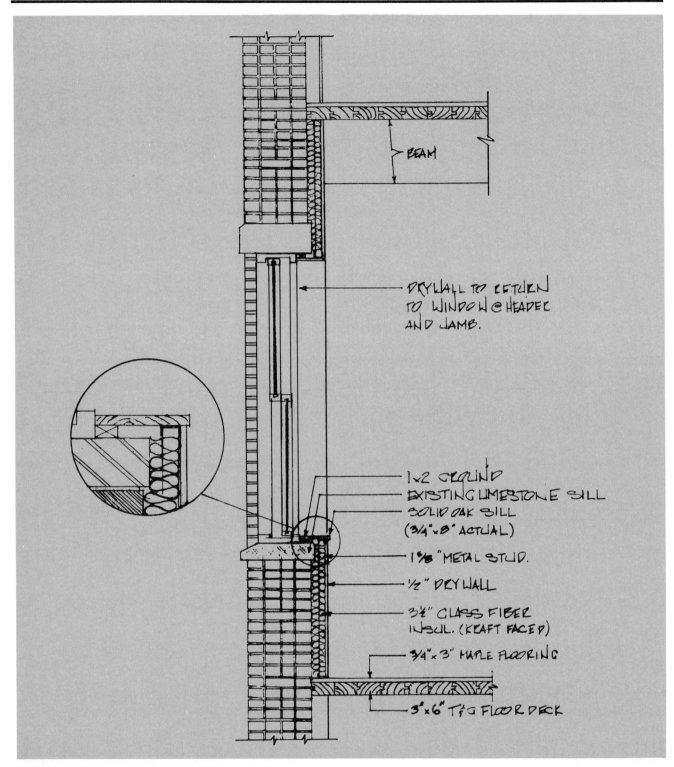

BEAM

DRYWALL TO RETURN
TO WINDOW @ HEADER
AND JAMB.

1×2 GROUND
EXISTING LIMESTONE SILL
SOLID OAK SILL
(3/4"×8" ACTUAL)

1⅝" METAL STUD.

½" DRY WALL

3¼" GLASS FIBER
INSUL. (KRAFT FACED)

3/4"×3" MAPLE FLOORING

3"×6" T+G FLOOR DECK

Figure II.17 Typical Section @ Window

186

6.2 Finish Carpentry

Stool Cap

		CREW	MAN-HOURS	UNIT	BARE COSTS MAT.	LABOR	EQUIP.	TOTAL	TOTAL INCL O&P	NOTES
51-001	**MOLDINGS, WINDOW AND DOOR**									
002										
280	Door moldings, stock, decorative, 1-1/8" wide, plain	1 Carp	.471	Set	17.40	9.20		26.60	33	
290	Detailed	"	.471	"	30	9.20		39.20	47	
310	Door trim, interior, including headers,									
315	stops and casings, 2 sides, pine, 2-1/2" wide	1 Carp	1.360	Opng.	18	27		45	61	
317	4-1/2" wide		1.510	"	23	30		53	71	
320	Glass beads, stock pine, 1/4" x 11/16"		.028	L.F.	.14	.55		.69	1	
325	3/8" x 1/2"		.029		.17	.57		.74	1.07	
327	3/8" x 7/8"		.030		.20	.58		.78	1.12	
485	Parting bead, stock pine, 3/8" x 3/4"		.029		.13	.57		.70	1.02	
487	1/2" x 3/4"		.031		.19	.61		.80	1.16	
500	Stool caps, stock pine, 11/16" x 3-1/2"		.040		.70	.78		1.48	1.98	
510	1-1/16" x 3-1/4"		.053		1.79	1.05		2.84	3.58	
530	Threshold, oak, 3' long, inside, 5/8" x 3-5/8"		.250	Ea.	3.94	4.90		8.84	11.90	
540	Outside, 1-1/2" x 7-5/8"		.500	"	14.70	9.80		24.50	31	
590	Window trim sets, including casings, header, stops,									
591	stool and apron, 2-1/2" wide, minimum	1 Carp	.615	Opng.	9	12.05		21.05	29	
595	Average		.800		11.50	15.70		27.20	37	
600	Maximum		1.330		14	26		40	56	
900	Minimum labor/equipment charge		2	Job		39		39	61L	
53-001	**PANELING, BOARDS**									
002										
640	Wood board paneling, 3/4" thick, knotty pine	F-2	.053	S.F.	.73	1.04	.05	1.82	2.47	
650	Rough sawn cedar		.053		1.42	1.04	.05	2.51	3.23	
670	Redwood, clear, 1" x 4" boards		.053		2.60	1.04	.05	3.69	4.52	
690	Aromatic cedar, closet lining, boards		.058		1.52	1.14	.05	2.71	3.49	
900	Minimum labor/equipment charge	1 Carp	4	Job		78		78	120L	
56-001	**PANELING, HARDBOARD**									
002	Not incl. furring or trim, hardboard, tempered, 1/8" thick	F-2	.032	S.F.	.22	.63	.03	.88	1.24	
010	1/4" thick		.032		.34	.63	.03	1	1.37	
030	Tempered pegboard, 1/8" thick		.032		.22	.63	.03	.88	1.24	
040	1/4" thick		.032		.35	.63	.03	1.01	1.38	
060	Untempered hardboard, natural finish, 1/8" thick		.032		.19	.63	.03	.85	1.21	
070	1/4" thick		.032		.25	.63	.03	.91	1.27	
090	Untempered pegboard, 1/8" thick		.032		.20	.63	.03	.86	1.22	
100	1/4" thick		.032		.33	.63	.03	.99	1.36	
120	Plastic faced hardboard, 1/8" thick		.032		.38	.63	.03	1.04	1.42	
130	1/4" thick		.032		.51	.63	.03	1.17	1.56	
150	Plastic faced pegboard, 1/8" thick		.032		.36	.63	.03	1.02	1.39	
160	1/4" thick		.032		.45	.63	.03	1.11	1.49	

For expanded coverage of these items see Means' *Interior Cost Data 1985*

Table II.33

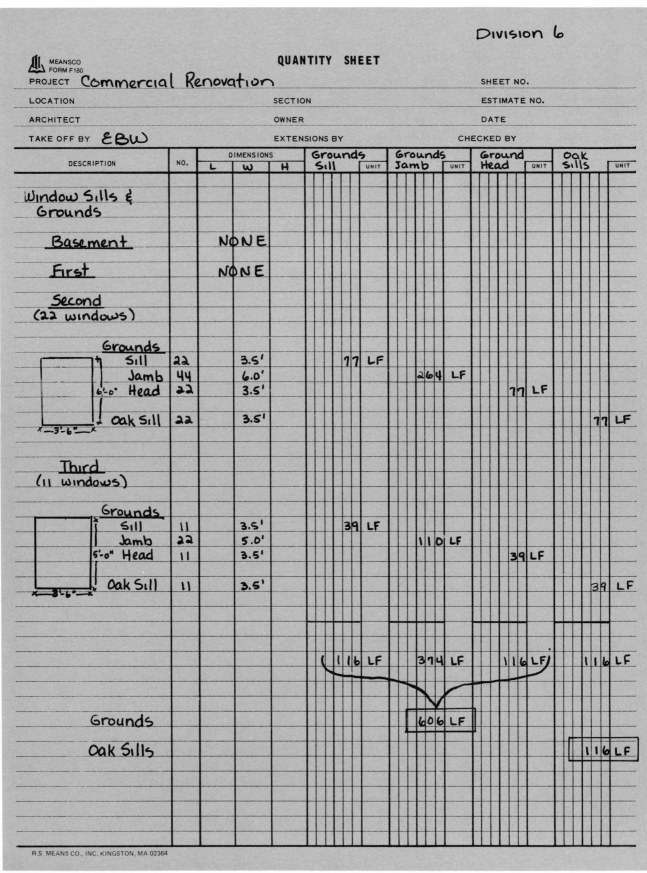

QUANTITY SHEET

MEANSCO FORM F180

PROJECT Commercial Renovation   SHEET NO.

LOCATION   SECTION   ESTIMATE NO.

ARCHITECT   OWNER   DATE

TAKE OFF BY EBW   EXTENSIONS BY   CHECKED BY

DESCRIPTION	NO.	L	W	H	Grounds Sill	UNIT	Grounds Jamb	UNIT	Ground Head	UNIT	Oak Sills	UNIT
Window Sills & Grounds												
Basement		NONE										
First		NONE										
Second (22 windows)												
Grounds Sill	22		3.5'		77	LF						
Jamb	44		6.0'				264	LF				
Head	22		3.5'						77	LF		
Oak Sill	22		3.5'								77	LF
Third (11 windows)												
Grounds Sill	11		3.5'		39	LF						
Jamb	22		5.0'				110	LF				
Head	11		3.5'						39	LF		
Oak Sill	11		3.5'								39	LF
					116	LF	374	LF	116	LF	116	LF
Grounds							606	LF				
Oak Sills											116	LF

R.S. MEANS CO., INC. KINGSTON, MA 02364

Table II.34

6.1 Rough Carpentry

		CREW	MAN-HOURS	UNIT	MAT.	LABOR	EQUIP.	TOTAL	TOTAL INCL O&P
						BARE COSTS			
070	Douglas fir, 3" thick	F-2	.050	S.F.	2.45	.98	.04	3.47	4.26
080	4" thick		.064		3.12	1.25	.06	4.43	5.45
100	Hemlock, 3" thick		.050		2.36	.98	.04	3.38	4.16
110	4" thick		.064		3.03	1.25	.06	4.34	5.35
130	Western white spruce, 3" thick		.050		2.45	.98	.04	3.47	4.26
140	4" thick		.064		3.12	1.25	.06	4.43	5.45
900	Minimum labor/equipment charge	F-1	4	Job		78.50	3.50	82	125
66-001	ROOF TRUSSES For timber connector trusses, see div. 5.8-35								
010	Fink (W) or King post type, 2'-0" O.C.								
020	Metal plate connected, 4 in 12 slope								
021	24' to 29' span	F-3	.013	S.F.Flr.	.87	.27	.08	1.22	1.45
030	30' to 43' span		.013		.93	.27	.08	1.28	1.52
040	44' to 60' span		.013		1.40	.27	.08	1.75	2.04
060	For change in roof pitch, add				.06			.06	.06M
070	Glued and nailed, add				50%				
68-001	ROUGH HARDWARE Average % of carpentry material, minimum			%	.50%				
020	Maximum			"	1.50%				
70-001	SHEATHING Plywood on roof, CDX								
003	5/16" thick	F-2	.010	S.F.	.26	.19	.01	.46	.60
005	3/8" thick		.010		.29	.20	.01	.50	.65
010	1/2" thick		.011		.37	.22	.01	.60	.76
020	5/8" thick		.012		.41	.24	.01	.66	.84
030	3/4" thick		.013		.46	.26	.01	.73	.92
050	Plywood on walls with exterior standard, 3/8" thick		.013		.29	.26	.01	.56	.74
060	1/2" thick		.014		.37	.28	.01	.66	.85
070	5/8" thick		.015		.41	.30	.01	.72	.93
080	3/4" thick		.016		.46	.33	.01	.80	1.02
100	For shear wall construction, add					20%			
120	For structural 1 exterior plywood, add				10%				
140	With boards, on roof 1" x 6" boards, laid horizontal	F-2	.022		.70	.43	.02	1.15	1.46
150	Laid diagonal		.025		.70	.48	.02	1.20	1.54
170	1" x 8" boards, laid horizontal		.018		.70	.35	.02	1.07	1.34
180	Laid diagonal		.022		.70	.43	.02	1.15	1.46
200	For steep roofs, add					40%			
220	For dormers, hips and valleys, add				5%	50%			
240	Boards on walls, 1" x 6" boards, laid regular	F-2	.025		.70	.48	.02	1.20	1.54
250	Laid diagonal		.027		.70	.54	.02	1.26	1.62
270	1" x 8" boards, laid regular		.021		.70	.41	.02	1.13	1.42
280	Laid diagonal		.025		.70	.48	.02	1.20	1.54
285	Gypsum, weatherproof, 1/2" thick		.015		.20	.30	.01	.51	.70
290	Sealed, 4/10" thick		.015		.18	.29	.01	.48	.65
300	Wood fiber, regular, no vapor barrier, 1/2" thick		.013		.36	.26	.01	.63	.81
310	5/8" thick		.013		.47	.26	.01	.74	.93

NOTES

WOOD ROOF TRUSSES: Material prices for trusses in lines 66-021 to 66-070 are based on a lumber price of $340 per MBF. Since the cost of lumber fluctuates, add or subtract 5% for every $50 differential in the current price of the lumber used in the manufacture of the truss.

For a 4 in 12 pitch some typical costs per truss for various spans are:

Span (Ft.)	Cost
24	$34.50
28	46.00
32	53.50
36	60.75
40	72.75

PLYWOOD: There are two types of plywood used in construction: interior, which is moisture-resistant but not waterproofed; and exterior, which is waterproofed.

The surface grade of plywood is designated by letters A to D. The first letter is the exterior surface.

A—Smooth surface with patches allowed.

B—Solid surface with patches and plugs allowed.

C—May be surface plugged or may have knot holes up to 1" wide.

D—Interior only with knot holes up to 2-1/2" allowed.

Typical uses for various plywood grades are as follows:

AA-AD Interior — cupboards, shelving, paneling, furniture.

B-B Plyform — concrete form plywood.

CDX — wall and roof sheathing.

Structural — box beams, girder, stressed skin panels.

AA-AC Exterior — fences, signs, siding, soffits, etc.

Underlayment — base for resilient floor coverings.

For expanded coverage of these items see Means' *Interior Cost Data 1985*

Table II.35

Division 7: Moisture and Thermal Protection

Four types of insulation are specified in the project. The urethane roof insulation is included in the roofing subcontract. The polystyrene foundation insulation is installed on the interior of the foundation walls at the crawl space. The take-off for these types is straight forward. The exterior wall fiberglass (for thermal protection) and the interior wall fiberglass (for reduced sound transmission) are an integral part of the drywall partition systems. As the quantities are calculated, the estimator should note and record the wall types and dimensions. This information will save time when estimating Division 9: Finishes. Tables II.36 to II.38 are the estimate sheets for Division 7.

The polyethylene vapor barrier in the basement is an item that might easily be overlooked. Many such items in a complex package of construction documents may be shown only once on the plans and not even mentioned directly in the specifications. The estimator must be careful and thorough in order to avoid omissions.

The roofing and roof insulation are estimated for the complete roof surface with no deductions for the hatches or skylights. This is because these accessories will require extra labor for cutting and flashing. When bids are submitted, the estimator must be sure that the quotes are for the roofing and materials exactly as specified. There are many materials and methods of installation, especially for single-ply roofs, as shown in Part I, Table I2.27.

In Division 7 is the first instance where work for the third floor tenant is included in the estimate. In Table II.38, the items are priced separately so that the total tenant costs can easily be determined at the end of the estimate. The tenant has requested that an additional skylight be installed. Table II.39b, line 40-900, shows a minimum labor and equipment charge. This cost does not apply to the tenant skylight because it will be installed at the same time as the other skylights and hatches. Note that curbs must be added to the cost of the skylights.

During the estimating process, the estimator should begin to think about scheduling and the progression of the work. Table II.40 is a preliminary schedule for Division 2 through Division 7. The schedule, at this point, is used only as a reference and will undoubtedly be changed as the estimate is completed. The estimator should note such items as the demolition of the freight elevator and shaft, which will occur out of a normal sequence. The sidewalk is scheduled near the end of the project because the scaffolding must be removed, and all exterior work completed, before installation. Proper preparation of an accurate Project Schedule is very important when determining the allocation of workers for a project. It is preferable to keep the work force as constant as possible throughout the project. The schedule also provides a basis for determining costs of time-related items in Division 1.

CONSOLIDATED ESTIMATE

PROJECT	Commercial Renovation			SHEET NO. 1 of 3
	PRICES BY RSM			ESTIMATE NO. 85-1
LOCATION				DATE 1985
TAKE OFF BY EBW	QUANTITIES BY EBW			
	CLASSIFICATION	ARCHITECT		CHECKED BY

DESCRIPTION	FLOOR	SOURCE	QUANTITY	UNIT	MATERIAL UNIT	MATERIAL TOTAL	LABOR UNIT	LABOR TOTAL	EQUIP. UNIT	EQUIP. TOTAL	SUBCONTRACTOR UNIT	TOTAL INCL O & P	MAN-HOURS UNIT	MAN-HOURS TOTAL
Division 7: Thermal & Moisture Protect.														
Insulation:														
Roof		7.2-50-224	8660	SF	SUBCONTRACT						1.08	9353	.010	87
Exterior Wall		7.2-85-008	4799	SF	18¢	864	10¢	480					.005	24
Interior Wall (soundproofing)		7.2-85-082	10,131	SF	16¢	1621	12¢	1216					.006	61
Foundation @ Crawl Space		7.2-30-090	880	SF	39¢	343	23¢	202					.012	11
2% Mat. 3% Labor					2%	7	3%	6					3%	1
Vapor Barrier	B	7.1-15-090	52	SQ	4.90	255	4.24	220					.216	11
Roofing		7.4-52-710	8660	SF	SUBCONTRACT						1.28	116281	.011	95
Copper Downspouts		7.6-10-250	204	LF	4.12	840	1.22	249					.550	11
Strainers		7.6-10-280	6	EA.	2.83	17	1.22	7					.60	1
Page Subtotals						3947		2380				256434		302

Table II.36

CONSOLIDATED ESTIMATE

PROJECT	Commercial Renovation
LOCATION	
PRICES BY	RSM
TAKE OFF BY	EBW
QUANTITIES BY	EBW

CLASSIFICATION

ARCHITECT

CHECKED BY

SHEET NO. 2 of 3
ESTIMATE NO. 85-1
DATE 1985

DESCRIPTION	FLOOR	SOURCE	QUANTITY	UNIT	MATERIAL UNIT	MATERIAL TOTAL	LABOR UNIT	LABOR TOTAL	EQUIPMENT UNIT	EQUIPMENT TOTAL	SUBCONTRACTOR UNIT	SUBCONTRACTOR TOTAL INCL. O & P	MAN-HOURS UNIT	MAN-HOURS TOTAL
Division 7 : (cont'd)														
Accessories														
Roof Hatch		7.8-20-050	1	Ea.	361	361	60.50	61	2.20	2			3.2	3
Skylights (14)		7.8-40-060	196	SF	14.70	2881	1.91	374	.07	14			.102	20
Curbs @ skylts.		7.8-40-180			30%	864								
Smoke Hatches		7.8-20-140	3	Ea.	850	2550	91.72	275	3.33	10			4.85	15
Add		7.8-55-030			10%	255	5%	14					5%	1
Page Subtotals						6911		724		26				39

Table II.37

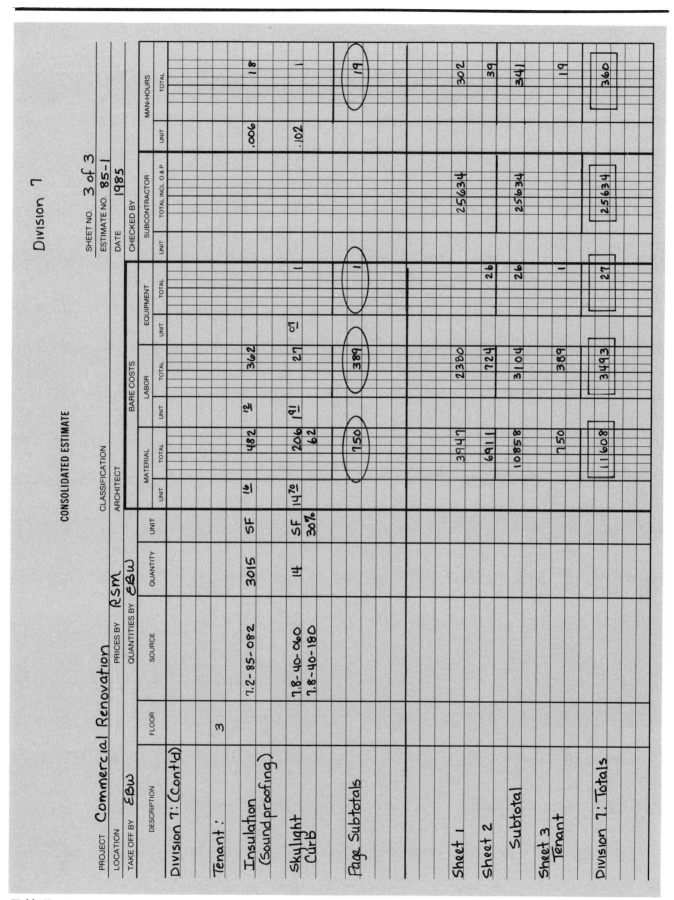

Table II.38

7.8 Roof Accessories

		CREW	MAN-HOURS	UNIT	BARE COSTS MAT.	BARE COSTS LABOR	BARE COSTS EQUIP.	BARE COSTS TOTAL	TOTAL INCL O&P	NOTES
10-001	CEILING HATCHES 2'-6" x 2'-6", single leaf, steel frame & cover									
010	Aluminum cover	G-3	2.910	Ea.	252	55	2	309	365	
030	2'-6" x 3'-0", single leaf, steel frame & steel cover		2.910		288	55	2	345	405	
040	Aluminum cover		2.910		326	55	2	383	445	
900	Minimum labor/equipment charge	F-2	8	Job		158	7	165	250	
15-001	ROOF DRAINS See division 15.1-16									
20-001	ROOF HATCHES With curb, 1" fiberglass insulation, 2'-6" x 3'-0"									
050	Aluminum curb and cover	G-3	3.200	Ea.	361	60.80	2.20	424	490	
052	Galvanized steel		3.200		340	60.80	2.20	403	470	
054	Plain steel, primed		3.200		304	60.80	2.20	367	430	
060	2'-6" x 4'-6", aluminum curb & cover		3.560		517	66.56	2.44	586	675	
080	Galvanized steel		3.560		489	66.56	2.44	558	645	
090	Plain steel, primed		3.560		430	66.56	2.44	499	580	
120	2'-6" x 8'-0", aluminum curb and cover		4.850		897	91.67	3.33	992	1,125	
140	Galvanized steel		4.850		850	91.67	3.33	945	1,075	
150	Plain steel, primed		4.850		742	91.67	3.33	837	960	
180	For plexiglass panels, add to above				197			197	215M	
200	For galv. curb and alum. cover, deduct from aluminum				14			14	15.40M	
900	Minimum labor/equipment charge	F-2	8	Job		158	7	165	250	
30-001	ROOF VENTS Mushroom for built-up roofs, aluminum	1 Rofc	.267	Ea.	17.95	4.89		22.84	28	
010	PVC, 6" high	"	.267		21.95	4.89		26.84	32	
100	Residential type (see division 7.6-42-301)	1 Carp	.667		9.70	13.05		22.75	31	
900	Minimum labor/equipment charge	1 Rofc	2.910	Job		53		53	86L	
40-001	SKYLIGHT Plastic roof domes, flush or curb mounted, ten or									
010	more units, curb not included, "L" frames									
030	Nominal size under 10 S.F., double	G-3	.246	S.F.	15.75	4.64	.17	20.56	25	
040	Single		.200		12.60	3.77	.14	16.51	19.75	
060	10 S.F. to 20 S.F., double		.102		14.70	1.91	.07	16.68	19.15	
070	Single		.081		10.50	1.52	.06	12.08	13.95	
090	20 S.F. to 30 S.F., double		.081		12.60	1.52	.06	14.18	16.25	
100	Single		.069		8.40	1.29	.05	9.74	11.25	
120	30 S.F. to 65 S.F., double		.069		9.45	1.29	.05	10.79	12.40	
130	Single		.052		6.30	.98	.04	7.32	8.50	
150	For insulated 4" curbs, double, add				15%					
160	Single, add				30%					
180	For integral insulated 9" curbs, double, add				30%					
190	Single, add				45%					
210	Ceiling plastic domes compared with single roof domes				95%	100%				
211										
212	Ventilating insulated plexiglass dome with									
213	curb mounting, 36" x 36"	G-3	2.670	Ea.	349	50.17	1.83	401	465	

Roof Hatch

Skylight, Single

Table II.39a

7.8 Roof Accessories

	CREW	MAN-HOURS	UNIT	MAT.	LABOR	EQUIP.	TOTAL	TOTAL INCL O&P	NOTES
215 52" x 52"	G-3	2.670	Ea.	467	50.17	1.83	519	590	
216 28" x 52"		3.200		386	60.80	2.20	449	520	
217 36" x 52"		3.200		410	60.80	2.20	473	545	
218 For electric opening system, add				210			210	230M	
220 Field fabricated, factory type, aluminum and wire glass	G-3	.267	S.F.	9.75	5.02	.18	14.95	18.60	
230 Insulated safety glass with aluminum frame		.200		63.25	3.77	.14	67.16	75	
240 Sandwich panels, fiberglass, for walls, 1-9/16" thick, to 250 S.F.		.160		11.20	3.02	.11	14.33	17.05	
250 250 S.F. and up		.121		9	2.28	.08	11.36	13.45	
270 As above, but for roofs, 2-3/4" thick, to 250 S.F.		.108		16.65	2.05	.07	18.77	22	
280 250 S.F. and up		.097		13.35	1.82	.07	15.24	17.55	
900 Minimum labor/equipment charge	F-2	8	Job		158	7	165	250	
50-001 SKYROOFS Translucent panels, 2-3/4" thick, under 5000 S.F.	G-3	.081	S.F.Hor.	12.95	1.52	.06	14.53	16.65	
010 Over 5000 S.F.		.069		11.50	1.29	.05	12.84	14.70	
030 Continuous vaulted, semi-circular, to 8' wide, double glazed		.221		24.75	4.16	.15	29.06	34	
040 Single glazed		.200		14.75	3.77	.14	18.66	22	
060 To 20' wide, single glazed		.183		21.70	3.44	.13	25.27	29	
070 Over 20' wide, single glazed		.160		23.10	3.02	.11	26.23	30	
090 Motorized opening type, single glazed, 1/3 opening		.221		27.85	4.16	.15	32.16	37	
100 Full opening		.246		33.15	4.64	.17	37.96	44	
120 Pyramid type units, self-supporting, to 30' clear opening,									
130 square or circular, single glazed, minimum	G-3	.160	S.F. Hor.	19.20	3.02	.11	22.33	26	
131 Average		.194		20.85	3.66	.13	24.64	29	
140 Maximum		.246		22.80	4.64	.17	27.61	32	
150 Grid type, 4' to 10' modules, single glass glazed, minimum		.160		17.50	3.02	.11	20.63	24	
155 Maximum		.250		23.40	4.71	.17	28.28	33	
160 Preformed acrylic, minimum		.107		12.05	2.02	.07	14.14	16.40	
165 Maximum		.184		22.15	3.46	.13	25.74	30	
900 Minimum labor/equipment charge	F-2	2	Job		39.25	1.75	41	62	
55-001 SMOKE HATCHES Unlabeled, not including hand winch operator									
010									
020 For 3'-0" long, add to roof hatches from division 7.8-20			Ea.	25%	5%				
030 For 8'-0" long, add to roof hatches from division 7.8-20			"	10%	5%				
60-001 SMOKE VENTS Metal cover, heavy duty, low profile, 4' x 4'									
010 Aluminum	G-3	2.460	Ea.	880	46.31	1.69	928	1,050	
020 Galvanized steel	"	2.460	"	762	46.31	1.69	810	910	
025									
030 4' x 8' aluminum	G-3	4	Ea.	1,125	75.25	2.75	1,203	1,350	
040 Galvanized steel	"	4	"	957	75.25	2.75	1,035	1,175	
050 Sloped cover style, deduct				10%					
900 Minimum labor/equipment charge	F-2	8	Job		158	7	165	250	
70-001 SNOW GUARDS Adjust., not incl. guard pipes, galv., 12" x 6" plate	G-3	.246	Ea.	32.15	4.64	.17	36.96	43	
020 24" x 12" plate	"	.246	"	39.60	4.64	.17	44.41	51	

Smoke Hatch

142

Table II.39b

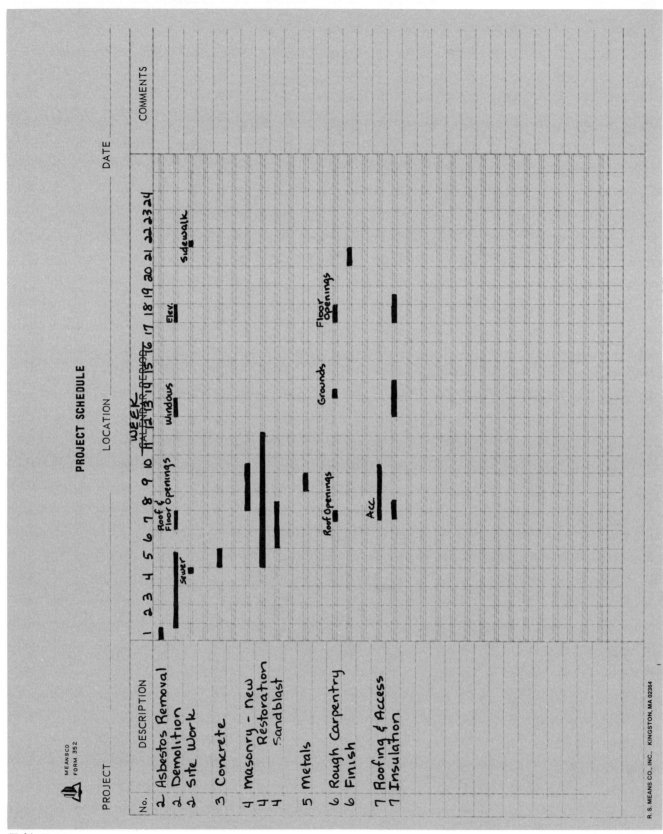

Table II.40

Division 8: Doors, Windows and Glass

A proper set of plans and specifications will have door, window and hardware schedules. These schedules should provide all information that is necessary for the quantity take-off. Table II.41 shows portions of the door schedule for the sample project. There are two common types of door schedules. The first, as in Table II.41, lists each door separately. The second lists each type of door (usually accompanied by elevations) that have common characteristics. Hardware is usually only designated by "set" on the schedules. These "sets" are described elsewhere on the plans or in the specifications. The estimator should cross-check quantities obtained from the schedules by counting and marking each item on the plans.

Table II.42 provides averages for finish hardware costs based on total job costs. These percentages should be used as another type of cross-check at the end of the estimate. If the actual estimated costs vary significantly from these figures, the estimator should determine the reason for the variation, whether it is caused by unusual project requirements or perhaps by omissions or duplications.

Specifications often state that all doors, frames, and hardware be as specified, or an "approved equal." This means that if the estimator can find similar quality products for less cost, the architect may accept these products as alternatives. Specifications usually require that the contractor submit shop drawings, schedules (as prepared by the contractor or supplier) or "cuts" (product literature). Most door, frame, and hardware suppliers provide these services to the contractor. It is recommended that the estimator obtain material prices from a supplier, because prices vary and fluctuate widely.

Door Schedule

Door	Size	Type	Rating	Frame	Depth	Rating	Hardware Set	Remarks
B01	$3^0 \times 6^8$	Flush Steel 18 ga.	"B" 1-1/2 Hr.	Exist'g.	—	—	HW-1	10" x 10" Vision Lite Shop-Primed
B02	$3^0 \times 6^8$	Flush Steel 18 ga.	"B" 1 Hr.	HMKD 16 ga.	4-7/8"	"B" 1 Hr.	HW-2	Shop-Primed
B03	$3^0 \times 6^8$	Flush Steel 18 ga.	"B" 1 Hr.	H.M. Welded 16 ga.	8"	"B" 1 Hr.	HW-3	w/Masonry Anchors Shop-Primed
B04	$3^0 \times 6^8$	Flush Steel 18 ga.	"B" 1-1/2 Hr.	H.M. Welded 16 ga.	8"	"B" 1-1/2 Hr.	HW-3	w/Masonry Anchors Shop-Primed
B05	$3^0 \times 6^8$	Flush Steel 18 ga.	"B" 1-1/2 Hr.	H.M. Welded 16 ga.	8"	"B" 1-1/2 Hr.	HW-3	w/Masonry Anchors Shop-Primed
B06	$3^0 \times 6^8$	Flush Steel 18 Ga.	"B" 1 Hr.	HMKD 16 ga.	4-7/8"	"B" 1 Hr.	HW-2	Shop-Primed
101	$3^0 \times 6^8$	Flush Steel 18 ga.	—	HMKD 16 Ga.	4-7/8"	—	HW-4	Transom Frame Above w/Masonry Anchors
102	$3^0 \times 6^8$	Flush Steel 18 ga.	"B" 1-1/2 Hr.	Exist'g.	—	—	HW-1	Shop-Primed
103	$3^0 \times 6^8$	Flush Oak Face	"B" 1 Hr.	HMKD 16 ga.	4-7/8"	"B" 1 Hr.	HW-5	
104	$2^6 \times 6^8$	Flush Oak Face SC	—	HMKD 16 ga.	4-5/8"	—	HW-6	
105	$3^0 \times 6^8$	Flush Oak Face	"B" 1 Hr.	HMKD 16 ga.	4-7/8"	"B" 1 Hr.	HW-5	

Table II.41

8.7 Finish Hardware & Specialties	CREW	MAN-HOURS	UNIT	BARE COSTS				TOTAL INCL O&P
				MAT.	LABOR	EQUIP.	TOTAL	
01-001 **AVERAGE** Percentage for hardware, total job cost, minimum							.75%	.75%
005　　　Maximum							3.50%	3.50%
050　　Total hardware for building, average distribution				85%	15%			
100　　Door hardware, apartment, interior			Door	66			66	73M
150　　　Hospital bedroom, minimum				90			90	99M
200　　　Maximum				425			425	470M

Table II.42

Division 8

CONSOLIDATED ESTIMATE

PROJECT Commercial Renovation
PRICES BY RSM
TAKE OFF BY EBW
QUANTITIES BY EBW

CLASSIFICATION
ARCHITECT

SHEET NO. 1 of 6
ESTIMATE NO. 85-1
DATE 1985
CHECKED BY

DESCRIPTION	FLOOR	SOURCE	QUANTITY	UNIT	MATERIAL UNIT	MATERIAL TOTAL	BARE COSTS LABOR UNIT	LABOR TOTAL	EQUIPMENT UNIT	EQUIPMENT TOTAL	SUBCONTRACTOR UNIT	TOTAL INCL. O & P	MAN-HOURS UNIT	MAN-HOURS TOTAL
Division 8: Door, Windows, Glass														
Metal Frames														
16 ga. to 5 3/4"		8.1-10-360	6	Ea.	60	360	21.07	126	.13	6			1.07	6
16 ga. "B" Label Welded		8.1-10-540	13	Ea.	66	858	21.07	274	.93	12			1.07	14
		8.1-10-490	3	Ea.	10	30								
16 ga. "B" Label Double		8.1-10-544	6	Ea.	76	456	25.92	155	.17	7			1.33	8
16 ga. "B" Label to 6 3/4"		8.1-10-580	3	Ea.	72	216	21.07	63	.93	3			1.1	3
16 ga. - Stair Exit "B" Label		8.1-10-540	2	Ea.	66	132	21.07	42	.93	2			1.07	2
Transoms		8.1-10-790	9	SF	6	54	2.3	18	.09	1			.103	1
16 ga. "B" Label to 8 3/4"		8.1-10-620	3	Ea.	77	231	21.07	63	.19	3			1.07	3
Page Subtotals						2337		741		34				37

Table II.43

CONSOLIDATED ESTIMATE

PROJECT: Commercial Renovation
LOCATION
TAKE OFF BY: EBW
PRICES BY: RSM
QUANTITIES BY: EBW
CLASSIFICATION
ARCHITECT

DESCRIPTION	FLOOR	SOURCE	QUANTITY	UNIT	MATERIAL UNIT	MATERIAL TOTAL	LABOR UNIT	LABOR TOTAL	EQUIP. UNIT	EQUIP. TOTAL	SUBCONTRACTOR UNIT	TOTAL INCL. O & P	MAN-HOURS UNIT	MAN-HOURS TOTAL
Division 8: (Cont'd)														
Doors														
Exterior Exit	1	8.1-21-114	2	Ea	140	280	19.12	38	1⁶	2			1	2
Stair (Exist'g Fr)		8.1-23-014	4	Ea.	165	660	19.12	76	fv	4			1	4
5% mat. 9% labor					5%	33	9%	7					9%	1
Stair & Basement (new frames)		8.1-23-014	8	Ea.	165	1320	19.12	153	5F	7			1	8
Vision Lites		8.1-23-024	7	Ea.	65	455								
Telephone Cl.		8.2-23-014	6	Ea.	105	630	22	132	1	6			1.14	7
Tenant Entrance Doors @ Corridor		8.2-23-019	17	Ea.	135 ↗ 121.50	2065	25.83	439	1⁷	20			1.33	23
6'-8" Deduct		8.2-23-246	(Deduct)		(10%)									
Retail - Interior		8.2-21-224	3	Ea.	90	270	22	66	1	3			1.14	3
Retail - Bath		8.2-21-222	3	Ea.	80	240	21.07	63	93	3			1.07	3
Page Subtotals						5953		974		45				15

Table II.44

CONSOLIDATED ESTIMATE

PROJECT	Commercial Renovation			CLASSIFICATION		SHEET NO. 3 of 6
LOCATION		PRICES BY RSM		ARCHITECT		ESTIMATE NO. 85-1
TAKE OFF BY EBW		QUANTITIES BY EBW				DATE 1985
						CHECKED BY

DESCRIPTION	FLOOR	SOURCE	QUANTITY	UNIT	MATERIAL UNIT	MATERIAL TOTAL	LABOR UNIT	LABOR TOTAL	EQUIPMENT UNIT	EQUIPMENT TOTAL	SUBCONTRACTOR UNIT	SUBCONTRACTOR TOTAL INCL O & P	MAN-HOURS UNIT	MAN-HOURS TOTAL
Division 8: (Cont'd)														
Windows:														
Subcontractor Quote			70	Ea.	427	Incl O & P 25					452	31,640	2	140
Hardware:														
Closers		8.7-15-240	28	Ea.	50	1400	26	728					1.33	37
Floor Bumpers		8.7-20-160	21	Ea.	2.50	52	6.55	138					.333	7
Hinges		8.7-33-140	33	Pr.	68	2244								
Kickplates		8.7-36-050	4	Ea.	33	132	10.45	42					.533	2
Locksets:														
Privacy		8.7-40-010	3	Ea.	29	87	13.05	39					.667	2
Keyed		8.7-40-040	13	Ea.	47	611	15.70	204					.80	10
Mortise		8.7-43-213	8	Ea.	295	2360	22	176					1.14	9
Exterior Panic		8.7-45-021	2	Ea.	370	740	39	78					2	4
Stair Panic		8.7-45-002	7	Ea.	245	1715	31	217					1.6	11
Push/Pull		8.7-50-050	4	Ea.	41	164	13.05	52					.667	3
Ext. Thresholds		8.7-60-010	2	Ea.	62	124	13.05	26					.667	1
Page Subtotals						9629		1700				31,640		226

Table II.45

CONSOLIDATED ESTIMATE

PROJECT Commercial Renovation
LOCATION
TAKE OFF BY EBW PRICES BY RSM QUANTITIES BY EBW
CLASSIFICATION
ARCHITECT
SHEET NO. 4 of 6
ESTIMATE NO. 85-1
DATE 1985
CHECKED BY

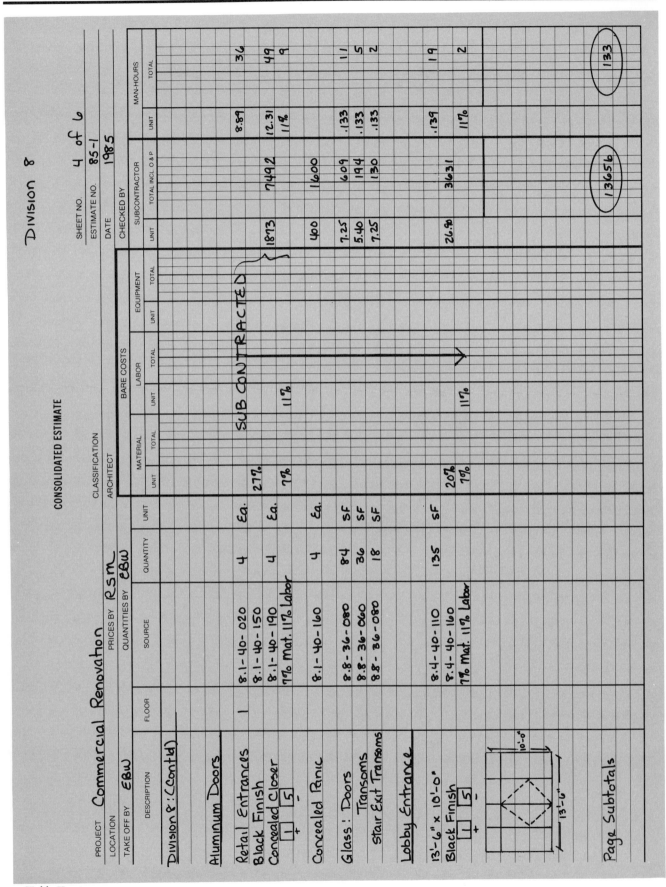

DESCRIPTION	FLOOR	SOURCE	QUANTITY	UNIT	MATERIAL UNIT	MATERIAL TOTAL	LABOR UNIT	LABOR TOTAL	EQUIPMENT UNIT	EQUIPMENT TOTAL	SUBCONTRACTOR UNIT	SUBCONTRACTOR TOTAL INCL. O & P	MAN-HOURS UNIT	MAN-HOURS TOTAL
Division 8: (Cont'd)														
Aluminum Doors														
Retail Entrances	1	8.1-40-020	4	Ea.	27%		SUB CONTRACTED →				1873	7492	8.89	36
Black Finish		8.1-40-150												
Concealed Closer [5] +		8.1-40-190	4	Ea.									12.31	49
7% Mat. 11% Labor					7%		11%						11%	9
Concealed Panic		8.1-40-160	4	Ea.							400	1600	.133	11
Glass: Doors		8.8-36-080	84	SF							7.25	609	.133	5
Transoms		8.8-36-060	36	SF							5.40	194	.133	
Stair Exit Transoms		8.8-36-080	18	SF							7.25	130	.135	2
Lobby Entrance		8.4-40-110	135	SF	20%						26.90	3631	.139	19
Black Finish [5] +		8.4-40-160			1%		11%						11%	2
1% Mat. 11% Labor														
Page Subtotals												13656		133

13'-6" x 10'-0"

Table II.46

CONSOLIDATED ESTIMATE

PROJECT Commercial Renovation
LOCATION
TAKE OFF BY EBW   PRICES BY RSM   QUANTITIES BY EBW

CLASSIFICATION
ARCHITECT

DESCRIPTION	FLOOR	SOURCE	QUANTITY	UNIT	MATERIAL UNIT	MATERIAL TOTAL	LABOR UNIT	LABOR TOTAL	EQUIPMENT UNIT	EQUIPMENT TOTAL	SUBCONTRACTOR UNIT	SUBCONTRACTOR TOTAL INCL. O & P	MAN-HOURS UNIT	MAN-HOURS TOTAL
Division 8: (Cont'd)														
Tenant:	3													
Doors		8.2-21-224	9	Ea.	90	810	22	198	1	9			1.14	10
Frames		8.1-10-360	9	Ea.	60	540	21.07	190	.93	10			1.07	10
Hinges		8.7-33-140	12	Pr.	68	816								
Floor Bumpers		8.7-20-160	9	Ea.	2.50	22	6.55	59					.333	3
Locksets:														
Passage		8.7-40-100	7	Ea.	81	567	13.95	91					.667	5
Keyed		8.7-40-140	2	Ea.	115	230	15.70	31					.80	2
Computer Window														
Frame		8.9-50-020	20	LF							16.69		.178	6
Glass Bead		8.9-50-045	20	LF								334	.067	1
Black Finish		8.9-50-802			277%			SUBCONTRACT →						
Glass		8.8-36-080	24	SF							7.25	174	.133	3
Page Subtotals						2986		569				508		40

Table II.47

CONSOLIDATED ESTIMATE

PROJECT **Commercial Renovation**
LOCATION
TAKE OFF BY **EBW** PRICES BY **RSM** QUANTITIES BY **EBW**
CLASSIFICATION
ARCHITECT
SHEET NO. **6 of 6**
ESTIMATE NO. **85-1**
DATE **1985**
CHECKED BY

DESCRIPTION	FLOOR	SOURCE	QUANTITY	UNIT	BARE COSTS — MATERIAL UNIT	MATERIAL TOTAL	LABOR UNIT	LABOR TOTAL	EQUIPMENT UNIT	EQUIPMENT TOTAL	SUBCONTRACTOR UNIT	TOTAL INCL O&P	MAN-HOURS UNIT	MAN-HOURS TOTAL
Division 8: (Cont'd)														
Totals														
Sheet 1 Frames						2337		747		34				37
Sheet 2 Doors						5953		974		45				51
Sheet 3 Hardware						9629		1700						86
Subtotal						17919		3415		79				174
Windows												31640		140
Sheet 4 Glazing												13656		133
Sheet 5 Tenant						2985		569				508		40
Division 8: Totals						20904		3984		79		45804		487

Table II.48

8.2 Wood & Plastic Doors

		CREW	MAN-HOURS	UNIT	BARE COSTS MAT.	LABOR	EQUIP.	TOTAL	TOTAL INCL O&P	NOTES
22	402	1-3/4" x 7'-0" x 3'-0" wide	F-2	1.140	Ea.	310	22	1	333	375	**WOOD FRAMES** are priced separately from doors so they can be combined with doors of other materials.
	404	3'-6" wide		1.230		405	23.92	1.08	430	485	
	420	Rosewood, 1-3/4" x 7'-0" x 3'-0" wide	↓	1.140		405	22	1	428	480	
	422	3'-6" wide		1.230		550	23.92	1.08	575	645	
	428	For 6'-8" high door, deduct from 7'-0" door				10%					
	432	For detailed design, add				50%					
	434	For hand carved back, add				20%					
	436	For ornate mahogany door, 2-1/4" thick, add				20%					
	438	For ornate rosewood door, 2-1/4" thick, add				20%					
	440	For custom finish, add				84			84	92M	
	460	Side panel, mahogany, simple design, 7'-0" x 1'-0" wide	F-2	.752		63	14.93	.67	78.60	93	
	462	1'-2" wide		.800		68	15.70	.70	84.40	100	
	464	1'-4" wide		.842		74	16.51	.74	91.25	110	
	480	Rosewood, simple design 7'-0" x 1'-0" wide	↓	.762		105	14.93	.67	120.60	140	
	482	1'-2" wide		.800		115	15.70	.70	131.40	150	
	484	1'-4" wide		.842		145	16.51	.74	162.25	185	
	490	For detailed design, add				50%					
	492	For hand carved back, add				20%					
	652	Interior cafe doors, 2'-6" opening, stock, panel pine	F-2	1		76	19.12	.88	96	115	
	654	3'-0" opening	"	1		84	19.12	.88	104	125	
	654	Custom hardwood or louvered pine									
	656	2'-6" opening	F-2	1	Ea.	65	19.12	.88	85	105	
	800	3'-0" opening	"	1	"	75	19.12	.88	95	115	
	880	Pre-hung doors, see division 8.2-50									
	900	Minimum labor/equipment charge	F-1	2	Job		39.25	1.75	41	62	
23-001		WOOD FIRE DOORS Mineral core, 3 ply stile, "B" label, 1 hour, birch face, 2'-6" x 6'-8"	F-2	1.140	Ea.	87	22	1	110	130	
	004										
	009	3'-0" x 7'-0"	"	1.330	"	115	25.83	1.17	142	170	
	011										
	014	Oak face, 2'-6" x 6'-8"	F-2	1.140	Ea.	105	22	1	128	150	
	019	3'-0" x 7'-0"		1.333		135	25.83	1.17	162	190	
	024	Walnut face, 2'-6" x 6'-8"		1.140		160	22	1	183	210	
	029	3'-0" x 7'-0"		1.330		185	25.83	1.17	212	245	
	044	M.D. overlay on hardboard, 2'-6" x 6'-8"		1.070		86	21.07	.93	108	130	
	049	3'-0" x 7'-0"		1.230		115	23.92	1.08	140	165	
	054	HP plastic laminate, 2'-6" x 6'-8"		1.230		185	23.92	1.08	210	240	
	059	3'-0" x 7'-0"	↓	1.450		210	28.73	1.27	240	275	
	246	For 6'-8" high door, deduct from 7'-0" door				10%					
	248	For oak veneer, add				50%					
	250	For walnut veneer, add				75%					
	900	Minimum labor/equipment charge	F-1	2	Job		39.25	1.75	41	62	
25-001		WOOD DOORS, PANELED Interior, six panel, hollow core, 1-3/4" thick									
	004	Molded hardboard, 2'-0" x 6'-8"	F-2	.941	Ea.	33	18.43	.82	52.25	66	

For expanded coverage of these items see Means' *Interior Cost Data 1985*

Table II.49

Installation costs, also, can vary due to restrictive existing conditions in commercial renovation. During the site evaluation the estimator should note any areas where such restrictions require the addition of factors. In the sample project, the metal frames with transoms at the stairway exits must be installed in existing masonry openings. (See Table II.43 and Figure II.9.) These openings most likely will not conform exactly to the sizes of new metal door frames. A factor is added to match existing conditions. The existing interior door frames at the west stairway are to remain and be reused. Again, a factor must be added to the appropriate door installations to match existing conditions. (See Table II.44.) Tables II.43 to II.48 are the estimate sheets for Division 8.

Note that the tenant entrance door costs in Table II.44 have a deduction for 6'-8" high doors. This is obtained from Table II.49. This deduction should be subtracted from the material price before extension of the costs. Otherwise, a minus figure in the "Total" column would be confusing and inconsistent.

The new windows for the project are not standard sizes and require a special black finish. A quotation from a subcontractor is obtained and is included in Table II.45. There are no factors added separately because any special installation or material costs should be included in the subcontract price. It is important, therefore, that the subcontractor examine the existing conditions thoroughly before submitting the quote. The estimator must be sure that no "surprises" will be encountered during installation.

As with the windows, the retail entrance doors and lobby entrance require a black finish. These items will be furnished and installed by a subcontractor. The added costs for the black finish are provided as a percentage of the bare material cost as shown in Table II.50. Also, the factors for matching existing conditions and protecting existing work in Table II.51 (applied to bare costs) must be added to the total including the installing subcontractor's overhead and profit. The calculations are shown in Table II.52.

8.1 Metal Doors		MAN-HOURS	UNIT	BARE COSTS				TOTAL INCL O&P
				MAT.	LABOR	EQUIP.	TOTAL	
40-001	ALUMINUM DOORS & FRAMES Entrance, narrow stile, including	CREW						
002	hardware & closer, clear finish, not incl. glass, 3' x 7' opening	2 Sswk	8	Ea.	505	170		675	835
010	3' x 10' opening, 3' high transom	2 Sswk	8.890	Ea.	585	190		775	955
020	3'-6" x 10' opening, 3' high transom	"	8.890	"	610	190		800	980
030	6' x 7' opening		12.310	Pr.	790	260		1,050	1,300
040	6' x 10' opening, 3' high transom	▼	14.550	"	990	310		1,300	1,600
100	Add to above for wide stile doors			Leaf	30%				
110	Full vision doors, with 1/2" glass, add				55%				
120	Non-standard size, add				35%				
130	Light bronze finish, add				15%				
140	Dark bronze finish, add				18%				
150	Black finish, add			▼	27%				
160	Concealed panic device, add				365			365	400M
170	Electric striker release, add			Opng.	260			260	285M
180	Floor check, add	2 Carp	5.330	Leaf	235	105		340	420
190	Concealed closer, add	"	12.310	"	150	240		390	535
900	Minimum labor/equipment charge	F-2	4	Job		78.50	3.50	82	125

Aluminum Door & Frame

Table II.50

17-001 010	**FACTORS** To be added to construction costs for particular job requirements									
050	**1** Cut & patch to match existing construction, add, minimum			Costs		2%	3%			
055	Maximum					5%	9%			
080	**2** Dust protection, add, minimum					1%	2%			
085	Maximum					4%	11%			
110	**3** Equipment usage curtailment, add, minimum					1%	1%			
115	Maximum					3%	10%			
140	**4** Material handling & storage limitation, add, minimum					1%	1%			
145	Maximum					6%	7%			
170	**5** Protection of existing work, add, minimum					2%	2%			
175	Maximum					5%	7%			
200	**6** Shift work requirements, add, minimum						5%			
205	Maximum						30%			
230	**7** Temporary shoring and bracing, add, minimum					2%	5%			
235	Maximum			▼		5%	12%			

Table II.51 Factors for Aluminum Entrance Doors

	Bare Costs			
	Material	**Labor**	**Total**	**Total Including O & P**
Entrance Door	$ 610	$190	$ 800	
Black Finish (27% of $610)	165			
Concealed Closer	150	240	390	
	925	430	$1,190	
Factors 1 5 +	(7%) 65	(11%) 47		
	990	477		
Overhead and Profit 10% Material 64.3% Labor*	(10%) 99	(64.3%) 307		
Totals Include Overhead and Profit	$1,089	$784		$1,873
*See Table II.22				

Table II.52

The factors do not apply to the costs for the concealed panic devices. These items are installed in the door and frame at the supplier's shop and affect only the material cost of the door units. The installation of the concealed closers, however, is affected by the existing conditions, so the factors do apply. The black finish cost is also included before the factors are calculated, because any required shims or spacers to conform to the existing opening will have the same black finish. Similar calculations are required for the lobby entrance storefront.

Storefront systems can be estimated in two ways, using *Repair and Remodeling Cost Data.* The first method is to separate the system into components, tube framing, glass, doors, and hardware, and to price each item individually. The second method is to use the data provided for complete systems as shown in Table II.53. The latter method is used in this example. When pricing is used for a system such as this, the estimator must be sure that all specified items are included in the system or added if necessary.

Table II.48 illustrates how the different components of Division 8 are totalled. The other estimate sheets (Tables II.43 to II.47) have been organized so that groups of similar items are priced together. The estimator is able to use this information to determine the percentage of total job costs, or the costs per square foot of the different components of commercial renovation. These percentages and square foot costs may be helpful when estimating future jobs.

As in Division 7, the tenant work for Division 8 is priced separately. The estimator must remember, for scheduling purposes, that all materials for the second and third floors should be in place before the freight elevator is removed.

Division 9: Finishes

In commercial renovation, Division 9 usually represents a major portion of the work. The seven estimate sheets for the finishes are shown in Tables II.54 to II.60.

The estimator must be careful when taking off quantities for metal stud and drywall partitions. It would be simple if each type and size of stud had a different drywall application. But different size studs will have the same drywall treatment and vice versa. Thoroughly complete plans and specifications will often have a schedule of the wall types as well as a Room Finish Schedule. In either case, the different wall types should be marked on the plans, with different colors, during the quantity take-off. The estimator should determine quantities for these "assembled" wall types before attempting to figure quantities of individual components. The estimator should also make notes during the take-off on existing conditions that will require added factors. In the sample project, the wood beams at the ceilings occur every 10'. The studs and drywall will have to be cut to fit around the beams. No deduction for material is made for this type of condition, but extra labor expense is included.

When the quantities of the different wall types have been determined, the estimator should list each individual component and the appropriate quantities. Then the total quantities of each component for all wall types are added and entered on the estimate sheet. As a cross-check, the resulting totals for studs and drywall can be compared. Remember, when comparing, that the drywall quantities will be twice those for some of the studs because of application on two sides. Table II.61 is the comparison for the sample project. Refer to Tables II.54 and II.55. This method will help to ensure that all items have been included.

8.4 Entrances & Storefronts

Sliding Entrance

10		Description	CREW	MAN-HOURS	UNIT	MAT.	LABOR	EQUIP.	TOTAL	TOTAL INCL O&P	NOTES
	900	Minimum labor/equipment charge	2 Sswk	16	Job		340		340	560L	
25-	001	SLIDING ENTRANCE 12' x 7'-6" opening, 5' x 7' door, two way traffic,									
	002	mat activated, panic pushout, incl. operator & hardware,									
	003	not incl. glass or glazing	2 Glaz	22.860	Opng.	6,275	455		6,730	7,600	
	900	Minimum labor/equipment charge		22.860	Job		455		455	690L	
30-	001	SLIDING PANEL Mall fronts, aluminum & glass, 15' x 9' high		12.310	Opng.	1,400	245		1,645	1,900	
	010	24' x 9' high		22.860		2,275	455		2,730	3,200	
	020	48' x 9' high, with fixed panels	↓	17.780	↓	4,575	355		4,930	5,575	
	050	For bronze finish, add				15%					
	900	Minimum labor/equipment charge	2 Glaz	16	Job		320		320	485L	
35-	001	STAINLESS STEEL and glass entrance unit, narrow stiles									
	002	3' x 7' opening, including hardware, minimum	2 Sswk	10	Opng.	1,200	215		1,415	1,675	
	005	Average		11.430		2,000	245		2,245	2,600	
	010	Maximum	↓	13.330	↓	3,200	285		3,485	3,975	
	100	For solid bronze entrance units, statuary finish, add				60%					
	110	Without statuary finish, add				40%					
	900	Minimum labor/equipment charge	2 Sswk	8	Job		170		170	280L	
40-	001	STOREFRONT SYSTEMS Aluminum frame, clear 3/8" plate glass,									
	002	incl. 3' x 7' door with hardware (400 sq. ft. max. wall)									
	050	Wall height to 12' high, commercial grade	2 Glaz	.107	S.F.	10.30	2.12		12.42	14.55	
	060	Institutional grade		.123		11.95	2.44		14.39	16.85	
	070	Monumental grade		.139		16.75	2.76		19.51	23	
	100	6' x 7' door with hardware, commercial grade		.119		13	2.35		15.35	17.90	
	110	Institutional grade		.139		15.75	2.76		18.51	22	
	120	Monumental grade	↓	.160	↓	21.50	3.18		24.68	28	
	150	For bronze anodized finish, add				15%					
	160	For black anodized finish, add				20%					
	170	For stainless steel framing, add to monumental				75%					
	200	For no 3' x 7' door and hardware, deduct				3.18			3.18	3.49M	
	250	For no 6' x 7' door and hardware, deduct				5.85			5.85	6.45M	
	900	Minimum labor/equipment charge	2 Glaz	16	Job		320		320	485L	
60-	001	SWING DOORS Aluminum entrance, 6' x 7', incl. hardware & operator	2 Sswk	22.860	Opng.	4,500	485		4,985	5,750	
	002	For anodized finish, add			"	380			380	420M	
	900	Minimum labor/equipment charge	2 Sswk	16	Job		340		340	560L	

For expanded coverage of these items see Means' *Interior Cost Data 1985*

Table II.53

CONSOLIDATED ESTIMATE

PROJECT Commercial Renovation

LOCATION

TAKE OFF BY EBW   QUANTITIES BY EBW   PRICES BY RSM

CLASSIFICATION

ARCHITECT

CHECKED BY

DESCRIPTION	FLOOR	SOURCE	QUANTITY	UNIT	MATERIAL		LABOR		EQUIPMENT		SUBCONTRACTOR		MAN-HOURS	
					UNIT	TOTAL	UNIT	TOTAL	UNIT	TOTAL	UNIT	TOTAL INCL. O & P	UNIT	TOTAL
Division 9: Finishes														
metal Studs														
Non-load Bearing 25 ga. 16" O.C.														
1 5/8"		9.2-20-200	7144	SF	20	1429	37	2643					.019	136
3 5/8"		9.2-20-230	11,775	SF	25	2944	39	4592					.02	235
6"		9.2-20-250	560	SF	37	207	44	246					.022	12
[1]		2% mat. 3% Labor			2%	92	3%	224					3%	11
Furring @ Stair & Elev.		9.2-02-090	26.38	CLF	17.30	456	60	1583					3.08	81
Shaft Wall @ Pipe Chase		9.2-45-003	552	SF	1.32	729	1.90	1049					.047	54
Tape & Finish from 9.2-07-210 & 215			255	SF	26	11	14	501					.019	01
Page Subtotals						58668		10442						539

Table II.54

Division 9

CONSOLIDATED ESTIMATE

PROJECT Commercial Renovation
LOCATION
TAKE OFF BY EBW
PRICES BY RSM
QUANTITIES BY EBW
CLASSIFICATION
ARCHITECT

SHEET NO. 2 of 7
ESTIMATE NO. 85-1
DATE 1985
CHECKED BY

DESCRIPTION	FLOOR	SOURCE	QUANTITY	UNIT	MATERIAL UNIT	MATERIAL TOTAL	LABOR UNIT	LABOR TOTAL	EQUIP. UNIT	EQUIP. TOTAL	SUBCONTRACTOR UNIT	SUBCONTRACTOR TOTAL INCL. O & P	MAN-HOURS UNIT	MAN-HOURS TOTAL
Division 9: (Cont'd)														
Drywall:														
1/2" Standard Taped		9.2-07-035	13,292	SF	.23	3057	.35	4652					.018	239
5/8" Fr No Finish		9.2-07-210	3288	SF	.26	855	.18	592					.009	30
5/8" Fr Taped		9.2-07-215	22,014	SF	.28	6164	.37	8145					.019	418
5/8" Fr Ceil. Taped		9.2-07-315	490	SF	.28	137	.42	206					.020	10
High Ceilings ☐ 4		9.2-07-520	39,084	SF	.10	3908	.10	3908					.005	195
3% Mat. 4% Labor					3%	424	4%	700					4%	36
Corner Bead		9.2-02-030	14.4	CLF	7.65	110	54	778					2.76	40
Finish Corners		9.2-07-535	2588	LF	.04	104	.29	751					.015	39
@ Windows														
1/2" Standard No Finish ☐ 4		9.2-07-030	404	SF	.21	85	.17	69					.009	4
3% Mat. 4% Labor					3%	3	3 4%	3					4%	1
Corner Bead		9.2-02-030	6.06	CLF	7.65	46	54	327					2.76	17
Finish Corners		9.2-07-535	1344	LF	.04	54	.29	390					.015	20
Page Subtotals						(14947)		(20521)						(1049)

Table II.55

CONSOLIDATED ESTIMATE

PROJECT Commercial Renovation							SHEET NO. 3 of 7				
LOCATION		PRICES BY RSM					ESTIMATE NO. 85-1				
TAKE OFF BY EBW		QUANTITIES BY EBW					DATE 1985				

CLASSIFICATION
ARCHITECT
CHECKED BY

DESCRIPTION	FLOOR	SOURCE	QUANTITY	UNIT	BARE COSTS — MATERIAL		BARE COSTS — LABOR		BARE COSTS — EQUIPMENT		SUBCONTRACTOR		MAN-HOURS	
					UNIT	TOTAL	UNIT	TOTAL	UNIT	TOTAL	UNIT	TOTAL INCL O & P	UNIT	TOTAL
Division 9 : (Cont'd)														
Ceramic Tile :														
Base		9.3-05-130	252	LF	SUBCONTRACT						5.10	1285	.129	32
Floor		9.3-05-340	684	SF							4.56	3119	.087	59
Wall		9.3-05-540	1008	SF							3.94	4012	.089	90
Bullnose		9.3-05-250	252	LF							4.86	1225	.125	31
Carpet :	3	9.6-05-320	129	SY	SUBCONTRACT						19.75	2548	.20	26
Resilient :														
Vct		9.6-20-735	153	SF							1.36	208	.015	2
Vinyl Base		9.6-20-115	993	LF							1.29	1281	.027	27
Corners		9.6-20-163	60	Ea.							1.43	86	.027	2
Page Subtotals												13764		269

Table II.56

Division 9

CONSOLIDATED ESTIMATE

PROJECT	Commercial Renovation
LOCATION	
TAKE OFF BY	EBW
PRICES BY	RSM
QUANTITIES BY	EBW
CLASSIFICATION	
ARCHITECT	
SHEET NO.	4 of 7
ESTIMATE NO.	85-1
DATE	1985
CHECKED BY	

DESCRIPTION	FLOOR	SOURCE	QUANTITY	UNIT	MATERIAL UNIT	MATERIAL TOTAL	LABOR UNIT	LABOR TOTAL	EQUIPMENT UNIT	EQUIPMENT TOTAL	SUBCONTRACTOR UNIT	SUBCONTRACTOR TOTAL INCL. O & P	MAN-HOURS UNIT	MAN-HOURS TOTAL
Division 9: (Cont'd)														
Ceiling:														
Tile		9.5-15-374	2837	SF	.78	2213	.27	766					.014	40
Grnd		9.5-20-030	2837	SF	.38	1078	.24	681					.012	34
Lobby: Walls		written Quote	876	SF										
Custom Floors			441	SF								14320		
Millwork Ceiling			441	SF										
Stair Treads		9.6-25-100	192	LF	4.60	883	1.34	257					.070	13
Risers		9.6-25-190	192	LF	1.45	278	.88	169					.046	9
Landings		9.6-25-130	108	SF	2.23	241	.56	60					.029	3
[1]		2% Mat. 3% Labor			2%	28	3%	15					3%	1
Refinish Wood Floor	1	9.6-40-760	3190	SF	.57	1818	1.21	3860					.062	198
Stucco @ Entrance Lintel	1	9.1-55-010	4	SY	1.80	7								
Min. Charge		9.1-55-155		Job			155	155					8	8
Special Finish		9.1-55-070	4	SY	.71	3								
Page Subtotals						6549		5963				14320		306

Table II.57

CONSOLIDATED ESTIMATE

PROJECT	Commercial Renovation						
LOCATION		PRICES BY RSM		CLASSIFICATION		SHEET NO. 5 of 7	
TAKE OFF BY EBW		QUANTITIES BY EBW		ARCHITECT		ESTIMATE NO. 85-1	
						DATE 1985	
						CHECKED BY	

DESCRIPTION	FLOOR	SOURCE	QUANTITY	UNIT	MATERIAL UNIT	MATERIAL TOTAL	LABOR UNIT	LABOR TOTAL	EQUIPMENT UNIT	EQUIPMENT TOTAL	SUBCONTRACTOR UNIT	SUBCONTRACTOR TOTAL INCL. O&P	MAN-HOURS UNIT	MAN-HOURS TOTAL
Division 9: (Cont'd)														
Paint:														
Doors - Oak } Each		9.8-17-180	58	Ea.	2^{70}	157	30	1740					1.6	93
metal } Side		9.8-17-100	28	Ea.	1^{31}	37	6^{25}	169					.32	9
Walls		9.6-21-024	6680	SF	.04	267	.07	468					.004	27
		9.8-21-084	6680	SF	.09	601	.13	868					.007	47
Sills		9.8-30-001	77	SF	.07	5	.17	13					.009	1
Wall Covering		9.8-40-330	7950	SF	.60	4770	.32	2544					.017	135
Spray Sandblast:														
Wood (Inc. 3rd Ceiling)		9.8-21-410	20,460	SF	.04	815	.17	3478					.009	184
Brick		9.8-21-410	2100	SF	.04	84	.17	357					.009	19
Existing Retail:														
Wall Covering		9.8-40-330	580	SF	.60	348	.32	186					.017	10
Ceiling - Tile		9.5-15-374	486	SF	.78	379	.27	131					.04	7
Grid		9.5-20-030	486	SF	.38	185	.24	117					.012	6
Carpet		9.6-05-110	54	SY	SUB	CON	TR	ACT			21	1134	.20	11
		14%Mat. 57% Labor			14%	128	67%	247			28%	318	279.	9
1 2 5 6 + + + +														
Page Subtotals						7779		10318				1453		558

Division 9

CONSOLIDATED ESTIMATE

PROJECT: Commercial Renovation
LOCATION:
TAKE OFF BY: EBW
PRICES BY: RSM
QUANTITIES BY: EBW
CLASSIFICATION:
ARCHITECT:

SHEET NO. 6 of 7
ESTIMATE NO. 85-1
DATE 1985
CHECKED BY:

DESCRIPTION	FLOOR	SOURCE	QUANTITY	UNIT	MATERIAL UNIT	MATERIAL TOTAL	LABOR UNIT	LABOR TOTAL	EQUIP UNIT	EQUIP TOTAL	SUBCONTR UNIT	SUBCONTR TOTAL INCL O&P	MAN-HRS UNIT	MAN-HRS TOTAL
Division 9: (Cont'd)														
Tenant:														
3 5/8" 25 ga. 16" o.c.		9.2-20-230	3015	SF	25	754	39	1176					.02	60
1/2" Drywall-Taped		9.2-07-635	6030	SF	23	1387	35	2110					.018	109
High Ceilings [1][5]		9.2-07-520	6030	SF	10	603	10	603					.005	30
4% mat. 5% Labor					4%	110	5%	194					5%	10
Corner Bead		9.2-02-030	.30	CLF	765	2	54	16					2.76	1
Finish Corners		9.2-07-535	615	LF	04	25	29	178					.015	9
Paint: Doors (Ea. Side)		9.8-17-180	16	Ea.	2.70	43	30	480					1.6	26
walls		9.8-21-024	2610	SF	04	104	07	183					.004	10
		9.8-21-084	2610	SF	09	235	13	339					.007	18
Wall Covering		9.8-40-300	4320	SF	40	1728	24	1037					.013	56
Ceiling		9.5-15-314	607	SF	78	473	27	164					.014	8
		9.5-20-030	607	SF	38	231	24	146					.012	7
VCT		9.6-20-735	607	SF			SUBCONTRACT				1.36	826	.015	9
Vinyl Base		9.6-20-115	482	LF							1.29	622	.027	13
Carpet		9.6-05-450	222	SY							33	7326	.20	44
Refinish Wood Floor		9.6-40-760	418	SF	51	238	12	506					.062	26
Page Subtotals						5935		7132				8774		436

Table II.59

CONSOLIDATED ESTIMATE

PROJECT	Commercial Renovation			CLASSIFICATION		SHEET NO.	7 of 7
LOCATION		PRICES BY RSM		ARCHITECT		ESTIMATE NO.	85-1
TAKE OFF BY EBW		QUANTITIES BY EBW				DATE	1985
						CHECKED BY	

DESCRIPTION	FLOOR	SOURCE	QUANTITY	UNIT	MATERIAL UNIT	MATERIAL TOTAL	LABOR UNIT	LABOR TOTAL	EQUIPMENT UNIT	EQUIPMENT TOTAL	SUBCONTRACTOR UNIT	SUBCONTRACTOR TOTAL INCL. O & P	MAN-HOURS UNIT	MAN-HOURS TOTAL
Division 9 : (Cont'd)														
Sheet 1						5868		10442						539
Sheet 2						19947		20521						1049
Subtotal : Drywall Partitions						20815		30963						1588
Sheet 3 : Floor Covering						6549		5963				13764		269
Sheet 4						7779		10318				14320		306
Sheet 5												1452		558
Subtotal						35143		47244				29536		2721
Sheet 6 : Tenant						5933		7132				8774		436
Division 9 : Totals						41076		54576				38310		3157

Table II.60

216

In Table II.55, the 5/8" fire-resistant drywall is listed in two ways, taped and with no finish. See also Table II.62. The drywall that requires no finish is the first layer of a two layer application, at the new stairway enclosure. The estimator should visualize the work in order to include the proper costs. The costs for shaftwall are shown in Table II.62. Taping and finishing is not included. Costs are derived from lines 210 and 215 in Table II.62.

The drywall returns at the window jambs and headers could easily be overlooked (Figure II.17). For quantities, refer back to Table II.34, the Quantity Sheet for the sills and grounds. The measurements have already been calculated and can be used for the drywall take-off. The drywall installation at the window is almost all corners, and the appropriate finish work is included in the estimate (Table II.55).

It is important, when estimating drywall, to be aware of units. Studs, drywall, and taping are priced by the square foot, furring and corner bead per one hundred linear feet, and finishing corners by the linear foot. Confusion of units can result in expensive mistakes.

The estimator must be constantly aware of how the existing conditions and factors will affect the costs. For example, the wallcovering, ceiling, and carpet in the existing retail space must be installed after business hours, and precautions are necessary. The appropriate factors are shown in Table II.63 and the costs included in Table II.58. The work, without factors, would cost $2,480. With the factors, however, the cost is $3,173, an increase of 28%.

Metal Studs (Table II.54)		Drywall (Table II.55)	
1-5/8"	7,144 S.F.	1/2"	13,292 S.F.
3-5/8" (x2)	23,550	5/8"	22,014
6" (x2)	1,120	(disregard one layer on	
Furring	3,492	two lower wall	
(convert to S.F.)		and ceiling)	
	35,306 S.F.		35,306 S.F.

Quantity Comparison of Studs vs. Drywall

Table II.61

217

Division 10: Specialties

Specialties are items of construction that do not fall within other divisions and are permanently attached or built into the work. Table I2.4 provides a check list for Division 10. The materials are usually pre-finished items installed at or near the end of the project. The estimate sheet for Division 10, Table II.64, does not include any factors. This is because previous work has "accounted for" or "corrected" discrepancies caused by existing conditions, and the items are installed at areas of new work. This is not to say that factors will never be applicable. For example, bathroom accessories may be specified at existing walls. If there is no backing, the wall must be cut and patched for proper installation.

The estimator must be very careful when examining the plans and specifications to be sure to include all required items that may be shown or described only once. Sometimes these items are included in a Room Finish Schedule. If there are no plans and specifications, the estimator should refer to past estimates or to a check list, as in Table I2.4b.

9.2 Drywall

			CREW	MAN-HOURS	UNIT	MAT.	LABOR	EQUIP.	TOTAL	TOTAL INCL O&P
07	200	5/8" thick, on walls, standard, no finish included		.009		.23	.18		.41	.54
	205	Taped and finished		.019		.25	.37		.62	.84
	210	Fire resistant, no finish included		.009		.26	.18		.44	.57
	215	Taped and finished		.019		.28	.37		.65	.88
	220	Water resistant, no finish included		.009		.30	.18		.48	.61
	225	Taped and finished		.019		.32	.37		.69	.92
	230	Prefinished, vinyl, clipped to studs	▼	.015	▼	.67	.30		.97	1.20
	235									
	300	On ceilings, standard, no finish included	2 Carp	.015	S.F.	.23	.29		.52	.69
	305	Taped and finished		.021		.25	.42		.67	.92
	310	Fire resistant, no finish included		.015		.26	.29		.55	.73
	315	Taped and finished		.021		.28	.42		.70	.95
	320	Water resistant, no finish included		.015		.30	.29		.59	.77
	325	Taped and finished		.021		.32	.42		.74	1
	350	On beams, columns, or soffits, standard, no finish included		.025		.23	.48		.71	1
	355	Taped and finished		.036		.25	.70		.95	1.35
	360	Fire resistant, no finish included		.025		.26	.48		.74	1.03
	365	Taped and finished		.036		.28	.70		.98	1.38
	370	Water resistant, no finish included		.025		.30	.48		.78	1.07
	375	Taped and finished		.036		.32	.70		1.02	1.43

9.2 Drywall

		CREW	MAN-HOURS	UNIT	MAT.	LABOR	EQUIP.	TOTAL	TOTAL INCL O&P
45-001	SHAFT WALL Cavity type, 1" steel C-H studs, with 2 layers 5/8"								
003	gypsum board 1 side, 2 hour fire rating	2 Carp	.097	S.F.	1.32	1.90		3.22	4.39
006	Laminated gypsum drywall, 2-1/2" solid or								
010	3-3/4" core with steel H sections								
030	24" wide units, to 10'-4" high	2 Carp	.148	S.F.	1.69	2.90		4.59	6.35
040	16" wide units, to 11'-7" high	"	.174	"	2.06	3.41		5.47	7.55
060	Solid 2" thick, steel edge gypsum in channels with								
070	1/2" fire resistant gypsum								
080	1 side, 2 hour fire rating	2 Carp	.107	S.F.	1.26	2.09		3.35	4.61
090	2 sides, 3 hour fire rating	"	.119	"	1.63	2.32		3.95	5.40

Table II.62

218

1.1 Overhead

	CREW	MAN-HOURS	UNIT	BARE COSTS MAT.	BARE COSTS LABOR	BARE COSTS EQUIP.	BARE COSTS TOTAL	TOTAL INCL O&P
09-001 CONSTRUCTION MANAGEMENT FEES								
006 For work to $10,000			Project					10%
007 To $25,000								9%
009 To $100,000								6%
010 To $500,000								5%
011 To $1,000,000								4%
11-001 CONTINGENCIES Allowance to add at conceptual stage								20%
005 Schematic stage								15%
010 Preliminary working drawing stage								10%
015 Final working drawing stage								2%
15-001 ENGINEERING FEES Educational planning consultant, minimum			Contract					4.10%
010 Maximum								10.10%
040 Elevator & conveying systems, minimum								2.50%
050 Maximum								5%
100 Mechanical (plumbing & HVAC), minimum								4.10%
110 Maximum								10.10%
120 Structural, minimum			Project					1%
130 Maximum			"					2.50%
17-001 FACTORS To be added to construction costs for particular job requirements								
010								
[1] 050 Cut & patch to match existing construction, add, minimum			Costs	2%	3%			
055 Maximum				5%	9%			
[2] 080 Dust protection, add, minimum				1%	2%			
085 Maximum				4%	11%			
[3] 110 Equipment usage curtailment, add, minimum				1%	1%			
115 Maximum				3%	10%			
[4] 140 Material handling & storage limitation, add, minimum				1%	1%			
145 Maximum				6%	7%			
[5] 170 Protection of existing work, add, minimum				2%	2%			
175 Maximum				5%	7%			
[6] 200 Shift work requirements, add, minimum				5%	5%			
205 Maximum					30%			
[7] 230 Temporary shoring and bracing, add, minimum				2%	5%			
235 Maximum				5%	12%			
18-001 INSURANCE Builders risk, standard, minimum			Job Cost					.10%
005 Maximum								.50%
020 All-risk type, minimum								12%
025 Maximum								68%
040 Contractor's equipment floater, minimum			Value					.90%
045 Maximum			"					1.60%
060 Public liability, average			Job Cost					.82%
081 Workers compensation & employer's liability								
200 Range of 36 trades in 50 states, excl. wrecking, min.			Payroll					1.04%
210 Average								9%

NOTES

FACTORS: In planning and estimating repair and remodeling projects, there are many factors that can affect the project cost more than material and labor. The economics of scale usually associated with new construction often has no influence on the cost of repair and remodeling. Small quantities of components may have to be custom fabricated at great expense. Work schedule coordination between trades frequently becomes difficult and work area restrictions can lead to subcontractor quotations with start-up and shutdown costs which are in excess of the cost of actual work involved. Some of the more prominent factors affecting repair and remodeling projects include:

1. Cutting and patching to match the existing construction can often lead to an economical trade-off of removing entire walls rather than creating new door and window openings. Substitutions for materials which are no longer manufactured can be expensive. Piping and ductwork runs may not be as straight as in new construction and wiring may have to be snaked through walls and floors.

2. Dust and noise protection of adjoining nonconstruction areas can alter usual construction methods.

3. Equipment usage curtailment resulting from physical limitations of the project may force workmen to use slow hand-operated equipment instead of power tools.

4. The confines of an enclosed building have a costly influence on movement and material handling. Low capacity elevators and stairwells may be the only access to upper floors of a multi-story building.

5. On some repair or remodeling projects completed work must be secured or otherwise protected from possible damage during construction. In certain areas completed work must be guarded to prevent theft and vandalism. (cont.)

For expanded coverage of these items see *Building Construction Cost Data 1985*

6

Table II.63

CONSOLIDATED ESTIMATE

PROJECT	Commercial Renovation				SHEET NO.	1 of 1
LOCATION		PRICES BY RSM		CLASSIFICATION	ESTIMATE NO.	85-1
TAKE OFF BY EBW		QUANTITIES BY EBW		ARCHITECT	DATE	1985
					CHECKED BY	

DESCRIPTION	FLOOR	SOURCE	QUANTITY	UNIT	BARE COSTS MATERIAL		LABOR		EQUIPMENT		SUBCONTRACTOR		MAN-HOURS	
					UNIT	TOTAL	UNIT	TOTAL	UNIT	TOTAL	UNIT	TOTAL INCL. O & P	UNIT	TOTAL
Division 10: Specialties														
Grab Bars 1¼" Dia.		10.1-02-110	8	Ea.	21	168	7.85	63					.4	3
		10.1-02-200			207%	34								
Mirrors		10.1-02-380	4	Ea.	265	1060	26	104					1.33	5
Napkin Dispenser		10.1-02-420	2	Ea.	245	490	10.45	21					.533	1
Soap Dispenser		10.1-02-460	11	Ea.	47	517	7.85	86					.40	4
T.P. Holder		10.1-02-610	13	Ea.	17.10	222	5.25	68					.261	3
Towel Dispenser		10.1-02-670	7	Ea.	41	287	9.80	69					.60	3
Waste Receptacle		10.1-02-800	4	Ea.	130	520	15.70	63					.80	3
Canvas Awnings		Written Quote	4	Ea.		SUBCONTRACTOR					725	2900	8	32
Medicine Cabinets		10.1-42-001	3	Ea.	41	123	11.20	34					.571	2
Toilet Partitions Handicapped		10.1-42-250	10	Ea.	190	1900	52	520					2.67	27
		10.1-60-290			66	264								
Urinal Screens		10.1-60-530	4	Ea.	115	460	39	156					2	8
Division 10: Totals						6045		1184				2900		91

Table II.64

Division 11: Architectural Equipment

This division includes prefabricated items or items that may be built and installed by specialty subcontractors. Often, the architect arranges to have the owner purchase architectural equipment. The estimator must include installation costs if necessary. Table II.65 is the estimate sheet for Divisions 11, 12, and 13. The only work in Division 11 is the installation of the kitchen unit in the third floor lounge. (see Figure II.11).

Division 12: Furnishings

Furnishings are usually purchased by the owner. In the sample project, the blinds are included in the project specifications because all windows receive the same treatment. A construction contract will most likely not include furniture, but the estimator may be asked to provide budget prices. *Repair and Remodeling Cost Data* provides cost data for such items as shown in Table II.66.

Division 13: Special Construction

The estimator must carefully examine and analyze work in Division 13 on an item by item basis, obtaining prices from appropriate specialty subcontractors. Special construction often requires preparation work, excavation, and unloading, which may not be included in the subcontract. All such requirements must be included in the estimate.

Division 14: Conveying Systems

Installation of elevators in commercial renovation is often difficult at best. The estimator and the installing subcontractor must be thoroughly aware of the existing conditions and be familiar with the complete installation process. Hydraulic elevators are used most often in commercial renovation, unless the buildings are tall.

In the sample project, the price is included in Table II.67 is a budget price only. A firm subcontract price must be obtained. Such a bid from the elevator installer will itemize what work is included and what is excluded. For the exclusions, the estimator must either determine and estimate the appropriate costs or define the exclusions in the final project bid. For example, ledge or rock encountered in drilling is very expensive. The potential extra costs must be included as a potential "extra" in the prime contract.

CONSOLIDATED ESTIMATE

PROJECT Commercial Renovation
LOCATION
TAKE OFF BY EBW PRICES BY RSM QUANTITIES BY EBW
CLASSIFICATION
ARCHITECT
SHEET NO. 1 of 1
ESTIMATE NO. 85-1
DATE 1985
CHECKED BY

| DESCRIPTION | FLOOR | SOURCE | QUANTITY | UNIT | BARE COSTS | | | | | | SUBCONTRACTOR | | MAN-HOURS | |
| | | | | | MATERIAL | | LABOR | | EQUIPMENT | | | | | |
					UNIT	TOTAL	UNIT	TOTAL	UNIT	TOTAL	UNIT	TOTAL INCL. O&P	UNIT	TOTAL
Division 11: Architectural Equipment														
Kitchen Unit Labor Only Tenant	3	11.1-03-166	1	Ea.			39	39					1.78	2
Division 12: Furnishings														
Blinds	1 & 2 (44)	12.1-10-001	924	SF	2	1848	.21	249					.014	13
	3 (26)	12.1-10-001	385	SF	2	770	.21	104					.014	5
Division 12: Totals						2618		353						18
Division 13: Special Construction														
No Work														

Table II.65

12.1 Furnishings

	CREW	MAN-HOURS	UNIT	MAT.	LABOR	EQUIP.	TOTAL	TOTAL INCL O&P	NOTES
10 445 18" x 40" each	1 Carp	.471	Pr.	43	9.20		52.20	62	
30-001 FURNITURE, DORMITORY Beds, free standing, minimum			Ea.	155			155	170M	
010 Maximum			"	375			375	415M	
205 Rule of thumb: Total cost for furniture, minimum			Student					1,200	
215 Maximum			"					2,100	
45-001 FURNITURE, HOSPITAL Beds, manual, minimum			Ea.	520			520	570M	
010 Maximum			"	905			905	995M	
110 Patient wall systems, not incl. plumbing, minimum			Room	520			520	570M	
120 Maximum				960			960	1,050M	
50-001 FURNITURE, HOTEL Standard quality, set, minimum			→	1,625			1,625	1,800M	
020 Maximum				4,850			4,850	5,325M	
53-001 FURNITURE, OFFICE									
002 Desks, 29" high, double pedestal, 30" x 60", metal, minimum			Ea.	205			205	225M	
003 Maximum			"	560			560	615M	
60-001 FURNITURE, RESTAURANT Bars, built-in, front bar	1 Carp	1.600	L.F.	125	31		156	185	
020 Back bar		1.600	"	90	31		121	145	
050 Booth unit, molded plastic, stub wall and 2 seats, minimum		4	Set	245	78		323	390	
060 Maximum		5.330	"	530	105		635	745	
080 Booth seat, upholstered, foursome, single (end) minimum		1.600	Ea.	355	31		386	440	
090 Maximum		2		740	39		779	875	
100 Foursome, double, minimum		2		530	39		569	645	
110 Maximum		2.670		1,050	52		1,102	1,225	
130 Circle booth, upholstered, 1/4 circle, minimum		2.670		585	52		637	725	
140 Maximum		4		1,175	78		1,253	1,425	
150 3/4 circle, minimum		5.330		1,050	105		1,155	1,325	
160 Maximum		8	→	2,850	155		3,005	3,375	
70-001 SHADES Basswood roll-up, stain finish, 3/8" slats		.027	S.F.	9.30	.52		9.82	11.05	
003 Double layered, heat reflective		.012		4.45	.23		4.68	5.25	
020 7/8" slats		.027		8.50	.52		9.02	10.15	
090 Mylar, single layer, non-heat reflective		.012		2.55	.23		2.78	3.16	
100 Double layered, heat reflective		.012		4.45	.23		4.68	5.25	
110 Triple layered, heat reflective		.012	→	5.20	.23		5.43	6.05	
500 Thermal, roll up, R-4		.182		4.75	3.56		8.31	10.75	
503 R-10.7		.182	→	6.40	3.56		9.96	12.55	
505 Magnetic clips, set of 20			Set	11			11	12.10M	

For expanded coverage of these items see Means' *Interior Cost Data 1985*

Table II.66

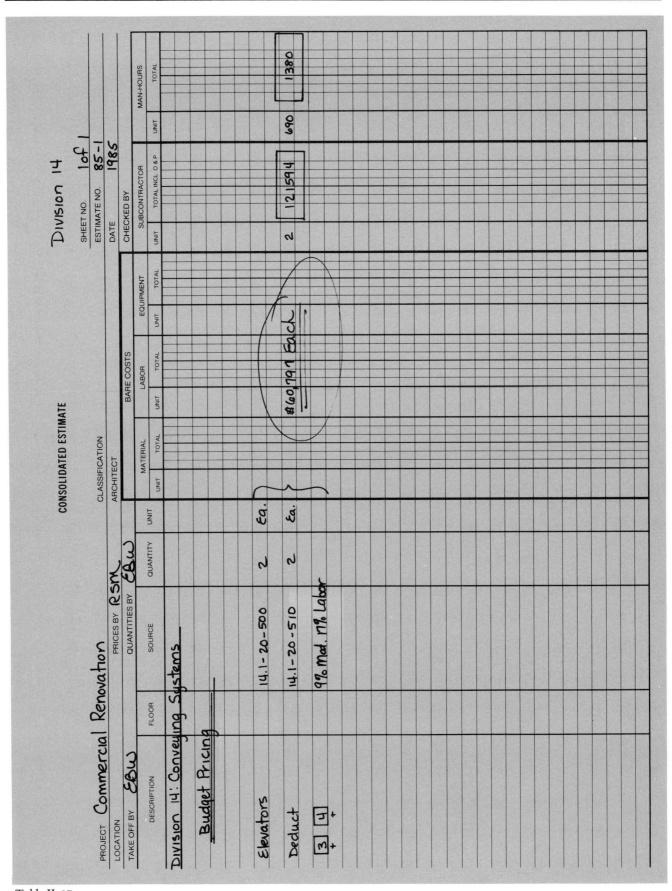

Table II.67

224

13.1 Special Construction

		CREW	MAN-HOURS	UNIT	BARE COSTS MAT.	BARE COSTS LABOR	BARE COSTS EQUIP.	BARE COSTS TOTAL	TOTAL INCL O&P	NOTES
75-001	SWIMMING POOLS. Outdoor, incl. equip. & houses, minimum			S.F.Surf					36	
030	Maximum								68	
040	Residential, incl. equipment, permanent type, minimum								12	
070	Maximum								25	
090	Municipal, including equipment only, over 5000 S.F., minimum								25	
100	Maximum								51	
130	Motel or apt., incl. equipment only, under 5000 S.F., minimum								22	
140	Maximum								34	

14.1 Conveying Systems

		CREW	MAN-HOURS	UNIT	BARE COSTS MAT.	BARE COSTS LABOR	BARE COSTS EQUIP.	BARE COSTS TOTAL	TOTAL INCL O&P
10-001	CORRESPONDENCE LIFT 1 floor 2 stop, 25 lb. capacity, electric	2 Elev	80	Ea.	3,400	1,775		5,175	6,400
010	Hand, 5 lb. capacity		80		1,000	1,775		2,775	3,750
15-001	DUMBWAITERS 2 stop, electric, minimum		123		1,750	2,725		4,475	5,875
010	Maximum		145		5,000	3,225		8,225	10,200
030	Hand, minimum		70		600	1,550		2,150	2,900
040	Maximum		84		1,025	1,875		2,900	3,825
060	For each additional stop, electric, add		30	Stop	750	655		1,405	1,775
070	Hand, add		27	"	545	590		1,135	1,450
20-001	ELEVATORS								
500	Passenger, pre-engineered, 5 story, hydraulic, 2,500 lb. capacity	M1	800	Ea.	43,400	18,300		61,700	74,000
510	For less than 5 stops, deduct	"	110	Stop	6,050	2,525		8,575	10,200
520	For 4,000 lb. capacity, general purpose, add			Ea.	1,925			1,925	2,125M
540	10 story, geared traction, 200 FPM, 2,500 lb. capacity	M1	1600	"	41,800	36,600		78,400	98,000
550	For less than 10 stops, deduct		94	Stop	1,875	2,150		4,025	5,125
560	For 4,500 lb. capacity, general purpose		1600	Ea.	46,100	36,600		82,700	103,000
580									
700	Residential, cab type, 1 floor, 2 stop, minimum	2 Elev	80	Ea.	5,200	1,775		6,975	8,300
710	Maximum		160		9,300	3,550		12,850	15,400
720	2 floor, 3 stop, minimum		133		6,300	2,950		9,250	11,200
730	Maximum		267		15,700	5,900		21,600	25,800
770	Stair climber (chair lift), single seat, minimum		16		1,900	355		2,255	2,600
780	Maximum		80		2,500	1,775		4,275	5,325
800	Wheelchair, porch lift, minimum		16		3,200	355		3,555	4,050
850	Maximum		32		6,375	710		7,085	8,075
870	Stair lift, minimum		16		5,000	355		5,355	6,025
890	Maximum		80		8,000	1,775		9,775	11,500
45-001	PNEUMATIC TUBE SYSTEM Single tube, 2 stations,								
002	100 ft. long, stock, economy,								

Table II.68

Table II.69

226

1.1 Overhead

		CREW	MAN-HOURS	UNIT	BARE COSTS MAT.	LABOR	EQUIP.	TOTAL	TOTAL INCL O&P
09-001	CONSTRUCTION MANAGEMENT FEES								
006	For work to $10,000			Project					10%
007	To $25,000								9%
009	To $100,000								6%
010	To $500,000								5%
011	To $1,000,000								4%
11-001	CONTINGENCIES Allowance to add at conceptual stage								20%
005	Schematic stage								15%
010	Preliminary working drawing stage								10%
015	Final working drawing stage								2%
15-001	ENGINEERING FEES Educational planning consultant, minimum			Contract					4.10%
010	Maximum								10.10%
040	Elevator & conveying systems, minimum								2.50%
050	Maximum								5%
100	Mechanical (plumbing & HVAC), minimum								4.10%
110	Maximum								10.10%
120	Structural, minimum			Project					1%
130	Maximum			"					2.50%
17-001	FACTORS To be added to construction costs for particular job requirements								
010									
[1] 050	Cut & patch to match existing construction, add, minimum			Costs	2%	3%			
055	Maximum				5%	9%			
[2] 080	Dust protection, add, minimum				1%	2%			
085	Maximum				4%	11%			
[3] 110	Equipment usage curtailment, add, minimum				1%	1%			
115	Maximum				3%	10%			
[4] 140	Material handling & storage limitation, add, minimum				1%	1%			
145	Maximum				6%	7%			
[5] 170	Protection of existing work, add, minimum				2%	2%			
175	Maximum				5%	7%			
[6] 200	Shift work requirements, add, minimum					5%			
205	Maximum					30%			
[7] 230	Temporary shoring and bracing, add, minimum				2%	5%			
235	Maximum				5%	12%			
18-001	INSURANCE Builders risk, standard, minimum			Job Cost					10%
005	Maximum								50%
020	All-risk type, minimum								12%
025	Maximum								68%
040	Contractor's equipment floater, minimum			Value					90%
045	Maximum			"					1.60%
060	Public liability, average			Job Cost					82%
081	Workers compensation & employer's liability								
200	Range of 36 trades in 50 states, excl. wrecking, min.			Payroll					1.04%
210	Average								9%

NOTES:

FACTORS: In planning and estimating repair and remodeling projects, there are many factors that can affect the project cost more than material and labor. The economics of scale usually associated with new construction often has no influence on the cost of repair and remodeling. Small quantities of components may have to be custom fabricated at great expense. Work schedule coordination between trades frequently becomes difficult and work area restrictions can lead to subcontractor quotations with start-up and shutdown costs which are in excess of the cost of actual work involved. Some of the more prominent factors affecting repair and remodeling projects include:

1. Cutting and patching to match the existing construction can often lead to an economical trade-off of removing entire walls rather than creating new door and window openings. Substitutions for materials which are no longer manufactured can be expensive. Piping and ductwork runs may not be as straight as in new construction and wiring may have to be snaked through walls and floors.

2. Dust and noise protection of adjoining nonconstruction areas can alter usual construction methods.

3. Equipment usage curtailment resulting from physical limitations of the project may force workmen to use slow hand-operated equipment instead of power tools.

4. The confines of an enclosed building have a costly influence on movement and material handling. Low capacity elevators and stairwells may be the only access to upper floors of a multi-story building.

5. On some repair or remodeling projects completed work must be secured or otherwise protected from possible damage during construction. In certain areas completed work must be guarded to prevent theft and vandalism. (cont.)

For expanded coverage of these items see Building Construction Cost Data 1985

The costs for the elevator budget price are derived from Table II.68. Note that there is a deduction for fewer than five stops. Factors from Table II.69 are applied to the budget price because access for drilling is very restricted and the handling of the drilling waste requires special consideration. The calculations for the budget price are shown in Table II.70. However ridiculous it may seem, a common error would be to forget to double the elevator cost to include the two elevators.

Division 15: Mechanical

When mechanical plans and specifications are provided, and prepared by an engineer, take-off and pricing can be relatively simple. If no plans are available, the work should be estimated by an experienced subcontractor who will be sure to include all requirements.

In the sample project, the plumbing work is itemized and estimated. A subcontractor will perform the work. Costs, including overhead and profit, are used. The estimator must visualize the whole system and follow the path of the piping to be sure that existing conditions will not restrict installation. If no plans are available, a quick riser diagram will be helpful.

Tables II.71 to II.74 are the estimate sheets for Division 15. In order to include all components, the estimator should make a list of all fixtures and equipment, complete with required faucets, fittings, and hanging hardware. All required backing should be included in Division 6.

	Bare Costs				Total Including O & P
		Material		Labor	
Elevator 14.1-20-500		$43,400		$18,300	
Deduct (2 Stops) 14.1-20-510		(12,100)		(5,050)	
		31,300		13,250	
Factors	(9%)	2,817	(17%)	2,252	
		34,117		15,502	
Overhead and Profit	(10%)	3,412	(50.1%)	7,766	
		$37,529		$23,268	$60,797
$60,797 x 2 Elevators = $121,594					

Calculations for Elevator Budget Price.

Table II.70

CONSOLIDATED ESTIMATE

PROJECT Commercial Renovation									SHEET NO. 1 of 4
LOCATION	PRICES BY RSM			CLASSIFICATION					ESTIMATE NO. 85-1
TAKE OFF BY EBW	QUANTITIES BY EBW			ARCHITECT					DATE 1985
									CHECKED BY

DESCRIPTION	FLOOR	SOURCE	QUANTITY	UNIT	BARE COSTS						SUBCONTRACTOR		MAN-HOURS	
					MATERIAL		LABOR		EQUIPMENT		UNIT	TOTAL INCL. O & P	UNIT	TOTAL
					UNIT	TOTAL	UNIT	TOTAL	UNIT	TOTAL				
Division 15: Mechanical														
Plumbing:														
Backflow Preventer	B	15.1-04-512	1	Ea.	SUBCONTRACT →						5175	5175	8	8
Faucets:														
Lavatory		15.1-22-210	15	Ea.	8⁹⁵						47	705	.80	12
w/Drain		15.1-22-220	15	Ea.	15%						13⁸⁴	207	156	2
Service		15.1-22-300	2	Ea.							61	122	.571	1
Fixtures:														
Drink Fountain		15.2-16-282	2	Ea.							675	1350	2.5	5
Rough		15.2-16-398	2	Ea.							260	520	6.45	13
Lavatories														
Vanity		15.2-32-060	6	Ea.							185	1110	2.5	15
Wall		15.2-32-418	9	Ea.							185	1665	2	18
Rough		15.2-32-696	15	Ea.							475	7125	11.76	176
Jan. Sink		15.2-36-010	2	Ea.							285	570	2.67	5
Rough		15.2-36-960	2	Ea.							440	880	11.94	24
Page Subtotals												(19429)		(279)

Table II.71

CONSOLIDATED ESTIMATE

PROJECT	Commercial Renovation							
LOCATION		PRICES BY RSM				SHEET NO. 2 of 4		
TAKE OFF BY EBW		QUANTITIES BY EBW			CLASSIFICATION	ESTIMATE NO. 85-1		
					ARCHITECT	DATE 1985 / CHECKED BY		

DESCRIPTION	FLOOR	SOURCE	QUANTITY	UNIT	BARE COSTS	SUBCONTRACTOR		MAN-HOURS	
					MATERIAL / LABOR / EQUIPMENT	UNIT	TOTAL INCL. O & P	UNIT	TOTAL
Division 15: Mechanical (Cont'd)									
Fixtures (Cont'd)									
Urinals		15.2-68-300	4	Ea.	SUBCONTRACT →	460	1840	5.33	21
Rough		15.2-68-330	4	Ea.		400	1600	10.74	43
Water Cl.									
Flush		15.2-80-310	10	Ea.		325	3250	2.76	28
Rough		15.2-80-320	10	Ea.		490	4900	10.53	105
Tank		15.2-80-110	3	Ea.		205	615	3.02	9
Rough		15.2-80-198	3	Ea.		375	1125	9.25	28
Water Heater		15.3-50-604	1	Ea.		895	895	5.71	6
Sump Pumps		15.2-54-710	2	Ea.		265	530	1.33	3
Floor Drains		15.1-16-204	1	Ea.		66	66	1.33	1
Page Subtotals							(11821)		(244)

Table II.72

CONSOLIDATED ESTIMATE

PROJECT	Commercial Renovation			
LOCATION		PRICES BY RSM		
TAKE OFF BY EBW		QUANTITIES BY EBW		

CLASSIFICATION
ARCHITECT
CHECKED BY

DESCRIPTION	FLOOR	SOURCE	QUANTITY	UNIT	BARE COSTS — MATERIAL UNIT	MATERIAL TOTAL	LABOR UNIT	LABOR TOTAL	EQUIPMENT UNIT	EQUIPMENT TOTAL	SUBCONTRACT UNIT	TOTAL INCL O&P	MAN-HOURS UNIT	MAN-HOURS TOTAL
Division 15: Mechanical-(Cont'd)														
Piping:														
6" PVC		15.1-49-449	132	LF			SUBCONTRACT				25	3300	.552	73
90° Elbows		15.1-50-062	16	Ea.							100	1600	2	52
Tees		15.1-50-089	12	Ea.							155	1860	3.2	38
Copper														
2½"		15.1-40-228	112	LF							21	2352	.485	54
1"		15.1-40-220	86	LF							9.15	787	.222	19
2½" Elbows		15.1-41-035	6	Ea.							45	270	1.23	7
1" Elbows		15.1-41-031	12	Ea.							17.90	215	.5	6
2½" Tees		15.1-41-055	4	Ea.							75	300	2	8
1" Tees		15.1-41-051	7	Ea.							29	203	.80	6
2½" Coupl.		15.1-41-075	8	Ea.							36	288	1.07	9
1" Coupl.		15.1-41-071	12	Ea.							15.65	188	.444	5
Factors		5% mat. 9% Labor			5%		9%				7%	795	9%	23
Page Subtotals												(12158)		(280)

Table II.73

Division 15

CONSOLIDATED ESTIMATE

PROJECT Commercial Renovation
LOCATION
TAKE OFF BY EBW   PRICES BY RSM   QUANTITIES BY EBW

CLASSIFICATION
ARCHITECT

DESCRIPTION	FLOOR	SOURCE	QUANTITY	UNIT	MATERIAL UNIT	MATERIAL TOTAL	LABOR UNIT	LABOR TOTAL	EQUIPMENT UNIT	EQUIPMENT TOTAL	SUBCONTRACTOR UNIT	SUBCONTRACTOR TOTAL INCL. O & P	MAN-HOURS UNIT	MAN-HOURS TOTAL
Division 15: Mechanical - (Cont'd)														
Heating & Air Conditioning		Written Quote										187813		1650
Tenant- HVAC												14563		
Page Subtotals												(202376)		(1650)
Sheet 1												19429		279
Sheet 2												14821		244
Sheet 3												12158		280
Plumbing Subtotal												46408		803
Sheet 4												202376		1650
Division 15: Totals												[248784]		[2453]

Table II.74

15.1 Pipe & Fittings

		CREW	MAN-HOURS	UNIT	BARE COSTS MAT.	LABOR	EQUIP.	TOTAL	TOTAL INCL O&P	NOTES
19	028	Female IPT to sweat, straight								
	034	3/4" pipe size	1 Plum	.400	Ea.	2.34	8.90		11.24	15.85
	078	Female IPT to female IPT, straight								
	080	1/2" pipe size	1 Plum	.333	Ea.	3.16	7.40		10.56	14.55
	084	3/4" pipe size		.400	"	3.52	8.90		12.42	17.15
	900	Minimum labor/equipment charge		2	Job		44		44	66L
22-001		**FAUCETS/FITTINGS**								
	002	Bath, faucets, diverter spout combination, sweat	1 Plum	1	Ea.	37	22		59	74
	015	For integral stops, IPS unions, add				18			18	19.80M
	050	Drain, central lift, 1-1/2" IPS male	1 Plum	.400		23	8.90		31.90	39
	060	Trip lever, 1-1/2" IPS male	"	.400		22	8.90		30.90	37
	084	Flush valves, with vacuum breaker								
	085	Water closet								
	086	Exposed, rear spud	1 Plum	1	Ea.	74	22		96	115
	087	Top spud		1		67	22		89	105
	088	Concealed, rear spud		1		76	22		98	115
	089	Top spud		1		87	22		109	130
	090	Wall hung		1		73	22		95	115
	091	Urinal								
	092	Exposed, stall	1 Plum	1	Ea.	67	22		89	105
	093	Wall, (washout)		1		67	22		89	105
	094	Pedestal, top spud		1		69	22		91	110
	095	Concealed, stall		1		69	22		91	110
	096	Wall (washout)		1		69	22		91	110
	100	Kitchen sink faucets, top mount, cast spout		.800		27	17.75		44.75	56
	110	For spray, add				8	10%			
	200	Laundry faucets, shelf type, I.P.S. or copper unions	1 Plum	.667		25	14.80		39.80	50
	210	Lavatory faucet, centerset, without drain	"	.800		19	17.75		36.75	47
	220	For pop-up drain, add				8.95	15%			
	280	Self-closing, center set	1 Plum	.800		53	17.75		70.75	85
	300	Service sink faucet, cast spout, pail hook, hose end		.571		38	12.70		50.70	61
	400	Shower by-pass valve with union		.444		29	9.85		38.85	47
	420	Shower thermostatic mixing valve, concealed	1 Plum	1		140	22		162	185
	430	For inlet strainer, check, and stops, add				40	5%			
	500	Sillcock, compact, brass, I.P.S. or copper to hose	1 Plum	.333		4.07	7.40		11.47	15.55
	900	Minimum labor/equipment charge	"	2	Job		44		44	66L
25-001	020	**FLOOR RECEPTORS** For connection to 2", 3" & 4" diameter pipe	Q-1	1.600	Ea.					
		12-1/2" square top, 25 sq. in. open area				155	32		187	220
	030	For grate with 4" diam. x 3-3/4" high funnel, add				23			23	25M
	040	For grate with 6" diameter x 6" high funnel, add				34			34	37M
	070	For acid-resisting bucket, add				33			33	36M
	090	For stainless steel mesh bucket liner, add				26			26	29M

Floor Receptor, Square Top

Floor Receptor, Round Top

For expanded coverage of these items see Means' *Mechanical Cost Data 1985*

Table II.75

In Section 15.2, Plumbing Fixtures, in *Repair and Remodeling Cost Data*, there are separate line items for rough-in of supply, waste, and vent for each fixture type. These include average costs for connecting to nearby risers and stacks. Also, faucets and valves are included in some fixture costs. With lavatories, however, faucets must be included as a separate item. Table II.75 lists prices for faucets. Note that while prices for water closet and urinal flush valves are listed, these costs are included in the fixture prices. Drains for lavatory faucets are listed as a separate item because in some commercial applications, drains are not required. The costs for the drains are included in the estimate as shown in Table II.76.

Costs for water supply risers and waste vent and stack, only, are estimated because rough-in piping is included with the fixtures. A factor for working around existing conditions is applied to the entire piping cost.

Because of the scope and size of the sample project, a subcontractor bids the cost of heating, ventilation, and air conditioning. The estimator must be sure that all necessary work is included in the bids. For example, since the third floor ceiling is open to the trusses and roof deck, ductwork will be exposed. The corridors must be heated and cooled, and the bathrooms require ventilation. The subcontractor should supply shop drawings of all work for clarification. At the owner's request, tenant costs are priced separately.

Division 16: Electrical

As with the heating, ventilation, and air conditioning, the electrical work is bid by a subcontractor (Table II.77). For purposes of this example, the itemized estimate for the tenant electrical work is included in Table II.78.

When estimating electrical work for commercial renovation, the estimator should visualize the installation and follow the proposed paths of the wiring during the site visit. Wrapping conduit around beams and columns can become very expensive. Such restrictive conditions exist in the tenant space. The ceiling is open to the roof deck. Light fixture wiring is exposed and carried in EMT. The conduit must be bent and neatly installed over, along, and around the exposed trusses. The exterior walls are sandblasted brick. Wiremold is specified. Factors must be applied to this work for conforming to existing conditions and for the protection of existing work, as shown in Table II.78.

	Bare Costs			Total Including O & P
	Material		Labor	
Lavatory Faucet 15.1-22-210		$19.00	$17.75	$47.00
Drain - add 15.1-22-220		8.95	(15%) 2.66	
Overhead and Profit	(10%)	.89	(49.5%) 1.31	
Total for Drain		$9.84	$3.97	$13.81

Calculations for Lavatory Drain Including Overhead and Profit.

Table II.76

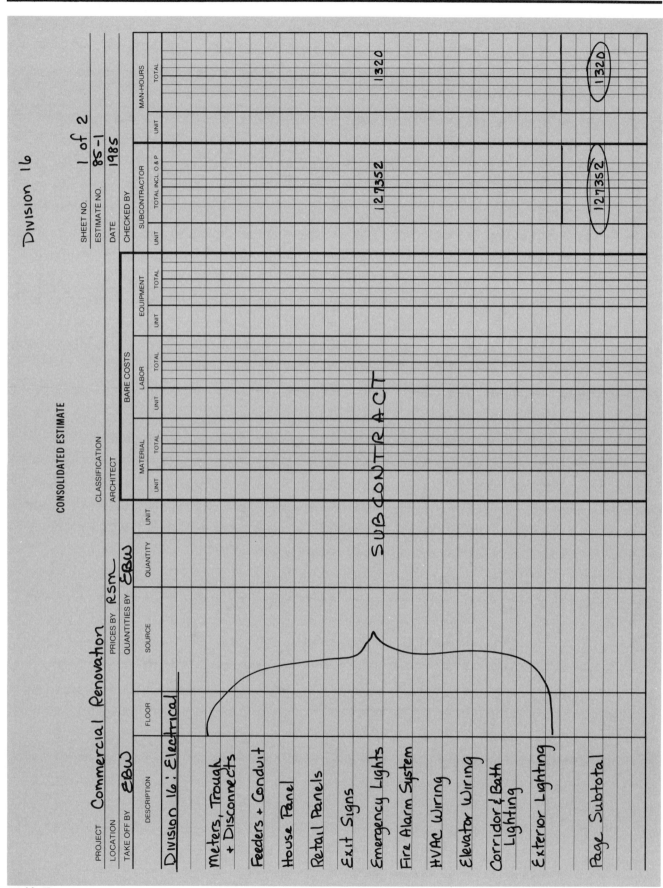

Table II.77

Division 16

CONSOLIDATED ESTIMATE

PROJECT: Commercial Renovation
LOCATION:
TAKE OFF BY: EBW
PRICES BY: RSM
QUANTITIES BY: EBW
CLASSIFICATION:
ARCHITECT:
SHEET NO. 1 of 2
ESTIMATE NO. 85-1
DATE: 1985
CHECKED BY:

DESCRIPTION	FLOOR	SOURCE	QUANTITY	UNIT	MATERIAL UNIT	MATERIAL TOTAL	LABOR UNIT	LABOR TOTAL	EQUIPMENT UNIT	EQUIPMENT TOTAL	SUBCONTRACTOR UNIT	TOTAL INCL. O & P	MAN-HOURS UNIT	MAN-HOURS TOTAL
Division 16: Electrical														
Meters, Trough + Disconnects														
Feeders + Conduit														
House Panel														
Retail Panels														
Exit Signs														
Emergency Lights												127352		1320
Fire Alarm System														
HVAC Wiring				SUBCONTRACT										
Elevator Wiring														
Corridor & Bath Lighting														
Exterior Lighting														
Page Subtotal												127352		1320

234

DIVISION 16

CONSOLIDATED ESTIMATE

PROJECT Commercial Renovation
LOCATION
TAKE OFF BY EBW   PRICES BY RSM   QUANTITIES BY EBW

CLASSIFICATION
ARCHITECT

SHEET NO. 2 of 2
ESTIMATE NO. 85-1
DATE 1985
CHECKED BY

DESCRIPTION	FLOOR	SOURCE	QUANTITY	UNIT	MATERIAL unit	MATERIAL total	LABOR unit	LABOR total	EQUIPMENT unit	EQUIPMENT total	SUBCONTRACTOR unit	SUBCONTRACTOR total INCL. O&P	MAN-HOURS unit	MAN-HOURS total
Division 16: Electrical (Cont'd)														
Tenant Work:														
EMT 3/4"		16.0-20-502	285	LF							2³⁷	675	.062	18
Bends		16.0-20-522	92	Ea.							3²⁹	303	.10	9
Wiremold		16.0-90-010	112	LF							3⁰⁹	346	.08	9
Boxes		16.0-90-300	16	Ea.				SUB CONTRACT			19²⁰	307	.50	8
11 5 +		10% Mat. 10% Labor			10%		16%				13%	212	16%	7
Panel		16.3-50-085	1	Ea.							1200	1200	17.78	18
Bx		16.1-20-015	4.6	CLF							155	713	3.81	18
Boxes		16.2-20-015	57	Ea.							15.70	895	.444	25
Rings		16.2-20-030	57	Ea.							4.76	271	.125	7
Switches		16.2-30-050	14	Ea.							17¹⁵	240	.296	4
Recept.		16.2-30-230	59	Ea.							15⁷⁰	926	.296	17
Lighting														
Recessed		16.6-10-060	10	Ea.							105	1050	1.7	17
Track Lighting		16.6-80-010	24	Ea.							90	2160	1.51	36
Fixtures		Quote	48	Ea.							86	4128		
Page Subtotals												(13426)		(193)
Sheet 1												127352		1320
Sheet 2 (Tenant)												13426		193
Division 16 Totals												140778		1513

Table II.78

The wiring for switches and receptacles in the perimeter offices must be concealed in the walls since there is no suspended ceiling. Much more wire is needed because straight runs are not possible.

The estimator must check to be sure that the subcontractor bids the work to conform to all code requirements. Even if the plans are prepared by an electrical engineer, approval by local authorities is usually necessary, especially for fire alarms.

Estimate Summary

When the work for all divisions is priced, the estimator should complete the Project Schedule so that time-related costs in the Project Overhead Summary can be determined. When preparing the schedule, the estimator must visualize the entire construction process so that the correct sequence of work is determined. Certain tasks must be completed before others are begun. Different trades will work simultaneously. Material deliveries will affect scheduling. All such variables must be incorporated into the Project Schedule, as shown in Table II.79. The man-hour figures, which have been calculated for each division, are used to assist with scheduling. The estimator must be careful not to use the man-hours for each division independently. Each division must be coordinated with related work.

The schedule shows that the project will last approximately six months. Time-dependent items, such as equipment rental and superintendent costs, can be included in the Project Overhead Summary. Some items are dependent on total job costs, such as permits and insurance. The total direct costs for the project must be determined as shown in the Condensed Estimated Summary, Table II.80. All costs can now be included and totalled on the Project Overhead Summary, Tables II.81a and II.81b.

The estimator is now able to complete the Estimate Summary as shown in Table II.82. Appropriate contingency, sales tax, and overhead and profit costs must be added to direct costs of the project. Ten percent is added to material, equipment, and subcontractor costs for handling and supervision. The overhead and profit percentage of 53.8% for labor is obtained from Table II.83, as the average mark-up for skilled workers. Contractors should determine appropriate mark-ups for their own companies as discussed in Part I, Chapter 4.3.

As part of the requirements for the estimate, the tenant improvement costs have been separated within each appropriate division and are included and totalled on a separate estimate sheet (Table II.84). Cost per square foot is shown at the top of the Estimate Summary. The owner can use this figure to budget costs for future tenant improvements in the building. This square foot cost figure must be used with reservations. Even in the same building, different areas will require special considerations because of existing conditions.

Note in Tables II.82 and II.84 that totals are recorded horizontally for each division, and vertically for the different cost categories. This method of recording the numbers provides a way for cross-checking the final calculations. A mistake at this final stage of the estimate could be very costly.

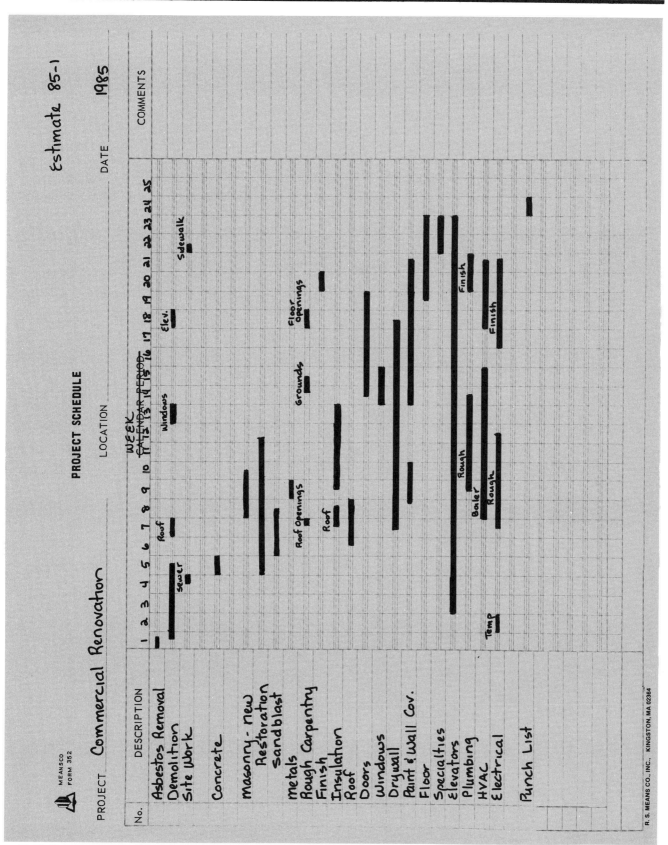

Table II.79

CONDENSED ESTIMATE SUMMARY

PROJECT **Commercial Renovation** TOTAL AREA **25,200 SF** SHEET NO. **1 of 1**
LOCATION TOTAL VOLUME **(Rentable)** ESTIMATE NO. **85-1**
ARCHITECT COST PER S.F. DATE **1985**
OWNER COST PER C.F. NO. OF STORIES **3**
QUANTITIES BY **EBW** PRICES BY **RSM** EXTENSIONS BY CHECKED BY

NO.	DESCRIPTION		Man Hours	MATERIAL	LABOR	EQUIPMENT	SUBCONTRACTOR	TOTAL
	SITE WORK		170	1792	2856			4648
	Excavation							
	Demolition		1183	442	17190	2341	4574	24547
	CONCRETE		140	5058	2827	293		8178
	MASONRY		972	5907	10831	179	16711	33628
	Restoration		1257	1253	22927	1833		26013
	METALS		15	393	157		11702	12252
	CARPENTRY	Rough	98	1310	1924	76		3310
		Finish	46	839	883	3		1725
	MOISTURE PROTECTION		341	10858	3104	26	25634	39622
		Tenant	19	750	389	1		1140
	DOORS, ~~WINDOWS, GLASS~~		174	17919	3415	79		21413
	Windows & Glass		273				45296	45296
		Tenant	40	2985	569		508	4062
	FINISHES		3157	41076	54376		38310	133762
		Tenant	436	5933	7132		8774	21839
	SPECIALTIES		91	6045	1184		2900	10129
	EQUIPMENT	Tenant	2		39			39
	FURNISHINGS		18	2618	353			2971
	SPECIAL CONSTRUCTION							
	CONVEYING SYSTEMS		1380				121594	121594
	BUDGET PRICE							
	MECHANICAL							
	Plumbing		803				46408	46408
	Heating, Ventilating, Air Conditioning		1650				187813	187813
		Tenant					14563	14563
	ELECTRICAL		1320				127352	127352
		Tenant	193				13426	13426
	Total Direct Costs			105178	130156	4831	665565	905730
	Proj. Overhead							
	Contingency 2%							
	Sales Tax 6%							
	Overhead & Profit 10/53.8/10/10							
	TOTAL BID							

Table II.80

	Man-Hours	QUANTITY	UNIT	MATERIAL		LABOR		EQUIPMENT	
DESCRIPTION				UNIT	TOTAL	UNIT	TOTAL	UNIT	TOTAL
Job Organization: Superintendent									
Accounting and bookkeeping									
Timekeeper and material clerk									
Clerical									
Shop									
Safety, watchman and first aid									
1.1-22-105	960	24	WK			765	18360		
Engineering: Layout									
Quantities									
Inspection									
Shop drawings									
Drafting & extra prints									
Testing: Soil									
Materials									
Structural									
Supplies: Office									
Shop									
Utilities: ~~Light and~~ power		28	MSF					84	2352
Water									
Heating									
Lighting 1.1-58-350	(66)	280	CSF	1⁴⁹	473	5²⁰	1456		
Equipment: Rental									
Light trucks									
Freight and hauling									
Loading, unloading, erecting, etc.									
Maintenance									
Dumpster 2.2-78-080		22	WK					150	3300
Travel Expense									
Main office personnel									
Freight and Express									
Demurrage									
Hauling, misc.									
Advertising Job Sign		1	Ea.		250				
Signs and Barricades									
Temporary fences									
Temporary stairs, ladders & floors									
Rails @ Stair & Elev.	(22)	270	LF	1²⁴	335	1⁵⁷	424		
~~Photos~~ 1.1-58-310									
Page total					1058		20240		5652

Table II.81a

DESCRIPTION	QUANTITY	UNIT	MATERIAL UNIT	MATERIAL TOTAL	LABOR UNIT	LABOR TOTAL	EQUIP., FEES, RENTAL UNIT	EQUIP., FEES, RENTAL TOTAL
Total Brought Forward				1058		20240		5652
Legal Contract Review							100	100
Medical and Hospitalization								
Field Offices								
Office furniture and equipment								
Telephones	6	Mo.					100	600
Heat and Light								
Temporary toilets								
Storage areas and sheds								
Permits: Building 1.1-36-001	0.5%							4529
Misc. Street Use	1	Ea.					50	50
Sewer Connection	1	Ea.					300	300
Insurance 1.1-18-020	.12%	Job						1087
Bonds								
Interest								
Taxes								
Cutting and Patching & Punch list								
Winter Protection								
Temporary heat								
Snow plowing								
Thawing materials								
Temporary Roads								
Rent 6 Parking Spaces Repairs to adjacent property	6	Mo.					300	1800
Pumping								
Scaffolding 1.1-44-010 (170)	119	CSF			28	3332		
Rental-381 Frames-$2 25/mo Small Tools	6	Mo.					851	5142
Stud Driver 5.8-32-001 Clean up	1	Ea.	285	285				
Final 1.1-04-010 (44)	28	MSF	1 52	43	24 76	693	1 24	35
Contingencies								
Main Office Expense								
Special Items								
Fire Exting. 15.4-20-208	4	Ea.	41	164				
Total:	1262 man-Hours			1550		24265		19295

Table II.81b

CONDENSED ESTIMATE SUMMARY

PROJECT	Commercial Renovation			TOTAL AREA 25,200 SF		SHEET NO. 1 of 1
LOCATION				TOTAL VOLUME (Rentable)		ESTIMATE NO. 85-1
ARCHITECT				COST PER S.F.		DATE 1985
OWNER				COST PER C.F.		NO. OF STORIES 3
QUANTITIES BY EBW		PRICES BY EBW		EXTENSIONS BY		CHECKED BY

NO.	DESCRIPTION	man-Hours	MATERIAL	LABOR	EQUIPMENT	SUBCONTRACTOR	TOTAL
	SITE WORK Excavation	170	1792	2856			4648
	Demolition	1183	442	17190	2341	4574	24547
	CONCRETE	140	5058	2827	293		8178
	MASONRY	972	5907	10831	179	16711	33628
	Restoration	1257	1253	22927	1833		26013
	METALS	15	393	157		11702	12252
	CARPENTRY Rough	98	1310	1924	76		3310
	Finish	46	839	883	3		1725
	MOISTURE PROTECTION	341	10858	3104	26	25634	39622
	Tenant	19	750	389	1		1140
	DOORS, ~~WINDOWS, GLASS~~	174	17919	3415	79		21413
	Windows & Glass	273				45296	45296
	Tenant	40	2985	569		508	4062
	FINISHES	3157	41076	54376		38310	133762
	Tenant	436	5933	7132		8774	21839
	SPECIALTIES	91	6045	1184		2900	10129
	EQUIPMENT Tenant	2		39			39
	FURNISHINGS	18	2618	353			2971
	SPECIAL CONSTRUCTION						
	CONVEYING SYSTEMS Budget Price	1380				121594	121594
	MECHANICAL Plumbing	803				46408	46408
	Heating, Ventilating, Air Conditioning	1650				187813	187813
	Tenant					14563	14563
	ELECTRICAL	1320				127352	127352
	Tenant	193				13426	13426
	Total Direct Costs		105178	130156	4831	665565	905730
	Proj. Overhead Summary	1262	1550	24265	19295		45110
	Contingency 2%		2135	3088	483	13311	19017
	Sales Tax 6%		6532				6532
	Overhead & Profit 10/53.8/10/10		11539	84740	2461	67888	166628
	TOTAL BID Man-Hours 15,100		126934	242249	27070	746764	1143017

Table II.82

241

CONTRACTOR'S OVERHEAD AND PROFIT
To the left are the average subcontractor's percentage mark-ups that should be applied directly to all labor rates in order to arrive at typical billing rates for subcontractors.

Column A:
Base rates including fringe benefits are described in Column A in hourly and daily terms. These figures are the sum of the base rate, employer-paid fringe benefits such as vacation pay, employer-paid health and welfare costs, pension costs, plus appropriate training and industry advancement funds costs.

Column B:
National average Workmen's Compensation rate by trade.

Column C:
Column C lists the average fixed overhead figures for all trades. In particular, Federal and State Unemployment costs are set at 5.5%; Social Security Taxes (FICA) are set at 7.05%, Builder's Risk Insurance costs are set at 0.38%; and Public Liability costs are set at 0.82%. These overhead costs are analyzed below. All the percentages except those for Social Security Taxes vary from state to state as well as from company to company.

Columns D & E:
Percentages in Columns D & E are based on the presumption that the subcontractor being used in any given project has an annual billing rate of $250,000. Smaller subcontractors' percentages for overhead are usually higher.
The overhead percentages for a subcontractor vary greatly and depend on a number of factors: the subcontractor's annual volume; his engineering and logistical support costs, his staff requirements, and the size of the equipment he is required to use on a particular construction project. The figures for overhead and profit will vary depending on the type of job, the job location, and the prevailing economic conditions. These factors should be examined very carefully for each job. For the purpose of estimating the cost of a project, it is reasonable to assume a 16% cost for the subcontractor's overhead, and a 15% cost for the subcontractor's profit.

Column F:
Column F lists the total of columns B, C, D, and E.

Column G:
Column G is Column A (hourly base labor rate) multiplied by the percentage in Column F (Sub's O&P percentage).

Column H:
Column H is the total of Column A (hourly base labor rate) plus Column G (Sub's O&P hourly rate).

Column I:
Column I is Column H multiplied by eight hours.

Mass. State Unemployment Tax ranges from 1.5% to 5.7% plus a small experience rating assessment the following year on the first $7,000. Federal Unemployment tax is 3.5% of the first $7,000 of wages. This is reduced by a credit for payment to the state. The minimum Federal Unemployment tax is 0.8% after all credits.

Combined rates in Mass. vary from 2.3% to 6.5% of the first $7,000 of wages. The combined average U.S. rate is about 5.5% of the first $7,000. Contractors with permanent workers will pay less, since the theoretical annual wage for skilled worker is $20.10 X 2,000 hours, or about $40,200 per year. The average combined rate for the U.S. would therefore be 5.50% x 7,000 ÷ 40,200 = 0.96% of total wages.

Abbr.	Trade	A Base Rate incl. fringes Hourly	A Daily	B Workers' Comp. Ins.	C Average Fixed Overhead	D Subs Overhead	E Subs Profit	F Subs Total Overhead & Profit %	G Amount	H Rate with Subs O. & P. Hourly	I Daily
Skwk	Skilled Workers Average (35 trades)	$20.10	$160.80	9.0%	13.8%	16%	15%	53.8%	$10.80	$30.90	$247.20
	Helpers Average (5 trades)	15.20	121.60	9.3				54.1	8.20	23.40	187.20
	Foremen Average, Inside (50¢ over trade)	20.60	164.80	9.0				53.8	11.10	31.70	253.60
	Foremen Average, Outside ($2.00 over trade)	22.10	176.80	9.0				53.8	11.90	34.00	272.00
Clab	Common Building Laborers	15.50	124.00	9.6				54.4	8.45	23.95	191.60
Asbe	Asbestos Workers	22.20	177.60	7.4				52.2	11.60	33.80	270.40
Boil	Boilermakers	22.30	178.40	6.7				51.5	11.50	33.80	270.40
Brc	Bricklayers	20.05	160.40	7.2				52.0	10.45	30.50	244.00
Brhe	Bricklayer Helpers	15.65	125.20	7.2				52.0	8.15	23.80	190.40
Carp	Carpenters	19.60	156.80	9.6				54.4	10.65	30.25	242.00
Cefi	Cement Finishers	18.80	150.40	5.5				50.3	9.45	28.25	226.00
Elec	Electricians	22.10	176.80	3.9				48.7	10.75	32.85	262.80
Elev	Elevator Constructors	22.15	177.20	5.3				50.1	11.10	33.25	266.00
Eqhv	Equipment Operators, Crane or Shovel	20.65	165.20	6.9				51.7	10.70	31.35	250.80
Eqmd	Equipment Operators, Medium Equipment	20.20	161.60	6.9				51.7	10.45	30.65	245.20
Eqlt	Equipment Operators, Light Equipment	19.05	152.40	6.9				51.7	9.85	28.90	231.20
Eqol	Equipment Operators, Oilers	17.10	136.80	6.9				51.7	8.85	25.95	207.60
Eqmm	Equipment Operators, Master Mechanics	21.45	171.60	6.9				51.7	11.10	32.55	260.40
Glaz	Glaziers	19.85	158.80	7.6				52.4	10.40	30.25	242.00
Lath	Lathers	19.75	158.00	5.8				50.6	10.00	29.75	238.00
Marb	Marble Setters	19.55	156.40	7.2				52.0	10.15	29.70	237.60
Mill	Millwrights	20.35	162.80	6.4				51.2	10.40	30.75	246.00
Mstz	Mosaic and Terrazzo Workers	19.35	154.80	5.2				50.0	9.70	29.05	232.40
Pord	Painters, Ordinary	18.85	150.80	7.2				52.0	9.80	28.65	229.20
Psst	Painters, Structural Steel	19.60	156.80	26.0				70.8	13.90	33.50	268.00
Pape	Paper Hangers	19.15	153.20	7.2				52.0	9.95	29.10	232.80
Pile	Pile Drivers	19.70	157.60	16.6				61.4	12.10	31.80	254.40
Plas	Plasterers	19.60	156.80	7.2				52.0	10.20	29.80	238.40
Plah	Plasterer Helpers	16.15	129.20	7.2				52.0	8.40	24.55	196.40
Plum	Plumbers	22.20	177.60	4.7				49.5	11.00	33.20	265.60
Rodm	Rodmen (Reinforcing)	21.30	170.40	15.9				60.7	12.95	34.25	274.00
Rotc	Roofers, Composition	18.35	146.80	17.1				61.9	11.35	29.70	237.60
Rots	Roofers, Tile & Slate	18.50	148.00	17.1				61.9	11.45	29.95	239.60
Rohe	Roofer Helpers (Composition)	13.45	107.60	17.1				61.9	8.35	21.80	174.40
Shee	Sheet Metal Workers	22.20	177.60	6.0				50.8	11.30	33.50	268.00
Spri	Sprinkler Installers	22.60	180.80	5.6				50.4	11.40	34.00	272.00
Stpi	Steamfitters or Pipefitters	22.30	178.40	4.7				49.5	11.05	33.35	266.80
Ston	Stone Masons	19.85	158.80	7.2				52.0	10.30	30.15	241.20
Sswk	Structural Steel Workers	21.30	170.40	19.5				64.3	13.70	35.00	280.00
Tilf	Tile Layers (Floor)	19.25	154.00	5.1				49.9	9.60	28.85	230.80
Tilh	Tile Layer Helpers	15.25	122.00	5.1				49.9	7.60	22.85	182.80
Trlt	Truck Drivers, Light	16.00	128.00	8.4				53.2	8.50	24.50	196.00
Trhv	Truck Drivers, Heavy	16.20	129.60	8.4				53.2	8.60	24.80	198.40
Sswl	Welders, Structural Steel	21.30	170.40	19.5				64.3	13.70	35.00	280.00
Wrck	*Wrecking	15.50	124.00	20.7				65.5	10.15	25.65	205.20

*Not included in Averages.

Table II.83

CONDENSED ESTIMATE SUMMARY

PROJECT **Tenant Improvements**
LOCATION **Commercial Renovation**
ARCHITECT
OWNER
QUANTITIES BY **EBW**   PRICES BY **EBW**

TOTAL AREA **2916 SF**
TOTAL VOLUME
COST PER S.F. **$23⁵⁶**
COST PER C.F.
EXTENSIONS BY

SHEET NO. **1 of 1**
ESTIMATE NO. **85-1**
DATE **1985**
NO. OF STORIES
CHECKED BY

NO.	DESCRIPTION	MATERIAL	LABOR	EQUIPMENT	SUBCONTRACTOR	TOTAL
	SITE WORK Excavation					
	CONCRETE					
	MASONRY					
	METALS					
	CARPENTRY					
	MOISTURE PROTECTION	750	389	1		1140
	DOORS, WINDOWS, GLASS	2985	569		508	4062
	FINISHES	5933	7132		8774	21839
	SPECIALTIES					
	EQUIPMENT		39			39
	FURNISHINGS					
	SPECIAL CONSTRUCTION					
	CONVEYING SYSTEMS					
	MECHANICAL Plumbing Heating, Ventilating, Air Conditioning				14563	14563
	ELECTRICAL				13426	13426
	Total Direct Costs	9668	8129	1	37271	55069
	Project Overhead 4%	387	325		1491	2203
	Contingencies 2%	201	169		775	1145
	Tax 6%	615				615
	O + P 10/53.8/10/10	1087	4639		3954	9680
	TOTAL BID	11958	13262	1	43491	68712

Table II.84

243

Part III:
Systems Estimating Example

Part III
Introduction

The Systems Estimate is useful during the design development stage of a project. The estimator needs only certain parameters and perhaps a preliminary floor plan to complete the estimate effectively. The advantage of using the Systems Estimate is the ability to develop costs quickly and to establish a budget before preparation of working drawings and specifications. The estimator can easily substitute one system for another to determine the most cost effective approach. The Systems Estimate can be completed in much less time than the Unit Price Estimate. Some accuracy is sacrificed, however, and the Systems Estimate should be used only for budgetary purposes.

In commercial renovation, costs vary greatly from project to project because of different requirements and the restrictions caused by existing conditions. Budgets and cost control are becoming increasingly more important before the project enters the final design process, and owners take on the expense of working drawings and specifications. It is crucial that the estimator combine a thorough evaluation of the existing conditions with the design parameters in order to properly complete the Systems Estimate. The estimator must use experience to be sure to include all requirements since little information is provided. Applicable building and fire codes and local regulations must also be considered.

Prices and costs used in the following example are from R.S. Mean' *Repair and Remodeling Cost Data*. A description of the use of the Systems pages is included in Part I, Chapter 4 of this book. The sample project below will vary in detail from actual projects. Every renovation must be treated individually.

Project Description

The sample project is the renovation of a twenty-five year old, two story suburban office building to eight apartments. The owner feels that the building is not profitable as office space and wants to know how much it will cost to convert to apartments. An architect has prepared a preliminary floor plan for only the ground level floor. The only information available to the estimator are the findings of the site visit, items passed on in a few discussions, and the floor plan, as shown in Figure III.1.

The exterior of the building is concrete block, with single pane, steel frame windows. The roof is wood trusses with old curling asphalt shingles. The ground floor is partially below grade. The ground floor structure is a concrete slab and the second floor is wood joist. The requirements for the project and existing conditions will be discussed throughout the appropriate divisions.

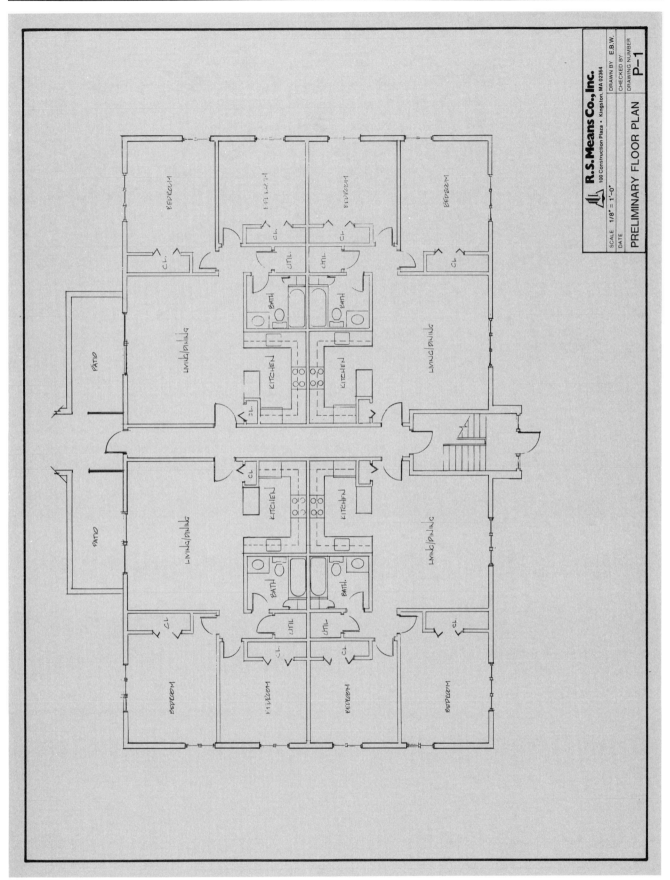

Figure III.1

FOUNDATIONS | 01.1-144 | Strip Footing

LINE NO.	DESCRIPTION	QUANTITY	MAT.	INST.	TOTAL
	SYSTEM		COST PER L.F.		
01	Strip footing, 2'-0" wide x 1'-0" thick, 2000 psi concrete including forms				
02	Reinforcing, keyway, and dowels.				
03					
04	Concrete, 2000 psi	.074 C.Y.	3.48		3.48
05	Placing concrete	.074 C.Y.		.78	.78
06	Forms, footing, 4 uses	2 S.F.	.51	3.87	4.38
07	Reinforcing	3.17 Lb.	.84	.81	1.65
08	Keyway, 2" x 4", 4 uses	1 L.F.	.08	.45	.53
09	Dowels, #4 bars, 2' long, 24" O.C.	.5 Ea.	.46	2.19	2.65
10	TOTAL	L.F.	5.37	8.10	13.47
11			3% .16	10% .81	
12			5.53	8.91	
13					
14	Above system with the following:				
15	2'-0" wide x 1' thick, 3000 psi concrete	L.F.	5.66	8.10	13.76
16	4000 psi concrete	"	5.89	8.10	13.99
17					
18	For alternate footing systems:				
19	2'-6" wide x 1' thick, 2000 psi concrete	L.F.	6.48	8.51	14.99
20	3000 psi concrete	→	6.85	8.51	15.36
21	4000 psi concrete		7.13	8.51	15.64
22					
23	3'-0" wide x 1' thick, 2000 psi concrete	L.F.	7.49	8.90	16.39
24	3000 psi concrete	→	7.93	8.90	16.83
25	4000 psi concrete		8.26	8.90	17.16
26					
27					
28					
29	Cut & patch to match existing construction, add, minimum		2%	3%	
30	Maximum		5%	9%	
31	Dust protection, add, minimum		1%	2%	
32	Maximum		4%	11%	
33	Equipment usage curtailment, add, minimum		1%	1%	
34	Maximum		3%	10%	
35	Material handling & storage limitation, add, minimum		1%	1%	
36	Maximum		6%	7%	
37	Protection of existing work, add, minimum		2%	2%	
38	Maximum		5%	7%	
39	Shift work requirements, add, minimum			5%	
40	Maximum			30%	
41					
42					

This page illustrates and describes a strip footing system including concrete, forms, reinforcing, keyway and dowels. Lines 01.1-144-04 thru 10 give the unit price and total price per linear foot for this system. Prices for alternate strip footing systems are on Line Items 01.1-144-15 thru 25. Both material quantities and labor costs have been adjusted for the system listed.

Example: 2'-6" wide x 1' thick, 3,000 psi concrete as an alternate system; choose Line Item 01.1-144-20, $6.85 MAT., $8.51 INST., $15.36 TOTAL. This price includes all materials compatible with the original system.

Factors: To adjust for job conditions other than normal working situations use Lines 01.1-144-29 thru 40.

Example: You are to install this footing, and due to a lack of accessibility, only hand tools can be used. Material handling is also a problem. Go to Lines 01.1-144-34 and 36 and apply these percentages to the appropriate MAT. and INST. costs.

Table III.1

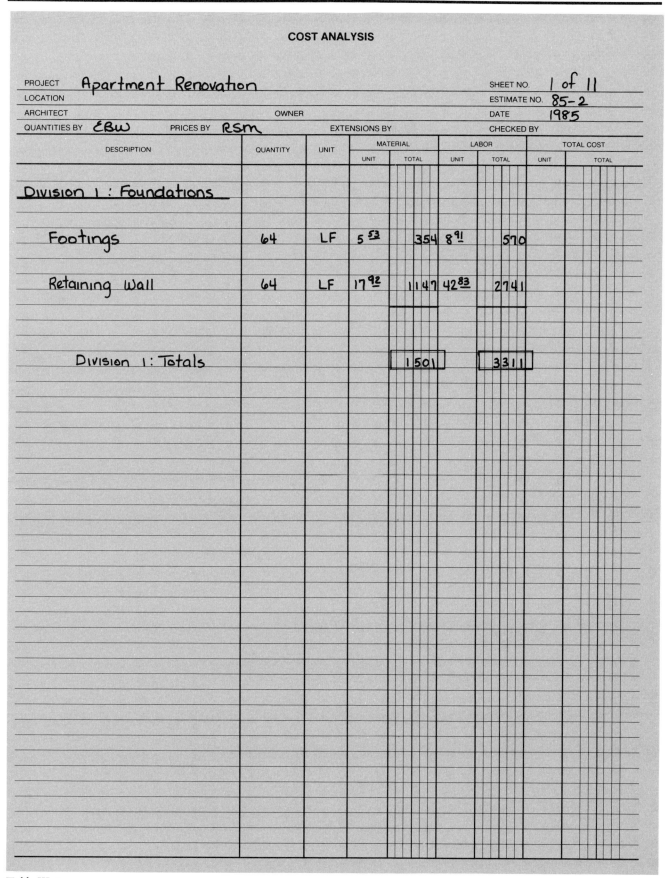

COST ANALYSIS

PROJECT Apartment Renovation						SHEET NO. 1 of 11			
LOCATION						ESTIMATE NO. 85-2			
ARCHITECT			OWNER			DATE 1985			
QUANTITIES BY EBW		PRICES BY RSM		EXTENSIONS BY		CHECKED BY			

DESCRIPTION	QUANTITY	UNIT	MATERIAL		LABOR		TOTAL COST	
			UNIT	TOTAL	UNIT	TOTAL	UNIT	TOTAL
Division 1 : Foundations								
Footings	64	LF	5⁵³	354	8⁹¹	570		
Retaining Wall	64	LF	17⁹²	1147	42⁸³	2741		
Division 1: Totals				1501		3311		

Table III.2

SYSTEM	LINE NO.	DESCRIPTION	QUANTITY	COST PER L.F.		
				MAT.	INST.	TOTAL
	01	Cast in place concrete foundation wall, 8" thick, 3' high, 2500 psi				
	02	Concrete including forms, reinforcing, waterproofing, and anchor bolts.				
	03					
	04	Concrete, 2500 psi, 8" thick, 3' high	.07 C.Y.	3.36		3.36
	05	Forms, wall, 4 uses	6 S.F.	3.37	17.33	20.70
	06	Reinforcing	6 Lb.	1.65	1.11	2.76
	07	Placing concrete	.07 C.Y.		1.82	1.82
	08	Waterproofing	3 S.F.	.50	1.42	1.92
	09	Rigid insulaton, 1" polystyrene	3 S.F.	.69	1.05	1.74
	10	Anchor bolts, 1/2" diameter, 4' O.C.	.25 Ea.	.14	.33	.47
	11	TOTAL	L.F.	9.71	23.06	32.77
	12					
	13					
	14	For alternate wall systems:				
	15	8" thick, 2500 psi concrete, 4' high	L.F.	13.21	30.82	44.03
	16	6' high		19.75	46.06	65.81
	17	8' high		26.29	61.30	87.59
	18	3500 psi concrete, 4' high		13.61	30.82	44.43
	19	6' high		20.35	46.06	66.41
	20	8' high		27.09	61.30	88.39
	21	12" thick, 2500 psi concrete, 4' high		16.71	32.86	49.57
	22	6' high		24.21	48.62	72.83
	23	8' high		32.19	64.64	96.83
	24	3500 psi concrete, 4' high		17.31	32.86	50.17
	25	8' high		33.39	64.64	98.03
	26	10' high		41.44	80.59	122.03
	27					
	28					
	29	Cut & patch to match existing construction, add, minimum		2%	3%	
	30	Maximum		5%	9%	
	31	Dust protection, add, minimum		1%	2%	
	32	Maximum		4%	11%	
	33	Equipment usage curtailment, add, minimum		1%	1%	
	34	Maximum		3%	10%	
	35	Material handling & storage limitation, add, minimum		1%	1%	
	36	Maximum		6%	7%	
	37	Protection of existing work, add, minimum		2%	2%	
	38	Maximum		5%	7%	
	39	Shift work requirements, add, minimum			5%	
	40	Maximum			30%	
	41			4%	5%	
	42					

Deduct

This page illustrates and describes a concrete wall system including concrete, placing concrete, forms, reinforcing, insulation, waterproofing and anchor bolts. Lines 01.1-214-04 thru 11 give the unit price and total price per linear foot for this system. Prices for alternate concrete wall systems are on Line Items 01.1-214-15 thru 26. Both material quantities and labor costs have been adjusted for the system listed.

Example: 12" thick, 2,500 psi concrete 4' high as an alternate system; choose Line Item 01.1-214-21, $16.71 MAT., $32.86 INST., $49.57 TOTAL. This price includes all materials compatible with the original system.

Factors: To adjust for job conditions other than normal working situations use Lines 01.1-214-29 thru 40.

Example: You are to install this wall system where delivery of material is difficult. Go to Line 01.1-214-36 and apply these percentages to the appropriate MAT. and INST. costs.

302

Table III.3

250

Division 1: Foundations

Preliminary floor plans often do not designate what is new work and what is existing. The estimator must determine the scope of work during the site visit. Footings are required for the retaining walls at the patios. Costs are determined from Table III.1. The footing system as shown is appropriate. Access for trucks, however, is restricted, so the concrete must be placed by hand. The appropriate factor for equipment usage curtailment is added. The quantities and costs are entered on the cost analysis in Table III.2.

Costs for the retaining wall are determined from Table III.3. The system, as shown, must be modified to meet the requirements of the project. The waterproofing, insulation, and anchor bolts are not needed. The costs for these items must be deducted from the complete system. Also the wall is 6' high and must be attached to the existing building foundation. The calculations, including the appropriate factors are shown in Table III.4. The costs are entered on the cost analysis (Table III.2).

		Material		Installation	Total
Concrete Wall		$19.75		$46.06	$65.81
01.1-214-16					
Deducts					
Waterproofing		(1.00)		(2.84)	(3.84)
Insulation		(1.38)		(2.10)	(3.48)
Anchor Bolts		(.14)		(.33)	(.47)
Subtotal		17.23		40.79	58.02
Factors	4%	.69	5%	2.04	2.73
4% Material					
5% Installation					
Total Costs per L.F.		$17.92		$42.83	$60.75

Calculations for Retaining Wall

Table III.4

SUBSTRUCTURE | 02.1-104 | Interior Slab on Grade

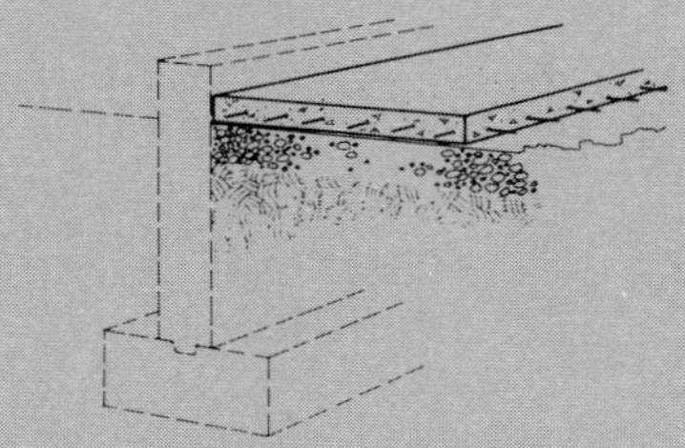

This page illustrates and describes a slab on grade system including slab, bank run gravel, bulkhead forms, placing concrete, welded wire fabric, vapor barrier, steel trowel finish and curing paper. Lines 02.1-104-04 thru 11 give the unit price and total price per square foot for this system. Prices for alternate slab on grade systems are on Line Items 02.1-104-15 thru 26. Both material quantities and labor costs have been adjusted for the system listed.

Example: 5" concrete slab with 12" gravel fill as an alternate system; choose Line Item 02.1-104-22, $1.27 MAT., $1.10 INST., $2.37 TOTAL. This price includes all materials compatible with the original system.

Factors: To adjust for job conditions other than normal working situations use Line 02.1-104-29 thru 40.

Example: You are to install the above slab system at a site where protection of the existing building is required. Go to Line 02.1-104-38 and apply these percentages to the appropriate MAT. and INST. costs.

LINE NO.	SYSTEM / DESCRIPTION	QUANTITY	COST PER S.F. MAT.	COST PER S.F. INST.	COST PER S.F. TOTAL
01	Ground slab, 4" thick, 3000 psi concrete, 4" granular base, vapor barrier				
02	Welded wire fabric, screed and steel trowel finish.				
03					
04	Concrete, 4" thick, 3000 psi concrete	.012 C.Y.	.61		.61
05	Bank run gravel, 4" deep	.074 C.Y.	.11	.03	.14
06	Polyethylene vapor barrier, 10 mil.	.011 C.S.F.	.07	.07	.14
07	Bulkhead forms, expansion material	.1 L.F.	.01	.16	.17
08	Welded wire fabric, 6 x 6 - #10/10	.011 C.S.F.	.09	.17	.26
09	Place concrete	.012 C.Y.		.14	.14
10	Screed & steel trowel finish	1 S.F.		.47	.47
11	TOTAL	S.F.	.89	1.04	1.93
12					
13					
14	Above system with the following:				
15	4" thick slab, 3000 psi concrete, 6" deep bank run gravel	S.F.	.95	1.04	1.99
16	12" deep bank run gravel	"	1.11	1.07	2.18
17					
18					
19					
20	For alternate slab systems:				
21	5" thick slab, 3000 psi concrete, 6" deep bank run gravel	S.F.	1.11	1.07	2.18
22	12" deep bank run gravel	"	1.27	1.10	2.37
23					
24					
25	6" thick slab, 3000 psi concrete, 6" deep bank run gravel	S.F.	1.31	1.12	2.43
26	12" deep bank run gravel	"	1.47	1.15	2.62
27					
28					
29	Cut & patch to match existing construction, add, minimum		2%	3%	
30	Maximum		5%	9%	
31	Dust protection, add, minimum		1%	2%	
32	Maximum		4%	11%	
33	Equipment usage curtailment, add, minimum		1%	1%	
34	Maximum		3%	10%	
35	Material handling & storage limitation, add, minimum		1%	1%	
36	Maximum		6%	7%	
37	Protection of existing work, add, minimum		2%	2%	
38	Maximum		5%	7%	
39	Shift work requirements, add, minimum			5%	
40	Maximum			30%	
41			147%		267%
42					

(Handwritten notes: "Deduct" beside lines 06–07; "147%" under MAT./INST.; "267%" under TOTAL.)

Table III.5

Division 2: Substructure

Sections of the ground floor slab must be cut and removed to install plumbing pipes. The estimator must be sure to include the demolition costs in Division 12 of the Systems portion of the Means' *Repair and Remodeling Cost Data*. The system used to replace the concrete is shown in Table III.5. The forms are not required and are deducted and the appropriate factors are added as shown in Table III.6. The total costs are entered in Table III.7.

Division 3: Superstructure

While no complete floor systems are specified for the project note that the superstructure systems in *Repair and Remodeling Cost Data* (Table III.8) include floor and ceiling finishes. The local building code requires that apartment ceilings have a one hour fire-rating. The "Floor and Ceiling Selective Price Sheet" in Table III.9 is used to determine the costs for the rated ceiling. Painting costs are taken from Table III.8. The floor finishes will be included in Division 6, Interior Construction of the Systems portion of the Means' *Repair and Remodeling Cost Data*.

During the site visit, the estimator must also determine the requirements for an exterior exit stairway from the second floor corridor. There is no indication of this item on the plan, so it is left to the estimator to itemize the requirements and calculate costs. Table III.10 is used to determine the costs for the stairway. The costs are entered on the cost analysis for Division 3 in Table III.11.

In Systems Estimating, the estimator must often make choices of methods and materials. Experience and a thorough evaluation of the existing conditions are important for making the correct choices.

	Material		Installation		Total
Interior Slab 02.1-104		$ .89		$1.04	$1.93
Deducts Forms		(.01)		(.16)	(.17)
Subtotal		.88		.88	1.76
Factors	14%	.12	26%	.23	.35
14% Material 26% Installation					
Total/S.F.		$1.00		$1.11	$2.11

Table III.6

PROJECT	Apartment Renovation						SHEET NO.	2 of 11		
LOCATION							ESTIMATE NO.	85-2		
ARCHITECT				OWNER			DATE	1985		
QUANTITIES BY EBW		PRICES BY RSM			EXTENSIONS BY		CHECKED BY			

DESCRIPTION	QUANTITY	UNIT	MATERIAL		LABOR		TOTAL COST	
			UNIT	TOTAL	UNIT	TOTAL	UNIT	TOTAL
Division 2: Substructure								
Interior Slab	160	SF	1	160	1"	178		
02.1-104								

Table III.7

Table III.8

SUPERSTRUCTURE 03.5-714 Floor - Ceiling, Wood Joists

This page illustrates and describes a wood joist floor system including wood joist, oak floor, sub-floor, bridging, sand and finish floor, furring, plasterboard, taped, finished and painted ceiling. Lines 03.5-714-04 thru 13 give the unit price and total price per square foot for this system. Prices for alternate wood joist floor systems are on Line Items 03.5-714-17 thru 23. Both material quantities and labor costs have been adjusted for the system listed.

Example: 2" x 12" joist 12" O.C. as an alternate system; choose Line Item 03.5-714-22, $3.76 MAT., $4.93 INST., $8.69 TOTAL. This price includes all materials compatible with the original system. For alternatives not listed, use the selective price sheet for this section (page 314). Substitute the new prices from the price sheet into the typical system and adjust the total to reflect each change.

Factors: To adjust for job conditions other than normal working situations use Lines 03.5-714-27 thru 40.

Example: You are to install the above system during off peak hours, 6 P.M. to 2 A.M. Go to Line 03.5-714-38 and apply this percentage to the appropriate INST. costs.

SYSTEM	LINE NO.	DESCRIPTION	QUANTITY	COST PER S.F.		
				MAT.	INST.	TOTAL
	01	Wood joists, 2" x 8", 16" O.C.,oak floor (sanded & finished),1/2" sub				
	02	Floor. 1" x 3" bridging, furring, 5/8" drywall. taped, finished, and painted.				
	03					
	04	Wood joists, 2" x 8", 16" O.C.	1 L.F.	.55	.53	1.08
	05	C.D.X. plywood sub floor, 1/2" thick	1 S.F.	.41	.33	.74
	06	Bridging 1" x 3"	.15 Pr.	.06	.29	.35
	07	Oak flooring, No. 1 common	1 S.F.	1.27	1.30	2.57
	08	Sand and finish floor	1 S.F.	.40	.82	1.22
	09	Wood furring, 1" x 3", 16" O.C.	1 L.F.	.09	.69	.78
	10	Gypsum drywall, 5/8" thick	1 S.F.	.25	.29	.54
	11	Tape and finishing	1 S.F.	.01	.24	.25
	12	Paint ceiling	1 S.F.	.10	.25	.35
	13	TOTAL	S.F.	3.14	4.74	7.88
	14					
	15					
	16	For alternate wood joist systems:				
	17	16" on center, 2" x 6" joists	S.F.	2.99	4.68	7.67
	18	2" x 10"		3.36	4.76	8.12
	19	2" x 12"		3.53	4.78	8.31
	20	2" x 14"		3.79	4.86	8.65
	21	12" on center, 2" x 10" joists		3.55	4.90	8.45
	22	2" x 12"		3.76	4.93	8.69
	23	2" x 14"		4.09	5.02	9.11
	24					
	25					
	26					
	27	Cut & patch to match existing construction, add, minimum		2%	3%	
	28	Maximum		5%	9%	
	29	Dust protector, add, minimum		1%	2%	
	30	Maximum		4%	11%	
	31	Equipment usage curtailment, add, minimum		1%	1%	
	32	Maximum		3%	10%	
	33	Material handling & storage limitation, add, minimum		1%	1%	
	34	Maximum		6%	7%	
	35	Protection of existing work, add, minimum		2%	2%	
	36	Maximum		5%	7%	
	37	Shift work requirements, add, minimum			5%	
	38	Maximum			30%	
	39	Temporary shoring and bracing, add, minimum		2%	5%	
	40	Maximum		5%	12%	
	41					
	42					

312

03.9-900 — Floor & Ceiling Selective Price Sheet

FLOORING

DESCRIPTION			MAT.	INST.	TOTAL
Carpet	Acrylic	26 oz. light traffic	1.27	.64	1.91
		35 oz. heavy traffic	1.74	.59	2.33
	Nylon	15 oz. light traffic	1.01	.65	1.66
	Anti-static	22 oz. medium traffic	1.33	.65	1.98
		26 oz. heavy traffic	1.54	.65	2.19
		28 oz. heavy traffic	1.65	.68	2.33
	Tile foamed back	Needle punch	.80	.36	1.16
		Tufted loop	1.43	.36	1.79
	Wool	36 oz. medium traffic	2.99	.64	3.63
		42 oz. heavy traffic	3.29	.60	3.89
Composition	Epoxy	With colored chips Min.	1.14	1.88	3.02
		Max.	1.78	2.59	4.37
		Trowelled Min.	1.44	2.26	3.70
		Max.	2.30	2.64	4.94
		Terrazzo, 1/4" thick chemical resistant Min.	3.81	3.39	7.20
		Max.	6.33	4.52	10.85
Resilient	Asphalt tile	1/8" thick	.68	.43	1.11
	Conductive flrg., rubber tile, plain	1/8" thick	2.99	.71	3.70
	Cork tile 1/8" thick	Standard finish	1.27	.71	1.98
		Urethane finish	1.55	.71	2.26
	PVC sheet goods for gyms	1/4" thick	2.31	2.89	5.20
		3/8" thick	2.60	3.85	6.45
	Vyl. comp. 12" x 12" tile, plain	1/16" thick	.58	.43	1.01
		1/8" thick	1.16	.42	1.58
	Vinyl tile, 12" x 12" 1/8" thick	Min.	1.99	.54	2.53
		Max.	7.98	.57	8.55
	Vinyl sheet goods backed	.093" thick	1.21	.36	1.57
		.250" thick	1.96	.35	2.31
Wood	Mple. strp. 25/32" x 2-1/4", finished	Select	1.89	1.43	3.32
		2nd & better	1.73	1.43	3.15
	Oak, 25/32" x 2-1/4" finished	Clear	1.60	1.42	3.02
		No. 1 common	1.27	1.30	2.57
	Parquet Standard, 5/16" thick finished	Min.	1.10	1.51	2.61
		Max.	5.72	2.43	8.15
	Custom, finished	Min.	11.88	2.42	14.30
		Max.	16.50	4.50	21.00
	Prefinished	Oak, 2-1/4" wide	1.85	1.42	3.27
	Prefinished	Ranch plank	3.16	1.67	4.83
Sleepers on concrete, treated, 24" O.C.	1" x 2"		.08	.17	.25
	1" x 3"		.11	.20	.31
	2" x 4"		.31	.27	.58
	2" x 6"		.46	.32	.78

CEILING

DESCRIPTION			MAT.	INST.	TOTAL
Plaster	Gypsum	2 coats	.31	1.39	1.70
		3 coats	.43	1.64	2.07
	Perlite or Vermiculite	2 coats	.31	1.62	1.93
		3 coats	.48	2.07	2.55
	Lath Gypsum	Plain 3/8" thick	.24	.32	.56
		1/2" thick	.26	.33	.59
		Firestop 1/2" thick	.34	.38	.72
		5/8" thick	.35	.42	.77
	Metal	Rib 2.75#	.26	.36	.62
		3.40#	.28	.38	.66
Drywall	Standard	Diamond 2.50#	.19	.36	.55
		3.40#	.24	.45	.69
		1/2" thick	.23	.27	.50
		5/8" thick	.20	.34	.54
	Fire resistant	1/2" thick	.26	.27	.53
		5/8" thick	.29	.28	.57
	Water resistant	1/2" thick	.30	.27	.57
		5/8" thick	.33	.28	.61
	Finish	Taping & finishing, add	.01	.24	.25
		thin coat plaster, add	.08	.38	.46
		textured spray, add	.10	.33	.43
Ceiling Tile	Stapled or Glued	Min. fiber 5/8" thick	.68	.61	1.29
		plastic coated 3/4" thick	.88	.61	1.49
		Wood fiber 1/2" thick	.57	.61	1.18
		3/4" thick	.86	.60	1.46
	Suspended	Fiberglass 5/8" thick	.34	.36	.70
		film faced 3" thick	.81	.49	1.30
		Min. fiber Standard	.36	.36	.72
		5/8" thick Aluminum	.75	.40	1.15
		Wood fiber 1" thick	1.32	.40	1.72
		Reveal edge 3" thick	2.88	.54	3.42
Suspension Systems	Ceiling Tile	"T" bar 2' x 4' grid	.40	.30	.70
		Class A 2' x 2' grid	.42	.37	.79
		Concealed "Z" 12" module	.51	.46	.97
Metal Furring	Plaster or Drywall	3/4" channels 16" O.C.	.25	.81	1.06
		24" O.C.	.19	.57	.76
		1-1/2" chan. 16" O.C.	.32	.91	1.23
		24" O.C.	.24	.62	.86
		2" x 4" studs 16" O.C.	.30	.42	.72
		24" O.C.	.23	.36	.59

314

Table III.9

Below are various stair systems based on cost per flight of stairs, no side Walls. Stairs are 4'-0" wide, railings are included unless otherwise noted.

LINE NO.	DESCRIPTION	QUANTITY	COST PER FLIGHT		
			MAT.	INST.	TOTAL
01	Below are various stair systems based on cost per flight of stairs, no side				
02	Walls. Stairs are 4'-0" wide, railings are included unless otherwise noted.				
03					
04					
05					
06					
07	Concrete, cast in place, no nosings, no railings, 12 risers	Flight	229.15	826.85	1056
08	24 risers		458.30	1653.70	2112
09	Add for 1 intermediate landing		61.95	235.65	297.60
10	Concrete, cast in place, with nosings, no railings, 12 risers		577.63	972.77	1550.40
11	24 risers		1155.26	1945.54	3100.80
12	Add for 1 intermediate landing		90.99	247.81	338.80
13	Steel, grating tread, safety nosing, 12 risers		1452	330	1782
14	24 risers		2904	660	3564
15	Add for intermediate landing		352	128	480
16	Steel, cement fill pan tread, 12 risers		1960.20	349.80	2310
17	24 risers		3920.40	699.60	4620
18	Add for intermediate landing		352	128	480
19	Spiral, industrial, 4'-6" diameter, 12 risers		1188	312	1500
20	24 risers		2376	624	3000
21	Wood, box stairs, oak treads, 12 risers		1154.45	378.55	1533
22	24 risers		2308.90	757.10	3066
23	Add for 1 intermediate landing		72.04	63.22	135.26
24	Wood, basement stairs, no risers, 12 steps		121	132	253
25	24 steps		242	264	506
26	Add for 1 intermediate landing		15.90	13.06	28.96
27	Wood, open, rough sawn cedar, 12 steps		(421.75)	(233.75)	1655.50
28	24 steps		2843.50	467.50	3311
29	Add for 1 intermediate landing		(25.06)	(19.24)	44.30
30	Wood, residential, oak treads, 12 risers		901.45	1216.05	2117.50
31	24 risers		1802.90	2432.10	4235
32	Add for 1 intermediate landing		64.10	56.73	120.83
33	→		1446.81	252.99	
34					
35	Dust protection, add, minimum		1%	2%	
36	Maximum		4%	11%	
37	Material handling & storage limitation, add, minimum		1%	1%	
38	Maximum		6%	7%	
39	Protection of existing work, add, minimum		2%	2%	
40	Maximum		5%	7%	
41	Shift work requirements, add, minimum			5%	
42	Maximum			30%	

This page illustrates and describes a stair system based on a cost per flight price. Prices for various stair systems are on Line Items 03.9-104-07 thru 32. Both material quantities and labor costs have been adjusted for the system listed.

Example: Spiral industrial, 4'-6" diameter, 24 risers as an alternate system; choose Line Item 03.9-104-20, $2376 MAT., $624 INST., $3000 TOTAL. This price includes all materials compatible with the original system. For alternatives not listed, use the selective price sheet for this section (page 314). Substitute the new prices from the price sheet into the typical system and adjust the total to reflect each change.

Factors: To adjust for job conditions other than normal working situations use Lines 03.9-104-35 thru 42.

Example: You are to install the above system during evenings only. Go to Line 03.9-104-42 and apply this percentage to the appropriate MAT. and INST. costs.

Table III.10

PROJECT Apartment Renovation								SHEET NO. 3 of 11	
LOCATION								ESTIMATE NO. 85-2	
ARCHITECT			OWNER					DATE 1985	
QUANTITIES BY EBW	PRICES BY RSM		EXTENSIONS BY					CHECKED BY	

DESCRIPTION	QUANTITY	UNIT	MATERIAL		LABOR		TOTAL COST	
			UNIT	TOTAL	UNIT	TOTAL	UNIT	TOTAL
Division 3: Superstructure								
Ceiling Drywall	5,808	SF	29	1684	28	1626		
Paint	5,808	SF	10	581	25	1452		
Stairs	1	Flight	1,447	1447	253	253		
Division 3: Totals				3712		3331		

Table III.11

Division 4: Exterior Closure

The requirements for the exterior of the building are determined through discussions with the owner:

1. Stucco over the existing concrete block
2. Insulation
3. New casement windows
4. New entrance door
5. New corridor exit doors
6. Patio doors at ground floor

These items can be easily priced but the existing conditions will have a great effect on the work. The quantity of the stucco finish must be determined at the site. New door and window openings must be deducted. The costs for stucco are found in Table III.12, and are included in the estimate in Table III.13.

04.9-200 Exterior Wall Selective Price Sheet

Exterior Surface / Interior Surface

DESCRIPTION				MAT.	INST.	TOTAL
Exterior Surface						
Masonry	Block Concrete	Standard	4"	.88	2.73	3.61
			6"	1.09	2.93	4.02
			8"	1.32	3.13	4.45
			12"	1.99	4.01	6.00
		Split Rib	4"	1.64	3.41	5.05
			8"	2.67	3.83	6.50
	Brick Running Bond	Standard	(6.75/S.F.)	1.76	5.34	7.10
		Buff	(6.75/S.F.)	2.20	5.60	7.80
	Stucco	On frame		.74	2.92	3.66
		On masonry		.21	2.34	2.55
Metal	Aluminum	Horizontal	Plain	1.27	.94	2.21
			Insulated	1.49	.94	2.43
		Vertical	Plain	1.32	.95	2.27
			Insulated	1.38	.99	2.37
Wood	Beveled Siding	"A" Grade Cedar	1/2" x 6"	1.45	.97	2.42
			1/2" x 8"	1.34	.88	2.22
	Shingles	16" #1 Red	7½" exposure	.97	1.18	2.15
		18" perfections	7½" exposure	1.12	.98	2.10
		Handsplit	10" exposure	1.20	.95	2.15
		White Cedar	7½" exposure	.77	1.23	2.00
	Vertical	Board and Batten	Redwood	2.38	.93	3.31
			White Pine	.52	.88	1.40
		Tongue & Groove	1" x 4" Redwood	2.57	1.67	4.24
			1" x 6" Redwood	2.37	1.20	3.57
Interior Surface						
Drywall taped & finished	Standard		1/2"	.21	.48	.69
			5/8"	.25	.52	.77
	Fire Resistant		1/2"	.24	.49	.73
			5/8"	.28	.51	.79
	Moisture Resistant		1/2"	.29	.48	.77
			5/8"	.33	.52	.85
	Core Board		1"	.41	1.01	1.42
Plaster	Gypsum		2 coats	.31	1.22	1.53
			3 coats	.43	1.47	1.90
	Perlite or Vermiculite		2 coats	.31	1.39	1.70
			3 coats	.48	1.73	2.21
Lath	Gypsum	Standard	3/8"	.24	.32	.56
			1/2"	.26	.33	.59
		Fire Resistant	1/2"	.34	.38	.72
			5/8"	.35	.42	.77
	Metal	Diamond	2.5 lb.	.19	.31	.50
		Rib	3.4 lb.	.28	.38	.66

Framing / Insulation

DESCRIPTION				MAT.	INST.	TOTAL
Framing						
Metal	Studs, including top & bottom runners, walls 10' high					
	24" O.C.	Non load bearing 20 gauge	2-1/2"	.24	.50	.74
			3-5/8"	.23	.52	.75
			4"	.28	.55	.83
			6"	.34	.57	.91
		Load bearing 18 gauge	2-1/2"	.80	.51	1.31
			3-5/8"	.85	.53	1.38
			4"	.92	.57	1.49
			6"	1.06	.59	1.65
	16" O.C.	Non load bearing 20 gauge	2-1/2"	.29	.60	.89
			3-5/8"	.32	.63	.95
			4"	.36	.67	1.03
			6"	.43	.68	1.11
		Load bearing 18 gauge	2-1/2"	.96	.61	1.57
			3-5/8"	1.01	.65	1.66
			4"	1.10	.69	1.79
			6"	1.27	.71	1.98
Wood	Studs, incl. double top plate and single bottom plate, walls 10' high					
	24" O.C.		2" x 4"	2.51	3.99	6.50
			2" x 6"	3.58	4.32	7.90
	16" O.C.		2" x 4"	3.32	4.98	8.30
			2" x 6"	4.82	5.53	10.35
	Sheathing	Boards	1" x 6"	.77	.77	1.54
			1" x 8"	.77	.65	1.42
		Plywood	3/8"	.32	.42	.74
			1/2"	.41	.44	.85
			5/8"	.45	.48	.93
			3/4"	.51	.51	1.02
		Wood fiber	5/8"	.52	.41	.93
		Gyp. weatherproof	1/2"	.22	.48	.70
Insulation	Batt	Fiberglass	R11	.22	.35	.57
			R19	.34	.40	.74
	Poured 4" thick	Fiberglass wool	R4/inch	.30	1.21	1.51
		Mineral wool	R3/inch	.80	1.21	2.01
		Polystyrene	R4/inch	1.49	1.21	2.70
		Perlite or vermiculite	R2.7/inch	1.53	1.21	2.74
	Rigid	Fiberglass	R4.3/inch	.44	.24	.68
			R8.7/inch	.88	.27	1.15
		Urethane	R5.8/inch	.44	.30	.74
			R11.7/inch	.88	.33	1.21

330

Table III.12

COST ANALYSIS

DESCRIPTION	QUANTITY	UNIT	MATERIAL UNIT	MATERIAL TOTAL	LABOR UNIT	LABOR TOTAL	TOTAL COST UNIT	TOTAL COST TOTAL
Division 4: Exterior Closure								
Stucco	3,120	SF	21	655	2^{34}	7301		
Interior Treatment	4,420	SF	97	4287	1^{65}	7293		
Patio Doors	2	Ea.	710	1420	234	468		
Windows- Type I	16	Ea.	316^{61}	5066	90^{28}	1444		
Type II	14	Ea.	554^{12}	7766	141^{35}	1979		
Entrance Door	1	Ea.	1202^{78}	1203	584^{83}	585		
Corridor Doors	2	Ea.	651^{88}	1304	254^{10}	508		
Division 4: Totals				21701		19578		

Table III.13

EXTERIOR CLOSURE | 04.1-258 | Masonry Wall, Brick - Stone

SYSTEM	LINE NO.	DESCRIPTION	QUANTITY	COST PER S.F.		
				MAT.	INST.	TOTAL
	01	Face brick, 4"thick, concrete block back-up, reinforce every second course.				
	02	3/4"insulation, furring, 1/2"drywall, taped, finish, and painted, baseboard.				
	03					
	04	Face brick, 4" brick @ $215 per M	1 S.F.	1.87	5.63	7.50
	05	Concrete back-up block, reinforced 8" thick	1 S.F.	1.39	2.93	4.32
	06	3/4" rigid polystyrene insulation	1 S.F.	.40	.30	.70
	07	Furring, 1" x 3", wood, 16" O.C.	1 S.F.	.12	.49	.61
	08	Drywall, 1/2" thick	1 S.F.	.23	.27	.50
	09	Taping & finishing	1 S.F.	.01	.24	.25
	10	Painting, 2 coats	1 S.F.	.10	.25	.35
	11	Baseboard, wood, 9/16" x 2-5/8"	1 L.F.	.06	.19	.25
	12	TOTAL	S.F.	4.18	10.30	14.48
	13					
	14	For alternate exterior wall systems:				
	15	Face brick, Norman, 4" x 2-2/3" x 12" (4.5 per S.F.) $385 per M	S.F.	4.64	8.54	13.18
	16	Roman, 4" x 2" x 12" (6.0 per S.F.) $460 per M		5.84	9.59	15.43
	17	Engineer, 4" x 3-1/5" x 8" (5.63 per S.F.) $255 per M		4.29	9.44	13.73
	18	S.C.R., 6" x 2-2/3" x 12" (4.5 per S.F.) $545 per M		5.56	8.67	14.23
	19	Jumbo, 6" x 4" x 12" (3.0 per S.F.)$900 per M		5.78	7.50	13.28
	20	Norwegian, 6" x 3-1/5" x 12" (3.75 per S.F.) $450 per M		4.57	7.96	12.53
	21					
	22					
	23	Stone, veneer, fieldstone, 6" thick	S.F.	7.12	8.61	15.73
	24	Marble, 2" thick		23.56	14.37	37.93
	25	Limestone, 2" thick		12.87	11.71	24.58
	26					
	27					
	28					
	29					
	30					
	31	Cut & patch to match existing construction, add, minimum		2%	3%	
	32	Maximum		5%	9%	
	33	Dust protection, add, minimum		1%	2%	
	34	Maximum		4%	11%	
	35	Equipment usage curtailment, adc, minimum		1%	1%	
	36	Maximum		3%	10%	
	37	Material handling & storage limitation, add, minimum		1%	1%	
	38	Maximum		6%	7%	
	39	Protection of existing work, add, minimum		2%	2%	
	40	Maximum		5%	7%	
	41	Shift work requirements, add, minimum			5%	
	42	Maximum			30%	

This page illustrates and describes a masonry wall, brick-stone system including brick, concrete block, durawall, insulation, plasterboard, taped and finished, furring, baseboard and painting interior. Lines 04.1-258-04 thru 12 give the unit price and total price per square foot for this system. Prices for alternate masonry wall, brick-stone systems are on Line 04.1-258-15 thru 25. Both material quantities and labor costs have been adjusted for the system listed.

Example: Norwegian, 6" x 3-1/5" x 12" (3.75 per S.F.) @ $450 per M as an alternate system; choose Line Item 04.1-258-20, $4.57 MAT., $7.96 INST., $12.53 TOTAL. This price includes all materials compatible with the original system. For alternatives not listed, use the selective price sheet for this section (page 330). Substitute the new prices from the price sheet into the typical system and adjust the total to reflect each change.

Factors: To adjust for job conditions other than normal working situations use Lines 04.1-258-31 thru 42.

Example: You are to install the above system without damaging the existing work. Go to Line 04.1-258-40 and apply these percentages to the appropriate MAT. and INST. costs.

Table III.14

This page illustrates and describes a wood frame exterior wall system including wood studs, sheathing, felt, insulation, plasterboard, taped and finished, baseboard and painted interior. Lines 04.1-416-05 thru 13 give the unit price and total price per square foot for this system. Prices for alternate wood frame exterior wall systems are on Line Items 04.1-416-17 thru 27. Both material quantities and labor costs have been adjusted for the system listed.

Example: Redwood siding 1" x 4" to 1" x 6" vertical T & G as an alternate system; choose Line Item 04.1-416-19, $3.30 MAT., $3.25 INST., $6.55 TOTAL. This price includes all materials compatible with the original system. For alternatives not listed, use the selective price sheet for this section (page 330). Substitute the new prices from the sheet into the typical system and adjust the total to reflect each change.

Factors: To adjust for job conditions other than normal working situations use Lines 04.1-416-31 thru 42.

Example: You are to install the above system with need for complete temporary bracing. Go to Line 04.1-416-42 and apply these percentages to the appropriate MAT. and INST. costs.

SYSTEM	LINE NO.	DESCRIPTION	QUANTITY	COST PER S.F.		
				MAT.	INST.	TOTAL
	01	Wood stud wall, cedar shingle siding, building paper, plywood sheathing,				
	02	Insulation, 5/8" drywall, taped, finished and painted, baseboard.				
	03					
	04					
	05	2" x 4" wood studs, 16" O.C.	.1 L.F.	.33	.50	.83
	06	1/2" CDX sheathing	1 S.F.	.41	.35	.76
	07	18" No. 1 red cedar shingles, 7-1/2" exposure	.008 C.S.F.	.97	.87	1.84
	08	15# felt paper	.01 C.S.F.	.03	.07	.10
	09	3-1/2" fiberglass insulation	1 S.F.	.22	.15	.37
	10	5/8" drywall, taped and finished	1 S.F.	.26	.53	.79
	11	Baseboard trim, stock pine, 9/16" x 3-1/2", painted	.1 L.F.	.06	.19	.25
	12	Paint, 2 coats, interior	1 S.F.	.10	.25	.35
	13	TOTAL	S.F.	2.38	2.91	5.29
	14					
	15					
	16	For alternate exterior wall systems:				
	17	Aluminum siding, horizontal clapboard	S.F.	2.68	2.98	5.66
	18	Cedar bevel siding, 1/2" x 6", vertical, painted		2.86	3.01	5.87
	19	Redwood siding 1" x 4" to 1" x 6" vertical, T & G		3.30	3.25	6.55
	20	Board and batten		2.46	2.97	5.43
	21	Ship lap siding		2.53	3.01	5.54
	22	Plywood, grooved (T1-11) fir		2	2.78	4.78
	23	Redwood		2.85	2.78	5.63
	24	Southern yellow pine		2	2.78	4.78
	25	Masonry on stud wall, stucco, wire and plaster		2.15	4.93	7.08
	26	Stone veneer		6.22	5.98	12.20
	27	Brick veneer, brick $200 per M		3.28	7.67	10.95
	28					
	29					
	30					
	31	Cut & patch to match existing construction, add, minimum		2%	3%	
	32	Maximum		5%	9%	
	33	Dust protection, add, minimum		1%	2%	
	34	Maximum		4%	11%	
	35	Material handling & storage limitation, add, minimum		1%	1%	
	36	Maximum		6%	7%	
	37	Protection of existing work, add, minimum		2%	2%	
	38	Maximum		5%	7%	
	39	Shift work requirements, add, minimum			5%	
	40	Maximum			30%	
	41	Temporary shoring and bracing, add, minimum		2%	5%	
	42	Maximum		5%	12%	

320

Table III.15

While the systems as described in *Repair and Remodeling Cost Data* may not conform exactly to job requirements, portions of the systems may be used as needed. The owner has requested that the building be well insulated, but has not specified the type of insulation. That choice is left to the estimator. Tables III.14 and III.15 illustrate two types of exterior wall systems that have different interior insulation and finish treatments. By comparing the costs of the two treatments (and also the R-Values) the estimator is able to determine which is better for the particular application. This cost comparison is demonstrated in Table III.16. Note that the drywall in System 2 is 1/2," substituted for 5/8" as shown, in order to compare the systems equally. The wood stud/fiberglass insulation system is chosen because of lower cost and higher R-value.

System from Table III.14:			
	Material	**Installation**	**Total**
Polystyrene Insulation (3/4")	$.40	$ .30	$ .70
Furring	.12	.49	.61
Drywall (1/2")	.23	.27	.50
Taping	.01	.24	.25
Paint	.10	.25	.35
Baseboard	.06	.19	.25
	$.92	$1.74	$2.66
Factors	.02	.05	.07
2% Material			
3% Installation			
Total per S.F. R-Value 4	$.94	$1.79	$2.73

System from Table III.15:			
	Material	**Installation**	**Total**
Wood Studs	$.33	$ .50	$ .83
Fiberglass Insulation (3-1/2")	.22	.15	.37
Drywall (Price for 1/2")	.23	.27	.50
Taping	.01	.24	.25
Paint	.10	.25	.35
Baseboard	.06	.19	.25
	$.95	$1.60	$2.55
Factors	.02	.05	.07
2% Material			
3% Installation			
Total per S.F., R-Valve 11	$.97	$1.65	$2.62

Table III.16

Table III.17

EXTERIOR CLOSURE | 04.6-152 | Doors, Sliding - Patio

This page illustrates and describes sliding door systems including a sliding door, frame, interior and exterior trim with exterior staining. Lines 04.6-152-04 thru 07 give the unit price and total price on a cost each basis for this system. Prices for alternate sliding door systems are on Line Items 04.6-152-11 thru 22. Both material quantities and labor costs have been adjusted for the system listed.

Example: Aluminum standard, 8'-0" x 6'-8" as an alternate system; choose Line Item 04.6-152-18, $377 MAT., $223 INST., $600 TOTAL. This price includes all materials compatible with the original system.

Factors: To adjust for job conditions other than normal working situations use Lines 04.6-152-27 thru 40.

Example: You are to install the above system with temporary shoring and bracing. Go to Line 04.6-152-40 and apply these percentages to the appropriate MAT. and INST. costs.

SYSTEM	LINE NO.	DESCRIPTION	QUANTITY	COST EACH MAT.	COST EACH INST.	TOTAL
	01	Sliding wood door, 6'-0" x 6'-8", with wood frame, interior and exterior				
	02	Trim, and exterior staining.				
	03					
	04	Sliding wood door, standard, 6'-0" x 6'-8", insulated glass	1 Ea.	385	120	505
	05	Interior & exterior trim	1 Set	10.78	20.22	31
	06	Stain door & trim	1 Ea.	4	31	35
	07	TOTAL		399.78	171.22	571
	08					
	09					
	10	For alternate sliding door systems:				
	11	Wood, standard, 8'-0" x 6'-8", insulated glass	Ea.	675.99	214.61	890.60
	12	12'-0" x 6'-8"		932.76	257.04	1189.80
	13	Vinyl coated, 6'-0" x 6'-8"		762.78	173.22	936
	14	8'-0" x 6'-8"		895.99	224.61	1120.60
	15	12'-0" x 6'-8"		1394.76	270.04	1664.80
	16					
	17	Aluminum, standard, 6'-0" x 6'-8", insulated glass	Ea.	319	177.20	496.20
	18	8'-0" x 6'-8"		377.30	223.02	600.32
	19	12'-0" x 6'-8"		444.40	269.16	713.56
	20	Anodized, 6'-0" x 6'-8"		374	177.20	551.20
	21	8'-0" x 6'-8"		437.80	227.52	665.32
	22	12'-0" x 6'-8"		499.40	269.16	768.56
	23					
	24	Deduct for single glazing	Ea.	50		50
	25					
	26					
	27	Cut & patch to match existing construction, add, minimum		2%	3%	
	28	Maximum		5%	9%	
	29	Dust protection, add, minimum		1%	2%	
	30	Maximum		4%	11%	
	31	Equipment usage curtailment, add, minimum		1%	1%	
	32	Maximum		3%	10%	
	33	Material handling & storage limitation, add, minimum		1%	1%	
	34	Maximum		6%	7%	
	35	Protection of existing, work, add, minimum		2%	2%	
	36	Maximum		5%	7%	
	37	Shift work requirements, add, minimum			5%	
	38	Maximum			30%	
	39	Temporary shoring and bracing, add, minimum		2%	5%	
	40	Maximum		5%	12%	
	41					
	42					

EXTERIOR CLOSURE 04.7-145 Windows - Wood

SYSTEM	LINE NO.	DESCRIPTION	QUANTITY	COST EACH MAT.	COST EACH INST.	COST EACH TOTAL
	01	Double hung wood window 2'-0" x 3'-0", exterior and interior trim.				
	02	Hardware, glazed with insulating glass.				
	03					
	04	2'-0" x 3'-0" double hung wood window, with insulating glass	1 Ea.	100.10	24.90	125
	05	Exterior and interior trim	1 Set	10.12	18.88	29
	06	Hardware	1 Set	.97	10.08	11.05
	07	TOTAL	Ea.	111.19	53.86	165.05
	08					
	09					
	10					
	11					
	12	For alternate window systems:				
	13	Double hung, 3'-0" x 4'-0"	Ea.	156.40	61.65	218.05
	14	4'-0" x 4'-6"		191.82	79.23	271.05
	15	Casement 2'-0" x 3'-0"		121.09	53.96	175.05
	16	2 leaf, 4'-0" x 4'-0" *Type I*		310.40	87.65	398.05
	17	3 leaf, 6'-0" x 6'-0" *Type II*		543.82	137.23	681.05
	18	Awning, 2'-10" x 1'-10"		94.69	55.36	150.05
	19	3'-6" x 2'-4"		122.30	60.75	183.05
	20	4'-0" x 3'-0"		147.82	78.23	226.05
	21	Horizontal siding 3'-0" x 2'-0"		104.59	50.46	155.05
	22	4'-0" x 3'-6"		145.40	62.65	208.05
	23	6'-0" x 5'-0"		230.32	80.73	311.05
	24					
	25					
	26					
	27					
	28					
	29					
	30					
	31	Cut & patch to match existing construction, add, minimum		2%	3%	
	32	Maximum		5%	9%	
	33	Dust protection, add, minimum		1%	2%	
	34	Maximum		4%	11%	
	35	Material handling & storage limitation, add, minimum		1%	1%	
	36	Maximum		6%	7%	
	37	Protection of existing work, add, minimum		2%	2%	
	38	Maximum		5%	7%	
	39	Shift work requirements, add, minimum			5%	
	40	Maximum			30%	
	41					
	42					

This page illustrates and describes a wood window system including double hung wood window, exterior and interior trim, hardware and insulating glass. Lines 04.7-145-04 thru 07 give the unit price and total price on a cost each basis for this system. Prices for alternate wood window systems are on Line Items 04.7-145-13 thru 23. Both material quantities and labor costs have been adjusted for the system listed.

Example: Awning 4'-0" x 3'-0" as an alternate system; choose Line Item 04.7-145-20, $148 MAT., $78 INST., $226 TOTAL. This price includes all materials compatible with the original system.

Factors: To adjust for job conditions other than normal working situations use Lines 04.7-145-31 thru 40.

Example: You are to install the above system during evening hours only. Go to Line 04.7-145-40 and apply this percentage to the appropriate INST. cost.

Table III.18

EXTERIOR CLOSURE — 04.6-142 — Doors, Metal - Commercial

SYSTEM	LINE NO.	DESCRIPTION	QUANTITY	COST EACH MAT.	INST.	TOTAL
	01	Single aluminum and glass door, 3'-0" x 7'-0", with narrow stiles, ext. jamb.				
	02	Weatherstripping, 1/2" tempered insul. glass, panic hardware and closer.				
	03					
	04	Aluminum door, 3'-0" x 7'-0" x 1-3/4", narrow stiles	1 Ea.	277.75	139.75	417.50
	05	Exterior jamb and trim	1 Set	166.65	83.85	250.50
	06	Hardware	1 Set	111.10	55.90	167
	07	Tempered insulating glass, 1/2" thick	20 S.F.	271.70	168.30	440
	08	Panic hardware	1 Set	220	80	300
	09	Automatic closer	1 Ea.	55	37	92
	10	*Entrance TOTAL*	Ea.	1102.20	564.80	1667
	11					
	12	For alternate door systems:				
	13	Single aluminum and glass with transom, 3'-0" x 10'-0"	Ea.	1298.88	664.12	1963
	14	Anodized aluminum and glass, 3'-0" x 7'-0"		1296.63	662.62	1959
	15	With transom, 3'-0" x 10'-0"		1524.11	773.14	2297
	16	Steel, deluxe, hollow metal 3'-0" x 7'-0" *Corridor*		639.10	246.70	886
	17	With transom 3'-0" x 10'-0"		700.98	275.72	977
	18	Fire door, "A" label, 3'-0" x 7'-0"		695.75	243.75	940
	19	Double, aluminum and glass, 6'-0" x 7'-0"		1797.40	961.60	2759
	20	With transom, 6'-0" x 10'-0"		2234.76	1176.24	3411
	21	Anodized aluminum and glass 6'-0" x 7'-0"		2101.55	1112.45	3214
	22	With transom, 6'-0" x 10'-0"		2615.91	1355.09	3971
	23	Steel, deluxe, hollow metal, 6'-0" x 7'-0"		1076.90	422.60	1500
	24	With transom, 6'-0" x 10'-0"		1200.65	480.65	1681
	25	Fire door, "A" label, 6'-0" x 7'-0"		1150.60	407.40	1558
	31	Cut & patch to match existing construction, add, minimum		2%	3%	
	32	Maximum		5%	9%	
	33	Dust protection, add, minimum		1%	2%	
	34	Maximum		4%	11%	
	35	Material handling & storage limitation, add, minimum		1%	1%	
	36	Maximum		6%	7%	
	37	Protection of existing work, add, minimum		2%	2%	
	38	Maximum		5%	7%	
	39	Shift work requirements, add, minimum			5%	
	40	Maximum			30%	

This page illustrates and describes a commercial metal door system, including a single aluminum and glass door, narrow stiles, jamb, hardware weatherstripping, panic hardware and closer. Lines 04.6-142-04 thru 10 give the unit price and total price on a cost each basis for this system. Prices for alternate commercial metal door systems are on Line Items 04.6-142-13 thru 25. Both material quantities and labor costs have been adjusted for the system listed.

Example: Anodized aluminum and glass with transom 6'-0" x 10'-0" as an alternate system; choose Line Item 04.6-142-22. $2,616 MAT., $1,355 INST., $3,971 TOTAL. This price includes all materials compatible with the original system. For alternatives not listed, use the selective price sheet for this section (page 330). Substitute the new prices from the price sheet into the typical system and adjust the total to reflect each change.

Factors: To adjust for job conditions other than normal working situations, use Lines 04.6-142-31 thru 40.

Example: You are to install the above system and cut and patch to match existing construction. Go to Line 04.6-142-32 and apply these percentages to the appropriate MAT. and INST. costs.

Table III.19

04.9-500 Hardware Selective Price Sheet

DESCRIPTION		UNIT	COST EACH		
			MAT.	INST.	TOTAL
DOOR CLOSER, Rack and Pinion, Backcheck and Adjustable Power					
REGULAR	Hinge face mount, all sizes, regular arm	Ea.	55.00	37.00	92.00
	Hold open arm		60.50	37.50	98.00
	Top jamb mount, all sizes, regular arm		60.50	37.50	98.00
	Hold open arm		60.50	39.50	100.00
	Stop face mount, all sizes, regular arm		55.00	37.00	92.00
	Hold open arm		60.50	37.50	98.00
FUSIBLE LINK	Hinge face mount, all sizes, regular arm		63.80	37.00	100.80
	Hold open arm		69.30	37.50	106.80
	Top jamb mount, all sizes, regular arm		63.80	40.00	103.80
	Hold open arm		69.30	39.50	108.80
	Stop face mount, all sizes, regular arm		63.00	37.00	100.00
	Hold open arm		69.30	37.50	106.80
DOOR STOPS	Holder & bumper, floor or wall	Ea.	17.60	10.40	28.00
	Wall bumper		3.30	10.10	13.40
	Floor bumper		2.75	10.10	12.85
	Plunger type, door mounted		13.20	9.80	23.00
HINGES, Material only					
3-1/2"x3-1/2" Interior	Full mortise, 1-3/8" doors	Set	16.70		16.70
	Steel plate ball bearing				
	Bronze, ball bearing		37.00		37.00
	Low frequency, steel, plated		5.15		5.15
4-1/2"x4-1/2" Exterior	Full mortise, 1-3/4" doors				
	Steel plate ball bearing		18.95		18.95
	Bronze, ball bearing		52.00		52.00
	Low frequency steel		8.60		8.60
KICK PLATE	6" high, for 3' door, aluminum	Ea.	13.75	16.25	30.00
	Bronze	"	36.30	15.70	52.00
PANIC DEVICE	For rim locks, single door, exit	Ea.	220.00	80.00	300.00
	Exit & entrance		247.50	82.50	330.00
	For mortise locks, single door, exit		286.00	79.00	365.00
	Exit & entrance		(297.00)	(83.00)	380.00

DESCRIPTION		UNIT	COST EACH		
			MAT.	INST.	TOTAL
LOCKSET					
Heavy duty, cylindrical	Passage doors	Ea.	74.80	24.20	99.00
	Classroom		115.50	24.50	140.00
	Bedroom, bathroom and inner office doors		95.70	24.30	120.00
	Apartment, office and corridor doors		121.00	24.00	145.00
Standard duty, cylindrical	Exit doors		49.50	24.50	74.00
	Inner office		16.50	17.50	34.00
	Passage doors		23.10	23.90	47.00
	Public restroom, classroom & office doors		23.10	23.90	47.00
Heavy duty mortise	Without lock knob		86.90	28.10	115.00
	Entrances		99.00	31.00	130.00
Heavy duty, deadbolt lock	Mortise, utility rooms		58.30	30.70	89.00
	Handicapped lever, add		87.00		87.00
Residential	Interior door, minimum		8.03	14.97	23.00
	Maximum		25.30	30.70	56.00
	Exterior door, minimum		16.50	24.50	41.00
	Maximum		88.00	22.00	110.00
PUSH PULL	Aluminum	Ea.	27.50	20.50	48.00
	Bronze		45.10	19.90	65.00
	Door pull, designer style, minimum		44.00	20.00	64.00
	Maximum		192.50	32.50	225.00
THRESHOLD					
3' long door saddles	Aluminum, minimum	Ea.	21.73	12.77	34.00
	Maximum		68.20	19.80	88.00
	Bronze, minimum		39.60	12.40	52.00
	Maximum		115.50	19.50	135.00
	Rubber, 1/2" thick, 5-1/2" wide		23.10	11.90	35.00
	2-3/4" wide		12.60	12.40	25.00
WEATHERSTRIPPING					
Doors	Wood frame, interlocking for 3x7' door, zinc	Set	20.02	79.98	100.00
	Bronze		33.00	82.00	115.00
	Wood frame, spring type for 3x7' door, bronze		9.74	32.26	42.00
	Metal frame, spring type for 3x7' door, bronze		38.50	81.50	120.00
	For stainless steel, spring type, add		100%		
	Metal frame, extruded sections,3x7' door, alum.	Set	27.50	122.50	150.00
	Bronze	"	72.60	122.40	195.00

Table III.20

By thinking ahead, the estimator should realize that the stud system will allow for easier installation of electrical receptacles and switches in the exterior walls. The furring system would require that the concrete block be chipped away at every box. This is a good example of the advantage of being able to visualize the whole job.

The doors and windows, with appropriate factors added, are taken from Tables III.17 to III.19. The entrance door and corridor exit door systems include panic hardware. The estimator must be sure that the hardware is as required. Table III.20, Hardware Selective Price Sheet, shows that the panic device is rim-type, exit only. A mortise lock for exit and entrance is required at the entrance and is substituted as shown in Table III.21.

	Material	Installation	Total
Entrance Door 04.6-142-10	$1,102.20	$564.80	$1,667.00
Deduct Panic 04.6-142-08	(220.00)	(80.00)	(300.00)
Add Mortise Panic (Table III.20)	297.00	83.00	380.00
	$1,179.20	$567.80	$1,747.00
Factors 2% Material 3% Installation	23.58	17.03	40.61
Total	$1,202.78	$584.83	$1,787.61

Hardware Substitution

Table III.21

This page illustrates and describes a wood frame roof system including rafters, ceiling joists, sheathing, building paper, asphalt shingles, roof trim, furring, insulation, plaster and paint. Lines 05.1-492-04 thru 15 give the unit price and total price per square foot for this system. Prices for alternate wood frame roof systems are on Line Items 05.1-492-19 thru 27. Both material quantities and labor costs have been adjusted for the system listed.

Example: Rafters 24" O.C., 2" x 10" as an alternate system; choose Line Item 05.1-492-24, $2.59 MAT., $3.96 INST., $6.55 TOTAL. This price includes all materials compatible with the original system. For alternatives not listed, use the selective price sheet for this section (pages 336 and 337). Substitute the new price from the price sheet into the typical system and adjust the total to reflect each change.

Factors: To adjust for job conditions other than normal working situations use Lines 05.1-492-33 thru 40.

Example: You are to install the above system while protecting existing work. Go to Line 05.1-492-38 and apply these percentages to the appropriate MAT. and INST. costs.

LINE NO.	DESCRIPTION	QUANTITY	COST PER S.F.		
			MAT.	INST.	TOTAL
01	Wood frame roof system, 4 in 12 pitch, including rafters, sheathing.				
02	Shingles, insulation, drywall, thin coat plaster, and painting.				
03					
04	Rafters, 2" x 6", 16" O.C., 4 in 12 pitch	1.08 L.F.	.42	.64	1.06
05	Ceiling joists, 2" x 6", 16" O.C.	1 L.F.	.40	.47	.87
06	Sheathing, 1/2" CDX	1.08 S.F.	.43	.39	.82
07	Building paper, 15# felt	.011 C.S.F.	.03	.08	.11
08	Asphalt shingles, 240#	.011 C.S.F.	.33	.53	.86
09	Roof trim	.1 L.F.	.06	.11	.17
10	Furring, 1" x 3", 16" O.C.	.1 L.F.	.09	.69	.78
11	Fiberglass insulation, 6" batts	1 S.F.	.35	.18	.53
12	Gypsum board, 1/2" thick	S.F.	.23	.36	.59
13	Thin coat plaster	1 S.F.	.08	.38	.46
14	Paint, roller, 2 coats	1 S.F.	.10	.25	.35
15	TOTAL	S.F.	2.52	4.08	6.60
16					
17					
18	For alternate roof systems:				
19	Rafters 16" O.C., 2" x 8"	S.F.	2.69	4.20	6.89
20	2" x 10"		2.90	4.30	7.20
21	2" x 12"		3.11	4.38	7.49
22	Rafters 24" O.C., 2" x 6"		2.31	3.79	6.10
23	2" x 8"		2.44	3.88	6.32
24	2" x 10"		2.59	3.96	6.55
25	2" x 12"		2.75	4.02	6.77
26	Roof pitch, 6 in 12, add		3%	10%	
27	8 in 12, add		5%	12%	
28					
29					
30					
31					
32					
33	Cut & patch to match existing construction, add, minimum		2%	3%	
34	Maximum		5%	9%	
35	Material handling & storage limitation, add, minimum		1%	1%	
36	Maximum		6%	7%	
37	Protection of existing work, add, minimum		2%	2%	
38	Maximum		5%	7%	
39	Shift work requirements, add, minimum			5%	
40	Maximum			30%	
41					
42					

Table III.22

05.9-300 | Roofing & Ceiling Finish Selective Price Sheet

ROOFING / INSULATION

	DESCRIPTION		MAT.	INST.	TOTAL
ROOFING					
Built-up	Asphalt	3 ply mineral surfaces	.42	.63	1.05
	Roll roofing	4 ply type I.V.	.64	.66	1.30
	Cold applied	3 ply	.80	.20	1.00
	Coal tar pitch	4 ply asbestos felt	1.05	.80	1.85
	Mopped	3 ply glass fiber	.75	.90	1.65
		4 ply organic felt	.87	.78	1.65
Elastomeric	Hypalon	Neoprene unreinforced	1.49	1.47	2.96
		Polyester reinforced	1.50	1.74	3.24
		Neoprene 5 coats 60 mils	3.74	2.97	6.71
		Over 10,000 S.F.	3.50	2.49	5.99
	PVC	Traffic deck sprayed	1.21	2.67	3.88
		With neoprene	1.13	1.02	2.15
Shingles	Asbestos	Strip 14" x 30", 325#/sq.	1.10	.60	1.70
		12" x 24", 167#/sq.	.90	.70	1.60
		Shake 9.35"x 16" 500#/sq.	1.62	1.08	2.70
	Asphalt	Strip 210-235 #/sq.	.31	.43	.74
		235-240 #/sq.	.31	.47	.78
		Class A laminated	.56	.54	1.10
		Class C laminated	.53	.57	1.10
	Slate	Buckingham 3/16" thick black	6.27	1.38	7.65
		1/4" thick	6.27	1.38	7.65
	Wood	Shingles 16" No. 1, 5" exp.	1.46	.99	2.43
		Red cedar 18" perfections	1.21	.89	2.10
		Shakes 24", 10" exposure	1.20	.95	2.15
		18", 8½" exposure	.92	1.23	2.15
INSULATION					
Ceiling Batts	Fiberglass	3-1/2" thick, R11	.20	.15	.35
		6" thick, R19	.33	.18	.51
		9" thick, R30	.53	.21	.74
		12" thick, R38	.72	.24	.96
	Mineral Fiber	3-1/2" thick, R13	.53	.15	.68
		6" thick, R19	.64	.15	.79
Roof Deck	Fiberboard	1" thick, R2.78	.28	.29	.57
		2" thick, R5.26	.55	.30	.85
	Perlite boards	3/4" thick, R2.08	.22	.30	.52
		2" thick, R5.26	.59	.34	.93
	Polystyrene extruded	1" thick, R4	.31	.16	.47
		2" thick, R8	.61	.19	.80
	Urethane paperbacked	1" thick, R6.7	.45	.24	.69
		3" thick, R20	.97	.30	1.27
	Foamglass sheets	1-1/2" thick, R3.95	1.56	.30	1.86
		2" thick, R5.26	2.07	.30	2.37

CEILING

	DESCRIPTION			MAT.	INST.	TOTAL
CEILING						
Plaster	Gypsum		2 coats	.31	1.39	1.70
			3 coats	.43	1.64	2.07
	Perlite or Vermiculite		2 coats	.31	1.62	1.93
			3 coats	.48	2.07	2.55
	Lath Gypsum	Plain	3/8" thick	.24	.32	.56
			1/2" thick	.26	.33	.59
		Firestop	1/2" thick	.34	.38	.72
			5/8" thick	.35	.42	.77
		Metal / Rib	2.75#	.26	.36	.62
			3.40#	.28	.38	.66
		Diamond	2.50#	.19	.36	.55
			3.40#	.24	.45	.69
Drywall	Standard		1/2" thick	.23	.40	.63
			5/8" thick	.25	.44	.69
	Fire resistant		1/2" thick	.26	.41	.67
			5/8" thick	.29	.44	.73
	Water resist.		1/2" thick	.30	.40	.70
			5/8" thick	.33	.44	.77
	Finish		Taping & finishing, add	.01	.24	.25
			thin coat plaster, add	.08	.38	.46
			textured spray, add	.10	.33	.43
Ceiling Tile	Stapled or Glued	Mineral fiber	5/8" thick	.68	.61	1.29
		plastic coated	3/4" thick	.88	.61	1.49
		Wood fiber	1/2" thick	.57	.61	1.18
			3/4" thick	.86	.60	1.46
	Suspended	Fiberglass film faced	5/8" thick	.34	.36	.70
			3" thick	.45	.49	.94
		Mineral fiber 5/8" thick	Standard	.36	.36	.72
			Aluminum	.75	.40	1.15
		Wood fiber Reveal edge	1" thick	1.32	.40	1.72
			3" thick	2.88	.54	3.42
Suspension Systems	Ceiling Tile	"T" bar Class A	2' x 4' grid	.40	.30	.70
			2' x 2' grid	.34	.36	.70
		Concealed "Z"	12" module	.51	.46	.97
	Plaster or Drywall	3/4" channels	16" O.C.	.25	.82	1.07
			24" O.C.	.19	.56	.75
		1-1/2" channels	16" O.C.	.32	.91	1.23
			24" O.C.	.24	.61	.81
		2" x 4" studs	16" O.C.	.25	.56	.81
			24" O.C.	.20	.45	.65

Table III.23

05.9-500 | Roof Accessory Selective Price Sheet

DESCRIPTION				COST PER L.F. MAT.	COST PER L.F. INST.	COST PER L.F. TOTAL
Downspouts	Aluminum	Enameled .024" thick	2" x 3"	.78	1.41	2.19
			3" x 4"	1.32	1.91	3.23
		Round .025" thick	3" diam.	1.05	1.40	2.45
			4" diam.	1.65	1.91	3.56
	Copper	Round 16 oz. stock	2" diam.	2.65	1.41	4.06
			3" diam.	3.41	1.41	4.82
			4" diam.	4.51	1.84	6.35
			5" diam.	4.80	2.05	6.85
		Rectangular	2" x 3"	3.72	1.43	5.15
			3" x 4"	4.53	1.87	6.40
	Lead-coated Copper	Round	2" diam.	4.75	1.40	6.15
			3" diam.	5.83	1.42	7.25
			4" diam.	7.10	1.85	8.95
			5" diam.	10.78	2.07	12.85
		Rectangular	2" x 3"	7.48	1.42	8.90
			3" x 4"	9.41	1.84	11.25
	Steel Galvanized	Round 28 gauge	3" diam.	.50	1.40	1.90
			4" diam.	.63	1.84	2.47
			5" diam.	.78	2.06	2.84
			6" diam.	1.13	2.55	3.68
		Rectangular	2" x 3"	.46	1.41	1.87
			3" x 4"	1.40	1.84	3.24
Elbows	Aluminum	Round	3" diam.	1.87	2.68	4.55
			4" diam.	2.04	2.67	4.71
		Rectangular	2" x 3"	1.93	2.67	4.60
			3" x 4"	2.26	2.67	4.93
	Copper	Round 16 oz.	2" diam.	6.60	2.70	9.30
			3" diam.	8.14	2.66	10.80
			4" diam.	10.78	2.67	13.45
			5" diam.	13.15	2.65	15.80
		Rectangular	2" x 3"	8.86	2.69	11.55
			3" x 4"	11.83	2.67	14.50
Drip Edge	Aluminum		5" girth	.14	.61	.75
			8" girth	.22	.61	.83
			28" girth	.99	2.42	3.41
	Steel Galvanized		5" girth	.17	.60	.77
			8" girth	.24	.61	.85

DESCRIPTION				COST PER L.F. MAT.	COST PER L.F. INST.	COST PER L.F. TOTAL
Flashing 12" wide	Aluminum	Mill finish	.013" thick	.30	1.84	2.14
			.019" thick	.69	1.85	2.54
			.040" thick	1.43	1.85	3.28
			.050" thick	1.76	1.85	3.61
	Copper		16 oz.	1.22	2.33	3.55
			20 oz.	1.54	2.43	3.97
			24 oz.	1.84	2.55	4.39
			32 oz.	2.44	2.66	5.10
	Lead	2.5 lb/S.F.	12" wide	2.42	1.76	4.18
			over 12" wide	3.25	1.75	5.00
	Lead-coated Copper	Fabric backed	2 oz.	1.01	.81	1.82
			5 oz.	1.49	.81	2.30
		Mastic backed	2 oz.	.65	.81	1.46
			5 oz.	1.12	.81	1.93
		Paper backed	2 oz.	.63	.81	1.44
			3 oz.	.91	.81	1.72
	Polyvinyl Chloride	Black	.010" thick	.52	.83	1.35
			.020" thick	.94	.83	1.77
			.030" thick	1.41	.83	2.24
			.056" thick	2.62	.83	3.45
	Steel	Galvanized	20 gauge	.55	2.06	2.61
			30 gauge	.20	1.67	1.87
		Stainless	32 ga. .010" thk.	1.87	1.73	3.60
			28 ga. .015" thk.	2.31	1.73	4.04
			26 ga. .018" thk.	2.86	1.73	4.59
			24 ga. .025" thk.	3.52	1.73	5.25
Gutters	Aluminum	5" box	.027" thick	(1.05)	(2.23)	3.28
			.032" thick	1.27	2.23	3.50
	Copper	Half round	4" wide	4.13	2.22	6.35
			6" wide	5.39	2.31	7.70
	Steel	26 gauge	5" wide	.86	2.23	3.09
		Galvanized	6" wide	.94	2.23	3.17
	Wood	Treated Hem-Fir	3" x 4"	4.02	2.43	6.45
			4" x 5"	5.23	2.42	7.65
Reglet	Aluminum	.025" thick	10 oz.	1.38	1.07	2.45
	Copper		10 oz.	1.30	1.07	2.37
	Steel	Galvanized	24 gauge	.46	1.08	1.54
		Stainless	.020" thick	1.93	1.07	3.00
Counter Flashing 12" wide	Aluminum		.032" thick	1.64	1.78	3.42
	Copper		10 oz.	1.53	1.78	3.31
	Steel		Galvanized 24 gauge	.65	1.78	2.43
			Stainless .020" thick	2.20	1.79	3.99

Table III.24

Division 5: Roofing

The existing roof truss system is to remain with some modifications. New shingles and roof trim are specified, and the owner wants 9″ of fiberglass insulation installed. The costs for these items are obtained from Tables III.22 and III.23. Remember that the drywall ceiling was included in Division 3. The costs for new aluminum gutters and downspouts are found in the "Roof Accessory Selective Price Sheet," Table III.24. The calculations for adding the appropriate factors are shown in Table III.25, and the total costs for Division 5 of the Systems portion of the Means' *Repair and Remodeling Cost Data*, are entered on Table III.26.

Already, the advantage of speed in Systems Estimating can be seen. In a relatively short period of time, a large portion of the renovation has been estimated.

Division 6: Interior Construction

The most important thing to remember when performing a Systems Estimate is to be sure to include all items. Since design data is usually limited, the estimator can easily overlook items that are assumed and must be anticipated. Each of the previous five divisions have included relatively few items. In commercial renovation, interior construction encompasses a great deal of work and must be carefully planned and estimated.

The major portion of the interior construction is wood stud partitions. Three types of partitions are required for the renovation: interior partitions within the apartments, one-hour firewalls between units and at the corridors, and furring and drywall at the existing stair enclosure. The appropriate system for the interior partitions is found in Table III.27. The insulation is included for soundproofing. The costs are entered on the estimate sheet for Division 6, in Table III.28. The firewalls are essentially the same system as the interior partitions. The drywall, however, must be 5/8″ fire resistant. Costs for the drywall are found in Table III.29 and incorporated into the system in Table III.30. Note that the costs in Table III.29 are per single square foot and must be doubled when substituted into the system price. The costs for the furring systems are determined by assembling the components from Tables III.31 and III.32. The calculations are shown in Table III.32.

	Material		Installation		Total
Shingles		$.33		$.53	$ .86
Roof Trim		.06		.11	.17
Subtotal		.39		.64	1.03
Factors	(5%)	.02	(9%)	.06	.08
Total/S.F.		$.41		$.70	$1.11
Insulation (9″)		$.53		$.21	$ .74
Factors	(8%)	.04	(10%)	.02	.06
Total/S.F.		$.57		$.23	$ .80

Division 5: Calculations

Table III.25

COST ANALYSIS

PROJECT	Apartment Renovation						SHEET NO.	5 of 11		

LOCATION — ESTIMATE NO. 85-2

ARCHITECT — OWNER — DATE 1985

QUANTITIES BY EBW — PRICES BY RSM — EXTENSIONS BY — CHECKED BY

DESCRIPTION	QUANTITY	UNIT	MATERIAL		LABOR		TOTAL COST	
			UNIT	TOTAL	UNIT	TOTAL	UNIT	TOTAL
Division 5: Roofing								
Shingles & Roof Trim	4,216	SF	41	1729	70	2951		
Insulation	4,000	SF	57	2280	23	920		
Downspouts	56	LF	78	44	1 41	79		
Gutters	164	LF	1 05	172	2 23	366		
Division 5: Totals				4225		4316		

Table III.26

INTERIOR CONSTRUCTION 06.1-592 — Partitions, Wood Stud

This page illustrates and describes a wood stud partition system including wood studs with plates, gypsum plasterboard – taped and finished, insulation, baseboard and painting. Lines 06.1-592-04 thru 10 give the unit price and total price per square foot for this system. Prices for alternate wood stud partition systems are on Line Items 06.1-592-13 thru 27. Both material quantities and labor costs have been adjusted for the system listed.

Example: 2" x 4" studs, 8' high, 24" O.C. as an alternate system; choose Line Item 06.1-592-17, $1.38 MAT., $2.58 INST., $3.96 TOTAL. This price includes all materials compatible with the original system. For alternatives not listed, use the selective price sheet for this section (pages 353, 354, 356). Substitute the new prices from the price sheet into the typical system and adjust the total to reflect each change.

Factors: To adjust for job conditions other than normal working situations use lines 06.1-592-29 thru 40.

Example: You are to install the above system where material handling and storage present a serious problem. Go to Line 06.1-592-34 and apply these percentages to the appropriate MAT. and INST. costs.

LINE NO.	DESCRIPTION	QUANTITY	MAT.	INST.	TOTAL
01	Wood stud wall, 2" x 4", 16" O.C., dbl. top plate, sngl bot. plate, 5/8" drywall.				
02	Taped, finished and painted on 2 faces, insulation, baseboard, wall 8' high				
03					
04	Wood studs, 2" x 4", 16" O.C., 8' high	.125 C.S.F.	.34	.64	.98
05	Gypsum drywall, 5/8" thick	2 S.F.	.51	.57	1.08
06	Taping and finishing	2 S.F.	.02	.48	.50
07	Insulation, 3-1/2" fiberglass batts	1 S.F.	.22	.15	.37
08	Baseboard, painted	.2 L.F.	.17	.38	.55
09	Painting, roller, 2 coats	2 S.F.	.20	.50	.70
10	TOTAL	S.F.	1.46	2.72	4.18
11					
12	For alternate wood stud systems:				
13	2" x 3" studs, 8' high, 16" O.C.	S.F.	1.45	2.67	4.12
14	24" O.C.		1.36	2.56	3.92
15	10' high, 16" O.C.		1.43	2.56	3.99
16	24" O.C.		1.35	2.47	3.82
17	2" x 4" studs, 8' high, 24" O.C.		1.38	2.58	3.96
18	10' high, 16" O.C.		1.45	2.58	4.03
19	24" O.C.		1.36	2.49	3.85
20	12' high, 16" O.C.		1.44	2.58	4.02
21	24" O.C.		1.35	2.49	3.84
22	2" x 6" studs, 8' high, 16" O.C.		1.62	2.78	4.40
23	24" O.C.		1.49	2.64	4.13
24	10' high, 16" O.C.		1.59	2.65	4.24
25	24" O.C.		1.47	2.52	3.99
26	12' high, 16" O.C.		1.56	2.65	4.21
27	24" O.C.		1.44	2.53	3.97
28					
29	Cut & patch to match existing construction, add, minimum		2%	3%	
30	Maximum		5%	9%	
31	Dust protection, add, minimum		1%	2%	
32	Maximum		4%	11%	
33	Material handling & storage limitation, add, minimum		1%	1%	
34	Maximum		6%	7%	
35	Protection of existing work, add, minimum		2%	2%	
36	Maximum		5%	7%	
37	Shift work requirements, add, minimum			5%	
38	Maximum			30%	
39	Temporary shoring and bracing, add, minimum		2%	5%	
40	Maximum		5%	12%	
41					
42					

340

Table III.27

275

COST ANALYSIS

PROJECT **Apartment Renovation**				SHEET NO. **6 of 11**	
LOCATION				ESTIMATE NO. **85-2**	
ARCHITECT		OWNER		DATE **1985**	
QUANTITIES BY **EBW**	PRICES BY **RSM**	EXTENSIONS BY		CHECKED BY	

DESCRIPTION	QUANTITY	UNIT	MATERIAL		LABOR		TOTAL COST	
			UNIT	TOTAL	UNIT	TOTAL	UNIT	TOTAL
Division 6: Interior Construction								
Interior Partitions	7,208	SF	1⁴⁶	10524	2⁷²	19606		
Firewalls	2,584	SF	1⁵³	3954	2⁷¹	7003		
Furring Wall	527	SF	³⁵	184	⁶⁸	358		
Interior Doors	24	Ea.	87⁴⁷	2099	116²⁸	2791		
Apartment & Stair Doors	10	Ea.	505⁶³	5056	146³²	1463		
Bathroom Closet Doors	8	Ea.	105¹⁴	841	112⁴⁵	900		
Utility Room Doors	8	Ea.	136⁹⁷	1096	114⁷⁸	918		
Bi-Folds - Coat Closets	8	Ea.	95⁵⁹	765	102⁸¹	822		
Bedroom Closets	16	Ea.	156⁰⁷	2497	143⁹³	2303		
Suspended Ceiling	1,216	SF	⁸¹	985	⁷⁶	924		
Painting	527	SF	¹⁰	53	²⁵	132		
Corridor Carpet	304	SF	1⁷⁴	529	⁵⁹	179		
Apartment Carpet	5,824	SF	1⁵⁴	8969	⁶⁵	3786		
Bathroom & Kitchen Vinyl	1,280	SF	1²¹	1549	³⁶	461		
Division 6: Totals				39101		41646		

Table III.28

06.9-300 | Plaster & Drywall Selective Price Sheet

DESCRIPTION			SIZE	COST PER S.F. MAT.	COST PER S.F. INST.	COST PER S.F. TOTAL
LATH	Gypsum Perforated	Regular	3/8"	.26	.33	.59
			1/2"	.28	.38	.66
		Fire Resistant	1/2"	.34	.38	.72
			5/8"	.35	.42	.77
		Moisture Resistant	1/2"	.36	.36	.72
			5/8"	.41	.38	.79
	Metal Lath	Diamond Painted	2.5 Lb.	.19	.31	.50
			3.4 Lb.	.24	.36	.60
		Rib Painted	2.75 Lb.	.26	.36	.62
			3.40 Lb.	.28	.38	.66
PLASTER	Gypsum		2 Coats	.31	1.22	1.53
			3 Coats	.43	1.47	1.90
	Perlite/Vermiculite		2 Coats	.31	1.39	1.70
			3 Coats	.48	1.73	2.21
	Bondcrete		1 Coat	.28	.53	.81
	Wood Fiber		2 Coats	.26	1.77	2.03
			3 Coats	.30	2.25	2.55
DRYWALL	Standard		3/8"	.20	.24	.44
			1/2"	.23	.27	.50
			5/8"	.25	.29	.54
	Fire Resistant		1/2"	.26	.27	.53
			5/8"	.29	.28	.57
	Water Resistant		1/2"	.30	.27	.57
			5/8"	.33	.28	.61
	Core Board		1"	.41	1.01	1.42
FINISH	Taping & Finishing			.01	.24	.25
	Thin Coat			.08	.38	.46
	Texture Spray			.10	.33	.43

Blank worksheet columns (right side):

DESCRIPTION	SIZE	COST PER S.F. MAT.	COST PER S.F. INST.	COST PER S.F. TOTAL

354

Table III.29

06.1-592 | Partitions, Wood Stud

SYSTEM	LINE NO.	DESCRIPTION	QUANTITY	COST PER S.F.		
				MAT.	INST.	TOTAL
	01	Wood stud wall, 2"x 4",16"O.C., dbl. top plate, sngl bot. plate, 5/8" drywall.				
	02	Taped, finished and painted on 2 faces, insulation, baseboard, wall 8' high				
	03					
	04	Wood studs, 2" x 4", 16" O.C., 8' high	.125 C.S.F.	.34	.64	.98
	05	Gypsum drywall, 5/8" thick Fire Resistant	2 S.F.	.58 ✗	.56 ✗	1.08
	06	Taping and finishing	2 S.F.	.02	.48	.50
	07	Insulation, 3-1/2" fiberglass batts	1 S.F.	.22	.15	.37
	08	Baseboard, painted	2 L.F.	.17	.38	.55
	09	Painting, roller, 2 coats	2 S.F.	.20	.50	.70
	10	TOTAL	S.F.	1.53	2.71	4.18
	11					
	12	For alternate wood stud systems:				
	13	2" x 3" studs, 8' high, 16" O.C.	S.F.	1.45	2.67	4.12
	14	24" O.C.		1.36	2.56	3.92
	15	10' high, 16" O.C.		1.43	2.56	3.99
	16	24" O.C.		1.35	2.47	3.82
	17	2" x 4" studs, 8' high, 24" O.C.		1.38	2.58	3.96
	18	10' high, 16" O.C.		1.45	2.58	4.03
	19	24" O.C.		1.36	2.49	3.85
	20	12' high, 16" O.C.		1.44	2.58	4.02
	21	24" O.C.		1.35	2.49	3.84
	22	2" x 6" studs, 8' high, 16" O.C.		1.62	2.78	4.40
	23	24" O.C.		1.49	2.64	4.13
	24	10' high, 16" O.C.		1.59	2.65	4.24
	25	24" O.C.		1.47	2.52	3.99
	26	12' high, 16" O.C.		1.56	2.65	4.21
	27	24" O.C.		1.44	2.53	3.97
	28					
	29	Cut & patch to match existing construction, add, minimum		2%	3%	
	30	Maximum		5%	9%	
	31	Dust protection, add, minimum		1%	2%	
	32	Maximum		4%	11%	
	33	Material handling & storage limitation, add, minimum		1%	1%	
	34	Maximum		6%	7%	
	35	Protection of existing work, add, minimum		2%	2%	
	36	Maximum		5%	7%	
	37	Shift work requirements, add, minimum			5%	
	38	Maximum			30%	
	39	Temporary shoring and bracing, add, minimum		2%	5%	
	40	Maximum		5%	12%	
	41					
	42					

This page illustrates and describes a wood stud partition system including wood studs with plates, gypsum plasterboard - taped and finished, insulation, baseboard and painting. Lines 06.1-592-04 thru 10 give the unit price and total price per square foot for this system. Prices for alternate wood stud partition systems are on Line Items 06.1-592-13 thru 27. Both material quantities and labor costs have been adjusted for the system listed.

Example: 2" x 4" studs, 8' high, 24" O.C. as an alternate system; choose Line Item 06.1-592-17, $1.38 MAT., $2.58 INST., $3.96 TOTAL. This price includes all materials compatible with the original system. For alternatives not listed, use the selective price sheet for this section (pages 353, 354, 356). Substitute the new prices from the price sheet into the typical system and adjust the total to reflect each change.

Factors: To adjust for job conditions other than normal working situations use lines 06.1-592-29 thru 40.

Example: You are to install the above system where material handling and storage present a serious problem. Go to Line 06.1-592-34 and apply these percentages to the appropriate MAT. and INST. costs.

340

Table III.30

06.9-100 | Stud & Furring Selective Price Sheet

STUDS — 24" O.C.

DESCRIPTION (10 ft. wall)		SIZE	COST PER S.F. MAT.	INST.	TOTAL
24" O.C., metal, including top and bottom runners					
Non load bearing	25 Ga.	1-5/8"	.18	.50	.68
		2-1/2"	.20	.50	.70
		3-5/8"	.23	.52	.75
		4"	.28	.55	.83
		6"	.34	.57	.91
	20 Ga.	2-1/2"	.24	.50	.74
		3-5/8"	.28	.52	.80
		4"	.31	.55	.86
		6"	.36	.57	.93
Load bearing	20 Ga.	2-1/2"	.40	.50	.90
		3-5/8"	.42	.52	.94
		4"	.46	.56	1.02
		6"	.52	.58	1.10
	18 Ga.	2-1/2"	.80	.51	1.31
		3-5/8"	.85	.53	1.38
		4"	.92	.57	1.49
		6"	1.06	.59	1.65
	16 Ga.	2-1/2"	.96	.52	1.48
		3-5/8"	.96	.55	1.51
		4"	1.07	.58	1.65
		6"	1.27	.60	1.87
		8"	1.61	.62	2.23
24" O.C., wood, including double top plate & shoe		2" x 4"	.29	.48	.77
		2" x 6"	.44	.51	.95

FURRING — 24" O.C.

DESCRIPTION (10 ft. wall)		SIZE	COST PER S.F. MAT.	INST.	TOTAL
24" O.C.	Metal	3/4"	.19	.57	.76
		1-1/2"	.24	.62	.86
	Wood — On wood	1" x 2"	.04	.21	.25
		1" x 3"	.06	.22	.28
	On masonry	1" x 2"	.04	.25	.29
		1" x 3"	.06	.25	.31
	On concrete	1" x 2"	.04	.46	.50
		1" x 3"	.04	.46	.50

STUDS — 16" O.C.

DESCRIPTION (10 ft. wall)		SIZE	COST PER S.F. MAT.	INST.	TOTAL
16" O.C., metal, including top and bottom runners					
Non load bearing	25 Ga.	1-5/8"	.21	.60	.81
		2-1/2"	.23	.60	.83
		3-5/8"	.28	.62	.90
		4"	.33	.67	1.00
		6"	.41	.68	1.09
	20 Ga.	2-1/2"	.29	.60	.89
		3-5/8"	.32	.63	.95
		4"	.36	.67	1.03
		6"	.43	.68	1.11
Load bearing	20 Ga.	2-1/2"	.47	.61	1.08
		3-5/8"	.50	.62	1.12
		4"	.55	.67	1.22
		6"	.62	.70	1.32
	18 Ga.	2-1/2"	.96	.61	1.57
		3-5/8"	1.01	.65	1.66
		4"	1.10	.69	1.79
		6"	1.27	.71	1.98
	16 Ga.	2-1/2"	1.14	.64	1.78
		3-5/8"	1.14	.68	1.82
		4"	1.28	.70	1.98
		6"	1.52	.73	2.25
		8"	1.91	.76	2.67
16" O.C., wood, including double top plate & shoe		2" x 3"	.30	.46	.76
		2" x 4"	.35	.55	.90
		2" x 6"	.45	.50	.95

FURRING — 16" O.C.

DESCRIPTION (10 ft. wall)		SIZE	COST PER S.F. MAT.	INST.	TOTAL
16" O.C.	Metal	3/4"	.25	.81	1.06
		1-1/2"	.32	.91	1.23
	Wood — On wood	1" x 2"	.06	.31	.37
		1" x 3"	.08	.33	.41
	On masonry	1" x 2"	.06	.37	.43
		1" x 3"	.09	.37	.46
	On concrete	1" x 2"	.07	.69	.76
		1" x 3"	.07	.69	.76

Table III.31

06.9-300 Plaster & Drywall Selective Price Sheet

DESCRIPTION			SIZE	COST PER S.F. MAT.	COST PER S.F. INST.	COST PER S.F. TOTAL
LATH	Gypsum Perforated					
		Regular	3/8"	.26	.33	.59
			1/2"	.28	.38	.66
		Fire Resistant	1/2"	.34	.38	.72
			5/8"	.35	.42	.77
		Moisture Resistant	1/2"	.36	.36	.72
			5/8"	.41	.38	.79
	Metal Lath					
		Diamond Painted	2.5 Lb.	.19	.31	.50
			3.4 Lb.	.24	.36	.60
		Rib Painted	2.75 Lb.	.26	.36	.62
			3.40 Lb.	.28	.38	.66
PLASTER	Gypsum		2 Coats	.31	1.22	1.53
			3 Coats	.43	1.47	1.90
	Perlite/Vermiculite		2 Coats	.31	1.39	1.70
			3 Coats	.48	1.73	2.21
	Bondcrete		1 Coat	.28	.53	.81
	Wood Fiber		2 Coats	.26	1.77	2.03
			3 Coats	.30	2.25	2.55
DRYWALL	Standard		3/8"	.20	.24	.44
			1/2"	.23	.27	.50
			5/8"	.25	.29	.54
	Fire Resistant		1/2"	.26	.27	.53
			5/8"	.29	.28	.57
	Water Resistant		1/2"	.30	.27	.57
			5/8"	.33	.28	.61
	Core Board		1"	.41	1.01	1.42
FINISH	Taping & Finishing			.01	.24	.25
	Thin Coat			.08	.38	.46
	Texture Spray			.10	.33	.43

DESCRIPTION	SIZE	COST PER S.F. MAT.	COST PER S.F. INST.	COST PER S.F. TOTAL

	mat.	Inst.
Furring (Table III.31)	.09	.37
Drywall	.25	.29
	.34	.66
Factors		
2% Mat.	.01	.02
3% Inst.		
Totals	.35	.68

Table III.32

LINE NO.	DESCRIPTION	QUANTITY	COST EACH MAT.	COST EACH INST.	COST EACH TOTAL
01	Single hollow core door, include jamb, header, trim and hardware, painted.				
02					
03					
04	Hollow core Lauan, 1-3/8" thick, 2'-0" x 6'-8", painted	1 Ea.	20.28	44.72	65
05	Wood jamb, 4-9/16" deep	1 Set	22.53	21.31	43.84
06	Trim, casing	1 Set	17.25	32.35	49.60
07	Hardware, hinges, lockset	1 Set	13.18	14.97	28.15
08	TOTAL		73.24	113.35	186.59
09					
10	For alternate door systems:				
11	Lauan (Mahogany) hollow core, 1-3/8" x 2'-6" x 6'-8"	Ea.	76.68	115.83	192.51
12	2'-8" x 6'-8"		78.67	117.08	195.75
13	3'-0" x 6'-8"		81.20	120.33	201.53
14					
15	Birch, hollow core, 1-3/8" x 2'-0" x 6'-8"		80.94	113.65	194.59
16	2'-6" x 6'-8"		85.48	115.03	200.51
17	2'-8" x 6'-8"		87.47	116.28	203.75
18	3'-0" x 6'-8"		91.10	120.43	211.53
19	Solid core, 1-3/8" x 2'-6" x 6'-8"		111.88	116.63	228.51
20	2'-8" x 6'-8"		113.87	117.88	231.75
21	3'-0" x 6'-8"		118.60	120.93	239.53
22					
23					
24	For metal frame instead of wood, add	Ea.	50%	20%	
25					
26					
27	Cut & patch to match existing construction, add, minimum		2%	3%	
28	Maximum		5%	9%	
29	Dust protection, add, minimum		1%	2%	
30	Maximum		4%	11%	
31	Equipment usage curtailment, add, minimum		1%	1%	
32	Maximum		3%	10%	
33	Material handling & storage limitation, add, minimum		1%	1%	
34	Maximum		6%	7%	
35	Protection of existing work, add, minimum		2%	2%	
36	Maximum		5%	7%	
37	Shift work requirements, add, minimum			5%	
38	Maximum			30%	
39					
40					
41					
42					

SYSTEM

This page illustrates and describes flush interior door systems including hollow core door, jamb, header and trim with hardware.

Lines 06.4-142-04 thru 08 give the unit price and total price on a cost each basis for this system. Prices for alternate flush interior door systems are on Line items 06.4-142-11 thru 24. Both material quantities and labor costs have been adjusted for the system listed.

Example: Birch, solid core, 3'-0" x 6'-8" as an alternate system; choose Line Item 06.4-142-21, $119.00 MAT.. $121.00 INST.. $240.00 TOTAL. This price includes all materials compatible with the original system. For alternatives not listed, use the selective price sheet for this section (page 355). Substitute the new prices from the price sheet into the typical system and adjust the total to reflect each change.

Factors: To adjust for job conditions other than normal working situations use Lines 06.1-142-27 thru 38.

Example: You are to install the above system in an area where dust protection is vital. Go to Line 06.4-142-30 and apply these percentages to the appropriate MAT. and INST. costs.

346

Table III.33

281

SYSTEM	LINE NO.	DESCRIPTION	QUANTITY	COST EACH		
				MAT.	INST.	TOTAL
	01	Single metal door, including frame and hardware.				
	02					
	03					
	04	Hollow metal door, 1-3/8" thck, 2'-6" x 6'-8", painted	1 Ea.	173.18	51.82	225
	05	Metal frame, 5-3/4" deep	1 Set	63.80	31.20	95
	06	Hinges and passage lockset	1 Set	(13.18)	(14.97)	28.15
	07	Deduct · TOTAL	Ea.	250.16	97.99	348.15
	08					
	09					
	10	For alternate systems:				
	11	Hollow metal doors, 1-3/8" thick, 2'-8" x 6'-8"	Ea.	257.86	97.29	355.15
	12	3'-0" x 7'-0"	"	257.86	99.29	357.15
	13					
	14	Interior fire door, 1-3/8" thick, 2'-6" x 6'-8"	Ea.	289.76	93.39	383.15
	15	2'-8" x 6'-8"	→	300.76	97.39	398.15
	16	3'-0" x 7'-0"		(318.36)	(99.79)	418.15
	17					
	18	Add to fire doors:				
	19	Baked enamel finish	Ea.	40%	90%	
	20	Galvanizing		10%		
	21	Porcelain finish	→	100%	150%	
	22					
	23					
	24					
	25					
	26					
	27					
	28					
	29	Cut & patch to match existing construction, add, minimum		2%	3%	
	30	Maximum		5%	9%	
	31	Dust protection, add, minimum		1%	2%	
	32	Maximum		4%	11%	
	33	Equipment usage curtailment, add, minimum		1%	1%	
	34	Maximum		3%	10%	
	35	Material handling & storage limitation, add, minimum		1%	1%	
	36	Maximum		6%	7%	
	37	Protection of existing work, add, minimum		2%	2%	
	38	Maximum		5%	7%	
	39	Shift work requirements, add, minimum			5%	
	40	Maximum			30%	
	41					
	42					

This page illustrates and describes interior metal door systems including a metal door, metal frame and hardware. Lines 06.4-146-04 thru 07 give the unit price and total price on a cost each for this system. Prices for alternate interior metal door systems are on Line Items 06.4-146-11 thru 21. Both material quantities and labor costs have been adjusted for the system listed.

Example: Interior fire door, 3'-0" x 7'-0" as an alternate system; choose Line Item 06.4-146-16, $318.00 MAT., $100.00 INST., $418.00 TOTAL. This price includes materials compatible with the original system. For alternatives not listed, use the selective price sheet for this section (page 355). Substitute the new prices from the price sheet into the typical system and adjust the total to reflect each change.

Factors: To adjust for job conditions other than normal working situations use Lines 06.5-146-29 thru 40.

Example: You are to install the above system while protecting existing construction. Go to Line 06.4-146-37 and apply these percentages to the appropriate MAT. and INST. costs.

348

Table III.34

06.9-500 | Hardware Selective Price Sheet

DESCRIPTION		UNIT	COST EACH		
			MAT.	INST.	TOTAL
DOOR CLOSER, Rack and Pinion, Backcheck and Adjustable Power					
REGULAR	Hinge face mount, all sizes, regular arm	Ea.	55.00	37.00	92.00
	Hold open arm		60.50	37.50	98.00
	Top jamb mount, all sizes, regular arm		60.50	37.50	98.00
	Hold open arm		60.50	39.50	100.00
	Stop face mount, all sizes, regular arm		55.00	37.00	92.00
	Hold open arm		60.50	37.50	98.00
FUSIBLE LINK	Hinge face mount, all sizes, regular arm		63.80	37.00	100.80
	Hold open arm		69.30	37.50	106.80
	Top jamb mount, all sizes, regular arm		63.80	40.00	103.80
	Hold open arm		69.30	39.50	108.80
	Stop face mount, all sizes, regular arm		63.00	37.00	100.00
	Hold open arm		69.30	37.50	106.80
DOOR STOPS	Holder & bumper, floor or wall	Ea.	17.60	10.40	28.00
	Wall bumper		3.30	10.10	13.40
	Floor bumper		2.75	10.10	12.85
	Plunger type, door mounted		13.20	9.80	23.00
HINGES, Material only					
3-1/2"x3-1/2" Interior	Full mortise, 1-3/8" doors	Set	16.70		16.70
	Steel plate ball bearing		37.00		37.00
	Bronze, ball bearing				
	Low frequency, steel, plated		5.15		5.15
4-1/2"x4-1/2" Exterior	Full mortise, 1-3/4" doors		18.95		18.95
	Steel plate ball bearing				
	Bronze, ball bearing		52.00		52.00
	Low frequency steel		8.60		8.60
KICK PLATE	6" high, for 3' door, aluminum	Ea.	13.75	16.25	30.00
	Bronze	"	36.30	15.70	52.00
PANIC DEVICE	For rim locks, single door, exit	Ea.	220.00	80.00	300.00
	Exit & entrance		247.50	82.50	330.00
	For mortise locks, single door, exit		286.00	79.00	365.00
	Exit & entrance		297.00	83.00	380.00

DESCRIPTION		UNIT	COST EACH		
			MAT.	INST.	TOTAL
LOCKSET					
Heavy duty, cylindrical	Passage doors	Ea.	74.80	24.20	99.00
	Classroom		115.50	24.50	140.00
	Bedroom, bathroom and inner office doors		95.70	24.30	120.00
	Apartment, office and corridor doors		121.00	24.00	145.00
Standard duty, cylindrical	Exit doors		49.50	24.50	74.00
	Inner office		16.50	17.50	34.00
	Passage doors		23.10	23.90	47.00
	Public restroom, classroom & office doors		23.10	23.90	47.00
Heavy duty mortise	Without lock knob		86.90	28.10	115.00
	Entrances		99.00	31.00	130.00
Heavy duty, deadbolt lock	Mortise, utility rooms		58.30	30.70	89.00
	Handicapped lever, add		87.00		87.00
Residential	Interior door, minimum		8.03	14.97	23.00
	Maximum		25.30	30.70	56.00
	Exterior door, minimum		16.50	24.50	41.00
	Maximum		88.00	22.00	110.00
PUSH PULL	Aluminum	Ea.	27.50	20.50	48.00
	Bronze		45.10	19.90	65.00
	Door pull, designer style, minimum		44.00	20.00	64.00
	Maximum		192.50	32.50	225.00
THRESHOLD					
3' long door saddles	Aluminum, minimum	Ea.	21.73	12.77	34.00
	Maximum		68.20	19.80	88.00
	Bronze, minimum		39.60	12.40	52.00
	Maximum		115.50	19.50	135.00
	Rubber, 1/2" thick, 5-1/2" wide		23.10	11.90	35.00
	2-3/4" wide		12.60	12.40	25.00
WEATHERSTRIPPING					
Doors	Wood frame, interlocking for 3x7 door, zinc	Set	20.02	79.98	100.00
	Bronze		33.00	82.00	115.00
	Wood frame, spring type for 3'x7' door, bronze		9.74	32.26	42.00
	Metal frame, spring type for 3'x7' door, bronze		38.50	81.50	120.00
	For stainless steel, spring type, add		100%		
	Metal frame, extruded sections, 3'x7' door, alum.	Set	27.50	122.50	150.00
	Bronze	"	72.60	122.40	195.00

Table III.35

There is no door schedule for the project. The estimator must be sure to establish the different door types, hardware sets, and quantities of each. When only one, or a "typical" floor plan is provided, it is easy to forget to multiply for repetitive floors. Cross-checking is necessary. The interior door system is found in Table III.33. The apartment entrance doors and stairway corridor doors must both be fire-rated, but different hardware sets are required from those as shown in Table III.34. The correct hardware is selected from Table III.35. The calculations are shown in Table III.36. Note that installation costs for the hinges are already included in the installation costs for the door. Costs for the remaining door types are obtained from Tables III.37 and III.38.

Throughout the estimate for Division 6, no factors have been added. This is because the interior construction for this project is similar to new construction, unimpeded by existing conditions. It is up to the estimator, using experience and discretion, to determine if and when factors are required for a particular project.

The estimator must be constantly aware of the project as a whole to be sure to include all requirements. The heating and cooling system is forced air. The ductwork will have to be concealed by a suspended ceiling. At this point or in Division 8, of the Systems portion of the *Means' Repair and Remodeling Cost Data*, a rough duct layout should be made to identify areas that will require a suspended ceiling. The system to be used is shown in Table III.39. A factor is added because the installation is in small spaces, in the bathrooms and closets. This will entail a high waste factor for materials as well as added labor expense.

Painting is included in the systems for all the required interior construction except for the furring and drywall system, which was "assembled." The ceilings, in Division 3, of the Systems portion of the *Means' Repair and Remodeling Cost Data*, also included painting. The costs for painting, and for other interior finishes that may be substituted for those included in the systems, are found in Table III.40.

Without specifications, the estimator must also choose the type of carpeting to be used. This decision should be based upon experience or with the advice of a floorcovering subcontractor. The costs are found in Table III.41.

	Material	Installation	Total
Apartment Entrance and Stairway Doors 06-4-146-16	$318.36	$ 99.79	$418.15
Deduct Hardware	13.18	14.97	28.15
Subtotal	305.18	84.82	390.00
Add:			
Closer	60.50	37.50	98.00
Hinges	18.95		18.95
Lockset	121.00	24.00	145.00
Total	$505.63	$146.32	$651.95

Calculations for Apartment and Stairway Doors

Table III.36

INTERIOR CONSTRUCTION | 06.4-144 | Doors, Interior Solid and Louvered

This page illustrates and describes interior, solid and louvered door systems including a pine panel door, wood jambs, header, and trim with hardware. Lines 06.4-144-04 thru 08 give the unit price and total price on a cost each basis for this system. Prices for alternate interior, solid and louvered systems are on Line Items 06.4-144-12 thru 24. Both material quantities and labor costs have been adjusted for the system listed.

Example: Louvered pine 2'-6" x 6'-8" as an alternate system; choose Line Item 06.4-144-18, $137.00 MAT., $115.00 INST., $252.00 TOTAL. This price includes all materials compatible with the original system. For alternatives not listed, use the selective price sheet for this section (page 355). Substitute the new prices from the price sheet into the typical system and adjust the total to reflect each change.

Factors: To adjust for job conditions other than normal working situations use Lines 06.4-144-29 thru 40.

Example: You are to install the above system during night hours only. Go to Line 06.4-144-40 and apply these percentages to the appropriate INST. costs.

LINE NO.	SYSTEM / DESCRIPTION	QUANTITY	MAT.	INST.	TOTAL
01	Single interior door, including jamb, header, trim and hardware, painted.				
02					
03					
04	Solid pine panel door, painted 1-3/8" thick, 2'-0" x 6'-8"	1 Ea.	96.18	43.82	140
05	Wooden jamb, 4-5/8" deep	1 Set	22.53	21.31	43.84
06	Trim, casing	1 Set	17.25	32.35	49.60
07	Hardware, hinges, lockset	1 Set	13.18	14.97	28.15
08	TOTAL	Ea.	149.14	112.45	261.59
09					
10					
11	For alternate door systems:				
12	Solid pine, painted raised panel, 1-3/8" x 2'-6" x 6'-8"	Ea.	155.88	113.63	269.51
13	2'-8" x 6'-8"	→	161.17	115.58	276.75
14	3'-0" x 6'-8"		174.70	120.83	295.53
15					
16	Louvered pine, painted 1'-6" x 6'-8" *Bath Closet*	Ea.	(105.14)	(112.45)	217.59
17	2'-0" x 6'-8"		117.38	115.13	232.51
18	2'-6" x 6'-8" *Utility Room*		(136.97)	(114.78)	251.75
19	3'-0" x 6'-8"	→	145	120.53	265.53
20					
21					
22	For prehung door, deduct	Ea.	5%	30%	
23					
24	For metal frame instead of wood, add	Ea.	50%	20%	
25					
26					
27					
28					
29	Cut & patch to match existing construction, add, minimum		2%	3%	
30	Maximum		5%	9%	
31	Dust protection, add, minimum		1%	2%	
32	Maximum		4%	11%	
33	Equipment usage curtailment, add, minimum		1%	1%	
34	Maximum		3%	10%	
35	Material handling & storage limitation, add, minimum		1%	1%	
36	Maximum		6%	7%	
37	Protection of existing work, add, minimum		2%	2%	
38	Maximum		5%	7%	
39	Shift work requirements, add, minimum			5%	
40	Maximum			30%	
41					
42					

Table III.37

LINE NO.	DESCRIPTION	QUANTITY	COST PER SET MAT.	INST.	TOTAL
01	Interior closet door painted, including frame, trim and hardware, prehung				
02					
03					
04	Bi-fold doors				
05	Pine paneled, 3'-0" x 6'-8"	Set	173.91	94.09	268
06	6'-0" x 6'-8"		324.59	130.41	455
07	Birch, hollow core, 3'-0" x 6'-8" *Coat Cl.*		95.59	102.81	198.40
08	6'-0" x 6'-8" *Bedroom Cl.*		156.07	143.93	300
09	Lauan, hollow core, 3'-0" x 6'-8"		84.81	95.19	180
10	6'-0" x 6'-8"		136.49	133.51	270
11	Louvered pine, 3'-0" x 6'-8"		127.71	95.29	223
12	6'-0" x 6'-8"	↓	225.59	129.41	355
13					
14	Sliding, bi-passing closet doors				
15	Pine paneled, 4'-0" x 6'-8"	Set	269.08	102.92	372
16	6'-0" x 6'-8"		324.59	130.41	455
17	Birch, hollow core, 4'-0" x 6'-8"		119.48	102.52	222
18	6'-0" x 6'-8"		154.09	130.91	285
19	Lauan, hollow core, 4'-0" x 6'-8"		100.78	101.22	202
20	6'-0" x 6'-8"		127.69	132.31	260
21	Louvered pine, 4'-0" x 6'-8"		153.58	103.42	257
22	6'-0" x 6'-8"	↓	192.59	132.41	325
23					
24					
25					
26					
27					
28					
29	Cut & patch to match existing construction, add, minimum		2%	3%	
30	Maximum		5%	9%	
31	Dust protection, add, minimum		1%	2%	
32	Maximum		4%	11%	
33	Equipment usage curtailment, add, minimum		1%	1%	
34	Maximum		3%	10%	
35	Material handling & storage limitation, add, minimum		1%	1%	
36	Maximum		6%	7%	
37	Protection of existing work, add, minimum		2%	2%	
38	Maximum		5%	7%	
39	Shift work requirements, add, minimum			5%	
40	Maximum			30%	
41					
42					

SYSTEM

This page illustrates and describes an interior closet door system including an interior closet door, painted, with trim and hardware. Prices for alternate interior closet door system are on Line Items 06.4-148-05 thru 22. Both material quantities and labor costs have been adjusted for the system listed.

Example: Bi-folding, louvered pine, 6'-0" x 6'-8" as an alternate system; choose Line Item 06.4-148-12, $226.00 MAT., $129.00 INST., $355.00 TOTAL. This price includes all materials compatible with the original system. For alternatives not listed, use the selective price sheet for this section (page 355). Substitute the new prices from the price sheet into the typical system and adjust the total to reflect each change.

Factors: To adjust for job conditions other than normal working situations use Lines 6-57-29 thru 40.

Example: You are to install the above system and match the existing construction. Go to Line 06.4-148-29 and apply these percentages to the appropriate MAT. and INST. costs.

Table III.38

349

INTERIOR CONSTRUCTION — 06.7-342 — Ceiling, Suspended Acoustical Boards

SYSTEM	LINE NO.	DESCRIPTION	QUANTITY	MAT.	INST.	TOTAL
				COST PER S.F.		
	01	Suspended acoustical ceiling board				
	02	Installed on exposed grid system.				
	03					
	04	Fiberglass boards, film faced, 2' x 4', 5/8" thick	1 S.F.	.34	.36	.70
	05	Hangers, #12 wire	1 S.F.	.03	.04	.07
	06	T bar suspension system, 2' x 4' grid	1 S.F.	.40	.30	.70
	07	TOTAL	S.F.	.77	.70	1.47
	08	Factors		.04	.06	
	09			.81	.76	
	10	For alternate suspended ceiling systems:				
	11	2' x 4' grid, mineral fiber board, aluminum faced, 5/8" thick	S.F.	1.18	.71	1.89
	12	Standard faced		.79	.70	1.49
	13	Plastic faced		.83	.94	1.77
	14	Fiberglass, film faced, 3" thick, R11		1.24	.83	2.07
	15	Grass cloth faced, 3/4" thick		1.26	.82	2.08
	16	1" thick		1.37	.82	2.19
	17	1-1/2" thick, nubby face		1.72	.82	2.54
	18	Wood fiber, reveal edge, painted, 1" thick		1.75	.74	2.49
	19	2" thick		2.70	.78	3.48
	20	2-1/2" thick		3.03	.82	3.85
	21	3" thick		3.31	.88	4.19
	22					
	23					
	24	Add for 2' x 2' grid system	S.F.	.08	.08	.16
	25					
	26					
	27					
	28					
	29	Cut & patch to match existing construction, add, minimum		2%	3%	
	30	Maximum		5%	9%	
	31	Dust protection, add, minimum		1%	2%	
	32	Maximum		4%	11%	
	33	Equipment usage curtailment, add, minimum		1%	1%	
	34	Maximum		3%	10%	
	35	Material handling & storage limitation, add, minimum		1%	1%	
	36	Maximum		6%	7%	
	37	Protection of existing work, add, minimum		2%	2%	
	38	Maximum		5%	7%	
	39	Shift work requirements, add, minimum			5%	
	40	Maximum			30%	
	41					
	42					

This page illustrates suspended acoustical board systems including acoustic ceiling board, hangers, and T bar suspension. Lines 06.7-342-04 thru 07 give the unit price and total price per square foot for this system. Prices for alternate suspended acoustical board systems are on Line Items 06.7-342-11 thru 24. Both material quantities and labor costs have been adjusted for the system listed.

Example: Fiberglass, film faced, 3" thick, R11 as an alternate system; choose Line Item 06.7-342-14, $1.24 MAT., $.83 INST., $2.07 TOTAL. This price includes all materials compatible with the original system. For alternatives not listed, use the selective price sheet for this section (page 357). Substitute the new price from the price sheet into the typical system and adjust the total to reflect each change.

Factors: To adjust for job conditions other than normal working situations use Lines 06.7-342-29 thru 40.

Example: You are to install the above system and protect existing construction. Go to Line 06.7-342-38 and apply these percentages to the appropriate MAT. and INST. costs.

Table III.39

06.9-600 | Interior Wall Finish Selective Price Sheet

(Left section)

DESCRIPTION				MAT.	INST.	TOTAL
Painting	On plaster or drywall	Brushwork	Primer & 1 ct.	.07	.32	.39
			Primer & 2 ct.	.09	.47	.56
		Rollerwork	Primer & 1 ct.	.07	.17	.24
			Primer & 2 ct.	.10	.25	.35
	Woodwork incl. puttying	Brushwork	Primer & 1 ct.	.09	.34	.43
			Primer & 2 ct.	.11	.46	.57
	Wood trim to 6" wide	Enamel	Primer & 1 ct.	.07	.68	.75
			Primer & 2 ct.	.09	.97	1.06
	Cabinets & casework	Enamel	Primer & 1 ct.	.09	.99	1.08
			Primer & 2 ct.	.11	1.35	1.46
	On masonry or concrete, latex	Brushwork	Primer & 1 ct.	.13	.47	.60
			Primer & 2 ct.	.15	.64	.79
		For block filler	Add	.09	.12	.21
Varnish	Wood trim, sealer & 1 coat	With sanding and puttying	Quality work	.08	.50	.58
			Medium work	.08	.38	.46
		Without sanding		.08	.25	.33
Wall Coverings	Wallpaper	@$8/dbl. roll	Average work	.18	.36	.54
		@$17/dbl. roll	Average work	.36	.44	.80
		@$40/dbl. roll	Quality work	.78	.54	1.32
		Grass cloths w/lining paper	Minimum	.61	.58	1.19
			Maximum	1.79	.67	2.46
	Vinyl	Fabric backed	Light weight	.44	.36	.80
			Medium weight	.66	.49	1.15
			Heavy weight	.88	.54	1.42
	Cork tiles	12" x 12"	3/16" thick	1.30	.97	2.27
			5/16" thick	1.62	.97	2.59
		12" x 36"	1/2" thick	.68	.61	1.29
		Granular surface	1" thick	.97	.60	1.57
	Aluminum foil			.74	.84	1.58
Tile	Ceramic, Adhesive set	4-1/4" x 4-1/4"		1.68	2.30	3.98
		6" x 6"		1.90	2.07	3.97
		Decorated 4-1/4" x 4-1/4"	Minimum	.95	.47	1.42
			Maximum	12.21	.69	12.90
		For epoxy grout	Add	.44	.43	.87
		Pregrouted sheets		2.21	1.72	3.93
	Plastic	4-1/4" x 4-1/4"	.050" thick	1.05	1.93	2.98
			.110" thick	1.28	1.93	3.21

(Right section)

DESCRIPTION				MAT.	INST.	TOTAL
	Tile, (cont.)	Metal, 4-1/4" x 4-1/4", thin set	Aluminum, plain	1.86	3.03	4.89
			Epoxy enameled	2.16	3.04	5.20
			Leather on aluminum	18.59	3.41	22.00
			Stainless steel	4.85	3.05	7.90
	Brick	Interior veneer ($178/M)	Minimum	1.71	5.74	7.45
			Maximum	1.71	5.74	7.45
		4" face brick, running bond		3.74	1.61	5.35
		Urethane pieces, set in mastic, Simulated		2.81	1.21	4.02
		Fiberglass panels				
	Wall Coatings	On drywall	Thin coat — Plain	.08	.38	.46
			Stipple	.08	.38	.46
			Textured spray	.10	.33	.43
	Paneling, not incl. furring or trim	Hardboard	Tempered 1/8" thick	.24	1.00	1.24
			Tempered 1/4" thick	.37	1.00	1.37
			Plastic faced 1/8" thick	.42	1.00	1.42
			Plastic faced 1/4" thick	.57	1.00	1.57
			Woodgrained 1/4" thick Minimum	.35	1.00	1.35
			Maximum	.67	1.18	1.85
		Plywood, 4'x8' sheets, 1/4" thick, prefinished, vertical grooves	Birch faced Minimum	.56	1.00	1.56
			Maximum	1.07	1.42	2.49
			Walnut Minimum	2.01	1.00	3.01
			Maximum	2.97	1.25	4.22
			Mahogany African	1.29	1.25	2.54
			Philippine	.39	.99	1.38
			Chestnut	3.37	1.33	4.70
			Pecan	1.34	1.25	2.59
			Rosewood	8.97	1.58	10.55
			Teak	2.35	1.25	3.60
			Aromatic Cedar Plywood	1.29	1.25	2.54
			Particle board	.56	1.25	1.81
		Wood board, 3/4" thick	Knotty pine	.84	1.66	2.50
			Rough sawn cedar	1.79	1.67	3.46
			Redwood, clear	3.07	1.66	4.73
			Aromatic cedar	1.71	1.81	3.52

Table III.40

06.9-800 | Floor Finish Selective Price Sheet

Left Table

FLOORING	DESCRIPTION				MAT.	INST.	TOTAL
FLOORING	Carpet	Acrylic	26 oz. light traffic		1.27	.64	1.91
			35 oz. heavy traffic		1.74	.59	2.33
		Nylon	15 oz. light traffic		1.01	.65	1.66
		Anti-static	22 oz. medium traffic		1.33	.65	1.98
			26 oz. heavy traffic		1.54	.65	2.19
			28 oz. heavy traffic		1.65	.68	2.33
		Tile	Needle punch		.80	.36	1.16
		foamed back	Tufted loop		1.43	.36	1.79
		Wool	36 oz. medium traffic		2.98	.68	3.66
			42 oz. heavy traffic		3.29	.60	3.89
	Composition	Epoxy	With colored chips	Min.	1.14	1.88	3.02
				Max.	1.78	2.59	4.37
			Trowelled	Min.	1.44	2.26	3.70
				Max.	2.30	2.64	4.94
			Terrazzo, 1/4" thick	Min.	3.81	3.39	7.20
			chemical resistant	Max.	6.33	4.52	10.85
	Resilient	Asphalt tile	1/8" thick		.68	.43	1.11
		Conductive flrg. rubber	1/8" thick		2.99	.71	3.70
		Cork tile	Standard finish		1.27	.71	1.98
		1/8" thick	Urethane finish		1.55	.71	2.26
		PVC sheet goods	1/4" thick		2.31	2.89	5.20
		for gyms	3/8" thick		2.60	3.85	6.45
		Vyl. comp. 12" x 12"	1/16" thick		.58	.43	1.01
		tile, plain	1/8" thick		1.16	.42	1.58
		Vinyl tile, 12" x 12"		Min.	1.99	.54	2.53
		1/8" thick		Max.	7.98	.57	8.55
		Vinyl sheet goods	.093" thick		1.21	.36	1.57
		backed	.250" thick		1.96	.35	2.31
	Slate	Random rectangular	1/4" thick		3.41	2.89	6.30
			1/2" thick		3.20	4.15	7.35
		Natural cleft, irregular, 3/4" thick			1.38	4.72	6.10
		For sand rubbed finish, add			2.26		2.26
	Terrazzo	Cast in Place	Bonded, 1-3/4" thick	Gray cement	1.89	5.21	7.10
				White cement	2.65	5.25	7.90
			Not bonded, 3" thick	Gray cement	2.32	5.23	7.55
				White cement	3.08	5.22	8.30
		Precast	12" x 12"	1" thick	6.11	7.24	13.35
				1-1/4" thick	7.21	7.24	14.45
			16" x 16"	1-1/4" thick	6.77	7.88	14.65
				1-1/2" thick	7.70	8.70	16.40
	Marble Travertine	Standard, 12" x 12" x 3/4" thick			5.23	6.47	11.70

(Handwritten annotations in left margin: "Corridors", "Apartments", "Bathrooms & Kitchens")

Right Table

FLOORING	DESCRIPTION				MAT.	INST.	TOTAL
FLOORING	Ceramic Tile	Natural Clay, thin set			1.84	2.26	4.10
		Porcelain, thin set			2.30	2.26	4.56
		Specialty, decorator finish			4.59	2.26	6.85
		Pregrouted sheets, unglazed			3.78	2.29	6.07
		Quarry	Red, mud set	4" x 4" x 1/2"	2.16	3.44	5.60
				6" x 6" x 1/2"	1.89	2.96	4.85
			Brown, imported	6" x 6" x 7/8"	4.19	3.46	7.65
				9" x 9" x 1-1/4"	5.72	3.78	9.50
		Slate	Vermont, thin set	6" x 6" x 1/4"	1.85	2.30	4.15
	Wood	Maple strip, 25/32" x 2-1/4", finished	Select		1.97	1.71	3.68
			2nd & better		1.81	1.70	3.51
		Oak, 25/32" x 2-1/4" finished	Clear		1.68	1.70	3.38
			No. 1 common		1.35	1.58	2.93
		Parquet Standard, 5/16" thick finished		Min.	1.18	1.79	2.97
				Max.	5.80	2.71	8.51
		Custom, finished		Min.	11.80	2.42	14.30
				Max.	16.50	4.50	21.00
		Prefinished Oak, 2-1/4" wide			1.85	1.42	3.27
		Ranch plank			3.16	1.67	4.83
	Subflooring	Sleepers on concrete, treated, 24" O.C.	1" x 2"		.07	.17	.24
			1" x 3"		.11	.22	.33
			2" x 4"		.34	.30	.64
			2" x 6"		.52	.34	.86
		Refinish old floors		Min.	.45	.61	1.06
				Max.	.63	1.86	2.49
		Plywood, CDX	1/2" thick		.41	.33	.74
			5/8" thick		.45	.37	.82
			3/4" thick		.51	.40	.91
	Underlayment	1" x 10" boards, S4S	Laid regular		.81	.46	1.27
			Laid diagonal		.81	.56	1.37
		1" x 8" boards, S4S	Laid regular		.83	.49	1.32
			Laid diagonal		.83	.58	1.41
		Plywood, underlayment grade	3/8" thick		.08	.91	.99
			1/2" thick		.46	.35	.81
			5/8" thick		.56	.36	.92
			3/4" thick		.08	.49	.57
		Particle board	3/8" thick		.23	.33	.56
			1/2" thick		.11	.44	.55
			5/8" thick		.09	.93	1.02
			3/4" thick		.08	.75	.83

Table III.41

Table III.42

13.1 Special Construction

		CREW	MAN-HOURS	UNIT	MAT.	LABOR	EQUIP.	TOTAL	TOTAL INCL O&P	NOTES
75-001	SWIMMING POOLS, Outdoor, incl. equip. & houses, minimum			S.F.Surf					36	
030	Maximum								68	
040	Residential, incl. equipment, permanent type, minimum								12	
070	Maximum								25	
090	Municipal, including equipment only, over 5000 S.F., minimum								25	
100	Maximum								51	
130	Motel or apt., incl. equipment only, under 5000 S.F., minimum								22	
140	Maximum			↓					34	

14.1 Conveying Systems

		CREW	MAN-HOURS	UNIT	MAT.	LABOR	EQUIP.	TOTAL	TOTAL INCL O&P
10-001	CORRESPONDENCE LIFT 1 floor 2 stop, 25 lb. capacity, electric	2 Elev	80	Ea.	3,400	1,775		5,175	6,400
010	Hand, 5 lb. capacity		80		1,000	1,775		2,775	3,750
15-001	DUMBWAITERS 2 stop, electric, minimum		123		1,750	2,725		4,475	5,875
010	Maximum		145		5,000	3,225		8,225	10,200
030	Hand, minimum		70		600	1,550		2,150	2,900
040	Maximum		84	↓	1,025	1,875		2,900	3,825
060	For each additional stop, electric, add		30	Stop	750	655		1,405	1,775
070	Hand, add	↓	27	"	545	590		1,135	1,450
20-001	ELEVATORS								
500	Passenger, pre-engineered, 5 story, hydraulic, 2,500 lb. capacity	M1	800	Ea.	43,400	18,300		61,700	74,000
510	For less than 5 stops, deduct	"	110	Stop	6,050	2,525		8,575	10,200
520	For 4,000 lb. capacity, general purpose, add			Ea.	1,925			1,925	2,125M
540	10 story, geared traction, 200 FPM, 2,500 lb. capacity	M1	1600	"	41,800	36,600		78,400	98,000
550	For less than 10 stops, deduct		94	Stop	1,875	2,150		4,025	5,125
560	For 4,500 lb. capacity, general purpose	↓	1600	Ea.	46,100	36,600		82,700	103,000
580									
700	Residential, cab type, 1 floor, 2 stop, minimum	2 Elev	80	Ea.	5,200	1,775		6,975	8,300
710	Maximum		160		9,300	3,550		12,850	15,400
720	2 floor, 3 stop, minimum		133		6,300	2,950		9,250	11,200
730	Maximum		267		15,700	5,900		21,600	25,800
770	Stair climber (chair lift), single seat, minimum		16		1,900	355		2,255	2,600
780	Maximum		80		2,500	1,775		4,275	5,325
800	Wheelchair, porch lift, minimum		16		3,200	355		3,555	4,050
850	Maximum		32		6,375	710		7,085	8,075
870	Stair lift, minimum		16		5,000	355		5,355	6,025
890	Maximum	↓	80	↓	8,000	1,775		9,775	11,500
45-001	PNEUMATIC TUBE SYSTEM Single tube, 2 stations,								
002	100 ft. long, stock, economy,								

| MECHANICAL | | 08.1-931 | Plumbing - Three Fixture Bathroom | | | |

This page illustrates and describes a three fixture bathroom system including a water closet, tub, lavatory, accessories and service piping. Lines 08.1-931-04 thru 14 give the unit price and total price on a cost each basis for this system. Prices for an alternate three fixture bathroom system are on Line Item 08.1-931-17. Both material quantities and labor costs have been adjusted for the system listed.

Example: Installed in one wall as an alternate system; choose Line Item 08.1-931-17. $910 MAT., $1,260 INST., $2,170 TOTAL. This price includes all materials compatible with the original system.

Factors: To adjust for job conditions other than normal working situations use Lines 08.1-931-29 thru 40.

Example: You are to install the above system and protect all existing work. Go to Line 08.1-931-38 and apply these percentages to the appropriate MAT. and INST. costs.

SYSTEM	LINE NO.	DESCRIPTION	QUANTITY	COST EACH MAT.	COST EACH INST.	TOTAL
	01	Three fixture bathroom incl. water closet, bathtub, lavatory, accessories,				
	02	And necessary service piping to install this system in 2 walls.				
	03					
	04	Water closet, floor mounted, 2 piece, close coupled	1 Ea.	115.50	89.50	205
	05	Rough-in waste & vent for water closet	1 Set	93.28	255.47	348.75
	06	Bathtub, P.E. cast iron 5' long with accessories	1 Ea.	269.50	110.50	380
	07	Rough-in waste & vent for bathtub	1 Set	91.80	387.95	479.75
	08	Lavatory, 20" x 18" P.E. cast iron with accessories	1 Ea.	126.50	58.50	185
	09	Rough-in waste & vent for lavatory	1 Set	121.81	353.19	475
	10	Accessories				
	11	Toilet tissue dispenser, chrome, single roll	1 Ea.	18.81	8.19	27
	12	18" long stainless steel towel bar	2 Ea.	37.62	20.38	58
	13	Medicine cabinet with mirror, 16" x 22", unlighted	1 Ea.	45.10	16.90	62
	14	TOTAL	System	919.92	1300.58	2220.50
	15					
	16					
	17	Above system installed in one wall with all necessary service piping	System	910.26	1259.74	2170
	18					
	19					
	20					
	21					
	22					
	23	Note: PLUMBING APPROXIMATIONS				
	24	WATER CONTROL: water meter, backflow preventer,				
	25	Shock absorbers, vacuum breakers, mixer ....10 to 15% of fixtures				
	26					
	27	PIPE AND FITTINGS:................................30 to 60% of fixtures		30%	30%	
	28					
	29	Cut & patch to match existing construction, add, minimum		2%	3%	
	30	Maximum		5%	9%	
	31	Dust protection, add, minimum		1%	2%	
	32	Maximum		4%	11%	
	33	Equipment usage curtailment, add, minimum		1%	1%	
	34	Maximum		3%	10%	
	35	Material handling & storage limitation, add, minimum		1%	1%	
	36	Maximum		6%	7%	
	37	Protection of existing work, add, minimum		2%	2%	
	38	Maximum		5%	7%	
	39	Shift work requirements, add, minimum		5%		
	40	Maximum			30%	
	41					
	42					

Table III.43

Division 7: Conveying Systems

While no conveying systems are specified for the sample project, such work is often included in commercial renovation. Accessibility for handicapped persons has become a consideration in most building codes, and wheelchair lifts are becoming more common. The Systems pages of *Repair and Remodeling Cost Data* contain costs for hydraulic elevators. When other conveying systems are required, refer to the Unit Price pages, of the *Means' Repair and Remodeling Cost Data,* as in Table III.42.

Division 8: Mechanical

The mechanical systems for the sample project include the bathrooms and HVAC systems.

A system similar to the bathrooms of the sample project is found in Table III.43. The water meter and controls are already in place and are not added to the costs. The calculations for the bathrooms are in Table III.44. The rough-in for the kitchen sink is not included in the systems price for kitchens (Division 11: Special) and is obtained from the Unit Price section (Division 15) of the *Means' Repair and Remodeling Cost Data.* Overhead and profit should be added to the bare material and labor costs. The plumbing costs are recorded on the estimate sheet in Table III.45.

The owner has requested that the estimate include cooling, so a ducted forced air system is the only choice. The estimator has learned from the site visit that the gas service is of adequate capacity. The system chosen is shown in Table III.46. Note that the flue, in Table III.46, is connected to an existing chimney. There are no chimneys in the existing building, so metal flues must be included in the estimate. The costs for the flues are obtained from Division 15 of the Unit Price section of the *Means' Repair and Remodeling Cost Data.* Overhead and profit must be added to the costs in Table III.47.

The mechanical and electrical work would, most likely, be performed by a subcontractor. The material and installation costs in the Systems pages of *Repair and Remodeling Cost Data* include the overhead and profit of the installing contractor. When certain work is to be done by a subcontractor, the estimator should add a percentage for supervision by the general contractor. This percentage is usually 10% and should be added within the appropriate division costs rather than at the estimate summary.

	Material	Installation	Total
Bathroom 08.1-931-17	$ 910.26	$1,259.74	$2,170.00
Pipe and Fittings (30%)	273.08	377.92	651.00
Subtotal	1,183.34	1,637.66	2,821.00
Factors 7% Material 11% Installation	82.83	180.14	262.97
Total	$1,266.17	$1,817.80	$3,083.97

Bathroom Calculations

Table III.44

COST ANALYSIS

PROJECT Apartment Renovation						SHEET NO. 7 of 11			
LOCATION						ESTIMATE NO. 85-2			
ARCHITECT			OWNER			DATE 1985			
QUANTITIES BY EBW	PRICES BY RSM		EXTENSIONS BY			CHECKED BY			

DESCRIPTION	QUANTITY	UNIT	MATERIAL		LABOR		TOTAL COST	
			UNIT	TOTAL	UNIT	TOTAL	UNIT	TOTAL
Division 8: mechanical								
Bathrooms	8	Ea.	1266^{17}	10129	1817^{80}	14542		
Kitchen Sink Rough-In								
15.2-60-498	8	Ea.	85^{75}	686	270	2160		
O&P	8	Ea.	8^{57}	69	133^{65}	1069		
HVAC Systems	7,296	SF	2^{45}	17875	2^{44}	17802		
Vent Chimney								
15.5-92-010	96	VLF	2^{43}	233	4^{70}	451		
O&P	96	VLF	24	23	2^{39}	229		
Subtotal				29015		36253		
GC Supervision	10%			2901		3625		
Division 8: Totals				31916		39878		

Table III.45

08.3-320 | Heating-Cooling, Gas Fired Forced Air System

LINE NO.	DESCRIPTION	QUANTITY	MAT.	INST.	TOTAL
	Gas fired hot air heating system including furnace, ductwork, registers And all necessary hookups.		*COST PER S.F.*		
01					
02					
03					
04	Area to 800 S.F., heat only				
05	Furnace, gas, AGA certified, direct drive, 44 MBH	1 Ea.	352	123	475
06	Gas piping	1 L.S.	88	30.75	118.75
07	Duct, galvanized steel	312 Lb.	408.41	995.59	1404
08	Insulation, blanket type, ductwork	270 S.F.	92.07	375.03	467.10
09	Flexible duct, 6" diameter, insulated	100 L.F.	152.90	185.10	338
10	Registers, baseboard, gravity, 12" x 6"	8 Ea.	47.96	93.24	141.20
11	Return, damper, 36" x 18"	1 Ea.	58.30	26.70	85
12	TOTAL	System	1199.64	1829.41	3029.05
13		S.F.	1.50	2.29	3.79
14	For alternate heating systems:				
15	Gas fired, area to 1000 S.F.	S.F.	1.23	1.86	3.09
16	To 1200 S.F.		1.10	1.64	2.74
17	To 1600 S.F.		1.03	1.54	2.57
18	To 2000 S.F.		.98	1.78	2.76
19	To 3000 S.F.		.82	1.42	2.24
20	For combined heating and cooling systems:				
21	Gas fired, heating and cooling, area to 800 S.F.	S.F.	2.82	2.75	5.57
22	To 1000 S.F.		2.33	2.24	4.57
23	To 1200 S.F.		2.02	1.96	3.98
24	To 1600 S.F.		1.75	1.79	3.54
25	To 2000 S.F.		1.61	1.99	3.60
26	To 3000 S.F.		1.42	1.58	3
27					
28					
29	Cut & patch to match existing construction, add, minimum		2%	3%	
30	Maximum		5%	9%	
31	Dust protection, add, minimum		1%	2%	
32	Maximum		4%	11%	
33	Equipment usage curtailment, add, minimum		1%	1%	
34	Maximum		3%	10%	
35	Material handling & storage limitation, add, minimum		1%	1%	
36	Maximum		6%	7%	
37	Protection of existing work, add, minimum		2%	2%	
38	Maximum		5%	7%	
39	Shift work requirements, add, minimum			5%	
40	Maximum			30%	
41					
42					

This page illustrates and describes a gas fired forced air system including a gas fired furnace, ductwork, registers and hookups. Lines 08.3-320-04 thru 13 give the unit price and total price per square foot for this system. Prices for alternate gas fired forced air systems are on Line Items 08.3-320-15 thru 26. Both material quantities and labor costs have been adjusted for the system listed.

Example: Combined heating and cooling system, gas fired, area to 1,600 S.F. as an alternate system; choose Line Item 08.3-320-24, $1.75 MAT., $1.79 INST., $3.54 TOTAL. This price includes all materials compatible with the original system.

Factors: To adjust for job conditions other than normal working situations use Lines 08.3-320-29 thru 40.

Example: You are to install the above system with material handling and storage limitations. Go to Line 08.3-320-35 and apply these percentages to the appropriate MAT. and INST. costs.

375

Table III.46

294

15.5 Heating

		CREW	MAN-HOURS	UNIT	BARE COSTS MAT.	LABOR	EQUIP.	TOTAL	TOTAL INCL O&P	NOTES
500	Steel underground, coated, set in place, incl. hold-down bars.									
550	Excavation, pad, pumps and piping not included									
552	1000 gallon capacity, 7 gauge shell	Q-7	8	Ea.	725	170		895	1,050	
554	5000 gallon capacity, 1/4" thick shell		32		2,625	680		3,305	3,900	
556	10,000 gallon capacity, 1/4" thick shell		45.710		3,875	975		4,850	5,725	
560	20,000 gallon capacity, 5/16" thick shell		107		7,650	2,275		9,925	11,800	
900	Minimum labor/equipment charge	Q-5	4	Job		80		80	120L	
92-001	**VENT CHIMNEY** Prefab metal, U.L. listed									
002	Gas, double wall, galvanized steel									
008	3" diameter	Q-9	.222	V.L.F.	2	4.44		6.44	8.90	
010	4" diameter		.235		2.43	4.70		7.13	9.75	
012	5" diameter		.250		2.88	5		7.88	10.70	
014	6" diameter		.267		3.38	5.35		8.73	11.75	
016	7" diameter		.286		4.59	5.70		10.29	13.65	
018	8" diameter		.308		5.10	6.15		11.25	14.90	
020	10" diameter		.333		10.80	6.65		17.45	22	
022	12" diameter		.364		14.40	7.25		21.65	27	
026	16" diameter		.400		32	8		40	47	
030	20" diameter	Q-10	.667		48	13.80		61.80	74	
034	24" diameter	"	.750		74	15.55		89.55	105	
300	All fuel, double wall, stainless steel, 6" diameter	Q-9	.267		13.95	5.35		19.30	23	
302	7" diameter		.286		17.25	5.70		22.95	28	
304	8" diameter		.308		21	6.15		27.15	32	
306	10" diameter		.333		29	6.65		35.65	42	
308	12" diameter		.364		38	7.25		45.25	53	
310	14" diameter		.381		50	7.60		57.60	66	
500	Vent damper bi-metal 6" flue		1	Ea.	49	20		69	84	
510	Gas, auto, electric		2		92	40		132	160	
512	Oil, auto, electric		2		135	40		175	210	
800	All fuel, double wall, stainless steel fittings									
801	Roof support 6" diameter	Q-9	.533	Ea.	35	10.65		45.65	55	
802	7" diameter		.571		39	11.40		50.40	60	
803	8" diameter		.615		42	12.30		54.30	65	
804	10" diameter		.667		54	13.30		67.30	80	
805	12" diameter		.727		65	14.55		79.55	93	
806	14" diameter		.762		81	15.20		96.20	110	
810	Elbow 15°, 6" diameter		.533		30	10.65		40.65	49	
812	7" diameter		.571		34	11.40		45.40	55	
814	8" diameter		.615		39	12.30		51.30	61	
816	10" diameter		.667		49	13.30		62.30	74	
818	12" diameter		.727		59	14.55		73.55	87	
820	14" diameter		.762		70	15.20		85.20	100	

Notes (diagram labels): Round Top, Roof Flashing, Joist Shield, Ceiling Support, Insulated Tee, Vent Chimney

For expanded coverage of these items see *Means' Mechanical Cost Data 1985*

Table III.47

LINE NO.	SYSTEM / DESCRIPTION	QUANTITY	COST EACH MAT.	COST EACH INST.	TOTAL
01	100 Amp Service, single phase				
02					
03	Weathercap	1 Ea.	3.52	21.48	25
04	Service entrance cable	2 C.L.F.	16.72	52.28	69
05	Meter socket	1 Ea.	19.80	80.20	100
06	Entrance disconnect switch	1 Ea.	110	140	250
07	Ground rod, with clamp	1 Ea.	17.27	49.73	67
08	Ground cable	1 C.L.F.	8.58	16.42	25
09	Panelboard, 12 circuit	1 Ea.	94.60	220.40	315
10	TOTAL	Ea.	270.49	580.51	851
11					
12					
13					
14	200 Amp Service, single phase				
15					
16					
17	Weathercap	1 Ea.	11	33	44
18	Service entrance cable	2 C.L.F.	41.80	75.20	117
19	Meter socket	1 Ea.	29.70	140.30	170
20	Entrance disconnect switch	1 Ea.	242	203	445
21	Ground rod, with clamp	1 Ea.	21.29	59.71	81
22	Ground cable	1 C.L.F.	7.15	8.85	16
23	3/4" EMT	10 L.F.	3.52	20.18	23.70
24	Panelboard, 24 circuit	1 Ea.	236.50	403.50	640
25	TOTAL	Ea.	592.96	943.74	1536.70
26					
27					
28					
29	Cut & patch to match existing construction, add, minimum		2%	3%	
30	Maximum		5%	9%	
31	Dust protection, add, minimum		1%	2%	
32	Maximum		4%	11%	
33	Equipment usage curtailment, add, minimum		1%	1%	
34	Maximum		3%	10%	
35	Material handling & storage limitation, add, minimum		1%	1%	
36	Maximum		6%	7%	
37	Protection of existing work, add, minimum		2%	2%	
38	Maximum		5%	7%	
39	Shift work requirements, add, minimum			5%	
40	Maximum			30%	
41					
42					

This page illustrates and describes a residential, single phase system including a weather cap, service entrance cable, meter socket, entrance switch, ground rod, ground cable, EMT, and panelboard. Lines 09.1-230-03 thru 10 give the unit price and total price on a cost each basis for this system. Prices for an alternate residential, single phase system are on Line Item 09.1-230-25. Both material quantities and labor costs have been adjusted for the system listed.

Example: 200 AMP service as an alternate system; choose Line Item 09.1-230-25, $593 MAT., $944 INST., $1,537 TOTAL. This price includes all materials compatible with the original system.

Factors: To adjust for job conditions other than normal working situations use Lines 09.1-230-29 thru 40.

Example: You are to install the above system with a minimum equipment usage curtailment. Go to Line 09.1-230-33 and apply these percentages to the appropriate MAT. and INST. costs.

378

Table III.48

Division 9: Electrical

Since there are no electrical plans, the estimator must use experience and sound judgement to determine the requirements and quantities of the electrical work.

The existing electrical service is old and inadequate and will be removed. The project calls for each apartment to be metered separately with a 100 Amp service. The appropriate system, as shown in Table III.48, must be modified. Obviously, the building will not have eight individual service entrances and grounding systems. The weathercap, service entrance cable, and grounding system are deleted. Each apartment will have a meter socket, disconnect, and panelboard. To replace the deleted items, the estimator must determine costs for one large service entrance, meter trough, and the distribution feeders to each remote panelboard. Since this is a unique installation, the estimator can get a budget price from an electrical subcontractor, usually with only a telephone call. The costs for one grounding rod, clamp, and cable must also be included. The calculations are shown in Table III.49.

The appropriate lighting fixtures are shown in Tables III.50 and III.51. The conduit is not required for this installation and is deleted from the cost.

Table III.52 gives wiring prices for various electrical devices using different types of wire. Note that wiring is included in costs for the lighting fixtures, so the costs for lighting wiring from Table III.52 are not included at this point. The cost analysis for Division 9 is shown in Table III.53. As with the mechanical costs, 10% is added for supervision of the electrical subcontractor.

	Material	Installation	Total
Service 09.1-230			
Meter Socket	$ 19.80	$ 80.20	$ 100.00
Disconnect	110.00	140.00	250.00
Panel Board	94.60	220.40	315.00
Subtotal	$ 224.40	$ 440.60	$ 665.00
Factors	11.22	39.65	50.87
5% Material			
9% Installation			
Total	$ 235.62	$ 480.25	$ 715.87
Entrance, Trough and Feeders	$2,000.00	$2,800.00	$4,800.00
Ground Rod	17.27	49.73	67.00
Ground Wire	8.58	16.42	25.00
Total	$2,025.85	$2,866.15	$4,892.00

Electrical Service Calculations

Table III.49

ELECTRICAL — 09.2-900 — Lighting, Fluorescent

LINE NO.	SYSTEM / DESCRIPTION	QUANTITY	COST EACH MAT.	COST EACH INST.	TOTAL
01	Fluorescent lighting, including fixture, lamp, outlet box and wiring.				
02					
03					
04	Recessed lighting fixture, on suspended system	1 Ea.	50.60	54.40	105
05	Outlet box	1 Ea.	1.52	18.71	20.23
06	Romex 12-2 with ground	2 C.L.F.	2.07	23.93	26
07	Conduit, EMT, 1/2" conduit *Deduct*	20 L.F.	(4.84)	(30.96)	35.80
08	TOTAL	Ea.	59.03	128	187.03
09					
10					
11					
12	For alternate lighting fixtures:				
13	Surface mounted, 2' x 4', acrylic prismatic diffuser	Ea.	(74.43)	(122.60)	197.03
14	Strip fixture, 8' long, two 8' lamps		46.93	116.10	163.03
15	Pendant mounted, industrial 8' long, with reflectors	→	86.53	135.50	222.03
16					
17				74.43	122.60
18					
19				− 4.84	30.96
20					
21				(69.59)	(91.64)
22					
23					
24					
25					
26					
27					
28					
29	Cut & patch to match existing construction, add, minimum		2%	3%	
30	Maximum		5%	9%	
31	Dust protection, add, minimum		1%	2%	
32	Maximum		4%	11%	
33	Equipment usage curtailment, add, minimum		1%	1%	
34	Maximum		3%	10%	
35	Material handling & storage limitation, add, minimum		1%	1%	
36	Maximum		6%	7%	
37	Protection of existing work, add, minimum		2%	2%	
38	Maximum		5%	7%	
39	Shift work requirements, add, minimum			5%	
40	Maximum			30%	
41					
42					

This page illustrates and describes fluorescent lighting systems including a fixture, lamp, outlet box and wiring. Lines 09.2-900-04 thru 08 give the unit price and total price on a cost each basis for this system. Prices for alternate fluorescent lighting systems are on Line Items 09.2-900-13 thru 15. Both material quantities and labor costs have been adjusted for the system listed.

Example: Strip fixture, 8' long, two 8' lamps as an alternate system; choose Line Item 09.2-900-14, $47 MAT., $116 INST., $163 TOTAL. This price includes all materials compatible with the original system.

Factors: To adjust for job conditions other than normal working situations use Lines 09.2-900-29 thru 40.

Example: You are to install the above system during evening hours. Go to Line 09.2-900-39 and apply this percentage to the appropriate INST. cost.

Table III.50

ELECTRICAL — 09.2-910 — Lighting, Incandescent

LINE NO.	DESCRIPTION	QUANTITY	COST EACH MAT.	COST EACH INST.	COST EACH TOTAL
01	Incandescent light fixture, including lamp, outlet box, conduit and wiring.				
02					
03					
04	Recessed wide reflector with flat glass lens	1 Ea.	27.50	39.50	67
05	Outlet box	1 Ea.	1.52	18.71	20.23
06	Romex, 12-2 with ground	.2 C.L.F.	2.07	23.93	26
07	Conduit, 1/2" EMT	20 L.F.	4.84	30.96	35.80
08	TOTAL	Ea.	35.93	113.10	149.03
09	*Deduct*		−4.84	−30.96	
10			31.09	82.14	
11					
12					
13	Recessed, R-40 flood lamp with reflector skirt	1 Ea.	40.70	33.30	74
14	150 watt R-40 flood lamp	.01 Ea.	4.13	2.02	6.15
15	Outlet box	1 Ea.	1.52	18.71	20.23
16	Romex, 12-2 with ground	.2 C.L.F.	2.07	23.93	26
17	Conduit, 1/2" EMT	20 L.F.	4.84	30.96	35.80
18	TOTAL	Ea.	53.26	108.92	162.18
19					
20					
21					
22					
23					
24					
25					
26					
27					
28					
29	Cut & patch to match existing construction, add, minimum		2%	3%	
30	Maximum		5%	9%	
31	Dust protection, add, minimum		1%	2%	
32	Maximum		4%	11%	
33	Equipment usage curtailment, add, minimum		1%	1%	
34	Maximum		3%	10%	
35	Material handling & storage limitation, add, minimum		1%	1%	
36	Maximum		6%	7%	
37	Protection of existing work, add, minimum		2%	2%	
38	Maximum		5%	7%	
39	Shift work requirements, add, minimum			5%	
40	Maximum			30%	
41					
42					

This page illustrates and describes incandescent lighting systems including a fixture, lamp, outlet box, conduit and wiring. Lines 09.2-910-04 thru 08 give the unit price and total price on a cost each basis for this system. Prices for an alternate incandescent lighting system are on Line Item 09.2-910-18. Both material quantities and labor costs have been adjusted for the system listed.

Example: Recessed, R-40 flood lamp with reflector skirt as an alternate system; choose Line Item 09.2-910-18, $53 MAT., $109 INST., $162 TOTAL. This price includes all materials compatible with the original system.

Factors: To adjust for conditions other than normal working situations use Lines 09.2-910-29 thru 40.

Example: You are to install the above system and cut and match existing construction. Go to Line 09.2-910-30 and apply this percentage to the appropriate INST. costs.

380

Table III.51

299

09.9-500 | Wiring Devices Selective Price Sheet

Using non metallic sheathed cable, BX cable, EMT conduit

DESCRIPTION		MAT.	INST. (COST EACH)	TOTAL
Using non metallic sheathed cable	Air conditioning receptacle	6.60	26.40	33.00
	Disposal wiring	5.50	29.50	35.00
	Dryer circuit	14.30	47.70	62.00
	Duplex receptacle	6.05	19.95	26.00
	Fire alarm or smoke detector	39.60	26.40	66.00
	Furnace circuit & switch	7.81	44.19	52.00
	Ground fault receptacle	39.60	32.40	72.00
	Heater circuit	5.50	32.50	38.00
	Lighting wiring	5.50	16.50	22.00
	Range circuit	33.00	66.00	99.00
	Switches, single pole	5.94	16.06	22.00
	3-way	7.70	22.30	30.00
	Water heater circuit	7.70	52.30	60.00
	Weatherproof receptacle	56.10	43.90	100.00
Using BX cable	Air conditioning receptacle	11.00	32.00	43.00
	Disposal wiring	8.80	35.20	44.00
	Dryer circuit	22.00	57.00	79.00
	Duplex receptacle	9.90	24.10	34.00
	Fire alarm or smoke detector	42.90	32.10	75.00
	Furnace circuit & switch	12.10	52.90	65.00
	Ground fault receptacle	45.10	39.90	85.00
	Heater circuit	8.80	40.20	49.00
	Lighting wiring	9.90	20.10	30.00
	Range circuit	46.20	78.80	125.00
	Switches, single pole	9.90	20.10	30.00
	3-way	13.20	25.80	39.00
	Water heater circuit	13.20	62.80	76.00
	Weatherproof receptacle	60.50	54.50	115.00
Using EMT conduit	Air conditioning receptacle	11.00	30.00	50.00
	Disposal wiring	8.80	44.20	53.00
	Dryer circuit	16.50	71.50	88.00
	Duplex receptacle	9.90	30.10	40.00
	Fire alarm or smoke detector	42.90	39.10	82.00
	Furnace circuit & switch	12.10	65.90	78.00
	Ground fault receptacle	45.10	48.90	94.00
	Heater circuit	8.80	48.20	57.00
	Lighting wiring	9.90	24.10	34.00
	Range circuit	28.60	96.40	125.00
	Switches, single pole	9.90	24.10	34.00
	3-way	13.20	32.80	46.00
	Water heater circuit	13.20	77.80	91.00
	Weatherproof receptacle	60.50	64.50	125.00

Using aluminum conduit, galvanized steel conduit

DESCRIPTION		MAT.	INST. (COST EACH)	TOTAL
Using aluminum conduit	Air conditioning receptacle	19.14	52.86	72.00
	Disposal wiring	17.60	58.40	76.00
	Dryer circuit	25.30	94.70	120.00
	Duplex receptacle	18.70	40.30	59.00
	Fire alarm or smoke detector	50.60	54.40	105.00
	Furnace circuit & switch	20.46	89.54	110.00
	Ground fault receptacle	52.80	67.20	120.00
	Heater circuit	17.60	65.40	83.00
	Lighting wiring	18.70	33.30	52.00
	Range circuit	37.40	132.60	170.00
	Switches, single pole	18.70	33.30	52.00
	3-way	19.80	44.20	64.00
	Water heater circuit	19.80	105.20	125.00
	Weatherproof receptacle	68.20	86.80	155.00
Using galvanized steel conduit	Air conditioning receptacle	18.26	55.74	74.00
	Disposal wiring	16.50	62.50	79.00
	Dryer circuit	24.20	100.80	125.00
	Duplex receptacle	17.60	43.40	61.00
	Fire alarm or smoke detector	49.50	55.50	105.00
	Furnace circuit & switch	19.36	95.64	115.00
	Ground fault receptacle	51.70	68.30	120.00
	Heater circuit	16.50	69.50	86.00
	Lighting wiring	17.60	35.40	53.00
	Range circuit	36.30	138.70	175.00
	Switches, single pole	17.60	35.40	53.00
	3-way	18.70	45.30	64.00
	Water heater circuit	18.70	111.30	130.00
	Weatherproof receptacle	66.00	94.00	160.00

Table III.52

COST ANALYSIS

PROJECT Apartment Renovation							SHEET NO. 8 of 11		
LOCATION							ESTIMATE NO. 85-2		
ARCHITECT			OWNER				DATE 1985		
QUANTITIES BY EBW	PRICES BY RSM			EXTENSIONS BY			CHECKED BY		

DESCRIPTION	QUANTITY	UNIT	MATERIAL		LABOR		TOTAL COST	
			UNIT	TOTAL	UNIT	TOTAL	UNIT	TOTAL
Division 9: Electrical								
Service: meter Socket								
Disconnect	8	Ea.	235^{62}	1885	480^{25}	3842		
Panel Board								
Entrance &								
Feeders	1	Ea.	2,026	2026	2,866	2866		
Ground								
Fixtures: Fluorescent	8	Ea.	69^{59}	557	91^{64}	733		
Incandescent	24	Ea.	31^{09}	746	82^{14}	1971		
Devices: Disposal	8	Ea.	5^{50}	44	29^{50}	236		
Receptacles	156	Ea.	6^{05}	944	19^{95}	3112		
Smoke Detectors	10	Ea.	39^{60}	396	26^{40}	264		
Furnace	8	Ea.	7^{81}	62	44^{19}	354		
GFI	8	Ea.	39^{60}	317	32^{40}	259		
Range	8	Ea.	33	264	66	528		
Switches	40	Ea.	5^{94}	238	16^{06}	642		
Subtotal				7479		14807		
GC Supervision	10%			748		1481		
Division 9: Totals				8227		16288		

Table III.53

11.1-242 Kitchens

LINE NO.	SYSTEM / DESCRIPTION	QUANTITY	COST EACH MAT.	COST EACH INST.	TOTAL
01	Kitchen cabinets including wall and base cabinets, custom laminated				
02	Plastic top, sink & appliances, no plumbing or electrical rough-in included.				
03					
04	Prefinished wood cabinets, average quality, wall and base *19 LF*	20 L.F.	1914	286	2200
05	Custom laminated plastic counter top *19 LF*	20 L.F.	119.90	161.10	281
06	Stainless steel sink, 22" x 25'	1 Ea.	242	148	390
07	Faucet, top mount	1 Ea.	29.70	26.30	56
08	Dishwasher, built-in	1 Ea.	297	68	365
09	Compactor, built-in *Delete*	1 Ea.	(374)	(31)	405
10	Range hood, 30", ductless	1 Ea.	121	77	198
11	TOTAL	Ea.	3097.60	797.40	3895
12					
13					
14	For alternate kitchen systems:				
15	Prefinished wood cabinets, high quality	Ea.	3977.60	896.40	4874
16	Custom cabinets, built in place, high quality	"	4924.70	1048.30	5973
17					
18					
19					
20					
21					
22	NOTE: No plumbing or electric rough-ins are included in the above				
23	Prices, for plumbing see Division A15, for electric see Division A16.				
24					
25					
26					
27					
28					
29	Cut & patch to match existing construction, add, minimum		2%	3%	
30	Maximum		5%	9%	
31	Dust protection, add, minimum		1%	2%	
32	Maximum		4%	11%	
33	Equipment usage curtailment, add, minimum		1%	1%	
34	Maximum		3%	10%	
35	Material handling & storage limitation, add, minimum		1%	1%	
36	Maximum		6%	7%	
37	Protection of existing work, add, minimum		2%	2%	
38	Maximum		5%	7%	
39	Shift work requirements, add, minimum			5%	
40	Maximum			30%	
41					
42					

This page illustrates and describes kitchen systems including top and bottom cabinets, custom laminated plastic top, single bowl sink, and appliances. Lines 11.1-242-04 thru 11 give the unit price and total price on a cost each basis for this system. Prices for alternate kitchen systems are on Line items 11.1-242-15 and 16. Both material quantities and labor costs have been adjusted for the system listed.

Example: Prefinished wood cabinets, high quality as an alternate system; choose Line Item 11.1-242-15, $3978 MAT., $896 INST., $4874 TOTAL. This price includes all materials compatible with the original system. For alternatives not listed, use the selective price sheet for this section (Page 395). Substitute the new price from the price sheet into the typical system and adjust the total to reflect each change.

Factors: To adjust for job conditions other than normal working situations use Lines 11.1-242-29 thru 40.

Example: You are to install the above system and protect the work area from dust. Go to Line 11.1-242-32 and apply these percentages to the appropriate MAT. and INST. costs.

392

Table III.54

11.9-100 | Kitchen Selective Price Sheet

Cabinets Standard Wood

DESCRIPTION					MAT.	INST. (COST EACH)	TOTAL
Base	One drawer	12" wide			93.50	21.50	115.00
	One door	15" wide			99.00	21.00	120.00
		18" wide			106.70	18.30	125.00
		21" wide			110.00	20.00	130.00
		24" wide			115.50	19.50	135.00
	Two drawers	27" wide			137.50	22.50	160.00
	Two doors	30" wide			154.00	21.00	175.00
		33" wide			159.50	25.50	185.00
		36" wide			165.00	25.00	190.00
		42" wide			176.00	24.00	200.00
		48" wide			187.00	28.00	215.00
	Drawer base (4 drawers)	12" wide			137.00	17.50	155.00
		15" wide			143.00	22.00	165.00
		18" wide			148.50	21.50	170.00
		24" wide			170.50	19.50	190.00
	Sink or Range base	30" wide			132.00	23.00	155.00
		33" wide			132.00	23.00	155.00
		36" wide			143.00	22.00	165.00
		42" wide			148.50	26.50	175.00
	Corner base	36" wide			148.50	26.50	175.00
	Lazy susan with revolving door				181.50	28.50	210.00
Wall	Two doors	12" high	30" wide		71.50	19.50	91.00
			36" wide		74.80	20.20	95.00
		15" high	30" wide		73.70	20.30	94.00
			36" wide		79.20	20.80	100.00
		24" high	30" wide		93.50	21.50	115.00
			36" wide		103.40	21.60	125.00
		30" high	30" wide		106.70	23.30	130.00
			36" wide		121.00	24.00	145.00
			42" wide		132.00	28.00	160.00
			48" wide		137.50	27.50	165.00
	One door	30" high	12" wide		64.90	22.10	87.00
			15" wide		68.20	22.80	91.00
			18" wide		75.90	23.10	99.00
			24" wide		82.50	22.50	105.00
	Corner	30" high	24" wide		82.50	27.50	110.00
			36" wide		101.20	28.80	130.00
	Broom, 84" high, 24" deep, 18" wide				209.00	46.00	255.00
	Oven, 84" high, 24" deep, 27" wide				225.50	59.50	285.00
	Valance board	4' long			24.64	4.96	29.60
		6' long			36.96	7.44	44.40

Counter tops — COST PER L.F.

DESCRIPTION				MAT.	INST.	TOTAL
Counter tops	Laminated plastic	Stock 25" wide with backsplash	Minimum	6.00	8.05	14.05
			Maximum	13.70	9.30	23.00
		Custom 7/8" thick	No splash	14.03	7.97	22.00
			Cove splash	18.59	8.41	27.00
		1-1/4" thick	No splash	16.28	8.72	25.00
			Square splash	20.85	8.15	29.00
		Post formed		8.80	8.05	16.85
		Maple	No splash	28.60	8.40	37.00
		Laminated 1-1/2" thick	Square splash	33.00	9.00	42.00

Appliances — COST EACH

DESCRIPTION				MAT.	INST.	TOTAL
Appliances	Range	Free standing	Minimum	352.00	23.00	375.00
			Maximum	1,320.00	30.00	1,350.00
		Built-in	Minimum	528.00	32.00	560.00
			Maximum	880.00	60.00	940.00
		Counter top range, 4 burner	Minimum	220.00	35.00	255.00
			Maximum	473.00	67.00	540.00
	Compactor	Built-in	Minimum	374.00	31.00	405.00
			Maximum	539.00	36.00	575.00
	Dishwasher	Built-in	Minimum	297.00	68.00	365.00
			Maximum	396.00	64.00	460.00
	Garbage Disposer	Sink-pipe	Minimum	55.00	55.00	110.00
			Maximum	198.00	52.00	250.00
	Range hood	30" wide, 2 speed	Vented	253.00	52.00	305.00
			Ductless	209.00	37.00	246.00
	Refrigerator	No frost	12 Cu. Ft.	385.00	40.00	425.00
			20 Cu. Ft.	638.00	57.00	695.00

Plumbing not incl. rough-ins — COST EACH

DESCRIPTION				MAT.	INST.	TOTAL
Plumbing not incl. rough-ins	Sinks	Porcelain Cast iron	Single bowl	21" x 24"	121.00	149.00	270.00
				21" x 30"	143.00	147.00	290.00
			Double bowl	20" x 32"	159.50	185.50	345.90
		Stainless Steel	Single bowl	19" x 18"	220.00	150.00	370.00
				22" x 25"	242.00	148.00	390.00

Table III.55

395

303

Division 10: General Conditions

In the Systems Estimating format, General Conditions are priced in Division 10. For convenience in our example, we have calculated the General Conditions at the end of the estimate (see page 314).

Division 11: Special

This division contains costs for various systems that are used in renovation but are not included in other divisions. The kitchen system, as shown in Table III.54 must be modified to meet the requirements of the sample project. A disposal unit, range and refrigerator must be added, the compactor deleted, and the cabinets changed. Costs for these items are found in Table III.55.

There are 19 L.F. of cabinets in each kitchen of the sample project. Since the types and sizes of the cabinets are not specified, costs for 20 L.F. in Table III.54 are adjusted. The calculations for the kitchen are found in Table III.56.

Mailboxes are to be installed. Costs for mailboxes are not found in the System pages so Unit Prices are used from Table III.57. The bare material and labor costs must be changed to include the installing contractor's overhead and profits. Table III.58 is the cost analysis for Division 11.

	Material	Installation	Total
Cabinets (adj. for 19 L.F.)	$1,818.30	$271.70	$2,090.00
Counter top	113.90	153.05	266.95
Sink	242.00	148.00	390.00
Faucet	29.70	26.30	56.00
Dishwasher	297.00	68.00	365.00
Range Hood	121.00	77.00	198.00
Range	352.00	23.00	375.00
Disposer	55.00	55.00	110.00
Refrigerator	385.00	40.00	425.00
Total	$3,413.90	$862.05	$4,275.95

Calculations for Kitchen

Table III.56

10.1 Specialties

Line	Description	CREW	MAN-HOURS	UNIT	MAT.	LABOR	EQUIP.	TOTAL	TOTAL INCL O&P	NOTES
090	Outdoor, weatherproof, black plastic, 36" x 24"	2 Carp	8	Ea.	420	155		575	705	
100	36" x 36"	"	10.670	"	470	210		680	840	
900	Minimum labor/equipment charge	1 Carp	8	Job		155		155	240L	
22-001	**DISAPPEARING STAIRWAY** No trim included									
002	Commercial, 8'-0" ceiling	2 Carp	4	Ea.	925	78		1,003	1,150	
003	9'-0" ceiling		4		950	78		1,028	1,175	
004	10'-0" ceiling		5.330		1,000	105		1,105	1,250	
005	11'-0" ceiling		5.330		1,175	105		1,280	1,450	
006	12'-0" ceiling		5.330		1,225	105		1,330	1,500	
010	Residential grade, pine, 8'-6" ceiling, minimum	1 Carp	2		62	39		101	130	
015	Average		2.290		145	45		190	230	
020	Maximum		2.670		225	52		277	330	
025										
050	Custom grade, pine, heavy duty, pivoted, 8'-6" ceiling pine	1 Carp	2.670	Ea.	270	52		322	380	
060	16'-0" ceiling		4		470	78		548	640	
080	Economy folding, pine, 8'-6" ceiling		2		54	39		93	120	
090	9'-6" ceiling		2		70	39		109	140	
100	Fire escape, galvanized steel, 8'-0" to 10'-4" ceiling	2 Carp	16		1,000	315		1,315	1,575	
101	10'-6" to 13'-6" ceiling		16		1,250	315		1,565	1,850	
110	Automatic electric, aluminum, floor to floor height, 8' to 9'		16		4,200	315		4,515	5,100	
150	11' to 12'		17.780		4,675	350		5,025	5,675	
170	14' x 15'		22.860		5,150	450		5,600	6,350	
900	Minimum labor/equipment charge	1 Carp	4	Job		78		78	120L	
37-001	**LOCKERS** Steel, baked enamel, 60" or 72", single tier, minimum	1 Shee	.571	Opng.	52	12.70		64.70	76	
010	Maximum		.667		95	14.80		109.80	125	
030	2 tier, 60" or 72" total height, minimum		.308		34	6.85		40.85	48	
040	Maximum		.400		49	8.90		57.90	67	
240	Teacher and pupil wardrobes, enameled									
250	22" x 15" x 61" high, minimum	1 Shee	.800	Ea.	90	17.75		107.75	125	
255	Average		.889		150	19.75		169.75	195	
270	Maximum		1		155	22		177	205	
360	For hanger rods, add				1.20			1.20	1.32M	
370	For stainless steel lockers, add				100%					
900	Minimum labor/equipment charge	1 Shee	3.200	Job		71		71	105L	
40-001	**MAIL** Boxes, horizontal, key lock, 5"H x 6"W x 15"D, alum., rear loading	1 Carp	.235	Ea.	50	4.61		54.61	62	
010	Front loading		.235		54	4.61		58.61	67	
020	Double, 5"H x 12"W x 15"D, rear loading		.308		92	6.05		98.05	110	
030	Front loading		.308		100	6.05		106.05	120	
050	Quadruple, 10"H x 12"W x 15"D, rear loading		.400		160	7.85		167.85	190	
060	Front loading		.400		170	7.85		177.85	200	
160	Vault type, horizontal, for apartments, 4" x 5"		.235		50	4.61		54.61	62	
170	Alphabetical directories, 50 names		.800		115	15.70		130.70	150	

Disappearing Stairway

20

208

Table III.57

COST ANALYSIS

PROJECT	Apartment Renovation			SHEET NO. 9 of 11
LOCATION				ESTIMATE NO. 85-2
ARCHITECT		OWNER		DATE 1985
QUANTITIES BY EBW	PRICES BY RSM	EXTENSIONS BY		CHECKED BY

DESCRIPTION	QUANTITY	UNIT	MATERIAL UNIT	MATERIAL TOTAL	LABOR UNIT	LABOR TOTAL	TOTAL COST UNIT	TOTAL COST TOTAL
Division 11: Special								
Kitchen (From Table III.56)	8	Ea.	3,414	27312	862	6896		
Mailboxes								
10.1-40-060	2	Ea.	170	340	7.85	16		
O&P	2	Ea.	17	34	4.27	9		
Division 11: Totals				27686		6921		

Table III.58

SITE WORK — 12.1-464 — Excavation, Foundation

SYSTEM	LINE NO.	DESCRIPTION	QUANTITY	COST PER C.Y. EQUIP.	LABOR	TOTAL
	01	Foundation excavation with 3/4 C.Y. backhoe-loader, incl. operator equip.				
	02	Rental, fuel, oil, and mobilization. Hauling of excavated materials is				
	03	Included. Prices based on one day's production of 360 C.Y. in medium soil				
	04	Without backfilling.				
	05					
	06	Equipment operator	8 Hrs.		107.00	
	07	Backhoe-loader, 3/4 C.Y.	1 Day	245.00		245.00
	08	Operating expense (fuel oil)	1 Day		107.00	107.00
	09	Hauling, 12 C.Y. trucks, 1 mile round trip	360 C.Y.	275.00	45.00	45.00
	10	Mobilization	1 Ea.		424.00	699.00
	11	TOTAL	360 C.Y.	520.00	140.00	140.00
	12	PER C.Y.	PER C.Y.	1.44	716.00	1,236.00
	13				1.99	3.43
	14	For alternate size excavations:				
	15		C.Y.			
	16	100 C.Y.		3.08	3.78	6.86
	17	200 C.Y.		1.94	2.52	4.46
	18	300 C.Y.		1.57	2.12	3.69
	19	400 C.Y.		1.39	1.93	3.32
	20	500 C.Y.		1.74	2.14	3.88
	21	600 C.Y.		1.60	2.06	3.66
	22	700 C.Y.		1.56	1.92	3.48
	29	Dust protection, add, minimum		1%	2%	
	30	Maximum		4%	11%	
	31	Equipment usage curtailment, add, minimum		1%	1%	
	32	Maximum		3%	10%	
	33	Material handling & storage limitation, add, minimum		1%	1%	
	34	Maximum		6%	7%	
	35	Protection pf existing work, add, minimum		2%	2%	
	36	Maximum		5%	7%	
	37	Shift work requirements, add, minimum			5%	
	38	Maximum			30%	
	39	Temporary shoring and bracing, add, minimum		2%	5%	
	40	Maximum		5%	12%	

(Handwritten annotations: "1 Day TOTAL", "1/2 Day", circled "358.00" and "260.00")

This page illustrates and describes foundation excavation systems including a backhoe-loader, operator, equipment rental, fuel, oil, mobilization, hauling material, no back filling. Lines 12.1-464-06 thru 12 give the unit price and total price per cubic yard for this system. Prices for alternate foundation excavation systems are on Line Items 12.1-464-16 thru 22. Both material quantities and labor costs have been adjusted for the system listed.

Example: 400 C.Y. as an alternate system; choose Line Item 12.1-464-19, $1.39 MAT., $1.93 INST., $3.32 TOTAL. This price includes all materials compatible with the original system.

Factors: To adjust for job conditions other than normal working situations use Lines 12.1-464-29 thru 40.

Example: You are to install the above system with the use of temporary shoring and bracing. Go to Line 12.1-464-39 and apply these percentages to the appropriate TOTAL costs.

Table III.59

12.7-104 Sidewalks

This page illustrates and describes sidewalk systems including concrete, welded wire and broom finish. Lines 12.7-104-05 thru 13 give unit price and total price per square foot for this system. Prices for alternate sidewalk systems are on Line Items 12.7-104-17 thru 19. Both material quantities and labor costs have been adjusted for the system listed.

Example: Flagstone, slate, 1" thick, rectangular as an alternate system; choose Line Item 12.7-104-19, $2.31 MAT., $4.74 INST., $7.05 TOTAL. This price includes all materials compatible with the original system.

Factors: To adjust for job conditions other than normal working situations use Lines 12.7-104-29 thru 40.

Example: You are to install the above system and match existing construction. Go to Line 12.7-104-29 and apply these percentages to the appropriate MAT. and INST. costs.

SYSTEM	DESCRIPTION	LINE NO.	QUANTITY	COST PER S.F.		
				MAT.	INST.	TOTAL
4" thick concrete sidewalk with welded wire fabric 3000 psi air entrained concrete, broom finish.		01				
		02				
		03				
		04				
	Gravel fill, 4" deep	05	.012 C.Y.	.03	.05	.08
	Compact fill	06	.012 C.Y.		.03	.03
	Hand grade	07	1 S.F.		.28	.28
	Edge form	08	.25 L.F.	.04	.40	.44
	Welded wire fabric	09	.011 S.F.	.09	.17	.26
	Concrete, 3000 psi air entrained	10	.012 C.Y.	.61		.61
	Place concrete	11	.012 C.Y.		.14	.14
	Broom finish	12	1 S.F.		.38	.38
	TOTAL	13	S.F.	.77	1.45	2.22
		14		-.04	-.40	
		15		.73	1.05	
	For alternate sidewalk systems:	16				
	Asphalt (bituminous), 2" thick	17	S.F.	.39	.58	.97
	Brick, on sand bed, 4.5 brick per S.F.	18		2.07	3.93	6
	Flagstone, slate, 1" thick, rectangular	19	→	2.31	4.74	7.05
		20				
		21				
		22				
		23				
		24				
		25				
		26				
		27				
		28				
	Cut & patch to match existing construction, add, minimum	29		2%	3%	
	Maximum	30		5%	9%	
	Dust protection, add, minimum	31		1%	2%	
	Maximum	32		4%	11%	
	Equipment usage curtailment, add, minimum	33		1%	1%	
	Maximum	34		3%	10%	
	Material handling & storage limitation, add, minimum	35		1%	1%	
	Maximum	36		6%	7%	
	Protection of existing work, add, minimum	37		2%	2%	
	Maximum	38		5%	7%	
	Shift work requirements, add, minimum	39		5%		
	Maximum	40			30%	
		41				
		42				
				9%	17%	

Deduct

404

Table III.60

Division 12: Site Work

The amount of site work in renovation will vary greatly from project to project. In the sample project, the site work is relatively extensive. The scope of work is developed through discussions with the owner. Excavation is required for the retaining wall and footing in Division 1, of the System portion of Means' *Repair and Remodeling Cost Data*. The existing parking lot is to be resurfaced and new loam and seeding is specified for the entire lawn. Demolition costs are also included in Division 12, of the System portion of Means' *Repair and Remodeling Cost Data*.

The estimator must be very careful when evaluating the site of an existing building for excavation work. Utility locations must be identified at the site. A water line break can be a very expensive mistake. After thorough examination, the estimator has determined that there should be no utilities at the area to be excavated. The costs are shown in Table III.59. Note that the costs as shown are for 360 CY (a full days cost) and per cubic yard. A half-day rental is usually a minimum for heavy equipment. Even though the amount to be excavated is 91 CY (less than one half of 360 CY) the costs for a half day are included in the estimate.

The concrete slab at the patios was not included in Division 2, Substructure, of the System portion of Means' *Repair and Remodeling Cost Data*, because the individual components required more closely resemble a sidewalk than an interior floor slab. The costs are derived from Table III.60. The edge forms are deducted because only a very small amount of forming will be necessary compared to a normal sidewalk. The factors are added because access for the truck is impossible and the concrete will be placed by hand. Calculations are shown in Table III.61.

The parking lot is to receive only a new topping coat. The existing base and binder are adequate. Therefore, only those costs that apply are taken from Table III.62. The loam and seed costs are shown in Table III.63. It is important that the estimator determine those areas that are to receive loam and seed to avoid any possible confusion. A quick sketch of the site will help to define the limits of the work.

	Material	Installation	Total
Sidewalk Slab	$ .77	$1.45	$2.22
Deduct Forms	(.04)	(.40)	(.44)
Subtotal	.73	1.05	1.78
Factors	.07	.18	.25
9% Material			
17% Installation			
Total	$.80	$1.23	$2.03

Calculations for Retaining Wall

Table III.61

SITE WORK — 12.5-514 — Parking Lots, Asphalt

SYSTEM	LINE NO.	DESCRIPTION	QUANTITY	COST PER S.Y. MAT.	INST.	TOTAL
	01	Parking lot consisting of 2" asphalt binder and 1" topping on 6"				
	02	Crushed stone base with painted parking stripes and concrete parking blocks				
	03					
	04	Fine grade and compact subgrade	1 S.Y.		1.71	1.71
	05	6" crushed stone base, stone at $11.55/ton	.32 Ton	3.69	.52	4.21
	06	2" asphalt binder, at $25.96/ton	1 S.Y.	2.96	1.23	4.19
	07	1" asphalt topping, at $29.26/ton	1 S.Y.	1.65	.73	2.38
	08	Paint parking stripes	.5 L.F.	.01	.04	.05
	09	6" x 10" x 6' precast concrete parking blocks	.02 Ea.	.40	.16	.56
	10	Mobilization of equipment	.005 Ea.		.73	.73
	11	TOTAL	S.Y.	8.71	5.12	13.83
	12					
	13					
	14	For alternate parking lot systems:				
	15	Above system on 9" crushed stone	S.Y.	10.52	5.30	15.82
	16	12" crushed stone		12.34	5.48	17.82
	17	On bank run gravel ($4.50/ton) 6" deep		6.53	4.94	11.47
	18	9" deep		7.28	5.06	12.34
	19	12" deep		8.02	5.17	13.19
	20	3" binder plus 1" topping on 6" crushed stone		10.19	5.60	15.79
	21	9" deep crushed stone		12	5.78	17.78
	22	12" deep crushed stone		13.82	5.96	19.78
	23	On bank run gravel, 6" deep		8.01	5.42	13.43
	24	9" deep		8.76	5.54	14.30
	25	12" deep	→	9.50	5.65	15.15
	26					
	27					
	28					
	29	Cut & patch to match existing construction, add, minimum		2%	3%	
	30	Maximum		5%	9%	
	31	Dust protection, add, minimum		1%	2%	
	32	Maximum		4%	11%	
	33	Equipment usage curtailment, add, minimum		1%	1%	
	34	Maximum		3%	10%	
	35	Material handling & storage limitation, add, minimum		1%	1%	
	36	Maximum		6%	7%	
	37	Protection of existing work, add, minimum		2%	2%	
	38	Maximum		5%	7%	
	39	Shift work requirements, add, minimum			5%	
	40	Maximum			30%	
	41					
	42					

This page illustrates and describes asphalt parking lot systems including asphalt binder, topping, crushed stone base, painted parking stripes and concrete parking blocks. Lines 12.5-514-04 thru 11 give the unit price and total price per square yard for this system. Prices for alternate asphalt parking lot systems are on Line Items 12.5-514-15 thru 25. Both material quantities and labor costs have been adjusted for the system listed.

Example: 3" binder plus 1" topping on 6" crushed stone as an alternate system; choose Line Item 12.5-514-20, $10.19 MAT., $5.60 INST., $15.79 TOTAL. This price includes all materials compatible with the original system.

Factors: To adjust for job conditions other than normal working situations use Lines 12.5-514-29 thru 40.

Example: You are to install the above system and match existing construction. Go to Line 12.5-514-29 and apply these percentages to the appropriate MAT. and INST. costs.

402

Table III.62

SITE WORK | 12.7-604 | Landscaping - Lawn Establishment

LINE NO.	DESCRIPTION	QUANTITY	COST PER S.Y.		
			MAT.	INST.	TOTAL
01	Establishing lawns with loam, lime, fertilizer, seed and top mulching				
02	On rough graded areas.				
03					
04	Furnish and place loam 4" deep	.11 C.Y.	1.17	.48	1.65
05	Fine grade, lime, fertilize and seed	1 S.Y.	.17	1.38	1.55
06	Hay mulch, 1 bale/M.S.F.	1 S.Y.	.02	.24	.26
07	Rolling with hand roller	1 S.Y.		.47	.47
08	TOTAL	S.Y.	1.36	2.57	3.93
09					
10	For alternate lawn systems:				
11	Above system with jute mesh in place of hay mulch	S.Y.	1.98	2.57	4.55
12	Above system with sod in place of seed	"	2.82	1.90	4.72
13					
14					
15					
16					
17					
18					
19					
20					
21					
22					
23					
24					
25					
26					
27					
28					
29	Cut & patch to match existing construction, add, minimum		2%	3%	
30	Maximum		5%	9%	
31	Dust protection, add, minimum		1%	2%	
32	Maximum		4%	11%	
33	Equipment usage curtailment, add, minimum		1%	1%	
34	Maximum		3%	10%	
35	Material handling & storage limitation, add, minimum		1%	1%	
36	Maximum		6%	7%	
37	Protection of existing work, add, minimum		2%	2%	
38	Maximum		5%	7%	
39	Shift work requirements, add, minimum			5%	
40	Maximum			30%	
41					
42					

This page describes landscaping—lawn establishment systems including loam, lime, fertilizer, side and top mulching. Lines 12.7-604-04 thru 08 give the unit price and total price per square yard for this system. Prices for alternate landscaping — lawn establishment systems are on Line Items 12.7-604-11 and 12. Both material quantities and labor costs have been adjusted for the system listed.

Example: Using sod in place of seed as an alternate system; choose Line Item 12.7-604-12, $2.82 MAT., $1.90 INST., $4.72 TOTAL. This price includes all materials compatible with the orginal system. For planting and gound cover alternatives not listed, use the selective price sheet for this section (page 407). Substitute the new price from the price sheet into the typical system and adjust the total to reflect each change.

Factors: To adjust for job conditions other than normal working situations use Lines 12.7-604-29 thru 40.

Example: You are to install the above system and provide dust protection. Go to Line 12.7-604-32 and apply these percentages to the appropriate MAT. and INST. costs.

Table III.63

405

311

12.9-300 Demolition Selective Price Sheet

Left section

Category	Description		UNIT	TOTAL COST
Cabinets	Base		L.F.	4.79
	Wall		"	4.79
Carpet	Bonded		S.F.	.19
	Tackless			.04
Ceiling	Tile	Adhesive bonded		.43
		On suspension system		.50
	Sheetrock	On furring		.48
		On suspension system		.53
	Plaster	On wire lath		.67
		On suspension system		.67
Chimney	Brick	16" x 16"	V.L.F.	12.80
		20" x 24"	"	23.00
Concrete	Footing	Plain	C.Y.	114.08
		Reinforced	"	125.49
	Slab, 6" thick	Plain	S.F.	3.03
		Mesh reinforced	"	3.35
	Wall, interior	Plain	C.Y.	307.80
		Reinforced	"	338.58
Door & frame	Wood		Ea.	28.40
	Hollow metal		"	40.95
Ducts	Small size, 4" x 8"		L.F.	.96
	Large size, 30" x 72"		"	3.85
Fascia	To 6" wide			.38
	To 10" wide			.48
Flooring	Brick		S.F.	.77
	Ceramic			.66
	Linoleum			.27
	Resilient tile			.38
	Terrazzo, cast in place			1.32
	Subflooring	Strip	S.F.	.71
	Wood	Block		.58
		T & G boards		.71
		Plywood		.38
Framing	Steel		L.F.	8.30
	Wood	Studs	B.F.	.28
		Roof structure	"	.67

Right section

Category	Description		UNIT	TOTAL COST
Gutters	Attached		L.F.	.90
	Built-in		"	1.91
Masonry	Veneer by hand	Brick to 4" thick	S.F.	1.65
		Marble to 2" thick		1.28
		Granite to 4" thick		1.35
		Stone to 8" thick		1.32
	Walls	Brick 4" thick		1.74
		8" thick		2.30
		12" thick		2.81
		16" thick		3.43
		Block 4" thick		1.15
		6" thick		1.21
		8" thick		1.28
		12" thick		1.32
Paneling	Plywood			.38
	Wood boards, tongue & groove			.55
Piping	To 2" diameter		L.F.	1.33
	To 4" diameter			1.77
	To 8" diameter			5.30
	To 16" diameter			8.85
Roofing	Built-up, 5 ply		S.F.	.61
	Shingles, asphalt strip		"	.28
Stairs	Wood	Minimum	Riser	9.55
		Maximum	"	14.75
Toilet fixtures	Bathtub		Ea.	66.00
	Sink			33.00
	Shower			53.00
	Toilet			38.00
	Urinal			38.00
	Vanity			27.00
Walls	Partitions	Studs & sheet rock	S.F.	.38
		Studs & plaster	"	.67
Windows	Wood	To 12 S.F.	Ea.	11.95
		To 50 S.F.		32.00
	Metal	To 12 S.F.		23.00
		To 50 S.F.		77.00

406

Table III.64

COST ANALYSIS

PROJECT	Apartment Renovation							SHEET NO.	10 of 11		
LOCATION								ESTIMATE NO.	85-2		
ARCHITECT				OWNER				DATE	1985		
QUANTITIES BY EBW		PRICES BY RSM			EXTENSIONS BY			CHECKED BY			

DESCRIPTION	QUANTITY	UNIT	MATERIAL		LABOR		TOTAL COST	
			UNIT	TOTAL	UNIT	TOTAL	UNIT	TOTAL
Division 12: Site Work								
Excavation (½ Day)	91	CY		260		358		
Sidewalk	356	SF	80	285	1 23	438		
Asphalt	467	SY	2 06	962	1 66	775		
Landscaping	890	SY	1 36	1210	2 57	2287		
Demolition	1	LS				12000		
Division 12: Totals				2717		15858		

Table III.65

313

Depending upon the precision necessary for the budget Systems Estimate, the estimator may elect to use a lump sum cost for demolition based upon past experience and the thorough evaluation of the site. If greater accuracy is required, Table III.64 provides costs for selective demolition. In this example, a lump sum figure is used.

The costs for Division 12, Site Work, are summarized on the estimate sheet in Table III.65.

Division 10: General Conditions

In the Systems Estimating format, the General Conditions Division is placed in the tenth position. This part of the estimate, however, is typically done after all other portions of the building project have been priced out. The prices shown in the Systems section of *Repair and Remodeling Cost Data* include the installing contractor's overhead and profit. Chapter 4.3 of this book provides a complete explanation of how labor rates, overhead, and profit are determined and used.

1. Project Overhead. It is necessary to identify those project overhead items that have not been included in the estimate. Items such as field supervision, tools, and minor equipment, field office, sheds, and photos. All have costs that must be included. Division 1 in the Unit Price section, of the Means' *Repair and Remodeling Cost Data*, lists many items that fall in the Project Overhead category. Depending on the estimating precision necessary, the estimator can be as specific or as general as the job dictates. Table III.66 may prove beneficial for general percentage markups only.

General Contractor's Overhead		
	% of Direct Costs	
Items of General Contractor's Indirect Costs	**As a Markup of Labor Only**	**As a Markup of Both Material and Labor**
Field Supervision	6.0%	2.4%
Main Office Expense	9.2	7.7
Tools and Minor Equipment	1.0	0.4
Field Office, Sheds, Photos, etc.	2.0	0.8
Performance and Payment Bond (0.5 to 1.2% Average)	0.7	0.7

Table III.66

2. Office Overhead. There are certain indirect expense items that are incurred by the requirement to keep the shop doors open and to attract business and bid work. The percentage of main office overhead expense declines with increased annual volume of the contractor. Overhead is not appreciably increased when there is an increase in the volume of work. Typical main office expenses range from 2% to 20% with the median being about 7% of the total volume (gross billings). Table III.67 shows approximate percentages for some of the different items usually included in a general contractor's main office overhead. These percentages may vary with different accounting procedures.

3. Profit. The profit assumed in *Repair and Remodeling Cost Data* is 10% on material and equipment, and 15% on labor. Since this is profit margin for the installing contractor, a percentage must be added to cover the profit of the general or prime contractor when subcontractors perform the work. A figure of 10% is used in the appropriate divisions of the sample estimate.

An allowance for the general or prime contractor's project and office overhead, project management, supervision, and markup should be added to the prices in *Repair and Remodeling Cost Data*. This markup ranges from approximately 10% to 20%. A figure of 15% is used for the sample project for general conditions in Table III.68.

General Contractor's Main Office Overhead		
Item	Typical Range	Average
Managers, clerical and estimators' salaries	40% to 55%	48%
Profit sharing, pension and bonus plans	2% to 20%	12%
Insurance	5% to 8%	6%
Estimating and project management (not including salaries)	5% to 9%	7%
Legal, accounting and data processing	0.5% to 5%	3%
Automobile and light truck expenses	2% to 8%	5%
Depreciation of overhead capital capital expenditures	2% to 6%	4%
Maintenance of office equipment	0.1% to 2%	1%
Office rental	3% to 5%	4%
Utilities including phone and light	1% to 3%	2%
Miscellaneous	5% to 15%	8%

Table III.67

COST ANALYSIS

PROJECT	Apartment Renovation					SHEET NO. 11 of 11		
LOCATION						ESTIMATE NO. 85-2		
ARCHITECT			OWNER			DATE 1985		
QUANTITIES BY EBW	PRICES BY RSM		EXTENSIONS BY			CHECKED BY		

DESCRIPTION	QUANTITY	UNIT	MATERIAL		LABOR		TOTAL COST	
			UNIT	TOTAL	UNIT	TOTAL	UNIT	TOTAL
Estimate Summary								
Foundations				1501		3311		4812
Substructure				160		178		338
Superstructure				3712		3331		7043
Exterior Closure				21701		19578		41279
Roofing				4225		4316		8541
Interior Construction				39101		41646		80747
Conveying Systems				—		—		—
Mechanical				31916		39878		71794
Electrical				8227		16288		24515
Special				27686		6921		34607
Site Work				2717		15858		18575
Subtotal				140946		151305		292251
General Conditions	15%			21142		22696		43838

Table III.68

Estimate Summary

It is common practice to include an allowance for contingencies to allow for unforeseen construction difficulties or for oversights during the estimating process. Different factors should be used for the various stages of design completion. The following serve as guides to determine contingency factors.

Conceptual Stage: add 15% to 20%

Preliminary Drawings: add 10% to 15%

Working Drawings,
60% Design Complete: add 7% to 10%

Final Working Drawings
100% Checked Finals: add 2% to 7%

Field Contingencies: add 0% to 3%

As far as the construction contract is concerned, changes in the project can and often will be covered by extras or change orders. The contractor should consider inflationary price trends and possible material shortages during the course of the job. Escalation factors depend on both economic conditions and the anticipated time between the estimate and actual construction. In the final summary, contingencies are a matter of estimating judgement.

Once the estimate is complete, an analysis is required of such items as sales tax on materials, rental equipment, as well as wheel and use taxes for the city, county and/or state where the project will be constructed. There are some locations that tax construction labor in addition to the above items. It is crucial that the estimator check the local regulations for the area of the project to seek the necessary tax information. Percentages for contingencies and sales tax are included in the cost analysis sheet in Table III.69.

A 10% figure for architectural and engineering fees is added to give the owner a better idea of the total project costs. The actual costs would be negotiated by the owner and architect.

The Systems Estimate for the sample project could be completed in less than one day, after initial discussions and a site evaluation. When performed with sound judgement and proper estimating practice, the Systems Estimate is an invaluable budgetary tool.

This book has stressed the importance of the site visit and evaluation. Every existing structure is different and must be treated accordingly. Only with a thorough understanding of how the existing conditions will affect the work will the estimator be properly prepared to analyze and estimate commercial renovations projects.

COST ANALYSIS

PROJECT	Apartment Renovation					SHEET NO.	11 of 11
LOCATION						ESTIMATE NO.	85-2
ARCHITECT		OWNER				DATE	1985
QUANTITIES BY EBW	PRICES BY RSM		EXTENSIONS BY			CHECKED BY	

DESCRIPTION	QUANTITY	UNIT	MATERIAL		LABOR		TOTAL COST	
			UNIT	TOTAL	UNIT	TOTAL	UNIT	TOTAL
Estimate Summary								
Foundations				1501		3311		4812
Substructure				160		178		338
Superstructure				3712		3331		7043
Exterior Closure				21701		19578		41279
Roofing				4225		4316		8541
Interior Construction				39101		41646		80747
Conveying Systems				—		—		—
Mechanical				31916		39878		71794
Electrical				8227		16288		24515
Special				27686		6921		34607
Site Work				2717		15858		18575
Subtotal				140946		151305		292251
General Conditions	15%			21142		22696		43838
Subtotal				162088		174001		336089
Contingencies	10%			16209		17400		33609
Sales Tax			6%	10698				10698
Total Construction Costs				188995		191401		380396
Arch. & Eng. Fees	10%							38040
Total Budget								418436

Table III.69